The Adolescent Idea

THE ADOLESCENT IDEA

Myths of Youth and the Adult Imagination

Patricia Meyer Spacks

Basic Books, Inc., Publishers　　*New York*

Grateful acknowledgment is made for the use of quotations from the following sources:

Jane Austen in a Social Context by David Monaghan, published by Barnes & Noble Books, Totowa, New Jersey, and The Macmillan Press, Ltd., London. By permission of the publishers.

"The Dangerous Age," *Eighteenth-Century Studies,* 11 (1978), 417–438. Used by permission.

"Us or Them," *The Hudson Review,* Vol. XXXI, No. 1 (Spring 1978).

Library of Congress Cataloging in Publication Data

Spacks, Patricia Ann Meyer.
  Adolescent idea.

  Includes bibliographical references and index.
  1. English fiction—History and criticism.
2. Adolescence in literature. 3. Youth in literature.
4. Myth in literature. I. Title.
PR830.A36S66   823'.009'352055   81–66103
ISBN: 0–465–00057–6   AACR2

For Judith

Contents

CONTENTS

Acknowledgments

Portions of this manuscript have been previously printed, in very different form. Part of chapter 4 appeared as "The Dangerous Age," in *Eighteenth-Century Studies* 11 (1978): 417–438; parts of chapters 6 and 7 as "Muted Discord: Generational Conflict in Jane Austen," in *Jane Austen in Her Social Context*, edited by David Monaghan (London: Macmillan, 1981); part of chapter 8 as "Us or Them," in the *Hudson Review* 31 (1978): 34–52.

I am grateful to the many people who have read parts of this work at various stages and have offered criticism, support, and suggestions. They include Elizabeth Ermarth, Wayne Fields, Irving Howe, Paul Hunter, Deborah Kaplan, Judith Kates, Donald Morton, Margery Sabin, Judith Spacks, and, at Basic Books, Phoebe Hoss and Jane Isay. I should add my more general indebtedness to the Fellows of the National Humanities Institute, 1976–77. At the institute I began work on this project; the intellectual stimulation and the supportiveness of the environment encouraged exploration and made ambitious undertakings seem possible. The American Council of Learned Societies supported a year of writing in 1978–79; for that help, too, I am grateful.

The Adolescent Idea

1

"Exploration, Becoming, Growth, and Pain"

To much of the public . . . , the mode of authority in America, the mode that deals with real experience, the mode that is neither dead (as the adult mode seems to be) nor compromised (as the childish world of television seems to be), is the *adolescent* mode—the mode of exploration, becoming, growth, and pain.

These words appear in the *New Yorker* of 29 May 1978, in a profile by George W. S. Trow, Jr., of the record company executive Ahmet Ertegun. They speak of an aspect of twentieth-century culture so familiar that it astonishes virtually no one. Although not everyone would wish to identify with a mode labeled *adolescent*, most middle-class adults attach value to exploration and growth; many believe, however reluctantly, that pain in some sense measures progress. Presumably, no one over the age of twenty-five considers pain the exclusive prerogative of the young; the middle-aged for the most part acknowledge that exploration and growth may characterize even the experience of the old. Yet Trow's abstractions associate themselves readily with that mysterious, powerful phenomenon that we have labeled *adolescence*. The notion of adolescence in our time almost necessarily includes ideas of exploration, becoming, and pain. If complaint about adolescent children forms a staple of middle-class, middle-aged conversation, such complaint often contains undertones of admiration or even awe. Right-thinking adult members of society may not understand adolescent slang or music or keep up with youthful styles in dance; they may rage at youth's recalcitrance in insisting on such manifestations of it-

3

self. But even the right-thinking recognize the young as style setters and at least occasionally envy and desire the apparent freedom they assert, the sense of possibility in their lives.

Exploration, becoming, growth, pain. If popular opinion assigns all these to the young, what remains for the rest of us? Stodginess, inertia, stasis, absence of feeling? So our juniors often imagine. I asked a class once what *adulthood* meant to them. No one much wanted to tell me; finally one young woman ventured, "It means having all your problems solved." I said that sounded like a state indistinguishable from death, and the students laughed; but that is, I think, what they in fact believed. And the conviction of the young has infected their elders. As Trow suggests, to "much of the public" the adult mode seems dead—or, at any rate, tenuously connected with "real experience."

Thinking about adolescence, for those of us who like to consider ourselves "grown-up," involves thinking about ourselves: what we were, might have been, hoped to be. Most people reminisce readily about their teen-age years, and we hear in such accounts the unmistakable note of the mythic. How miserable one felt back then, or how rebellious, foolhardy, popular, isolated! How much one wanted, how much one dreamed! Women in particular say they wouldn't live that time over again for anything, but even memories stressing youthful unhappiness evoke a nostalgic sense of *aliveness*. As during those adolescent years one endlessly re-created oneself, trying out in one's head—sometimes even tentatively in the real world—different possible roles, so now one re-invents those past selves, converting the shifting shapes of adolescence into images that make retrospective sense. Individual fantasies of adolescence in some respects have more power than have those of childhood, a time of life associated with innocence but also with helplessness; about adolescence we can imagine not only the infinite power of untested potential but the gathering force of actual human capacity.

Such imagining, of course, belongs mainly to the middle class, where the young have more real choices than their working-class contemporaries; but it persists in the face of economic stringencies that may make new college graduates, for example, feel possessed of far fewer opportunities than their elders had. Those elders often insist, despite all evidence to the contrary, on believing the world open to youth. Unlike youth's fantasy of middle age as living death, the view of adolescence as a time of limitless opportunity does not originate with them. The parental generation see intelligence, strength, sexual energy, all reaching a high pitch in the postpuberty years. They see youth's suffering, too, but consider it a small price to pay. The selves they remember, the young they live with and worry about, possess all that adults lack—except for worldly power and economic security. Grown-ups know their middle-aged brains to be losing neurons every day—and feel as though they lose them to the young.

However much the popular press, the images of film, television, and advertising, and the energies of nostalgia encourage the glorification of youth, twentieth-century Western culture manifests also a comparably potent countertrend. Freud wrote, in his essay "Family Romances," that "the whole progress of society rests upon the opposition between successive generations."[1] If one does not believe that opposition universal, one must yet acknowledge its ubiquity. Adolescents may possess the "mode of authority," but their elders wield actual social, political, pedagogical, and economic power. The young flaunt their beauty, energy, and freedom; the middle-aged assert their experience, wisdom, and parental dominance. The young press forward, the old press them back. Conflict prevails.

Seventeen-year-old Joseph, Genesis recounts, dreams that he and his much older brothers are binding sheaves in a field: "and, lo, my sheaf arose, and also stood upright; and, behold, your sheaves stood round about, and made obeisance to my sheaf."[2] A typical adolescent fantasy, we may feel—a *male* adolescent fantasy. Then the boy dreams again: "behold, the sun and the moon and the eleven stars made obeisance to me."[3] In such dreams his father and his elder brothers have no difficulty discerning the will to power. His father rebukes him, his brothers sell him into slavery—and thus become instruments for the fulfillment of Joseph's fantasies of dominion. Not a twentieth-century story, this, but a parable still full of meaning for our time—perhaps an illustration of Freud's thesis. Joseph, we are told, has God on his side: consolation for the father and brothers, who, in the end, profit from his eminence—but only after bowing down to their junior.

Intergenerational politics evokes energies as potent as those of intersexual politics. Like women, adolescents constitute, in their own perception, an oppressed class; like women, they possess hidden weapons. Unlike women, they inevitably win in the long run, if only by growing up and succeeding their parents. Their challenge precedes their winning. Bruno Bettelheim has suggested far-reaching psychological consequences of the fact that children now rarely follow the occupations of their parents; they no longer affirm the choices of previous generations even as they succeed to adult places in the social order.[4] The challenge of youth, however, as myth and drama and fiction attest, does not depend on social mobility. Antigone speaks passionately for the moral certainty of the young; Romeo and Juliet claim the authority of their passion against the rigid antagonism of their parents. Antigone and Romeo and Juliet die in the course of the fictional actions that contain them: dying, they assert their power, imply the inevitability of cultural change.

The storyteller, the mythmaker, causes them to die: the young cannot have things all their own way, even in fiction. The conflict between young and old, an apparent fact of past and present, implies profound antagonisms, hostility coexisting with the envy and glorification of youth implied by the quotation from Trow. Hostility, envy, and glorification, moreover, all on occasion yield to—or hide behind—nostalgic identification. However incomprehensible, repellent, or exciting adolescents appear, they remain the children of grownups—a fact that domesticates their strangeness. We (I write as one of the middle-aged) were young once ourselves; and the young belong to us, though they may seek to deny the connection. We can take pleasure in their growth, grieve for their sorrows, identify with their joy, remembering our comparable experience, reassuring ourselves that eventually they will turn into our counterparts. Such reassurance, of course, derives from unconfirmable fantasy, the source also of such other typical responses as glorification and hostility.

These three ways of reacting to adolescents, all vivid in the twentieth century, do not belong uniquely to our moment in history—nor does adolescence as a phenomenon, a phenomenon still presenting difficulties of definition. Although the *Oxford English Dictionary*, with its customary assurance, concludes its splendid elucidation by pronouncing that the "condition of growing up" usually lasts from twelve to twenty-one in females, from fourteen to twenty-five in males, most authorities feel less certain. John and Virginia Demos have pointed out that adolescence constitutes an idea masquerading as a fact; they believe the idea to have originated in the late nineteenth century and to be "on the whole an American discovery."[5] It has a curious vagueness, this idea. The beginning of adolescence coincides with the beginning of puberty, but we have no clear way of locating its end.[6] The psychoanalyst Helene Deutsch is said to have remarked, in her eighties, that she was proceeding directly from adolescence to senility; other people deny ever having had an adolescence at all. Moreover, like *narcissism*, the term has gradually enlarged its metaphoric reference and become a generalized designation, usually of blame: the middle-aged man who abandons wife and job, we say, is

6

behaving in adolescent fashion, although teen-agers rarely have wives and jobs to abandon.

Despite its historical, semantic, and referential perplexities, adolescence provides an idea as valuable for analysis of the past as of the present. Lawrence Stone demonstrates that adolescence has been a viable notion ever since the Renaissance.[7] Even in medieval times, the seven ages of man included a period called adolescence, beginning at fourteen, uncertain as to termination.

> Afterwards follows the third age, which is called adolescence, which ends according to Constantine in his viaticum in the twenty-first year, but according to Isidore it lasts till twenty-eight, . . . and it can go on till thirty or thirty-five. This age is called adolescence because the person is big enough to beget children, says Isidore.[8]

Our special vision of adolescence belongs to the twentieth century, but preceding periods had their own concepts of its phenomena.

Let me formulate a conveniently vague definition: *adolescence* designates the time of life when the individual has developed full sexual capacity but has not assumed a full adult role in society. I emphasize sexuality because real and imagined sexual energy, crucial in the mythology of the teen-age years, accounts for much of the imaginative power implicit in the idea of adolescence. In 1755, Samuel Johnson's *Dictionary* defined *puberty*, touchingly, as "The time of life in which the two sexes begin first to be acquainted." In our day Erik Erikson has spoken of a moratorium between childhood and adulthood, a space for testing and discovery.[9] His formulation suggests the association of adolescence with the middle class; but the apprentices of seventeenth-century London, for example, displayed the characteristics we have come to consider typical of this lifestage; and the institution of apprenticeship itself amounts to a social objectification of the moratorium idea. The anomalous behavior of those with more energy than ready outlet occurs not only in the bourgeoisie. On the other hand, leisure encourages adolescent manifestations. From the eighteenth century to the twentieth in England, as the middle class has enlarged, more and more young people have found themselves without significant occupation. We tell our young now that education is a meaningful pursuit for their time of life; they tell us, in increasing numbers, that it is not. Their dilemma and their conduct have roots in the past.

If adolescence as an observable stage of life has a long history, adolescence as a distinct idea has a short one. Seventeenth- and eighteenth-century thinkers lacked clear concepts to rationalize youth's

7

disturbing displays. John Locke, for example, at the very end of the seventeenth century, in his influential *Some Thoughts Concerning Education*, reflected on the custom of sending young men on the Grand Tour between the ages of sixteen and twenty-one—precisely the time of life "the least suited to these Improvements."[10] At fifteen or sixteen, a boy "begins to consort himself with Men, and think himself one"; he "thinks it a shame to be any longer under the Controul and Conduct of another." Under such circumstances,

what can be hoped from even the most careful and discreet Governour, when neither he has Power to compel, nor his Pupil a disposition to be perswaded; but on the contrary, has the advice of warm Blood, and prevailing Fashion, to hearken to the Temptations of his companions, just as Wise as himself, rather than to the perswasions of his Tutor, who is now looked on as the Enemy to his Freedom? And when is a Man so like to miscarry, as when at the same time he is both raw and unruly? This is the Season of all his Life, that most requires the Eye and Authority of his Parents, and Friends to govern it. The flexibleness of the former part of a Man's Age, not yet grown up to be head-strong, makes it more governable and safe; and in the after-part, Reason and Foresight begin a little to take place, and mind a Man of his Safety and Improvement. (Pp. 255–56)

These words were published in 1693. The definition of the teen-age years as "both raw and unruly," the frustration at the impossibility of imposing wise parental constraint on this developmental stage, have continued unchanged. William Cobbett wrote in 1829:

Every man, and especially every Englishman (for here we seldom love or hate by halves), will recollect how many mad pranks he has played; how many wild and ridiculous things he has said and done between the age of sixteen and that of twenty-two; how many times a kind glance has scattered all his reasoning and resolution to the winds; how many times a cool look has plunged him into the deepest misery![11]

No use trying to reason with those whose minds are thus overwhelmed by passion, he concluded. Almost a century and a half later, in 1968, the British sociologist Cyril Smith observed that youth provides a contrast to the dreariness and restriction of adult life, "for it appears exciting, unrestrained, engaged in conflicts with authority, and deeply involved in meaningful relationships with the opposite sex. It is envied for this drama and preyed upon by adults who wish to prolong their own adolescence."[12] The explicit value judgments have altered far more than have the descriptions: each writer perceives the same energy, the same conflict with adult authority.

What do such responses tell us? Not necessarily a great deal about how the young live and act, but much about how adults think and feel. Cyril Smith implicitly acknowledges the necessary distortions in adult description of the young when he uses the verb *appears*. Adolescence *appears* to us in distinct, definable ways; many of its appearances have remained more or less constant for at least three centuries. Most of us, however, can remember or glimpse enough to suspect how dramatically the experience differs from its most visible appearances; and the shifting reactions to these appearances testify to altering configurations of young and old. Locke's irritation; Cobbett's amused, nostalgic indulgence; Cyril Smith's effort to separate himself from the conflict he evokes: such tonal divergences reflect changes in social as well as personal assumptions and remind us that observers as well as what they observe alter over time. In other eras, exploration, growth, becoming might seem life's painful necessities rather than states associated with any idea of authority; then the condition ultimately achieved, not the process of achieving it, would locate value. Examining views of adolescence in our cultural past helps us to understand the views we hold in the present—and to understand that they are only views.

"Only" implies no deprecation. What we can see largely determines what we consider to be reality. The shifting meanings of adolescence correspond to perceptual shifts about the nature as well as the value of society and of individuals within it. Although in the period that mainly concerns me—roughly the mid-eighteenth to the mid-twentieth centuries—thinkers have consistently assumed the importance of the individual, the reasons for that importance and its context have changed. From glorifying personal achievement, we have moved to celebrating personal fulfillment. The adolescent can claim little in the way of achievement but need yield to no one in his or her capacity to concentrate on, and in some ways to attain, self-gratification and self-development. Compound nouns beginning with *self* almost all apply readily to adolescents, immersed in a life stage of heightened narcissistic energy. The young person's absorption with his or her own growth, discovery, and pain are reason enough for proclaiming ours the century of the adolescent.

One can imagine other, equally plausible, reasons for the contemporary fascination with the image of the adolescent and for historical shifts of attitude toward pre-adult life. Corresponding to the emphasis on self-fulfillment is an increased skepticism about the positive value—although not about the power—of society. Even the satiric energy with which eighteenth-century poets, dramatists, and novelists attacked social corruption speaks of faith in the possibility of a society that would support the best in individuals. In our time, on the other hand, adults often concur with the young in a vague notion that the "Establishment" represents forces of stultification if not of active criminality. Adolescents function as social outsiders, not yet accepted into the established order; their separation from the realm of social power now constitutes their virtue. Not so two centuries ago, when the powerlessness of the young implied that they need not be taken altogether seriously.

Both these sociological observations—the increasing stress on self-fulfillment, the increasing distrust of society—suggest that twentieth-century commentators might value adolescence more highly than did their historical predecessors. The truth, however, proves less simple. The grand polarities that surface repeatedly in the thought of any given historical period help to determine that period's understanding and evaluation of adolescence. Thus the eighteenth-century debate between reason and passion, with reason the society's normative ideal, reverberates through discussions of youth that reveal the culture's ambivalence about values it explicitly celebrates. Adulthood can be optimistically summarized as the time when reason has the power to prevail, since the human being then possesses fully developed reasoning capacity; in adolescence, one's passions overbalance one's rational faculties—a weakness of the young. In the eighteenth century, however, as in our own, the old often envied the young their relatively unconstricted (at least in adult fantasy) capability for expressing what mature consciousness strove to control and to submerge. As a result, a punitive attitude toward youth emerged—along with a desire to sentimentalize and to protect the young. The eighteenth century supplies evidence alike for high and low esteem of adolescence. So does the nineteenth century, when attitudes toward the polarities of innocence and experience help to shape responses to youth; and the twentieth century, when evaluations of youth reflect ideological positions about authenticity versus worldly wisdom (which the young call "hypocrisy") or engagement versus disengagement. If we celebrate adolescence now, we also, with equal vigor, condemn it; sometimes we fear it. "The hatred with which the mature of Western society regard the young," English sociologist Frank Musgrove commented in the 1960's, "is a testimony to the latter's importance, to their power potential and actual."[13] The eighteenth century, too, both celebrated and condemned. Every period supplies evidence for a wide range of opposed ideas and feelings.

Some ideas and feelings, however, possess more importance than others. In the eighteenth century, much written material enforces and celebrates the subordination of young to old. Samuel Richardson's Pamela behaves as her parents wish; her fictional comtemporary Tom Jones acts in ways his guardian disapproves: he remains an adolescent rebel through much of Fielding's novel. Tom wins reward only after he has learned compliance, and Pamela's obedience accounts for her rise: thus, adolescent subservience emerges as a more significant eighteenth-century theme than adolescent rebellion, although writers describe both. Conversely, in the twentieth century one can still find non-ironic presentations of the ideally compliant young person—but only at the level of low culture. Doris Lessing's teen-aged Martha Quest, who wishes to believe nothing her mother believes, is a more typical literary heroine. To isolate adolescent submissiveness as a crucial issue for the eighteenth century reveals fears familiar to us in the present; the particular expressions of such fears contribute to defining a culture. By locating salient themes in a particular historical period, one can organize the culture's fantasies about adolescence and thus can see more clearly their social implications—ultimately their literary significance as well. The revealed fantasies can focus investigation of how cultural assumption helps determine literary form: one of the main purposes of this study.

Erik Erikson has written, "We who know so much about the child in the adult know so much less about the fate of the adolescent in him, whether as a continued source of renewal or as a split-off younger self alternately idealized and repudiated, revived and 'murdered'—and, of course, reprojected on the young."[14] The first-person pronoun here refers specifically to psychoanalysts, but historians, and every intelligent person concerned with the life of his time, too, need to know about those idealizations, repudiations, and projections. Such mental processes, the more powerful because largely unconscious, help to determine modes of conceptualization; they therefore contain social as well as psychological import. The ambiguities inherent in the adolescent state allow adults to project fears, hopes, and accurate or distorted memories onto their juniors. To the extent that such projections may be generalized, they help to clarify a culture's values and thus its literature.

"In the long run," Kenneth Keniston has argued, "developmental concepts are likely to prove more useful than concepts of socialization, acculturation, and national character in explaining historical change, and ... the relationship between historical context and psychological

11

development is far more intimate than we have heretofore suspected."[15] "Developmental concepts" should not be taken as identical with descriptions of development, as Keniston goes on to emphasize: "an account of social expectations about age-appropriate behavior is not an account of development" (p. 336). It is, rather, a partial account of how a society sees itself. Definitions of developmental norms reveal one kind of history in the making. Such definitions reflect interpretations of personal and collective experience, impositions of order on the confusion of growing up. As cultural mythology generalizes the experience, it distances the confusion, containing it within a justifying sequence. The chaos of politics, of custom, of incomprehensible event all yields to the organization imposed by historians; theorists of human development similarly organize the disorder of individual experience.

Sometimes theories emerge without apparent theorists. In the eighteenth and early nineteenth centuries, people got along without psychologists to explain them to themselves—but not without explanations. Didactic and imaginative texts nominally concerned with other matters often imply theories of human development. What people claim to see reveals what they imagine. Our forebears, too, saw a great deal in the young. Their testimony survives in sermons and manuals intended for youth or for parents—documents revealing, through prescriptions of conduct, assumptions about pre-adult moral and psychological development. Another sort of testimony—no more informative, though far more compelling—derives from the vast imaginative literature of adolescence, particularly novels that tell stories of the young man or young woman preparing for entrance into what eighteenth-century writers called "the world." (I begin this study specifically with the eighteenth century rather than earlier because in this period the novel first emerged as a significant literary form.) Novels, too, imply theories of development and powerfully reinforce them, but—unlike didactic manuals—they do not necessarily describe idealized developmental sequences. On the contrary, from Tom Jones onward, many young fictional heroes and heroines postponed growing up in socially acceptable fashion, insisting on dangerous excursions from the path of steadily strengthening reason and morality. Many young people read and enjoyed the books about such heroes and heroines; eighteenth-century critics and moralists, in fact, imagined a largely adolescent (and almost entirely female) audience for the novel, although the haphazard evidence of surviving letters suggests that most adult members of the educated middle class, including even Dr. Johnson, also read current fiction in the eighteenth and nineteenth centuries. So the moralists who concerned themselves with prescriptions to and for the young worried about novels as potential rivals to their own unexceptionable advice. Moralists instruct youth, novelists corrupt it: so traditional wisdom had it, until well into the nineteenth century.

The surveyor of the past, however, can see, more clearly there than in the present, what novels and moralizing have in common. Both purport to describe something conceivable as reality; neither confines itself to actuality. The historian Charles Rosenberg, discussing the task of extrapolating "behavior from formal admonition" in documents from the past, points out that "formal role prescriptions are always more uniform than the behavior which may—or may not—incorporate them."[16] The uniformity of generalization and idealization obscures actualities of behavior; so does the idiosyncrasy of imagined character. Yet both novel and didactic tract bear a probably unrecoverable relation to the ways in which people really act and think and feel. One cannot recapture all the facts from which they derive, but the works themselves reveal the feelings and fantasies that largely determine their shapes. Juxtaposing the fantasies of moralists about the young with those of novelists, investigating how they diverge and how they coincide, we may discover more both about how representatives of various versions of Western culture have perceived and valued themselves, and about how fiction and nonnarrative prose create their effects.

My interest in fantasy—a word that I use in general as psychoanalysts do, to designate mental productions serving the purpose of wish fulfillment and often substituting for action or effort in the realm outside the self—implies a concern with latent as well as with manifest content, with meanings a writer never consciously intended, although he or she would not necessarily disavow them. To detect in the sentence by Cobbett quoted earlier, for example, a wistful or nostalgic glorification of youth's romantic intensity does not deny, but reinforces, the message he consciously offers, about the difficulty of reasoning with the young. The focus on fantasy also implies a relative absence of concern with matters of fact. The crucial question becomes not, What is adolescence? but, How has adolescence been perceived, remembered, imagined? Although the second question allows a vast range of responses, it does not, like the first, seem utterly unanswerable. The flood of writing—description, prescription, rhapsody, polemic—that purports to delineate youth evokes the predispositions of its creators far more dependably than the nature of its subject.

13

The history of fantasies, of social mythology, does not lend itself to orderly arrangement. As contradictions effortlessly coexist in the individual unconscious, so, too, the collective imagination of a culture simultaneously contains opposing ideas. The late twentieth century provides abundant examples: our society believes that the young embody a dangerous force (Geoffrey Hartman refers to "the demonic energy of adolescence"[17]) and equally believes them to contain the principle of our salvation. Similarly in the eighteenth century and in the nineteenth, not only the range of published material but even on occasion a single work may provide images utterly antithetical to one another. If the same themes emerge everywhere, it is equally true that works of every period reveal multiple contradictory attitudes. Generalizations about dominant views in various epochs at best register an emotional atmosphere.

But the tenable generalizations in any case hold less interest than the individual texts that generate them. Even didactic works of thin or clotted verbal texture, works of predictable content, take on new richness when examined for their implicit meanings; and familiar novels show unexpected aspects as one asks fresh questions about them. Sociologists and historians have used imaginative literature as evidence of cultural fact; the literary critic's skills at reading texts can map new contours in terrain long claimed by social scientists. By weakening the force of established categories, "literary" readings of sententious works uncover startling connections. Lord Chesterfield's worldly letters to his son turn out to bear an unexpected affinity to Isaac Watt's pieties for youth; Mary Wollstonecraft in some respects resembles the clergyman John Gregory, whom she loathed. Minor writers, composers of bad prose, prove rewarding: for instance, the forger William Dodd, before his exposure a prolific producer of advice in which language, precariously controlled, reveals a rich store of fantasies just beneath the surface. Even the sociology and psychologizing of our own time repay literary inquiry: a study of the morality of British working-class youth becomes far more compelling as its language provides clues to what its authors really feel about the young people they depict.

When one inquires about the uses to which fantasy is put, avowedly imaginative literature provides the most compelling—because the most complex and evocative—material. Novels obviously "use" fantasy for aesthetic as well as for social and psychological ends. If Erik Erikson reveals in his psychological analyses of youth an uneasy substratum of guilt because adults have failed their offspring, the fiction of Anthony Burgess and Muriel Spark suggests how that guilt, and the imaginings it encourages, can provide a basis for novelistic structure, and thus hints the importance of such experience for individuals and for cultures. Questions about how adolescence has been perceived justify themselves partly by the illumination they provide for well-known works of literature, the ways in which they make the familiar new.

Many important novels of the eighteenth, nineteenth, and twentieth centuries deal with adolescent turmoil and shape their plots by typical psychological patterns of youthful growth and resolution. This fact itself suggests how consistently in our culture notions of imaginative vitality have clung about the young, in whom novelists—like the rest of us—perceive meaningful conflict internal and external. Novels take the young seriously. From *Tom Jones* to *The Catcher in the Rye*, they have evoked adolescents who oppose the existent social order, enjoy more vital passional involvements than their elders, face in their lives crucial and compelling decisions—the stuff of drama. The adolescent's efforts alternately to resist the adult world and to find a place in it focus sharply on that intersection of the personal and the social often declared the novel's central concern.

So ubiquitous is the subject of adolescence in major fiction that few of us wonder why this should be so. Yet why have the problems of adolescence appeared more useful for fiction than have those of the middle-aged? Adolescents in real life change their minds a lot; their commitments often fail to endure; why should they matter so much? Adults have always had more at stake, yet the drama of their decisions, through the early history of the novel, seldom attracted fictional attention. Something in the notion of youth, clearly, supports the fantasies that make fiction.

To investigate novels in relation to this subject matter establishes a nexus of new relationships comparable to that uncovered in didactic texts. *The Vicar of Wakefield* reveals ideological connections with *Roderick Random; Tristram Shandy* generates new questions (does adolescence provide a useful metaphor for the indeterminate sensibility?). Jane Austen and Sir Walter Scott illuminate one another, their contemporaneity becoming freshly meaningful; the same is true of D. H. Lawrence and James Joyce. The frequent occurrence of youth as subject suggests a way of looking at a large and important body of fiction. What is it about? can be a crude or a profound question—but is rarely irrelevant. Novels can be "about" the young in many different ways; both identities and differences prove worth investigating.

15

Adolescent issues as novelistic content lead to problems of novelistic form, and conversely. One may wonder, for instance, about the endings of many important novels of adolescence. How odd that, after an elaborate sequence of events apparently designed to educate the youthful protagonist for his place in the world, Tom Jones decides that he belongs *out* of the world and chooses, like his mentor, Squire Allworthy, the life of rural isolation. His education, in other words, has prepared him—as Joseph Andrews's and Roderick Random's educations prepare them—not to survive in the world but to escape it. The familiarity of this pattern may obscure its significance: the novelistic action declares the rightness of the widespread adolescent rejection of grown-up corruption, and justifies the young man's repudiation of much that adults have created. *The Catcher in the Rye* displays the same sequence, with the same moral point. The shape of such novels, in every century, manifestly depends upon adult attitudes toward youth.

The novel's efflorescence in the eighteenth century, some commentators feel, reflects the period's increasing stress on individualism, its more highly developed ideas of selfhood; other commentators have asserted a connection between the rise of the novel and that of the middle class. The novelistic preoccupation with adolescence relates to both emphases. Adolescence became a more conspicuous social issue with the enlargement of the population of prosperous, idle young; fiction explored the situation of this group. Since puberty has traditionally involved self-discovery, the subject of adolescence lent itself readily to concentration on selfhood. The form of a novel about the teen-age years may derive less from an individual author's sense of fictional structure than from general notions about the shape of human life, invented actions of self-definition duplicating processes believed inherent in development to adulthood. If literature bears some relation to life, if verbal constructs convey ideas and feelings with reference beyond themselves, then formal questions may elicit social answers. Ideas about adolescence suggest useful solutions to a number of problems about the nature of particular novelistic actions. Yet this fact itself implies further questions: To what extent do psychological and social assumptions determine novelistic structures? How much can we understand about the structures by investigating the assumptions? The present case study begins to confront such issues.

Novels, like other cultural manifestations, assume different shapes from different angles. The idea of adolescence provides a distinct perspective. We have become accustomed to believing that the battle of the sexes, with the complexities of love and hate it implies, underlies

16

many or most plots of Western fiction. The battle of the generations, with *its* loves and hates, plays a comparably crucial role, determining structure as well as content not only in the *Bildungsroman* but often in the novel of initiation, in the Gothic romance and the anti-Gothic it spawned, in much social satire, in much realistic fiction by no means solely concerned with youth. The question of how this fiction confronts adolescence implies a wide range of answers, involving plot, tone, structure, characterization, ideological and psychological context.

Despite the subversive energies of the imagination, the novel flourishes in the garden of the taken-for-granted. It reflects social values while proclaiming its iconoclasm: Joyce and Lawrence, celebrating adolescent nonconformity, demonstrate their own participation in their generation's convictions. And novels imitate actions dependent on a world of social interchange: *The Mysteries of Udolpho* describes events of wonderful implausibility which move the reader because of their recognizable, although skewed, relation to ordinary patterns of action and feeling. Fiction helps to focus shifting conceptions of the important, and adolescence, in our conception, is a time when important things happen. Novels, of the past and the present, document the conceptualizations through which society comes to terms with its young and the ways society assigns value.

Novels, and for that matter didactic works, about the young focus attention on memory's ambiguities. Memory, preserving the past, reverses the emphasis of hope, usually directed toward the future. Works of admonition or imagination conventionally acknowledge no reliance on memory. Yet how can one evoke or advise the young without recalling one's youth? Hope and fear can reach backward as well as forward. One imagines one's earlier selves in forms shaped by apprehension ("perhaps that girl I used to be was a monster") or wish ("maybe after all she was a saint"). Comparable distortions inform the literature of adolescence, shape the myths with whose aid we purport to understand the young. Examining those myths, we examine ourselves.

Not by initial intent, but by necessity, this is a book about politics, about power relations. The reinterpretations by which our culture keeps its balance obsessively define and locate, redefine and relocate, power. We see the young—feared antagonists, beloved children—as weak or as strong; we, like our ancestors, ponder the nature and the limits of our children's strength in comparison with their elders, ourselves. The conflict model that governs Western conceptions of society, family, and individual limits understanding of generational se-

17

quence. As writers explore the dramatic possibilities of youth or didactically diagnose its weaknesses and failures, they consistently perceive open or concealed struggles for dominance between generations. The literature of adolescence documents that struggle.

It documents also a sequence of concern with other issues basic to our society: the proper relation of outer-directed and inner-directed, public and private life, for example. The young, in adult perception, almost invariably align themselves with "private," "inner" values, even when they engage ardently in grand causes. What we now call "adolescent narcissism" guarantees youthful attention to inner experience; it constitutes one of youth's challenges to age. Another, closely related, comes from the persistent association of adolescence with "romanticism" and "idealism," in opposition to adult "pragmatism." The appropriate direction and limitation of ambition, yet another crux of adolescent experience, troubles adults as well; in its youthful resolutions often it opposes their values. Because in adolescence men and women alike typically confirm their sexual roles, writings about the young often convey with particular sharpness the dichotomies and inequalities between male and female experience.

The topic of adult attitudes toward, fantasies about, adolescence, in short, implies responses to a series of perceived challenges. I propose to investigate these challenges and their consequences by considering a group of major novels in the context of didactic discussions of youth, seeking in both kinds of text to uncover assumptions about those younger human beings whom grown-ups alternately protect and battle. The approach will reveal something about how novels organize sequences of events and how they convey values and attitudes. It will also clarify—if only by defining questions—an aspect of the complex relation between cultural and literary change, and may explain why a time of life when few individuals accomplish anything of note has assumed such consistent importance in our culture, and how narrative, description, and advice have reiterated that importance.

2

''Nobody's Power''

Fantasies and facts of youthful power alike disturb many grown-ups. Facts are bad enough: the rippling muscles of the twenty-year-old male tennis player, the gleaming hair of his female counterpart, visible emblems of vitality. Fantasies are worse: the lovers those tennis players surely attract. Sex focuses the true issue, defines the crucial power—a fact denied, avoided, transformed; the central fact of adolescence.

Western social structures have always assumed the authority—hence, implicitly, the power—of adults and granted the young at most the status of rebels. Yet adolescents have not always claimed, or been allowed, even so much. For young women in particular, compliance has often constituted a satisfactory norm. If the physical appearance of a late adolescent girl speaks eloquently of sexuality, her rhetoric and her conduct may deny it; the rhetoric of her culture, reflecting communal wishes, shared adult disturbance, may insist that her concerns lie elsewhere. The written records of the last three centuries reveal an intricate counterpoint of assertion and denial, coexistent contradictory fantasies finding expression in different literary forms.

As recent feminist criticism has revealed, ambivalent attitudes toward women of all ages have been conveyed by the written word. Woman as temptress and as saint, as powerful mother and as helpless child, as manipulator and as victim, inhabits Western fiction and moralizing alike; her roles shift sometimes within a paragraph, even within a sentence. Woman on the brink of adulthood evokes special perplexity—particularly about her power. Lacking the wifehood that would assign her comprehensible, measurable status by virtue of her association with a more or less powerful man, she may partake of her father's status but has none of her own. On the other hand, she pos-

19

sesses certain strengths: at least some degree of attractiveness, energy, and physical self-awareness. A sexual being yet unpossessed, she wields a power independent of social position. But she may not allow herself to know this. How potent is such power, unacknowledged? Does the unmarried girl have more or less force than the woman she will become? How does the social condition of women in general determine literary imagining or understanding of the young, unmarried female?

In the eighteenth century, we think, women had fewer opportunities than they have today. Their marriages determined their fates. The moralists who advised them stressed their necessary subordination at every stage of life. A hundred years later, didactic writers had begun to glorify the power of the mother, and journalistic debate raged over the desirability of intellectual independence for women. One might imagine that a young woman could find more room for herself, could exercise more force in the society. By the 1960s, the literature of advice for girls proclaimed that the world lay all before them, they could go anywhere, do anything, explore their sexual, moral, intellectual, and vocational freedoms. Didactic texts of the past three centuries speak of steady progress, steady enlargement of women's sphere and therefore of their power.

Novels, however, suggest that the public position of women does not necessarily correspond to their private experience. To begin the investigation of fantasies about adolescence by examining in sequence an eighteenth-, a nineteenth-, and a twentieth-century novel about a young woman will adumbrate the complexities of the subject. Samuel Richardson's *Pamela* (1740), Elizabeth Gaskell's *Wives and Daughters* (1866), and Doris Lessing's *Martha Quest* (1964) all assert that the unmarried girl exercises diminishing power as her social freedom increases.

Pamela's culture assumed that a young woman who achieved by her own endeavors risked betraying her womanhood. "Good" marriage—Pamela's triumph—represented a desirable goal for every female, but one should not work openly to bring it about. Marriage would simply *happen* to the virtuous girl, perhaps partly the result of efforts by her family, mainly the reward of her passive goodness; after marriage she would subside once more into docility, obedient to the will of her husband as previously to that of her parents. "Women," Lord Kames wrote in 1782, "destined by nature to be obedient, ought to be disci-

plined early to bear wrongs, without murmuring. This is a hard lesson; and yet it is necessary even for their own sake: sullenness or
peevishness may alienate the husband, but tend not to sooth his
roughness, nor to moderate his impetuosity."[1]

The double message of this advice echoes through many utterances
of the middle and even late eighteenth century. On the one hand, the
pedagogue declares obedience to be women's natural destiny; on the
other, he acknowledges it "a hard lesson," to be enforced by threats
about the unruly propensities of husbands. The hidden issue, in either
case, concerns ambiguous female sexuality: perhaps a "natural" mode
of submission, perhaps a dangerous impulse needing constant discipline. A French text translated and adapted into English in the early
1740s suggests the problem yet more clearly—although still without
mentioning it:

It has been justly observed, that young People of your Sex, who are suffered to
be Mistresses of their own Inclinations, very seldom succeed in the nice and
important Business of Matrimony. They are apt to surrender at the first Attack,
without reflecting of what moment it is to deliberate upon their Choice; they
look upon Matrimony as the Period to the filial Subjection they are uneasy
under, and as a State of more Freedom and Independency than that which it
delivers them from, and therefore rush into it with Transport the very first
Opportunity.[2]

A vocabulary of power controls this commentary, pointing again to
the ambiguities of female action and impulse. A woman allowed to
function as mistress of her "own Inclinations," with power over her
own life, eagerly will "surrender"; but her asserted status as mistress
of herself in any case has little substance, since her desire to surrender
reflects impatience with her "filial Subjection." Women wish independence: the commentator hints they will find slavery. They make an
equally fundamental mistake in their apparent failure to understand
matrimony as a "Business" properly conducted with sobriety rather
than with the "Transport" that marks youthful emotional energy.
Emotional energy and, presumably, sexual energy as well: hence the
eagerness, the transport, the danger. To interpret marriage as business
removes it at least verbally from the chancy dominion of sexual
impulse.

Michel Foucault has argued—mainly on the basis of French texts—
the inadequacy of any theory of repression to explain social attitudes
toward sexuality from the eighteenth century onward. He insists that
"a steady proliferation of discourses concerned with sex" accompanied

the change in mores toward the end of the seventeenth century. More important, he claims, than any tightening of decorum "was the multiplication of discourse concerning sex in the field of exercise of power itself: an institutional incitement to speak about it, and to do so more and more; a determination on the part of the agencies of power to hear it spoken about."[3] Commentary about the nature and proper conduct of girls supports his thesis: sex was their subterranean subject; powerlessness, their prescription. The girl should, must, submit in order to escape the destructive potential of inner forces. Even as they preached discipline and obedience, the male and female moralists who advised the young woman betrayed their anxiety about what Eliza Haywood called "the Torrent of Inclinations" within her awaiting release. Hence the importance of "inspiring her with those just Notions, which will prevent her from giving way at first to any Inclinations unbefitting her Rank and Station in Life" by "cultivating her Genius, improving her Understanding, finding such Employments for her as will rectify her Mind."[4] The same author pointed out the dangers for the girl of that "Vanity and Pride . . . perpetually endeavouring to force their Way into the Heart"; those who care for her welfare must offer the strongest possible arguments to convince her of the "little Value she should set upon" beauty (IV,320). Beauty would endanger the adolescent female by supplying pretext for vanity, by causing her to ignore more important concerns, by attracting the wrong suitors. Two issues of the *Rambler* contain letters from "Victoria," a girl who, reared by a mother who valued only beauty, assessed her own worth by her appearance. At nineteen she suffered a disfiguring attack of smallpox, about which she commented, "when I looked again at that face which had been often flushed with transport at its own reflexion, and saw all that I had learned to value, all that I had endeavoured to improve, all that had procured me honours or praises, irrecoverably destroyed, I sunk at once into melancholy and despondence."[5] Small wonder! As the second letter makes clear, the destruction of such a girl's beauty deprived her at once "of all that gave her eminence or power; of all that elated her pride, or animated her activity; all that filled her days with pleasure and her nights with hope." The writer suggested that no man could "image to himself such helpless destitution, such dismal inanity," because no man feels "accustomed to derive from others much of his happiness."[6]

This comparison of male and female destinies helps to focus the central issue of many discussions of beauty: reliance on beauty as power constitutes dependency, since beauty has value only by controlling others' perceptions. Men, who *do* more, may base self-respect on accomplishment; not so the woman who relies on a lovely face. The "honours or praises" attendant on beauty may generate self-love, but beauty's primary gratifications depend on the approval it wins. As a source of "eminence or power," it has little stability; it epitomizes the precariousness of female dominance.

Taking eighteenth-century advice to young women at face value, one must conclude that a girl could aspire, at most, to the power inherent in being loved; that love based on beauty wouldn't last; that she could cultivate even her more substantial qualities—virtue, wit— for their effect on others. Many moralists encouraged a young woman to engage in conspicuous prayer and to perform acts of piety specifically as a mode of attractiveness. Conversely, they also warned against her shining in public, thus becoming conscious of her force and valuing its effects. Wit, unless rigorously controlled, "is the most dangerous Companion that can lurk in a Female Bosom," Wetenhall Wilkes insisted in 1744. It threatens the young lady because "it softens her Sentiments; makes her fond of being politely addrest; curious of fine Speeches; impatient of Praise; and exposes her to all the Temptations of Flattery and Deceit."[7] The essence of youthful female goodness resided in inconspicuousness. Why, we may wonder, did this message demand such lavish inculcation?

One teen-aged girl who appeared to take it very seriously, Fanny Burney, began her diary in 1768 at the age of fifteen with an elaborate invocation to "Nobody." "To *whom* dare I reveal my private opinion of my nearest relations? my secret thoughts of my dearest friends? my own hopes, fears, reflections, and dislikes?—Nobody!"[8] She meditated at length on the virtues of Nobody: an ideal recipient of confidence, an ideal object of love, an intimate incapable of betrayal, one who will feel pity rather than contempt for the writer. Then she concluded, "From this moment, then, my dear girl—but why, permit me to ask, must a *female* be made Nobody? Ah! my dear, what were this would good for, *were* Nobody a female?" (I, 5). Five years later, opening her journal for 1773, Burney spoke of it as a document "addressed to Myself." The entry ends, "But now to events, which will otherwise crowd so fast upon me, that I shall not be able to recollect them: what a loss would that be! to my dear—Nobody!" (I, 181). The identification between herself and the image of nonentity, implicit from the first, has become clear and more or less conscious. By the end of the next year, she wrote that she would abandon her account of one adventure for the sake of recording other events "by way of *amende honorable*—to

23

whom? why to myself, that is to Nobody! Heigh-ho! poor me! Are Nobody and I one and the same person?" (I, 327). The anger hinted by the question recalls the earlier query—"why must a female be made Nobody?"—which has been answered by the account of trivial happenings composing the writer's life. Through her insistence on the trivial she makes herself a nobody, remarking obsessively her own lack of importance. The original address to Nobody emanates from the diarist's consciousness of a social world in which one can trust no companion. If a shadow of arrogance breathes through the joking rhetorical question about what the world would be good for without females, explicit assertion, throughout the diary, reiterates the girl's claim that she has significant value for no one. Playing the role of Nobody, she plays it safe.

Readers of the early diary, however, may react to a less open message. The insistent claims of insignificance relate oddly to a subterranean assertion of the author's power as observer of and commentator on the familial and social scene. As unmistakably as the youthful James Boswell of the *London Journal*, Fanny Burney appears in her diary as someone forever playing a part: ingenue, obedient daughter . . . Nobody. Her dramatizations of her unwillingness to make claims finally imply that her reluctance constitutes a claim in itself. Denying the power of her youth, attractiveness, intelligence, perception, she avoids responsibility for the force she exercises. A familiar female mode—the mode of an oppressed class; its manifestations in adolescence have special intensity because of the strength with which the young experience the paradox of insubordinate energies, social suppression.

In 1740, more than a quarter-century before Fanny Burney began her diary, Samuel Richardson published a novel that explored— among other things—precisely this aspect of the adolescent female psyche. Fifteen-year-old Pamela Andrews claims no social significance, although her soul, she remarks, is as important as that of a princess. The theological argument supplies a plausible basis for self-assertion, but Pamela finds other grounds for self-glorification, always more or less in disguise. Never wanting to put herself forward, Pamela nonetheless manages to get herself noticed. She possesses only the lowly status of servant girl; even that position becomes precarious when her mistress, Lady B, dies, leaving an unmarried son as sole ruler of the household. Pamela shrinks from all attention, makes no claim of secular rights; yet, in the course of the novel, she achieves powerful self-assertion.

Pamela's preoccupation with her own identity focuses much of the novel's action—a theme familiar from twentieth-century discussions of adolescence but in eighteenth-century fiction often subordinated to the social problems and maneuvers of the young. Pamela, too, has abundant social problems and a conscious or unconscious social goal: the marriage that will elevate her class status. But her concern with who she really is, and how her selfhood can be communicated, controls many of her actions and reactions. She manufactures and enforces an identity through her letters, of course, but also through her behavior. Her projected self, unfailingly virtuous in expressed motive and intent, has hidden dimensions and hidden power. If Pamela wants to dress in ways appropriate to her station in life, she wants even more that others should see her doing so; if her garb dramatizes humility, it also expresses both vanity and pride; her costume exemplifies her integrity, a selfhood of resistance as well as of stability. Or should we say it exemplifies her *pose* of integrity? A long literary tradition of dress as obscuring naked truth stands behind Richardson's use of clothes as emblem. His heroine's pleasure in the alluring aspects of her apparel suggests that she consciously plays the part of country girl—and she uses her playing of the part to help reinforce the evolving reality of her selfhood. The positive reaction to her "honest" apparel, by no means a response simply to honesty, encourages her insistence on moral uprightness: a viable social as well as personal position, or so this optimistic fable would have it.

The character Pamela resembles the young diarist Fanny Burney, insisting on her status as Nobody and endowing that status with power. Like Burney, she proclaims her reluctance to be looked at and makes herself worth seeing. To her parents she presents herself in letters as the ideal adolescent, embodying without question the values of her elders. Chastity, piety, service to others: these admirable grown-up principles govern Pamela's behavior. Unlike the adolescents evoked by didactic writers, she presents herself as virtually devoid of passional impulse—or at least as having such impulse under control. Moreover, she manifests highly developed reasoning power, apparent most often in her canny assessments of others. Far more aware of human possibility than the naïve Parson Williams, she declares her adulthood by her calculation. If her cool head sometimes gives way—as when she allows herself to be terrorized by cows—it dominates sufficiently that her parents can congratulate themselves on remarkable success in child rearing. She seems to fulfill the fantasies implicit in many moralistic texts: she combines the rationality of the adult with the compliance of the child and seeks parental advice and approval, acknowledging the superior wisdom of her elders.

Compliance as well as rationality proves intermittent, yields to incompletely acknowledged impulse. Both qualities, like Pamela's integrity, amount to poses as well as realities, convenient modes of acting that allow the performer to discover herself with their protection—"real" enough, but not altogether definitive. Readers other than Pamela's parents find different messages in these letters. To Mr. B, the letters reveal not only Pamela's virtue but her cleverness and her increasing preoccupation with him. For twentieth-century readers, they have a yet more complicated effect: we respond both to the messages offered the avowed writer's consciously and unconsciously intended readers, and to Richardson's evocation of realistic adolescent conflict.

Adolescents are a socially subordinated class; so are women and servants. Pamela belongs to all three groups. Faced with the adolescent problems of gratifying narcissism, discovering identity, establishing intimate relationship, she also faces a situation that apparently forbids her—fifteen years old, female, a servant—clear self-assertion. She can, or course, resist; to find means of self-affirmation presents more vexing problems. Her triumph, in fact, involves her accumulation of power—power paradoxically greatest while she remains an adolescent servant girl, significantly decreased after her achievement of adult, upper-class status. She not only succeeds in getting her man, she conquers him—only to lose her power almost as she gains it.

Two episodes in which Pamela's power seems virtually nonexistent may suggest the dynamics of her ascendancy: her near decision to commit suicide, and a subsequent incident in which her master forces her to wait on him at table. The "suicide" drama illustrates how the girl's force derives from just those elements in her situation that apparently declare her lack of power. Abducted to Mr. B's Lincolnshire estate under the guardianship of a sadistic, prurient housekeeper, Mrs. Jewkes, Pamela has become the object of her master's lust. Mrs. Jewkes threatens his imminent arrival, and Pamela realizes her own absolute physical helplessness. She has appealed to the local parson, who proves ineffectual; she has tried to get help from the villagers, who deny it; wherever she turns, she has found evidence of Mr. B's immense social power. An earlier attempt to escape failed because she thought she saw two bulls (actually cows) menacing her. Now she plans to crawl between the bars of her window and to foil her pursuers by pretending to drown herself. Her description of this plan emphasizes the hidden issue of power: she remembers "a great captain" who confused his enemies by luring them to shoot at his discarded upper garments—"and so he escaped, and lived to truimph over them all."[9] Pamela, too, hopes to triumph over others, not merely to evade them. But nothing goes right, she injures herself trying to climb a wall, and she thinks of suicide as the ultimate evasion and triumph.

Her mental dialogue on the subject, as she reports it, amounts to a debate between forces of salvation and damnation; her final decision to trust to Providence involves giving up the intent of saving herself by her own means. Granting the theological and the dramatic importance of this account, one may also discern another level in Pamela's vacillations and decision. She attributes her impulse toward suicide to "the impetuousness of my passions" (p.180), a weakness often associated with adolescence; and her fantasies of how sorry everyone will be reflect another attribute of her time of life—indulged and elaborated narcissism. She says that she hopes no one will make ballads and elegies about her; clearly she means just the opposite. Gradually she begins to talk herself out of the desperate act, setting forth conventional religious arguments against self-destruction. God can help her, she recalls; God has given her strength to help herself. Then the crucial insight:

And who knows, but that the very presence I so much dread of my angry and designing master, (for he has had me in his power before, and yet I have escaped,) may be better for me, than these persecuting emissaries of his, who, for his money, are true to their wicked trust, and are hardened by that, and a long habit of wickedness, against compunction of heart? God *can* touch his heart in an instant; and if this should *not* be done, I can *then* but put an end to my life by some other means, if I am so resolved. (P.181)

The illogic of this argument reveals Pamela's real—and accurate—understanding of her situation. If God can touch the heart of wicked Mr. B, He can equally well convert Mr. B's servants, the "persecuting emissaries." The true distinction between Mr. B and his minions has to do with their vulnerability not to God but to Pamela. The girl has been in her master's power before and has escaped because of the force of her unacknowledged sexuality, which reduces Mr. B to ineffectual bluster. Pamela's accurate perception that she will be better off with her master than with Mrs. Jewkes depends on the resource she cannot allow herself to recognize. She reflects further: "Hitherto, Pamela, thought I, thou art the innocent, the suffering Pamela; and wilt thou, to avoid thy sufferings, be the guilty aggressor?" (p.182). Her position as innocent sufferer provides moral leverage that she would lose in any direct claim of power; her insistence on her helpless vulnerability (young, female, a servant . . .) sustains the stand-off between her and the grown-up aristocratic male, her master. By insisting that she has nothing, is nobody, she baffles his efforts.

A slightly later scene reiterates the paradox that all Mr. B's power proves futile in the face of Pamela's powerlessness. Mr. B comes to Lincolnshire, reducing his intended victim to a paralysis of terror: "I laid me down on the floor, and had no power to stir, till the clock struck nine; and then the wicked woman came up again" (pp.192–93). Mrs. Jewkes commands her to attend her master; Pamela claims she cannot stand up, but trembles her way downstairs, where Mr. B orders her to wait on him at table. She does so, holding on to a chair in order to keep herself upright, her hand shaking so that she spills the wine. Forced to listen to Mrs. Jewkes's false accounts of her, and to remain silent; falling on her knees to beg mercy; interrupted, ridiculed, and contradicted in her attempts at self-justification, Pamela feels utterly helpless. Mr. B forcibly kisses her and tries to put his hand into her bosom; Pamela struggles and says she would rather die than be used thus. Her master emphasizes his absolute control of her fate. He subsequently sends her a written proposal that she should become his mistress, a proposal eliciting Pamela's contemptuous refusal. The refusal includes her reminder "that I, a poor, weak, friendless, unhappy creature, am too full in your power!" (p.201). Soon afterward comes the second rape attempt, but by now the reader finds it unsurprising that Mr. B cannot carry it through: Pamela has unmanned him.

The dynamics of these situations repeat themselves over and over. The more helpless Pamela seems, the more ineffectual her master proves. His claim of social authority works as badly as his efforts at sexual authority. The last-ditch attempt to bribe the girl into becoming his mistress involves a desperate effort to get her to acknowledge a want he can gratify—perhaps for wealth or jewels or finery, some metaphoric equivalent for the sexual desire she steadfastly refuses to admit. Mr. B sees Pamela as sexual object, but she will not admit a sexual identity, declaring her selfhood dependent, rather, on her *moral* identity. Hence B's total frustration. Unlike Lovelace in *Clarissa*, he does not imagine himself as conqueror. He would prefer the role of seducer—a role Pamela makes it impossible for him to play. By withholding herself, psychologicaly as well as physically, she nullifies her master's aggressive self-assertion. She declares herself only her parents' daughter, not an independent sexual being; in the face of such denial, Mr. B becomes powerless.

After the second bedroom episode, B's sexual purposes having been frustrated once more by Pamel's lapse into unconsciousness—emblematic nonbeing—the young woman's superior power becomes increasingly apparent. Mr. B implores her to tell him what to do; she tells him not to marry her. She begins a literal journey back to her parents; he humbly begs her to return, to have mercy on the aggressive male now prostrated on a sickbed by his yearning for this servant girl. She makes the decision to go back to him; he can only feel grateful. She stops being merely her parents' daughter. Her father understands precisely what is going on (Pamela's adolescence ending as she separates from her parents) and deals with it by another instance of denial: he refuses to believe that Pamela would willingly choose another man, and comes himself in search of her. She declares a symbolic identity between lover and father (Mr. B's clothes fit her father perfectly), but chooses the lover; her power to choose, to dispose, to manifest and exploit her attractiveness, has now reached its high point.

After her marriage, that power steadily diminishes. If she curtseys at the altar and says, "Thank you, sir," to her husband's vows, these facts suggest future realities. Socially sealed as adult rather than as adolescent, and elevated in class, Pamela no longer has so many causes for subordination. She can distribute largesse to the servants and control their employment; she can assert herself with Lady Davers; she can triumph over all the neighbors through her beauty, her virtue, and her narrative. No longer, however, has she the same substantive power over Mr. B. Now her sexuality is known, her selfhood revealed; she lacks the potent force of the unknowable. Her subordination becomes increasingly vivid. She provides a pattern for other ladies by alluding to her husband as her master, and his mastery now has far more efficacy than before. Furious at the very idea that she might take his anger lightly, he reminds her of his absolute dominance. Now he lays down rules and makes conditions that she experiences as binding, despite some private reservations. Before our eyes, Pamela dwindles into a wife.

As girl and woman, Pamela obeys the advice books; indeed, the novel itself, the narrator explicitly maintains, constitutes a didactic text. Pamela relies on virtue rather than on beauty, she behaves as her parents have taught her, she acknowledges no "Torrent of Inclinations." But the parabolic curve of her power elucidates a hidden message of the didactic texts. Young women must keep themselves firmly under control in the pubertal years because they have so much to control. The beauty on which they should not depend symbolizes the sexual power they dare not openly acknowledge. However virtuous, they possess potent resources for captivating, even dominating, men. But they lose their power when they accept full adult status. As Mrs. Peachum had sung earlier in the century,

> A Maid is like the golden Our,
> Which hath Guineas intrinsical in't,
> Whose Worth is never known, before
> It is try'd and imprest in the Mint.[10]

Unmeasured worth vanishes with marriage. Richardson's investigation of Pamela's postmarital career, overtly demonstrating the heroine's capacity for fulfilling the responsibilities of the class to which she has risen, reveals her losses more vividly than her gains and suggests an aspect of eighteenth-century ambivalence about adolescence. Maturity may define the proper goal of the young—but adolescents (at least adolescent women) have more fun, and, paradoxically, more power than their elders.

A century or so later, adolescent women, as described by moralists and novelists alike, led lives seldom characterized by either fun or power. The parabola of power in *Pamela* gave way, in much Victorian fiction, to a slightly rising, or even slightly descending, straight line. In Charlotte Yonge's immensely popular novel for the young, *The Daisy Chain* (1856), adolescents learn the necessity of giving up what they want for the sake of service to others. "I like Greek so much," teenaged Ethel remarks plaintively, to be rebuked by her elder sister Margaret: "And for that would you give up being a useful, steady daughter and sister at home? The sort of woman that dear mama wished to make you, and a comfort to papa."[11] A new fantasy dominated. If sexual power remained the latent issue, the culture found fresh forms of concealment for it in defining as threat brains rather than bodies. What a girl should do with her intelligence presented difficulties comparable to those implicit in the question of what she should do with her beauty. The primary form of power conceivable for women remained power over men. Most discussions of either the dangers or the advantages of female education returned compulsively to the problem of relations between the sexes. Some, indeed, started there. The twentieth-century reader may feel tempted to discern irony, but certainly none is intended in an essay by the anonymous father of six sons bemoaning the consequences of female education:

The pretty ignorance, the fascinating helplessness, the charming unconsciousness that enslaved us bachelors of long ago—where are they all gone to?
Where is the graceful weakness that appealed so eloquently to our awkward
strength; where the delicious unreasonableness that so subtly flattered our
logical profundity; where the enthusiastic romance that seemed designed ex-
pressly to temper and balance the matter-of-fact worldliness inevitable more
or less to the nature of the masculine animal which has to work for its living?
Where, I ask in eager anxiety, for the sake of my six boys?[12]

The presence of such spokesmen for a potent cultural attitude helps to
explain why even female apologists for intellectual self-development
implicitly justified themselves by what they could give to men. De-
fenses of female education adopted a serious, straightforward tone in
marked contrast to the coy attempt at charm in the concerned father's
utterance. But the defenders carried in their heads the arguments of
the other side. "There is a feeling that since education develops the
powers, it increases the dangers, and that our object with girls should
rather be to seclude, to administer sedatives, than to develop those
powers of mind and character, which are the media of temptation."[13]
The association between "powers of mind and character" and "temptation" erupted repeatedly. Dorothea Beale, author of the sentence just
quoted, argued for the desirability of encouraging rather than repressing the young woman's capacities; but she felt obliged to acknowledge
the danger of such a course.

More explicitly than anyone in the preceding century, mid-nine-
teenth-century thinkers recognized the special psychic stress of
adolescence.

The mature woman, of whatever age or fortunes, can hardly look without
keenest sympathy and trembling pity on those who have yet to go through it
all. . . . The years between twelve and twenty are, to most, a season anything
but pleasant; a crisis in which the whole heart and brain are full of tumult,
when all life looks strange and bewildering—delirious with exquisite unreali-
ties,—and agonized with griefs equally chimerical and unnatural. . . . Most
girls' characters are stamped for life by the associations they form, and the
circumstances by which they are surrounded, during their teens.[14]

The notion that the adolescent years have crucial importance for later
development appears frequently from the end of the seventeenth century on. Dinah Mulock's stress on the "tumult" of internal experience
during the pubertal years, however, embodies a newer perception of
far-reaching implications: the delirium and agony of the teen-aged
girl make her a dubious judge of her own welfare; her unstable emo-

tional state implies her vulnerability to the potential seducer. More-over, the nineteenth-century vocabulary of crisis, tumult, bewilder-ment, delirium, suggests that she contains within herself contending powers that victimize her. Reason does not necessarily help the victim of feeling. Indeed, the cultivation of intellectual qualities, particularly in young women, may intensify the danger created by volatile emo-tion. The issue, once more, relates to power: if a girl develops her intellectual capacities, she may claim not only independence but—a point never openly stated—perhaps even dominance; and although she may have the capacity for power, she cannot be allowed the right. What, after all, are young women *for*?

Certainly not to function in the world:

If, indeed, parents expected their daughters to fill the situations that their degenerate sons ought to occupy, it might be well to send them to these "min-iature worlds" [that is, boarding schools], to acquire a spirit of hardy self-dependence; but if woman is still to be the kind and delightful companion of our homes, the refiner and tranquiliser of our minds, . . . we think that a pub-lic seminary can hardly be regarded as the likeliest place for the cultivation of qualities such as these.[15]

British education, Charles Kingsley pointed out late in the nineteenth century, "has been most certainly a splendid moral success. It has made, by the grace of God, British women the best wives, mothers, daughters, sisters, aunts that the world, as far as I can discover, has yet seen."[16] God presumably intended women to function as wives, moth-ers, aunts, to refine and tranquilize. But how were girls to become women, moving from adolescent tumult to adult roles as sources of tranquillity? The ironic recommendation to administer sedatives has obvious plausibility. More serious recommendations took characteris-tic negative forms. Victorian moralists felt quite sure what they want-ed young women to turn into (wives, mothers, aunts . . .) and what they wanted them to avoid ("hardy self-dependence"), but were con-siderably less certain what exactly girls should *do*.

"Does a man fall in love with artist, novelist, mathematician, or poli-tician? No, he doesn't."[17] Therefore, a girl should avoid becoming any-thing of the sort. Dinah Mulock, herself a successful commercial writ-er, denounced "that frantic craving for literary reputation, which lures a girl from her natural duties, her safe shut-up home life, to join the band of writing women—of which the very highest, noblest, and most successful feel, that to them, as women, what has been gained is at best a poor equivalent for what has been lost" (Mulock, p. 220). To the girl herself belongs the choice between safety—dependent on "shut-up home life"—and the danger of intellectual adventure, symbolizing less mentionable dangers. Mulock's emphatic language, her stress on "what has been lost" by literary commitment, underlines the implicit equation between intellectuality and sexuality. The status of writing women appears to coincide with that of fallen women.

The countercase also depends on a partly concealed preoccupation with the sexual. Young women become vulnerable to sexual danger, a more radical argument went, not through intellectuality but through boredom.

From the purely physiological point of view, it is difficult to believe that study much more serious than that usually pursued by young men would do a girl's health as much harm as a life directly calculated to over-stimulate the emotional and sexual instincts, and to weaken the guiding and controlling forces which these instincts so imperatively need. The stimulus found in novel-reading, in the theatre and ball-room, the excitement which attends a premature entry into society, the competition of vanity and frivolity, these involve far more real dangers to the health of young women than the competition for knowledge, or for scientific or literary honours, ever has done, or is ever likely to do. And even if, in the absence of real culture, dissipation be avoided, there is another danger still more difficult to escape, of which the evil physical results are scarcely less grave, and that is dulness. It is not easy for those whose lives are full to realize how insupportably dull the life of a young woman just out of the schoolroom is apt to be, nor the powerful influence for evil this dulness has upon her health and morals.[18]

The winner in "the competition of vanity and frivolity" presumably would triumph in attracting male attention; the winner in "the competition for knowledge" might actually triumph over men. The female author of this account, Dr. Elizabeth Anderson, faced the possibility with equanimity, but male commentators on young women's yearning for intellectual achievement wielded powerful sexual weapons, threatening that female breasts would atrophy and that a woman who insisted on leaving her proper sphere would develop hard "masculine" lines in her face. One female apologist suggested that the girl who had been working for scholarships instead of reading novels "might easily have affections as unhackneyed as those of a convent-bred *ingenue*": she would be more virginal than *anybody*.[19] The very presence of such an argument indicates the potency and the ubiquity of the sexual issue concealed behind the intellectual one.

Many nineteenth-century novels contain book-reading heroines: from Jane Eyre and Lucy Snowe to Dorothea Brooke. Pamela's education included enough literary texts to supply her with conveniently highfalutin rhetoric on occasion, but Richardson's novel stresses the social rather than the intellectual value of that education: Pamela knows how to carve gracefully and to sing a little, so she can support her rise in station. Molly Gibson, heroine of Elizabeth Gaskell's *Wives and Daughters* (1866), has had little formal education, her father believing it preferable to keep girls ignorant and good. She reads, however, and thinks about what she reads—a fact that accumulates symbolic weight and helps to determine her sexual, therefore her social, fate.

Two contemporary comments, one on the situation of women, the other on that of the young, locate important concerns of *Wives and Daughters*. The remark about women occurs in an anonymous 1869 essay: "Novels of various shades, sensational, domestic, sentimental, or philosophical, reflect the discontent prevalent amongst women of all classes, and considering the enormous proportion of feminine authors, must be allowed to possess a considerable authority."[20] The more extended observations on the situation of the young, by Harriet Martineau, date from twenty years earlier but sound timeless.

It should be remembered that the young creature is half-living in a new world; and that the difficulty of reconciling this beloved new world with the familiar old one is naturally very trying to one who is just entering upon the struggles of the mind and of life. He cannot reconcile the world and its ways and its people with the ideals which are presenting themselves to him; and he becomes, for a time, irritable, or scornful, or depressed. One will be fanatical, for a time, and sleep on the boards, and make and keep a vow never to smile. . . . Another looks down already on all his neighbors on account of the great deeds he is to do by and by: and all are convinced,—every youth and maiden of them all,—that nobody can enter into their feelings,—nobody understand their minds,—nobody conceive of emotions and aspirations like theirs. At the moment, this is likely to be true; for their ideas and emotions are vast and stirring, beyond their own power to express; and it can scarcely happen that any one is at hand, just at the right season, to receive their outpourings, and give them credit for more than they can tell.[21]

Women and young people, one might conclude, have in common their discontent. The tone of the 1869 essayist suggests that women's problems reflect a specific historical situation; Martineau's unusually sympathetic and inward description of the young makes a more universal claim. Martineau went on to hint, however, that, if simply left alone, the youths and maidens would outgrow their difficulties. The painful discrepancy between feeling and expression, aspiration and actuality, would diminish as the feelings and aspirations dwindled: Martineau did not comment on the pain of *that* fact.

Nor, directly, did Elizabeth Gaskell, who created in Molly Gibson a character both epitomizing and repressing the special discontents of the female young. Like Pamela, Molly achieves power—considerably less than Pamela's—while steadily denying the achievement; unlike Pamela, she shares a household with another girl who takes a different, apparently more successful, course, and whose sexual and social power manifests itself vividly at every turn. As imagined by Gaskell, Molly cannot choose to imitate her glamorous stepsister Cynthia: character is fate. And she comes out well in the long run. On the other hand, this novel explicitly preaching repression—for young and old, male and female—conveys a submerged consciousness of disturbance. It stands among the nineteenth-century documents of feminine dissatisfaction, and it dramatizes a Victorian pattern of youthful dissatisfaction; it also explores the relation between sexual power and bookishness.

The novel opens with a characteristically veiled announcement of the power issue. Molly Gibson, a very young twelve-year-old, wakens in her bedroom.

To begin with the old rigmarole of childhood. In a country there was a shire, and in that shire there was a town, and in that town there was a house, and in that house there was a room, and in that room there was a bed, and in that bed there lay a little girl; wide awake and longing to get up, but not daring to do so for fear of the unseen power in the next room—a certain Betty, whose slumbers must not be disturbed until six o'clock struck. [22]

The pleasure of that rigmarole, when used by children, involves declaring oneself the center of the universe, seeing the world organized, in enlarging circles, around the self. But for a narrator to locate "a little girl" in a bed in a house in a town in a country reminds the reader, rather, of the child's *unimportance* in any large scheme of things. Precisely this tension, between the sense of a young woman's utter insignificance and a rebellious insistence on her importance, dominates the narrative. Moreover, the conflict between Molly's longing to get up and her immobilization by an "unseen power," internalized in her overwhelming desire to be good, epitomizes all the plot's intricacies insofar as they concern Molly.

The disingenuousness of the slightly arch narrator, ostentatiously relying on innocuous convention, also continues. The novel takes a predictable form, supplying a "good" girl in Molly and a "bad" one in Cynthia, whose badness, however, never gets out of hand; she acts provocative, but not loose. The good girl subordinates herself to the needs of others and is overlooked by Roger Hamley, the man she loves, who proposes instead to the bad girl. Cynthia has triumphed casually over every male she encounters; she accepts Roger. When events conspire to expose her shoddy past, she rapidly finds another man who suits her better—rich, stylish, superficial. Good Molly then gets her reward in good Roger; her father, who has mistakenly remarried for prudential reasons, must live with the consequences of his misguided choice.

Does Molly's getting the man she wants sufficiently compensate for what she has previously endured? At a deeper level, the happy-ending match seems virtually irrelevant—an effect intensified by the fact that the happy ending was never actually written, as Gaskell died before completing the last chapter. The more profound story, pessimistic in a different way from *Pamela*, shows Molly turning inward rather than outward, learning not to seek her fulfillment in the responses of others, developing psychological rather than sexual power: the power of limited needs. This theme does not find full articulation: Gaskell drew back from the implications of her narrative, making Molly apologize for and deny her own serious reading.

At the outset, Molly suffers for her lack of literary sophistication. On her first visit to Cumnor Towers at the age of twelve, she fails to understand Lord Cumnor's allusion to "The Three Bears," which she has never read; to her his attempts at friendliness register as terrifying patriarchal power. She clings closer to her own father, who willingly accepts total responsibility for her; her mother has died some years earlier. On the way home from this excursion among the aristocracy, Molly announces, "Papa, I should like to get a chain like Ponto's, just as long as your longest [medical] round, and then I could fasten us two to each end of it, and when I wanted you I could pull, and if you didn't want to come, you could pull back again; but I should know you knew I wanted you, and we could never lose each other" (p.58). That desire never to lose each other long controls Molly. This fantasy of passive power—Molly would not *hold* her father's chain, she would only attach herself to it—for years defines her conscious aspiration.

Dr. Gibson, content with his daughter's passivity, sees no desire for power in her utterances. Later, when she is seventeen, and his apprentice declares himself in love with her, the doctor conceals the fact from the girl and ships her off to live with the neighboring Hamley family. His propensities for denial manifest themselves also in his ill-considered plans for marriage; meanwhile Molly, with the same propensities, avoids awareness of the very possibility that her father might remarry.

At the age of seventeen, Molly, unlike Pamela, has no real power at all. Her social class does not subordinate her, but her role as good daughter—literal and symbolic—in her own and in the Hamley family, does. She has no sexual force. Squire Hamley worries lest his sons fall in love with her; Mrs. Hamley points out, accurately, that Molly is not the kind of girl young men fall in love with. She does not possess Pamela's subterranean sexual awareness; although she spins romantic fantasies about Osborne Hamley, the elder son whom she has never met, they lack physicality: two angels holding hands. Despite her selfless devotion to her father, she has no power over him: he marries out of some fantasy of his own about taking care of her, but never considers her unexpressed wishes and needs. Not having discovered, defined, or come to terms with herself, she lacks even the power of articulated personality. Molly has a large problem: how to find and use power—both "great ability to do, act, or affect strongly" and "the ability to control others."

Her father's remarriage creates for Molly a sexual crisis, although she does not understand it as such. Grief and rage utterly incapacitate her.

She was afraid of saying anything, lest the passion of anger, dislike, indignation—whatever it was that was boiling up in her breast—should find vent in cries and screams, or worse, in raging words that could never be forgotten. It was as if the piece of solid ground on which she stood had broken from the stone, and she was drifting out to the infinite sea alone. (P. 145)

The sea of adult life and love has never attracted her; her attachment to her father has found comfortable embodiment in her continued position as child. Now the experience of losing her moorings coincides with the discovery of inexpressible passions within herself. She must find new ground to stand on and figure out what to do with her unknown passions.

The social dimensions of Pamela's drama help to control its possibilities. At every stage of events, Pamela understands the precise social meaning of each eventuality; her highly developed social awareness largely determines her course of action. Molly has no equivalent resource. Superficially, her situation presents no such vivid dangers as Pamela's; yet she has more truly been set adrift. As deeply committed as Pamela to an image of her own goodness (though less obviously concerned to promulgate it), she therefore finds herself severely restricted. Most of the novel dramatizes, in painful detail, the minutiae of that restriction. Roger Hamley, a friend rather than a lover, and her strongest ally, insists that she must try to consider others' needs rather than her own; she attempts to do so. Her father's second marriage connects her with a woman embodying all she detests—falsity, frivolity, pretension; she must subordinate herself to this woman. She must relinquish the pleasures of daily association with her father as well as the deeper gratifications of standing always first with him. She must see her stepsister eclipsing her at every turn, must listen to Cynthia's praise from others, must know that Roger loves Cynthia more than Cynthia loves him. She must always refrain from using or saying what she knows. Under the increasingly intolerable discipline of refraining, she falls into a Victorian decline. With no conspicuous hardships in her life, Molly has yet endured a great deal.

The contrast with Cynthia becomes ever more clearly focused on questions of power. Cynthia's mother, who tyrannizes over Molly, feels afraid of her own daughter and avoids confrontation with her. A vocabulary of domination and control evokes Cynthia's charm. "In the short time since they had met, Cynthia's unconscious power of fascination had been exercised upon her. Some people have this power. Of course, its effects are only manifested in the susceptible" (p. 254). "Cynthia missed her slave, although she did not care for Roger one thousandth part of what he did for her; yet she had found it not unpleasant to have a man whom she thoroughly respected, and whom men in general respected, the subject of her eye, the glad ministrant to each scarce-spoken wish" (p. 398). The equivalence between charm and power impresses itself even upon Molly, forced to realize her own relative helplessness as she sees her stepsister controlling the responses of others.

The language and the structure of *Wives and Daughters* consistently emphasize Molly's ineffectuality and its psychic costs, registered not in active rebellion but in a magnifying sense of dullness. Dr. Elizabeth Anderson's comment about the extreme dullness of life for a girl just out of the schoolroom applies to Molly, who becomes ever more conscious of the meaninglessness of her existence, however ardently she tries to focus her attention on the needs of others. Harriet Martineau's description also applies: Molly has high ideals and aspirations—aspirations directed mainly toward the achievement of flawless virtue; she finds actualities draining her ideals of significance. Frustration, boredom, futility: such is Molly's lot, a paradigm of the female adolescent's situation—unless, like Cynthia, the adolescent risks self-indulgence.

Yet *Wives and Daughters* does not present itself finally as a story of failure: it gets almost to its happy ending. Its dark side, however, embodies Gaskell's most original contribution to the fiction of adolescence. *Wives and Daughters* testifies to at least one adult's perception or memory or imagining of the emotional dreariness associated with the life of a good girl, in the Victorian definition, as she experiences puberty with no circumstantial freedom. But the novelist also allows Molly to discover her own kind of power. Its nature emerges for the reader, if not for Molly herself, in two striking episodes.

Although the girl's life of frustration has driven her inward, to a steady moral dialogue with herself (she has literally no one else to talk to about serious matters), her power registers itself in relation to men. The incident with moral and psychological reverberations second only to those of Dr. Gibson's marriage involves the stereotypical Victorian bounder, Mr. Preston, who, like Cynthia, commits no real sexual sin but displays dangerous inclinations. Cynthia has got herself into a compromising position in relation to him. Earlier she has borrowed money from him and, from gratitude and ignorance, agreed to marry him. Now she has repaid Preston, but he refuses to return the early letters in which she professed her love and made damaging allegations about her mother. Desperate for liberation from a man she has grown to detest, Cynthia gladly accepts Molly's offer to try to procure the letters. Molly meets Preston by appointment and triumphs over him in a direct battle of wills: he relinquishes the letters.

As Molly sets out on her heroic enterprise, her emotions foretell no triumph. "Not really knowing what she should say, hating the errand, not satisfied with Cynthia's manner of speaking about her relations to Roger, oppressed with shame and complicity in conduct which appeared to her deceitful, yet willing to bear all and brave all, if she could once set Cynthia on a straight path—in a clear space, . . . Molly set out" (p. 528). Characteristically motivated by empathetic concern for another's welfare, characteristically dominated by negative feelings ("not . . . knowing," "hating," "not satisfied," "oppressed"), expecting her fate to involve *bearing* as well as *braving*, Molly has little sense of herself as heroine; nor, at the end of her encounter with Preston, does she even realize that she has won. Cynthia's sexuality provides her power; Molly's asexuality provides hers. It derives from unconsciousness, Gaskell tells us; we would say today, from denial.

There she stood, frightened, yet brave, not letting go her hold on what she meant to do, even when things seemed most against her; and besides, there was something that struck him most of all perhaps, and which shows the kind of man he was—he perceived that Molly was as unconscious that he was a young man, and she a young woman, as if she had been a pure angel of heaven. . . . He felt that he would have to yield, and give up the letters. (P. 533)

He yields not because Molly resembles a pure angel of heaven but because she has stumbled upon an authoritative strategy—a strategy (turning to a father figure: she threatens to inform Preston's employer, Lord Cumnor, of the situation) also derived from her innocence: she by no means perceives its implications. Cynthia's knowingness makes her effective; Molly's unknowingness saves her. The equation of innocence with power means something very different from its implications in Richardson's novel. Pamela's technical innocence underlines her sexual potential; Molly appears to have no sexual potential. Gaskell implicitly reproaches Preston for his awareness of sexual possibility—that's the sort of man he is: a bad sort—thus apparently endorsing Molly's system of denial. The "good" adolescent, in this fantasy, achieves total separation from sexuality.

Yet asexual triumph over a man cannot bring the plot to a satisfactory conclusion; only marriage will do that. Molly becomes marriageable partly by virtue of her reading. (And partly by her beauty: she lacks the sexy vividness of Cynthia, but has a pale distinction, which eventually Roger notices.) At a charity ball, Molly appeals to shy Lord Hollingford by asking questions; and he compliments her father on having a "well-read" daughter (p. 339). Her stepmother concludes that reading somehow generates sexual attractiveness and recommends it to Cynthia as preferable to millinery. Molly blushes and disclaims intellectual seriousness; but the interests that she has developed as a result of her affection for Roger stand her in good stead. In the climactic scene where she returns as a young woman to Cumnor Towers, where at the age of twelve she had felt humiliated for not having read "The Three Bears," Roger sees her as the cynosure of an admiring group of men. When two members of the aristocratic household discuss the possibility of a match between Roger and Molly, Molly's high intelligence and her capacity to appreciate Roger provide arguments in its favor. Intelligence and reading have become forms of deference to the superior male; yet Molly also exercises genuine power over Roger, and he feels unsure of himself as he begins to realize his interest in her.

But Molly in fact—here she differs most sharply from Pamela—does not really *want* the power that for a brief moment she has. As the novel has revealed earlier, hers is the "great power of loving," as opposed to Cynthia's power to charm (p. 389). Unconscious alike of sexual and social dynamics, unconscious of how completely she has defeated Mr. Preston and of how fully she has appealed to Roger, she revels in subordination. Because of the danger of infection from scarlet fever at Hamley Hall, she cannot even speak to her lover before he leaves for Africa on a scientific expedition; she tries to wave to him from the window and is forced to dodge around her stepmother, who thinks his attentions intended for herself. But Molly has effectively transferred her interest—at last—from father to lover; and her father, even more explicitly than Pamela's, feels the pain. "'Lover *versus* father!' thought he, half sadly. 'Lover wins.' And he, too, became indifferent to all that remained of his dinner" (p. 701). The transfer, as for Pamela, amounts to a transition from one master to another. Molly has grown, has defined herself as a separate moral being, has even defied her father, in a mild way, when he wishes to protect her from the gossip provoked by her private interview with Preston: she refuses to tell him how and why she has acted for Cynthia. More than many youthful novelistic heroines, Molly has established an identity separate from that of love and marriage: an elaboration of her role as good daughter, but also a distinct personality. Yet the consistent association of separateness with sadness, the melancholy that attends the girl's growth, her inability to take pleasure in her power, sexual or asexual: these conspicuous emotional facts support the view that *Wives and Daughters* depicts a youthful heroine who wishes most to remain a daughter, whose wifehood will amount to a version of daughterhood, whose shift of affection from father to lover seems more a necessity than a source of excitement. A sad parable.

A single novel can hardly demonstrate a universal shift of sensibility from the mid-eighteenth to the mid-nineteenth century. On the other hand, *Wives and Daughters* belongs clearly to its time: if it does not embody the totality of Victorian opinion about female adolescence, it does exemplify a kind of imagining inconceivable a century earlier. Richardson envisioned a girl whose gathering sexual force generates power enabling her to circumvent social restrictions. Although Pamela acknowledges the laws governing the conduct of servant girls and of pious young women, she makes a sharp distinction between her self and her social roles. Her soul is as important as that of a princess: the statement has psychological as well as theological import. Gaskell's Molly, although she develops a more highly elaborated and more morally individual sense of self, has internalized more of her society's prescriptions—the society's moral preaching, not its practice. Denying her sexuality, refusing to acknowledge the power she can have, Molly welcomes powerlessness as her native condition. Her creator seems to approve—but she also conveys the sadness of the situation. Cynthia gets what she deserves, in her glittering young man; but she and her mother, Mrs. Gibson, although both suffer as well, undeniably achieve more pleasure than do upright Molly and her upright father. Pleasure is not everything, we may piously agree, but the systematic association of virtue with repression and depression implies a sad recognition of realities unacknowledged a century before. If Pamela loses real power in marriage, she gains the social power she wants. Molly wins in marriage the opportunity to exercise her great power of loving; her virtue must be her reward. Female adolescence no longer seems a joyous time of life.

A century later, matters appear yet worse. Doris Lessing's Martha Quest—free to express her sexuality, free to have a career, free to leave home when she wants to—feels miserable. For a time she obscures her unhappiness by dissipation, but misery remains the substratum of her experience. Her marriage at the novel's end expresses failure rather than success, and little in Martha's adolescence foretells anything but continuing failure. She knows her own sexual power far more vividly than her fictional predecessors, but its open acknowledgment makes it meaningless. Everyone has it, everyone recognizes it, it does not really matter. The novel, which takes its heroine from the age of fifteen to eighteen, charts a decline in her power—a power that in any case always existed mainly in fantasy.

Unlike her eighteenth- and nineteenth-century equivalents, Martha knows that she is adolescent and feels the condition as a doom. Literature tells her of adolescence as misery:

in a hundred years' time people will read the novels of this century and conclude that everyone (no less) suffered adolescence like a disease, for they will hardly be able to lay hands on a novel which does not describe the condition. ... Perhaps, [Martha] thought (retreating into the sour humour that was her refuge at such moments), one should simply take the years from, let us say, fourteen to twenty as read, until those happier times arrive when adolescents may, and with a perfectly clear conscience, again enjoy themselves?[23]

Her own adolescent career demonstrates in elaborate detail the utter impossibility of enjoyment.

Published originally in 1964, *Martha Quest* reports imagined events in the late 1930s in Rhodesia. The vision of adolescence the novel offers, however, reflects fantasies implicit in the work of sociologists and psychologists of the early sixties, who wrote about English and American adolescents as constituting a separate culture. Collectively, the representatives of that culture have immense social power. Even sober commentary often betrays not the fear *for* the young characteristic of the eighteenth century but a vivid fear *of* the young as utterly alien. "If you were given a Hottentot to bring up I think you would have a bit of a job, because I do not think you would begin to understand how the Hottentot mind works. As far as we are concerned, I think this teenage group is a Hottentot group."[24] The sense of difference gives rise to grandiose prophecies of doom:

The so-called youth problem is not confined to young people and . . . it is intimately associated with the whole life of the community. It arises from ordinary social processes and trends in contemporary western civilisation and cannot be evaluated in isolation. . . . The cleavage between the generations, because it involves inability and refusal to accept and comprehend necessary differences, could be called a state of cultural *anomie*. In so far as this is true it is a threat to the stability of the social structure.[25]

Observers found in the young an absence of what adults "regarded as appropriate feelings of guilt and shame" and a "growing disinclination to take on trust the moral system and values—the Rules—handed down by the adult world" (Hopkins, p. 439). They looked on their juniors with blind and altogether irrational awe:

By 15 or 16, middle-class youths have developed a psychological stability that was rare in earlier generations of this strata. Having put personal tasks of development behind them by the time they reach the later stages of secondary education or the first years of university, they are able to cope with social and political questions that their forerunners gladly left to adult authority.[26]

Or they described them with extravagant sympathy: "to appreciate properly how the young can feel, one has to imagine living in a foreign country whose language you cannot properly speak, whose inhabitants look at you with suspicion, and impute dreadful crimes to you. You are expected to be polite, deferent, quiet and to spend your life standing up out of doors."[27]

We write more books than our ancestors did, and as more books survive from the 1950s and 1960s than from earlier centuries, one can easily multiply examples of historical or social-scientific observation shaped by emotional preconceptions about the young. The most conspicuous difference between mid-twentieth-century fantasies about youth and those of previous generations involves the degree of distance asserted to divide young and old. Moralists of the eighteenth and the nineteenth centuries apparently believed that, given proper guidance, their juniors would grow into respectable citizens. Moralists of the twentieth century, representing purportedly value-free intellectual disciplines, hope for the same result but appear less sure of its occurring. They believe in the collective power of the young: to effect social change, to resist established ideas, to cope with difficult problems, to do the unpredictable. The assumed antagonism between young and old derives not from idiosyncrasies of differing developmental stages but from clashes of well-defined value. When social scientists ask English working-class adolescents to complete a sentence beginning, "The older generation," the latter make negative responses.

It may be seen at once that the majority of these subjects, particularly the boys, feel that adults are unduly critical of young people, do not understand them, and stand in their way, blocking their road to independence. The predominant feeling is that adults are against them, jealous of them, critical of their clothes, their taste in music, their love of excitement and adventure, and ready to condemn them on mere hearsay or gossip.[28]

Surely adolescents have always felt that grown-ups are in some fundamental way *against* them. But now such fantasies, publicized, solidified, gain authority by promulgation; and we hear little of the counterfantasy of adults as allies.

The adolescent conviction that adults are against them reinforces the corresponding grown-up fantasy that the young are against *them*. But those young show themselves unwilling to grant significant power to the old (authority, yes—but not lasting power), whereas by the mid-twentieth century, their elders, in the hints of fear that suffuse much published prose, suggest that, in their minds, the much-discussed economic power of the young corresponds to some vague but threatening massing of adolescent force. Anthony Burgess's *A Clock-*

work Orange (1963) provides a clear fictional expression of this notion, which emerges also in less likely contexts.

The great power implicitly assigned to adolescents in social science studies belongs to them only as a group. As individuals, psychological commentary makes clear, they suffer uncertainty, absence of power. Doris Lessing emphasizes much suffering in her portrayal of Martha Quest, whose character epitomizes two typical adolescent manifestations: the need of the young person to invent himself or herself, and the problematic relation of reality and fantasy in youthful experience. A recent formulation generalizes such situations as Martha's: "The adolescent's search for himself appears, then, to be more than merely an attempt to find something that is already there. More basically, it is also an active attempt to create a personality. As he tries on various roles and manners, his interior experience crystallizes and becomes his own to feel, to think about, to change, to conceptualize, and to act upon."[29] A condition full of possibility—but precarious. Cyril Smith, writing in the early 1960s, remarks that "the extraordinary feature of the contemporary situation is the contrast between the continuity and conformity which individuals experience in family life and the variety of possibilities demonstrated to him [sic] in fantasy."[30] Fantasy becomes available to everyone, as Martha's experience testifies, not only through the operations of the individual imagination but through the offerings of the popular press, the proliferating abundance of books. The uncertainties of twentieth-century adolescence derive not only from ambiguities inherent in the search for identity but from the conflicting images offered by the culture.

Martha Quest issues from an imagination of the 1960s informed by memories from the 1930s. An isolated young woman on a farm, she experiences herself as more or less powerless (although with occasional small triumphs) in reality, if not in fantasy. When she goes to town, she becomes part of a youthful group with considerable social force; yet her grotesque inability to take command even of her own life continues. Her early sexual experiences, her marriage itself, dramatize the impossibility of control.

The narrative tone of the novel emphasizes a special perspective on the young woman's situation. Richardson, in the eighteenth century, attempted to imagine Pamela imagining her self; except in rare interludes, hers is the voice the reader hears. A century and a quarter later, Gaskell incorporated Molly Gibson into a third-person narrative, the voice of the narrator speaking for adult wisdom and common sense.

Sometimes this voice speaks of Molly with gentle amusement; always it assumes—as I have argued thinkers of the past characteristically assume—the inevitability of youth's turning to age and accepting the values of previous generations. Although Molly's unhappiness has social roots, Gaskell did not use it to suggest serious social criticism. Lessing's point of view on Martha Quest reflects the ambiguities of recent attitudes toward adolescence. Despite the fact (or because of it) that *Martha Quest* has obvious autobiographical components, the author often adopts a sardonic tone toward her protagonist. Her "voice" does not embody conventional adult wisdom and morality; it questions the validity of such notions. On the other hand, it by no means endorses the adolescent sensibility. Its authority depends partly on its refusal to acknowledge public sanctions; it mingles admiration and condescension toward the young.

In trying to define how Martha is understood by the narrator, let us start with the facts of her experience, where lines of power seem relatively simple to describe. Power defines itself in relationship, and the girl has few relationships: principally the tie with parents so crucial to adolescent realization. To separate from and to triumph over her mother and father are her crucial tasks. Her own explicit consciousness of this fact, and the narrator's tacit strong endorsement of the undertaking, mark conspicuous differences between the twentieth-century novel and its predecessors. Pamela and Molly had to shift allegiance from father to lover, but with no shift of values. Martha considers it self-evident that, in order to start living, she must free herself from her parents' assumptions about life. Pamela's shadowy mother presents no problems to her. Molly's mother, conveniently dead, also offers no difficulties; the girl can permissibly direct hostile feelings toward her stepmother. Moreover, her detestation of that stepmother's moral laxity reflects what her father has taught her; in action she remains subservient. Not so Martha, locked in conscious struggle with a mother antagonist whose power seems out of all proportion to any personal strength. Martha's apparent victories prove illusory; the novel ends with Martha's defeat, in this and other battles. Her limited power accomplishes almost nothing for her; her fate suggests a dark view of adolescent experience.

Even with her parents, Martha's body provides a source of power. As the girl develops breasts and hips, she begins to perceive her sexuality as a weapon. She refuses to wear childish dresses; she buys material and makes herself a glamorous (although inappropriate) gown for dancing; before she goes to town, she has turned herself into an imitation of women in magazines. These acts of defiant self-assertion help her to claim an independent identity, to impress herself on the world. Her parents feel the force of her assertions: her mother twittering in futile efforts at restraint, her father denying the facts as long as possible and refusing to bestow the unambiguous approval she needs for emotional release.

Martha's sexuality does not liberate her, nor does it lead her to any definitive power over men. For, more openly than in Pamela's world or in Molly's, men acknowledge the force of female attractiveness. Hordes of youths at the Sports Club manifest toward Martha ritualized agonies of longing which mean nothing. Donovan, who claims her as his "girl," treats her only as an object for display. Perry wishes to admire her body but not to make love to her. Dolly, to whom she loses her virginity, feels little interest in her and no real passion. Douglas, whom she marries, makes love out of a book. On occasion Martha admires herself, but the admiration of others has too little energy to affect the dynamics of relationship. Sexuality, no longer a concealed locus of power, makes little happen.

If the body provides no power, what of the mind? Martha reads a lot, and her reading creates and reinforces potent fantasies. When she wishes, at fifteen, to dramatize resistance to her mother and her mother's friend, Mrs. Van Rensberg, she pretends to read Havelock Ellis. She expresses her alliance with the Cohen boys by reading what they tell her to read—even as Molly educated herself under the guidance of Roger. Molly, however, makes no intellectual claims; Martha presumes an extravagant valuation of her own mental capacities, despite the fact that she has hardly exercised them. She reads mainly to confirm what she already believes, not to expand her mind or understanding; if she occasionally seeks something new from books, she rarely sustains the effort for long. Her alliance with Douglas, initially based on her belief that they share reading and convictions, proves as superficial as the reading and convictions. Her intellectual pretensions do not even enable her to take a matriculation examination; her reading does not help her deal with reality.

Only in fantasy does Martha possess power. Her vision of "a noble city" where all races live harmoniously together, a city "fabulous and ancient," depends on the idea of exclusion (p. 11). Functioning as authority in her imaginary city, possessed sometimes by the imagined potency of her beauty, dreaming of effectiveness in hypothetical careers, Martha substitutes for actual control the power supplied by daydreams. She has less mastery than she realizes, hurried as she is from one activity to the next by the conventions of social groups to which she has never consciously chosen to belong, playing expected roles, and experiencing sharp disapproval if she steps out of her established part. At the beginning of the novel, Martha looks through the window to a sky "flooded with wild colour. She was facing, with dubious confidence, what she knew would be a long fight. She was saying to herself, I won't give in, I won't; though it would have been hard for her to define what it was she fought" (p. 19). At the end, she marries Douglas. "Mrs. Quest waited anxiously immediately behind Martha's left shoulder, and at the crucial moment when the ring must be put on she grasped Martha's elbow and pushed forward her arm, so that everyone was able to see how Martha turned around and said in a loud, angry whisper, 'Who's getting married, me or you?' " (p. 246). The long fight for separate identity, for power at least over her own life, has ended in Martha's effective merging with her mother, accepting such a marriage as that mother might have arranged: Martha's rebellion has somehow produced perfect conformity.

Pamela and Molly content themselves with the status of Nobody, and behind its protection, they consolidate their gains. Martha Quest insists on being *Somebody* but cannot substantiate her claim. Pamela and Molly have internalized the professed values of their societies, including the low valuation placed on women; they assume such values as the necessary condition of self-fulfillment. If Molly feels rather less happy than Pamela about the emotional implications of her moralistic self-subordination, she too manages to find some measure of satisfaction within the restrictions she accepts and endorses. Not so Martha Quest, whose satisfactions prove evanescent and minimal, who cannot feel herself part of any viable society, who makes the adolescent state of "outsider" into the apparent guiding principle of her life. The angry, rebellious, questioning twentieth-century adolescent accomplishes little; the compliant eighteenth-century girl gets precisely what she wants.

Yet Martha, like Pamela, functions as heroine of a narrative action—functions thus mainly by the effect of the narrative point of view which evaluates and "places" the characters. Much of the time, the narrative voice simply tells the reader—in language often rather different from Martha's—what the protagonist feels and thinks, what forces impel her. Sometimes the voice comments from a judicious distance on the implications of Martha's thought and action. Always dictional choices suggest a system of values—perhaps not altogether coherent—by which the action may be judged.

"Nobody's Power"

To begin with the ending: "The group then dissolved in tears, kisses, congratulations, and alcohol. In this manner, therefore, was Martha Quest married, on a warm Thursday afternoon in the month of March, 1939, in the capital city of a British colony in the centre of the great African continent" (p. 246). The formulation of the second sentence recalls the opening lines of *Wives and Daughters*, but it serves a very different purpose. Molly's domestic setting (her house and room and bed) will shape her life far more than will the town and shire and country that lie beyond; she both centers her universe and takes comfort from her insignificance. Discomfort dominates the sentence evoking Martha's chronological and geographical setting: discomfort epitomized in the passive construction that makes the girl victim rather than actor in her own marriage, and reinforced by the political reverberations of the date and of the discrepancy between small "British colony" and "great African continent." However unconscious she may temporarily remain, Martha inhabits a political—not, as do Pamela and Molly, only a social—world. The disturbances latent in that world both foretell and dwarf the disturbances implicit in the match she has made. The zeugma of the first sentence, equalizing kisses and alcohol as dissolving agents, undercuts any positive sentiment associated with this marriage. In conjunction, the two sentences convey the narrator's opinion of Martha's wedding: a mindless pairing, made insignificant by events of larger scope, involving little volition and little real feeling on the part of its protagonists.

The ironic consciousness of the narrator undercuts many forms of adolescent extravagance or moral and intellectual inadequacy, but its critical force does not depend on unanimity of adult values. In the sentences about Martha's wedding, Martha is not the only target. The adult spectators of her marriage dissolve equally in congratulations and alcohol; adults lead the world toward war; adults have created the colony in the vast continent. The sharp eye of the judging narrator sees folly and evil everywhere. She (I shall consider this narrator female, although the voice seems predominantly sexless) belongs to some collectivity, but not to so large a one as Gaskell's narrator assumes: this is a political collectivity mainly, assuming the necessity of political awareness and equality, and the corollary desirability of awareness of all kinds, at all levels.

Most of the time, the narrator's awareness far exceeds Martha's. Sometimes she offers wry sympathy for Martha's plight, as when she points out that her heroine belongs to an enormous group of aspiring writers motivated by nothing more than discontent with their present lot, yet feels herself utterly unique; or when she comments, "alas for the romantic disposition, always waiting for these 'moments,' these exquisite turning points where everything is clear . . . !" (p. 241). Sometimes the tone partakes more strongly of condemnation. In either case, the narrator, although embodying the values of a vaguely political adult group, speaks essentially with an individual voice. She affirms most strongly the value of perception—a shared standard but in its nature an individual achievement. No powerful realized community exists in the foreground or the background of *Martha Quest*. Martha allies herself with her peers, the group as a whole exercising considerable force in the community, a subsociety of youth like those the sociologists describe and fear—but although she makes this alliance in action, she experiences herself in isolation. The narrator sympathizes with her specifically inasmuch as the girl herself struggles with the problem of perception.

> Even more painful than this cold-minded analysis was the knowledge that it was all so banal; just as the stare from that dispassionate cool eye, which judged herself as adolescent, and therefore contradictory and dissatisfied, was harder to bear than the condition of adolescence itself. She was, in fact, suffering from the form of moral exhaustion which is caused by seeing a great many facts without knowing the cause for them. (P. 165)

And the narrator tends—rather inconsistently—to glorify the character for her truly visionary moments, her painful semimystical experiences of communion with the universe. Beneath the skepticism of the narrative tone lurks another level of romanticism: a yearning to glorify some possibility having nothing at all to do with the mundane actualities of daily life.

Inasmuch as they reflect an attitude toward adolescence, skepticism and romanticism affirm the same position. Martha Quest, an exemplary adolescent girl, is condemned to the extent that she lacks equipment to avoid growing up into a conforming member of her society, and praised for her will to refuse conformity—a will that requires clear vision to be realized. To the degree that she resembles her mother and her father, Martha has failed—by her own standards and by those of the narrator. Because she wishes not to resemble them, she merits the role of heroine, admirable for her struggles, her painful efforts at self-education, her yearning to validate her private experience. She lacks the power to control her own destiny, the only power that counts; her "heroism" is severely compromised. Her alienation and her helplessness, however, allow her to exemplify not only a time of life but a moral and psychological condition extending far beyond adolescence. Like other twentieth-century protagonists, she attests her heroism partly by her failure.

The subject of adolescence encourages fantasies of potentiality, and the heroines of the three novels here considered display great potential power—sexual (Pamela), moral (Molly), or perceptual (Martha). Actual power, on the other hand, operates within a context. The novelists differ more sharply in their imagining of context than in their understanding of their protagonists. Meanings assignable to adolescence must derive from the culture that surrounds it. "Adolescence is a period of transition with little independent reality. It draws its meaning from the past and from its relationship to some future adulthood toward which it aims and unfolds. . . . Adolescence in all cultures, especially in our own, is bound inextricably to adult reality."[31] Writers with faith in the established social, moral, and psychological system can generate plots in which the growth of the young enables them to participate in the adult order—a happy ending. Pamela moves from one social level to another and immediately sets about reaffirming the intricacies of hierarchy. She rises without disrupting anything; her gains, in her apparent view, compensate for her losses. Molly, inhabiting a darker world, feels the cost of her moral choices; but her struggle to affirm her integrity lends dignity to her final elevation to adult female status, such as it is. She will manage, presumably, a decent marriage, a decent life. For Martha, the odds look bad. She belongs to a society in which adolescents do not necessarily grow up at all, they only grow older; and growing up is not necessarily an improvement. No real order governs the adult world, and certainly none governs the adolescent. Power has hardened into tyranny, political, social, familial. The indeterminacy of adolescence makes it perhaps preferable to the rigidities that succeed it, but adolescents live in as much confusion and ignorance and blindness as do their elders. *Martha Quest* endorses little—mainly the narrator's sardonic tone.

The shifts of sensibility and perception expressed by these three novels suggest not only a change of feeling about adolescence but altering perspectives on women, diminishing optimism about possibilities for the individual, increasing skepticism about happy endings. *Marth Quest* parodies the familiar structures of earlier novels about young women entering the world and finding a man. Like *Evelina,* Lessing's novel reports a girl's leaving home, her uncertainties in a new social world, her confusion among false suitors, her marriage to one of the community's most eligible young men—and evaluates each of these happenings in a new and dismal way. The point concerns adolescence less than society.

Observations about adolescence *always* imply comments on society, on the sexes, on the structures—acknowledged and unacknowledged fictions—by which we order experience: which brings us back where we started. Even a single book tells something about the world from which it comes; and the three books I have been discussing share characteristics with many of their contemporaries. Richardson's capacity to suggest without appearing to emphasize the sexual sets him apart from most of his fellow novelists in the eighteenth century; but even decorous Fanny Burney, even the host of undistinguished women writers who stocked the circulating libraries, made beauty a metaphor for sexuality and conveyed through their accounts of lovely heroines the power of female attraction not yet fully measured. A century after Richardson, in 1847, *Wuthering Heights* established a nineteenth-century pattern. Freedom and power recede to childhood (as they do for Maggie Tulliver in that very different novel, *The Mill on the Floss*); in adolescence, the pressures toward conformity kill the first Catherine Earnshaw and transform the second Catherine into a paragon of selflessness, force Maggie to deny herself, send Gaskell's Molly into a decline. And by the mid-twentieth century, dozens of novels evoke beauty as a trap—for its possessor as much as for its victim. Alix Shulman's *Memoirs of an Ex-Prom Queen* (1972) exemplifies the pattern: a girl *seems* to have power in her sexuality, but she thus conspires in her own diminution and guarantees her misery.

The increasing stress on a girl's powerlessness corresponds to the much-reported twentieth-century phenomena of alienation and experienced powerlessness for all ages, all conditions: the adolescent girl thus provides a metaphor for her elders as well as, on occasion, a target for their vindictiveness. But the kinds of perception recorded by Richardson, Gaskell, and Lessing by no means embody the only possible ways of seeing and rendering adolescence. Novelists committed in different ways to a resolutely adult point of view—though sometimes apparently struggling against their commitment—offer strikingly different images.

3

"Straight from Mother Nature"

Youth has power, a kind of divine power straight from mother nature. All the old tax-payers know of this because, of course, for one thing, the poor old sordids recollect their own glorious teenage days, but yet they're so jealous of us, they hide this fact, and whisper it among themselves. As for the boys and girls, the dear young absolute beginners, I sometimes feel that if they only *knew* this fact, this very simple fact, namely how powerful they really are, then they could rise up overnight and enslave the old tax-payers, the whole dam lot of them—toupets and falsies and rejuvenators and all—even though they number millions and sit in the seats of strength.[1]

Colin MacInnes published *Absolute Beginners* in 1969, when Great Britain and the rest of the Western world had discovered in their midst a flourishing and dismaying Youth Culture. The novel's protagonist, who makes the observations above, is aged eighteen-going-on-nineteen; he prospers by taking and selling pornographic photographs. At the end of a lurid sequence of events, mostly connected with race riots in London, he gets his girl: a seventeen-year-old who goes to bed with any black man who will have her, but has recently married a middle-aged homosexual dress designer. The young man's father dies, leaving him money, but he discovers he does not want to do what he thought he wanted; he works at nothing new; and he therefore changes nothing in his life. Such a plot measures a long distance from *Tom Jones*, ostensibly a less ambiguous account of a young man's growing up.

MacInnes's youth who asserts teenage power apparently resembles Martha Quest as little as Tom Jones, although Lessing's novel was published at almost the same historical moment as MacInnes's. Martha experiences utter ineffectuality; this speaker claims "divine power"—a claim, however, that rests more on wish than on perception. The "old tax-payers" in actuality "sit in the seats of strength." Although the young "really" possess great strength, they don't know it, they don't

53

use it, it tests itself only in fantasy—corresponding thus to Martha's vision of the ideal city that she will absolutely control. Despite its surface differences, *Absolute Beginners*, too, would support a generalization that mid-twentieth-century views of the young accord them little force, although writers pay them obsessive attention.

The contrast in tone between *Martha Quest* and *Absolute Beginners*, the contrast in plot between *Tom Jones* and the latter novel, also call attention to a particular angle of vision controlling this and other fiction of adolescence—an angle from which the young, however individualized, appear also as members of an age-defined class. In such fiction, attitudes toward adolescents as a species dominate the presentation of youthful development. Pamela in her rise offers vicarious satisfaction for readers of any age; Molly Gibson exemplifies the situation of Victorian women; Martha Quest articulates twentieth-century alienation. But other novels in every period present adolescent characters in ways forbidding such large identifications. The feelings these characters express reflect clearly the wishes and the fears that the young arouse in the adult world. Imagining Pamela as a remarkable girl, Richardson could fulfill fantasies of control in his authorial role as he manipulated his character through her fairy tale career. To understand a youthful figure as representing a generation changes the possibilities and the meaning of authorial manipulation. A second group of novels from three centuries adumbrates the intricate balance of sympathies such works reflect and generate.

One theme that emerges more vividly from these novels—*The Vicar of Wakefield, Pendennis, Absolute Beginners*—than from those treated in the last chapter is the fundamental conflict of generations, expressed in plot or narrative stance, or both. "I cannot but fancy," Dr. Johnson wrote, " . . . that the young and the old were always at variance."[2] Writers for two centuries after him have sometimes fancied the same thing. In fiction, journalism, and "objective" description, they render the anger and envy the old feel toward the young, and they attribute to youth the same feelings. As persistent as the battle of the sexes, the struggle of generations displays comparable ambiguities and concealments. Everyone knows about it, although some have a stake in covering it up.

Despite the differences that divide *Pamela, Wives and Daughters*, and *Martha Quest*, all three assume common concerns between "good" adult and worthy adolescent. Pamela will incur losses, but she still wishes to grow up and participate in established society; the narrator of Gaskell's novel shares the protagonist's interest in behaving well;

Martha's efforts to discriminate, however dubious their success, unite her with the ironic narrator who perceives her inadequacies. In other fiction, however, adolescents and adults pursue antithetic agendas. The speaker in *Absolute Beginners* perceives the conflict of youth and age as a class war, the basic assumption of the novel. Earlier novelists, too, often noted a vast gap between generations; they therefore made power relations of central importance in their fiction. Didactic writers also realize the power struggle between old and young and uneasily try to come to terms with it.

Conventional morality, particularly in the eighteenth century, encouraged moralists to record their uneasiness in the form of disapproval as they described the basic conflict, insisting that matters *should* be otherwise. Richard Steele declared the misunderstanding between young and old "unnatural": "But though every old man has been a young, and every young one hopes to be old, there seems to be a most unnatural misunderstanding between those two stages of life. This unhappy want of commerce arises from the insolent arrogance or exultation in youth, and the irrational despondence or self-pity in age."[3] Keeping himself as writer distant alike from age and youth, he attributes the conflict to individual insolence and irrationality rather than to the nature of things. Describing arrogant youth and irrational age as appropriate objects of "contempt and derision," insisting that no other terms adequately convey the condemnation appropriate to such violation of norms, Steele's essay elaborates the situation of the older man who wishes himself younger—a situation dominated by tension between "the course of things" and human beings' distress at that course. Over and over Steele specifies what "should be." "One would think it should be no small satisfaction to have gone so far in our journey that the heat of the day is over with us. When life itself is a fever, as it is in licentious youth, the pleasures of it are no other than the dreams of a man in that distemper . . ." (p. 343). The more he argues the absurdity of repining at the processes of aging, the more eloquently he conveys the energy and hints the universality of such repining. The latter part of life, he insists, "in the eye of reason, is certainly the more eligible" (p. 344), marked by possession of authority that generates pleasure. But such assertions echo with uncertainty. "If to be saluted, attended, and consulted with deference, are instances of pleasure, they are such as never fail a virtuous old age" (p. 345). The sentence's conditional form contradicts its insistence. "The natural course of our minds," Steele tells us, "should build their approbations and dislikes upon what nature and reason dictate" (p. 344); but the essay reveals his bewilderment that minds rarely follow their "natural course," and that the dictates of nature and reason prove easy to avoid.

Many eighteenth-century thinkers besides Steele got into difficulties by assuming necessary correspondence between the "reasonable" and the "natural." For age and youth to live constantly at odds defies rationality, but Steele's condemnation could hardly obviate the conflict; it could only encourage repression of hostile manifestations. Less than half a century later, Dr. Johnson declared the clash of generations inevitable because of the constant "revolution of sentiments" that "occasions a perpetual contest between the old and young."[4] People change their minds with age; looking back, we can all see such changes in ourselves, although we may not know how or when they happened. The most fundamental alteration of perspective derives from the steady lessening of hope. The young man, controlled by his faith in appearances, "never imagines that there may be greatness without safety, affluence without content, jollity without friendship, and solitude without peace" (p. 259). Despite the inevitability of such benign blindness, Johnson cannot note youth's naïveté without "pity and contempt"—contempt less emphatically stated than Steele's, but equally inherent in the nature of things. The old see the dangers of youthful innocence, self-importance, narcissism; but the old fall prey to their own dangers. The *Rambler* concludes with depressed summary: "In youth we have warm hopes, which are soon blasted by rashness and negligence, and great designs which are defeated by inexperience. In age we have knowledge and prudence without spirit to exert, or motives to prompt them; we are able to plan schemes and regulate measures, but have not time remaining to bring them to completion" (p. 261). "We" belong successively to each group; both groups experience the same discrepancy between the capacities to imagine and to do; both exemplify the poignance of the human condition, for which the misunderstandings between generations become an emblem.

Most eighteenth-century commentators on the conflict between young and old appeared to believe it remediable, although they differed about the remedies and who should apply them. An anonymous midcentury essay in the *Connoisseur* distributes responsibility equally between the generations:

Old men are perpetually commenting on the extreme levity of the times, and blaming the young, because they do not admire and court their company; which, indeed, is no wonder, since they generally treat their youthful companions as mere children, and expect such a slavish deference to their years, as destroys that equality by which cheerfulness and society subsists. Young men do not like to be chid by a proverb, or approved by a wrinkle; but though they do not choose to be corrected by their grave seniors like school-boys, they would be proud to consult them as friends. . . . Youth . . . shun the company of age, complaining of the small regard and respect paid to them, though they often act with so little reserve and such unbecoming confidence, as not to deserve it.[5]

The old isolate themselves from the young, the essay explains; the young run "into dissipation and debauchery, rather than associate with age." If both sides would try for reconciliation, both would profit: the young would gain instruction, the old, vicarious "cheerfulness" (p. 77). But the implicit recommendation to the old to treat the young as equals counters deep emotional biases. Virtually all descriptions of generational relationships stress the insubordination of the young and assume the rightness of their elders' firm control. Fear that youth might elude this control governs fictional, descriptive, and prescriptive utterance.

Fear, and also rage: the young possess too much power. "It is a frequent and growing Folly in our Age, that *pert young Disciples soon fancy themselves wiser than those who teach them.*"[6] "It is enough to be of an advanced Age, without any other Failing, to be looked at as a proper Object for *Raillery*, if no worse."[7] "Young people never shew their folly and ignorance more conspicuously, than by this over-confidence in their own judgment, and this haughty disdain of the opinion of those who have known more days."[8] "Oh! how unhandsome it is, as well as irreligious and unchristian, for a young Man or Woman, when their Parents are old, and perhaps full of Aches and Pains, or otherwise in Years and in bad Health, to treat them with Scorn and contempt."[9] These commentators sound exasperated and frustrated and self-righteous. They represent experience, civilization, and Christianity, which oppose folly, ignorance, petulance, and irreligion. But the fierce denunciations breathe a sense of futility: one cannot order back the tide. Knowing themselves right, the moralists yet feel themselves helpless.

They offer advice in abundance: warnings to adults to attend to their children's development in order to avoid the horrors of rebellion, and strictures to the young about their obligation to respect the old. Both approaches resist any claim of youthful autonomy: the young should be thought of, should think of themselves, as children until the moment they assume full adult responsibility. Parents must monitor every detail of youthful conduct; children must cultivate self-subordination. I shall quote only one example, from a book of advice to a sixteen-year-old girl:

Let your Obedience to your Mother be . . . your Delight and Exercise. . . . She was the Guardian of your Childhood, and is the Guide of your yet unexperienc'd Youth, and never was a Trust discharged with greater Tenderness and Fidelity. . . . Therefore let filial Affection be your governing Principle; and behave yourself towards her with all Humility and Observance. Let no Pretence of your being in the Right ever provoke you to answer her with Indifference or Contempt. . . . You are to please her in all Circumstances, to comfort her on all Occasions, to obey her Commands with Pleasure, to consult her in all Affairs, and to reverence all her Precepts.[10]

The adolescent state, by adult definition, makes "being in the Right" irrelevant. Categorical assertions ("You are to please her in all Circumstances . . . "); a language of emotional blackmail; imperative syntax and sentimental vocabulary; a refusal to acknowledge any rights belonging to adolescence: such resources strengthened the eighteenth-century moralist. An additional heavy weapon belonged to writers appealing to religious impulse, as many did.

Whatever sanctions the writer invoked, he or she often urged in particular the obligation to love. Psychological theorists in our own time have taught us that children dread above all else the withdrawal of parental love; eighteenth-century moralists conveyed the obverse terror. If the young think and act for themselves, the subterranean argument went, they will stop loving their parents; if they no longer feel the need for parental care—for guidance in the practical and the moral affairs of life—they may cease to pay for what they get in the coin of filial devotion. Hence the panicky note of the frequent reminders about all that parents do for their offspring in the early years; hence too, perhaps, the sense of sinister possibility in the perceived unlikeness of young and old. The gap between generations must at all costs be papered over—if not between youth and age in general, at any rate between parents and children. For aging implies weakening, loss of energy and capacity for action, as Steele and Johnson and many others noted; the young, therefore, will win if warfare opposes parental and filial generations. Thus fear fuels the anger of the avowedly mature.

The wish for control, the fear of defeat, implicit in the frantic commands and pleas of adult moralists presumably countered comparable wishes and fears in the young. Little direct testimony from youth survives, although Boswell's journals from the 1760s, written in his early twenties, testify to at least one intense father-son struggle for control.

Fiction most often imagines events from the young person's point of view: *Pamela* in this respect typifies many eighteenth-century novels. One of the century's most popular works, on the other hand, commits itself to the perspective of a father rather than of a son or daughter. *The Vicar of Wakefield* (1766) allows its father-narrator to report the adventures of four adolescent children—two male, two female. (Fictions based on what I am calling a class perspective usually concentrate more attention on young men than on young women, perhaps because a mythology of conflict associates itself more readily with males. Goldsmith, however, imagined the struggle for control as involving both sexes equally.)

The Reverend Primrose relies heavily on denial. Never does he acknowledge the strength of his conflict with his growing sons and daughters; he assumes always the rightness of his dominance and the continuing necessity of his control. None of his children ultimately challenges his right or his capacity to determine their fates: the fantasy answers the wish for adult dominance. On the other hand, the action has meanings of which its reporter remains sublimely unaware. One set of meanings concerns the relation of parents and children on the verge of adulthood, a relation of mutual unacknowledged hostility in which parents appear to possess all the weapons.

The Vicar defines his parenthood as inherently virtuous in the novel's opening sentence: "I was ever of opinion, that the honest man who married and brought up a large family, did more service than he who continued single, and only talked of population."[11] The plot's major catastrophes result from actions of the young. For the loss of money that initiates the train of dire events and the fire that leaves the family homeless, youth bears no responsibility; but Olivia's fall from virtue precipitates a series of disasters, and George's rashness results in more.

No individualized detail marks the description of the young people: in their father's opinion, the young have virtually no character at all. "It is needless," he observes, "to attempt describing the particular characters of young people that had seen but very little of the world. In short, a family likeness prevailed through all, and properly speaking, they had but one character, that of being all equally generous, credulous, simple, and inoffensive" (IV, 21). The young, however, behave in conspicuously different ways. George has already graduated from Oxford at the beginning of the novel; he then travels on the Continent, supporting himself by various ingenious expedients, and makes his own way in England. (His career thus bears analogies to

Goldsmith's own—a fact that raises provocative psychological questions about the apparent authorial hostility toward him.) Presumably in his early twenties, George assertedly shares with his younger siblings the generic credulity and worldy inadequacy of the adolescent. If the father demonstrates at least equal credulity, when he is tricked—like his sixteen-year-old son—by a sharper, he still claims clerical and paternal authority. George, despite his success at supporting himself through considerable difficulty, must submit, acknowledging his own moral inadequacy (he has twice got himself in trouble by dueling) before he can accomplish the marriage he desires.

The young need not to grow but to submit: *The Vicar of Wakefield* openly reveals an adult wish more ingeniously concealed in other fiction. Sophia, wise in her innocence, yields from the beginning to the guidance of her elders. Although she dissolves in tears when Sir William, the man she loves, pretends to give her to another, she offers little resistance to anyone from beginning to end; she accordingly wins the richest spouse. Olivia, led astray by her compelling desire to please, must confess the error of her ways, submit to her father's religious instruction, and do what she is told. She learns nothing but submission. Sixteen-year-old Moses wins only rebuke for his precocious intellectual pretension and effort. His father explains the boy's proper role: "Thou art now sixteen years old, and hast strength, and it was given thee, my son, for very useful purposes; for it must save from famine your helpless parents and family" (IV, 144). Never does the father express gratitude for the son's help, which he considers his due. He will, however, in due time bestow a farmer's daughter on worthy Moses. George, having repented his youthful rashness, receives reward. A rich man functions as *deus ex machina*; the young learn their dependence on the mature, the rich, the powerful.

The Reverend Primrose's political vision of the state perceives contention for power as motivating all who possess any wealth, with only the presence of a monarch at the head of the contenders moderating competing tyrannies. Considering the idea of kingship far more important than that of liberty, the Vicar defends it almost as stoutly as he advocates monogamy. His familial politics derive from similar principles, although he calls his family "a little republic." The young find occasional modes of rebellion—the girls, for example, brewing surreptitious complexion washes—but their father assumes his right of absolute control, treating even his wife like an adolescent girl. Power matters immensely to him, freedom not at all. He delights in his daughters' humiliations when they attempt to indulge their vanity; he feels no sympathy for their emotional turmoils. Although he welcomes back his repentant eldest daughter with much rhetoric of forgiveness, he stresses his goodness more than her need. More important for his aggrandizement of power: he accepts responsibility only for his children's virtues, none at all for their misdoings and difficulties. Moses's intellectual folly, Olivia's moral weakness, George's impetuosity: such weaknesses may, he hints, derive from his wife's inadequacies, but certainly not from his own. On the other hand, he stresses the good instruction that Olivia and the rest have received. "Sure it was no small temptation," he remarks to Olivia, "that could thus obliterate all the impressions of such an education, and so virtuous a disposition as thine" (IV, 127).

This rather crude summary of Primrose's relations with his children ignores the father's conspicuous virtues to suggest one special effect of the story's being told from a parent's point of view. Variations on the theme of Olivia's fall and repentance are staples for minor eighteenth-century novels; George's attempts to make his way in the world parallel the youthful careers of Smollett's protagonists and Fielding's; even Sophia's uneventful course finds equivalents in novels about young women aspiring to places in the world. But these other fictions rely on sympathetic identification with adolescent dilemmas and emotions, even though the narrator characteristically represents either an adult version of the central youthful character or a wise adult commentator on the latter's career. The use of a father as narrator emphasizes the strength of parental ambivalence toward maturing children—not, presumably, as a result of conscious authorial intention but as a reflection of more or less universal fantasy. *The Vicar of Wakefield's* plot fulfills the wish implicit in many adjurations of the moralists—the wish for absolute adolescent submission. Fielding and Smollett and Burney, identifying themselves more closely with a youthful point of view, depicted young people as gaining and growing from knowledge of "the world," which enables them to assume adult places in society (or, on occasion, outside it). From Goldsmith's perspective in this novel, "the world" constitutes only an enemy; although the worldly goal of financial prosperity, however disavowed, measures the children's ultimate success—success depending specifically on acts of compliance.

The uncertain relation between author and narrator makes it difficult to ascertain how fully the former endorsed the position the latter expounds. Certainly the fiction dramatizes the moral consequences of considering adolescents as objects rather than as subjects. A particularly chilling instance occurs when erring Olivia returns home with her forgiving father, who tries to comfort her:

As we travelled along, I strove, by every persuasion, to calm her sorrows and fears, and to arm her with resolution to bear the presence of her offended mother. I took every opportunity, from the prospect of a fine country, through which we passed, to observe how much kinder heaven was to us, than we to each other, and that the misfortunes of nature's making were very few. I assured her, that she should never perceive any change in my affections, and that during my life, which yet might be long, she might depend upon a guardian and an instructor. I armed her against the censures of the world, shewed her that books were sweet unreproaching companions to the miserable, and that if they could not bring us to enjoy life, they would at least teach us to endure it. (IV, 129)

Olivia neither flees nor commits suicide under such verbiage; her sad experience, presumably, has cowed her. The Reverend Primrose wishes to cow her further. He assumes that she wants "a guardian and instructor" because she has not prospered without one; he speaks of repression and constriction and thinks he is making his daughter feel better. He even hints the withdrawal of love: Olivia shall never *perceive* any change in his affections, but he has raised the possibility of affectional diminution. The girl has no special reason to worry about misfortunes of nature's making. But her father's sententiousness ignores her needs. His promise that books will help her to endure life takes on new specificity when, a little later, he provides an example of instructive narrative, telling her a long story about a young woman of wondrous virtue and devotion who wins for herself and her family "all the happiness that love, friendship, and duty could confer" (IV, 134). When Olivia fails to respond cheerfully, he complains that her self-pity blocks her feelings of compassion.

Olivia's adolescent sexuality, of course, encourages her father to indulge this moral sadism. Unlike Pamela, she has lost control, become a fallen woman. The novel grants her little psychology and no power; more than the other young people, she embodies the adolescent as victim, allowed only her moment of attractiveness. Her crude female narcissism—the simple desire to be admired—makes her vulnerable; her father's more intricate narcissism finds frequent unreproved opportunities for expression. The Reverend Primrose's insistence on doing good always partakes of (although it is not entirely defined by) his desire to display his goodness. His self-satisfaction has abundant justification, but one would not want to live with him. His children, however, in this narrative shaped by paternal consciousness, never comment on their experience of his benevolent despotism. Those who attempt to evade it only get in trouble. The force of youth, as embodied by the Primrose children, has no effective power in comparison with that of age, bolstered by social and religious sanctions.

Yet this novel's extremities of language and action have long encouraged ironic readings, and the evoked relations of age and youth raise particularly vivid ironic possibilities. What logic, for instance, justifies the gratuitous cruelty of the scene in which Sir William pretends to give the young woman who loves him to another man? Sophia, like many eighteenth-century heroines, has no recourse but refusal. First she demonstrates intense passive resistance, "almost sinking into her mother's arms," crying out "faintly," "scarcely able to speak." Finally she responds "angrily," "I'd sooner die first"; and her lover claims her, rewarding her first show of spirit (IV, 180–81). Neither she nor anyone else reproaches him for needlessly tormenting her.

The episode emblemizes the adolescent situation in the novel. Powerless before the authority of wealth, symbol of adult force, the girl may refuse to be disposed of, but she cannot dispose of herself. When Sir William proclaims his devotion, he says not that she has conquered him but that he feels "rapture to have made a conquest over such sense and such heavenly beauty!" (IV, 181); he has reduced sense and beauty to trophies. Those qualities, however, have won the girl the prize she seeks, despite her passive self-presentation: maybe Sophia has, after all, the gifts of a Pamela. Elevated to a share in adult prosperity, she will assume social ascendancy over her parents. Neither the Reverend Primrose nor his surrogates can rule forever.

When, echoing Dr. Johnson, Primrose mentions endurance and enjoyment as alternative human possibilities, the reader feels the discrepancy between Johnson's measured assessment and Primrose's didactic pieties. Perceiving life as morality play, he enforces his dominance over youth by proclaiming the unalterable laws of his moral universe, which generate misery for him and his family but allow him to display his pious capacity to accept suffering. The inadequacy of his perception to encompass the needs or feelings of others, particularly *young* others, produces no visible negative effects in the novel, which explicitly celebrates his moral triumphs and neglects his insufficiencies.

Primrose's point of view controls the narrative. He ignores not only the struggle of old and young but the capitalistic struggle also inherent in the events he reports, in which poor and rich oppose one another and wealth corresponds precisely to power. If the young prove helpless to govern their own lives, and require rescue by their elders, Primrose also demonstrates his ineffectuality, helplessly imprisoned (with the compensation, however, of a captive audience for his preaching). Only when wealthy Sir William Thornhill arrives can the narrator's burned arm, his confinement, his wretched family find relief. A rich man appears: false evidence gives way to true, servants shift loyalties, the rude turn polite. The obsequiousness of Primrose and his wife testifies that, compared with financial power, moral force has little efficacy. The clergyman's insistence on dominating his family, denying his children's individuality, imposing his certainties on the young compensates for his powerlessness in the larger social context. He can feel confident of reward in heaven and of dominion on earth, within his tiny sphere. And he avoids the pain of experiencing his children as challenges by perceiving only their inadequacies, mistakes, and sins and by praising only their submissiveness, celebrating Sophia's passive compliance but not George's enterprise, Moses's curiosity, or Olivia's eagerness to love. The conflict of generations, as the Vicar understands it, consists in the opposition of the misguided to the wise.

Even a cursory look at contemporary moral manuals reveals the same assumptions about generational hierarchy, and one would hardly suspect irony *there*. Minds conditioned by twentieth-century psychological theory will deduce ambivalence beneath the moral assurance of eighteenth-century prescriptions for youth and for parents, and will perceive an excessive insistence on the utter rightness and authority of adults, the necessary subordination of the young. Surely these writers protest too much; their rigidity covers their fear of that insubordination they desperately oppose. They allow the young no room because of their terror about what, given space, youth might do. The texts themselves, however, offer little direct evidence of fear; it lurks beneath the surface. We know it is there because of our understanding of how people work; we cannot prove its presence.

Fictional texts confirm the latent meanings of the moralizing. Given an imagined action and imagined persons, a novel's happenings and characters support or challenge its announced doctrine. *The Vicar of Wakefield* reveals the discrepancies between collective and individualized views of the young. The Vicar himself insists on generalizing, obviating distinctions of character. He appears to control the narrative, yet the narrative reveals more than he knows; he appears to control his children, but they too show unexpected aspects. Like the other ironies twentieth-century readers have perceived in the novel, the ambiguities associated with adolescence cannot be confidently declared under Goldsmith's conscious control. Perhaps these ironies blossom in the intersection between the twentieth-century reader's consciousness, infused with lore about oedipal strivings, and the eighteenth-century writer's moral surety, resting on his capacity to imagine congruence between matters as they should and as they might be, between the generalized adolescent of the moralists and a conceivable individual human being. On the other hand, many eighteenth-century novels allow youngsters more freedom for self-discovery: perhaps Goldsmith's imagining of a father—a good, in some respects even saintly, man, whose self-esteem depends partly on his tyranny—derives from awareness of the necessary tragi-comic disparity between what fathers want (power) and what sons and daughters need (freedom). The politics of adolescence, as evoked by *The Vicar of Wakefield*, allows the young only covert victories. With or without ironic awareness, the novel expresses the view emphatically reiterated in almost all eighteenth-century discussions of youth in general: it should not, must not, cannot have power.

Despite its insistence on adult control, *The Vicar of Wakefield* acknowledges more threatening possibilities than does *Pamela*, that tale of a girl who loses her power at the point when it gets her what she wants. Pamela can exercise some freedom because she has left home. But she uses it only toward conventional goals and relinquishes it to a surrogate father when she marries. Richardson allows himself to imagine a young woman using her sexual force, but he imagines her as utterly compliant to adult values, not in conflict with an older generation: a relatively helpless individual, not a member of a powerful class. *The Vicar of Wakefield* bludgeons its adolescents into submission but tacitly recognizes that they will not always remain passive. Unlike Pamela, George and Moses will more than superficially widen their possibilities in marriage; so, presumably, will Sophia: her husband can hardly be such a tyrant as her father. Even erring Olivia, when her spouse finishes learning to play the French horn, may take advantage of a more powerful social position than she has known in her youth. The novel, as I have suggested, clearly documents the wish implicit in the fantasy of generational warfare: the wish for complete adult control and for adolescent acceptance of control's necessity. But *The Vicar of Wakefield* also realizes the corresponding fear: in the long run the young will grow up and take away their parents' power. Every "happy ending" of a novel of adolescence implies such a threat. In works understanding adolescents as a class, the threat seems particularly clear.

Such works, in every period, attest the same wish for dominance, the same fear of loss.

Emphases change, though, as time passes. The Victorians expressed their fears more openly; they also dealt with them differently. "I have been led to think deeply and to speak openly upon this solemn matter, my friends," Charles Kingsley wrote,

> by seeing, as who can help seeing, the great division and estrangement between the old and the young which is growing up in our days. I do not, alas! I cannot, deny the complaints which old people commonly make. Old people complain that young people are grown too independent, disobedient, saucy, and what not. It is too true, frightfully, miserably true, that there is not the same reverence for parents as there was a generation back;—that the children break loose from their parents, spend their parents' money, choose their own road in life, their own politics, their own religion, alas! too often, for themselves;—that young people now presume to do and say a hundred things which they would not have done in old times.[12]

Perhaps they should not, perhaps they must not, but the young unquestionably *do* have power—to break loose, to choose their own road. Kingsley's every *alas!*, however rhetorical, speaks of pain and fear. As one of "the old tax-payers," almost a century before Colin MacInnes's novel, he contemplates his juniors' "divine power" and finds it appalling. The frightful truth that children insist on their own politics seems yet more dreadful, given the fantasy that such things did not happen "in old times"; but even without such a contrast, the sight of presumptuous youth challenging parental wisdom and authority must arouse anxiety and frustration. Kingsley's tone of wretched bafflement—how could all this have happened?—underlines the desperation of the predicament, from the adult point of view, and helps to explain the punitive insistence with which Victorian moralizers berated the young. It also accounts for the intense rhetoric even of milder modes of persuasion.

Kingsley himself constructed a compelling syllogism addressed to filial love and guilt: "a good son loves and obeys his father, and the better son he is, the more he loves and obeys his father; and therefore a perfect son will perfectly love and perfectly obey his father." Animal children do not take care of their parents; "the love and obedience of full-grown sons to their fathers is so utterly human a thing . . . that we must believe it to be part of man's immortal soul, part of God's likeness in man."[13] Christ, perfect Son of a perfect Father, exemplifies the possibility all should strive for. Herbert Spencer, on the other hand, addressed parents rather than children. Preaching the value of a "discipline of natural consequences," he argued that it would prevent the "mutual exasperations and estrangements" between the generations which other modes of discipline encourage. "Seeing, then, as all must do, that estrangement of this kind is fatal to a salutary moral culture, it follows that parents cannot be too solicitous in avoiding occasions of direct antagonism with their children—occasions of personal resentment."[14] The emotional penalties of estrangement may trouble young as well as old, or so the old hopefully imagine. When Tom Brown at Oxford has an ideological quarrel with his father, he promptly finds himself "dejected and melancholy; now accusing his father of injustice and bigotry, now longing to go after him, and give up everything. What were all his opinions and convictions compared with his father's confidence and love?"[15] Like the explicit didacticism of Spencer and Kingsley, this fictional evocation of antagonism between father and son warns of emotional danger.

Like their eighteenth-century equivalents, these comments imply a political understanding of the situation between generations, but they offer little political clarity. The earlier texts express anxiety about youth's threat to age but no doubt about the locus of authority. Spencer's recommendation that parents "avoid" direct antagonism betrays a weaker political position. Kingsley's account of how the young break away, his overheated injunctions to imitate Christ, and the emotional blackmail implicit in the narrative of Tom Brown's situation also reflect adult insecurities. However certain that grown-ups *should* control the young, these writers betray doubt about whether they *can*. At the very least, the young must cooperate to make possible their elders' dominion.

By promulgating an imagery of alliance rather than hegemony, commentators might evade the problem of assigning power. That perceptive observer Harriet Martineau, for example, points out that young people leaving the family circle for the first time often feel attracted to others by qualities radically different from those embodied in their own families. She implicitly acknowledges the threat of such shifts of allegiance and offers a remedy: Don't let them leave you. Join them! Parents, she explains, must avoid feeling reproached by their children's psychological departure. "[Parents] may make sure of an increased reverence and love from their children if they have the magnanimity to go hand in hand with them into new fields of moral exercise and enterprise, and to admit the beauty and desirableness of what they see."[16] Go hand in hand whether they want you to or not. Martineau does not, of course, conceive that the young folks' "new fields" would involve anything radically antipathetic to their parents' values; she refuses to imagine so threatening an eventuality. The poignance of her prescription comes from its insistence that everything will work out all right if parents do the proper thing: no apparent responsibility rests with the children, presumably because parents have the motivating force that their sons and daughters lack. Children want to get away: Victorian writers realized that.

Twentieth-century parents dutifully try to let go. Victorian parents told themselves and one another to find ways to hold on. They insisted on their continued pre-eminence in their children's lives by presenting themselves as models. William Cobbett's published letters of advice to his sons reiterate his own virtues: "How little of eating and drinking is sufficient for me! How wholesome is my sleep! How early do I rise!"[17] He could help his sons best, he apparently thought, by reminding them of his extraordinary gifts and achievements: "for my part, I can truly say, that I owe more of my great labours to my strict adherence to the precepts that I have here given you, than to all the natural abilities with which I have been endowed" (p. 39). Samuel Smiles, in his famous manual on *Self-Help*, quotes a philanthropist named Sir T. Fowell Buxton writing to his teen-aged son, urging "principle, determination, and strength of mind," and justifying his advice by his own experience. "I am sure that a young man may be very much what he pleases. In my own case it was so. . . . Much of my happiness, and all my prosperity in life, have resulted from the change I made at your age."[18]

To offer oneself as model emphasizes parental primacy in time but implies mutuality of goal, an abstract equivalent to walking hand in hand. The ideal relation of generations hinted by many nineteenth-century didactic texts depends on comradeship more than on hierarchy. Granted, children should obey parents; on the other hand, parents should avoid offending children. In generalized advice to either generation, talk of Christ, of love, of piety often covers over dangerous emotional possibility. More individualized discussions—like the advice from fathers to sons—sometimes directly reveals awareness of subterranean struggle. A particularly rich text involves a father's reflections on his daughter's marriage. The essay uncovers the hidden competition between generations and suggests its sexual elements.

The father (he did not identify himself in the *Cornhill Magazine*, but twentieth-century research has named him as Frederick Greenwood), a widower, responds to his abandonment by a twenty-year-old daughter and complains that no one worries about his emotions. Open anger marks his commentary—anger only faintly disguised by a self-mocking tone as he writes of himself in the third person:

This is an affair of love and youth: does he understand them even? It seems not. Opinion is against any such presumption. The young, who are authoritative on the subject, are more than sceptical—they are saucy in their hearts; and of all the story-tellers whom I have read, not one has ever deemed it worth while to consider what an old fellow's thoughts and sentiments may be when his daughter has kissed him farewell and is gone from his house.[19]

He, too, wants to be young; he wants, in fact, to compete with the groom for his daughter's love. Although he openly expresses his yearning for youth, he adopts devious tactics for revealing his competitive wishes: he transfers them to the opposite sex.

Suppose we *were* all young together, fathers, daughters, uncles, cousins—would that profit us? Suppose our mothers could keep the freshness, and innocence, and beauty of their youth for their sons to see when they in turn come to twenty years: it would indeed be a delightful wholesome dispensation for the sons, but for the daughters it would be a different thing, wouldn't it? (Pp. 805–66)

Why, one may wonder, a *wholesome* dispensation? To get the reader off the track by proclaiming that this father does not mean anything sexy? But, of course, he does. He wants to be young so that he can win; he rages at the sexual advantage of adolescent men over grown-ups. The young, "saucy in their hearts," possess sexual power. Nothing else matters.

Anger and anxiety merge in this oblique narrative of loss. It expresses emotions more or less imperfectly concealed by other didactic texts of the mid-nineteenth century, responses to the experienced threat of the young. The responses invariably involve denial. Offering visions of benign cooperation or pious devotion, claiming or relinquishing authority, declaring the unfairness of the universe, they admit more uneasiness than do their eighteenth-century equivalents, an uneasiness implicit in a society of less secure generational hierarchy. The questions implied by this commentary—how much power, really, do the young possess? what should their elders do about it?—emerge also, in different form, in the period's fiction.

William Thackeray's *Pendennis*, for example, provides a confused adolescent hero and a confused perspective on him. At the novel's end, its eponymous protagonist has reached the age of twenty-six. He has not yet figured out who he is or what course he should follow. His cousin Laura tells him what to do (someone has always told him what to do); he marries her, and we may hope that eventually he will grow up, after an adolescence remarkably prolonged.

A long-winded chap fond of direct addresses to the reader tells the story. Unlike the narrator of *The Vicar of Wakefield*, he has no acknowledged stake in the action; but he proclaims powerful feelings and convictions. Often his commentary concerns appropriate attitudes toward youth:

Of course here Mr. Pen went off into a rhapsody through which, as we have perfect command over our own feelings, we have no reason to follow the lad. Of course, love, truth, and eternity were produced; and words were tried but found impossible to plumb the tremendous depth of his affection. This speech, we say, is no business of ours. It was most likely not very wise, but what right have we to overhear? Let the poor boy fling out his simple heart at the woman's feet, and deal gently with him. It is best to love wisely, no doubt; but to love foolishly is better than not to be able to love at all. Some of us can't; and are proud of our impotence too.[20]

The tone resembles that of Frederick Greenwood's remarks about his daughter—perhaps for similar reasons of self-protection. Read as a political document, the statement insists on the utter dominance of the adult speaker, whose condescension contains affection and even admiration but nonetheless insists on how much more grown-ups know, for better or worse, than Pen can know. "We"—the adults invoked in this patronizing and indulgent commentary—command our feelings, therefore the world.

On the other hand, sterility, repression, and narrowness characterize adulthood. If foolish impetuosity marks the young, emotional authenticity accompanies it. "Wise" virtually transforms itself into a negative term: Pen's inexperience prevents his loving wisely, but his capacity to feel marks his superiority to those limited by their wisdom. "Impotence," a malady of grown-ups, suggests unsureness about where, after all, the power lies. If command over feelings becomes impotence, perhaps command over the world, more specifically over the young, also has aspects of impotence. The balance of power wavers; amused condescension covers severe misgivings.

In tone, this paragraph belongs to its time; in substance it anticipates the twentieth century. If you can't lick 'em, join 'em, Harriet Martineau recommended; and her colleagues in advice giving found devious ways to disguise the same recommendation. Thackeray's narrator implicitly goes one step farther, taking the young as models or ideals of conduct. "We" who cannot love may learn from those whose simple hearts allow extremities of passion. If impotence prevents passion, "we" can at least respect, even reverence, intensities we cannot imitate.

Yet the tonal assertion of adult superiority mocks what the lad will surely outgrow as he inevitably joins the officially mature. The narrator's feelings about himself and his kind manifestly determine his feelings about "the other," as exemplified in Pen. His ambivalence about adulthood corresponds to his perplexity about adolescence: ambivalence pervades the novel. The book repays attention as an exemplary nineteenth-century text about the power and the weakness of the young.

The action of *Pendennis* involves an adult struggle for Arthur Pendennis's soul—a struggle given scope by the young man's passivity. The old wish to "help" the young. More accurately, they wish to possess them. Pen's worldly uncle, Major Pendennis, urges him to seek social and financial advancement; his saintly mother wants him to marry his cousin, another maternal angel in the house who will keep him virtuous, ensuring his heavenly as well as earthly satisfaction. Other influences come and go: Miss Costigan, for example, his first love, eight years older than he and distinctly grown-up in comparison to the naïve eighteen-year-old who casts himself at her feet. Even his near contemporaries—Foker, endorsing the Major's worldly gospel, and Warrington, disciple of his mother's view—think of themselves, and are presented by the narrator, as adults in comparison with Pendennis, whose main interest for the storyteller resides in his embodiment of archetypal youth.

Look back, good friend, to your own youth, and ask how was that? I like to think of a well-nurtured boy, brave and gentle, warm-hearted and loving, and looking the world in the face with kind honest eyes. What bright colours it wore then, and how you enjoyed it! A man has not many years of such time. He does not know them whilst they are with him. It is only when they are passed long away that he remembers how dear and happy they were. (Pp. 26–27)

The language of such commentary on Pendennis's adolescent state belongs to Romantic rhetoric about childhood. The bright-colored world, the attributed virtues of the protagonist ("brave and gentle, warm-hearted and loving . . . kind honest eyes"), the stress on the fleeting moment—these *topoi* appear in nineteenth-century poems celebrating prepuberty. Although the novel reveals little about the preadolescent Pendennis, one might surmise that the man described between the ages of eighteen and twenty-six differs from his earlier self mainly in his enlarged opportunities and sexual capacities and in his superficial acquaintance with sophisticated modes of behavior. These aspects of his personality represent by the novel's standards defects or impediments. The brave, gentle, loving, kind, honest youth returns happily to childhood in his marriage. When Laura accepts his proposal, "Pen's head sinks down in the girl's lap, as he sobs out, 'Come and bless us, dear mother,' and arms as tender as Helen's [his mother] once more enfold him" (p. 820). The maternal rather than the sexual nature of the embrace, the explicit comparison between fiancée and mother, the childlike physical attitude Pendennis assumes: all emphasize the novel's equation of virtue and childhood. The equation holds only for men: *female* virtue is maternal. The final evocation of the Pendennises' married life stresses this discrepancy. Laura takes care of the Major as well as of her husband: "For this sweet lady is the friend of the young and the old: and her life is always passed in making other lives happy" (p. 849). Pendennis, on the other hand, remains full of "faults and wayward moods," to be dealt with by Laura "with the most constant affection" (p. 849). Although he himself explicitly connects the prospect of marriage with the end of youth, it appears that he need after all never grow up.

The Victorian propensity for glorifying childhood hardly needs further documentation. To say that it controls much of the presentation of Pendennis as young man, however, does not adequately describe the novel's psychological and moral complexities, which depend partly on Pendennis's literal status as adolescent rather than child. The enlarged sexual capacities and opportunities, the new sophistication, make it impossible to evaluate Pendennis in simple terms. Inasmuch as he resembles a child, he can provide a subject for benign reminiscence and indulgence of the sort represented by the narrative interpolations already cited, which appeal to the reader's memories of his own youth. (The imagined reader is almost always male, and invariably adult, despite the historical fact that the young avidly read novels and that females had from the beginning dominated the novelistic audience. Thackeray himself had written a warning to "lazy boys": If they read too many novels before the age of twenty, they will get sick. "As surely as the cadet drinks too much pale ale, it will disagree with him; and so surely, dear youth, will too much novels cloy on thee."[21] He does not admit such youths to the company of readers he address- es.) These interpolations effectively condense adolescence into child- hood: both states belonging to a dimly remembered historical past for the posited reader; both sharing innocence, enthusiasm, and authen- ticity, both (given a rather blurry focus) supplying pretexts for nostal- gia. Fiction implicitly justifies itself by restoring to memory—or en- couraging memory to manufacture—a glorious past time.

But the narrative reveals Pendennis's young manhood as well as his childishness and hints the narrator's rage at that manhood's implicit threat. Children, by nineteenth-century convention, are incorruptible. Not so Pendennis. Ambition makes him vulnerable. Only one fully delineated male in the novel retains virtue equivalent to that of the good women; he also lacks ambition. Warrington's untested aspira- tions have been thwarted by his early, unwise marriage (which conve- niently removes him from competition for love as well as for worldly accomplishment). Deprived of incentive for self-betterment, he em- bodies a wistful simulacrum of maturity, boyish in his continued ca- pacity for pleasure but burdened by a wisdom declaring the futility of endeavor. He can guide Pendennis with almost paternal concern, pro- tecting and instructing him as need arises; but because he does not compete, he does not embody a fully enfranchised member of adult male society. The other grown-up men include a convict, a gambler, a drunkard (all appropriate objects of disgust, the narrative tone makes clear), and Major Pendennis, a focus for sympathy inasmuch as he sac- rifices immediate self-interest for Arthur and his mother, but more generally the target of the narrator's disapproval.

To the degree that he succumbs to his uncle's guidance, Arthur too becomes an object of contempt. When Foker reveals to the youth his own infatuation with Blanche Amory, young Pendennis discovers that his friend's rivalry "gave a zest and an impetus to his own pursuit of Blanche" (p. 520). The narrator directs the reader's response:

Ah! is this the boy that prayed at his mother's knee but a few years since, and for whom very likely at this hour of morning she is praying? Is this jaded and selfish worldling the lad who, a short while back, was ready to fling away his worldly all, his hope, his ambition, his chance of life, for his love? This is the man you are proud of, old Pendennis. You boast of having formed him, and of having reasoned him out of his absurd romance and folly—and groaning in your bed over your pains and rheumatisms, satisfy yourself still by thinking that at last that lad will do something to better himself in life, and that the

Pendennises will take a good place in the world. And is he the only one who in his progress through this dark life goes wilfully or fatally astray, whilst the natural truth and love which should illumine him grow dim in the poisoned air, and suffice to light him no more? (P. 520)

Goodness and safety inhere in childish dependency; "the world" (which turns a "lad" into a "jaded and selfish worldling"), that world constituted most importantly of adult males, guarantees moral depreciation. Although the narrator has earlier invited readers to smile at the boy's romantic folly, he has also stressed its nostalgic charm; now he unambiguously endorses it as morally preferable to the effort to "take a good place in the world." As a "man" ("the man you are proud of, old Pendennis"), Arthur seems altogether reprehensible; as a boy praying at his mother's knee, he can engage our sympathy (remaining thus in a securely subordinate position). The final rhetorical question also appeals for our sympathetic identification with the corrupted lad, by locating blame for his deterioration in "the poisoned air" of the adult world and suggesting that few escape the evil effects of such environment.

But most poisons have antidotes; why not Pen's? The antidote must come from the depths of character; Pen's character is too flawed to resist the world's destructiveness. "The world had got hold of Pen in the shape of his selfish old Mentor: and those who have any interest in his character must have perceived ere now, that this lad was very weak as well as very impetuous, very vain as well as very frank, and if of a generous disposition, not a little selfish in the midst of his profuseness, and also rather fickle, as all eager pursuers of self-gratification are" (p. 192). The faults and the virtues here assigned to Pen belong almost generically to youth, although the narrator does not say so. Pen succumbs, in other words, because he is young. A later summary concludes, "our friend had been bred up like a young prince as yet, or as a child in arms whom his mother feeds when it cries out" (p. 352). He has never earned a living, never even thought of doing so. The analogies to young prince and child in arms stress his passivity and explain it by his upbringing; like the description of opposing elements in Pen's character, they carry contemptuous overtones.

Children belong to the world of women, a realm of assumed moral virtue which endures by virtue of its fugitive and cloistered state. Inasmuch as Pen remains identified with his mother, he stays in that world. By now we know a good deal about the mixture of reverence and contempt the Victorians accorded their women; the instabilities of value in Pendennis suggest that the problem of evaluating adolescents provided even greater difficulty. The narrator scorns Pen for showing signs of "worldliness": competitiveness, ambition, suspicion, cynicism—hallmarks of the fully functioning adult male in a capitalist society. But he scorns him also for his unworldliness, his prolonged infantilism, his lack of awareness about how people operate in the marketplace. (The book shows as much ambivalence about capitalism as about adulthood.) If the narrative finally endorses Pendennis as large-size little boy, it also has undercut its own sentimentalities by making one feel the moral insufficiency of Pen's immaturity. Like *The Vicar of Wakefield*, it brings a young person to the conventional happy ending in a fashion that underlines the superiority of grown-ups (exemplified by the knowing narrator) to youth. Under the guise of reporting a young man's growing up, it insists that the young man can never grow up.

The double view finds no resolution in the novel. On the one hand, the fiction exploits the nostalgic associations of innocence and freshness with those uncontaminated by "the world"; it stresses the sense of possibility inherent in life's early stages and invites the reader's regret for the losses of time. On the other hand, it emphasizes the narcissism, susceptibility to pressure, passivity also associated with early life. At twenty-six, Pendennis has outgrown none of these characteristics, and the narrator's moralizing interpolations emphasize the moral inadequacies implicit in youthful self-absorption and weakness. Even Pen's assertions of extreme cynicism testify to his youth and inexperience rather than to the knowledge he claims. His young manhood implies weakness and wrong—as well as virtue and ease. He cannot repel the poisoned air.

Like the adolescents in *The Vicar of Wakefield*, Pen lacks moral and practical sufficiency; he needs help and guidance. Or perhaps one should say, rather, that the narrator presents him as inadequate, thus emphasizing by implication his own moral superiority; and that the narrator in this respect resembles the father of *The Vicar*, whose motivation for this mode of presentation emerges in the structure of the novel. We can readily understand why the Reverend Primrose should wish to say that adolescents present no real threat because they have no real power. *Pendennis* says much the same thing.

Nineteenth-century moralists registered their fear of antagonism between young and old, hinted the competitive element built into the relation of generations, and recommended comradeship. *Pendennis* conveys the same fear, as the narrator manipulates the story to declare the absolute ascendancy of the adult, for good (Pen's mother) or evil (his uncle). In the story's telling, Arthur is systematically infantilized. No matter what the fiction allows him to do—and he pursues a successful journalistic career after his university years, although that seems hard to believe—the storyteller removes all power from him by consistent emphasis, in action and image ("a child in arms whom his mother . . . "; "Pen's head sinks down in the girl's lap . . . "), on his passive nonage. This portrait of the artist as young man makes of its central character recipient rather than agent. It nullifies the adolescent threat by its vision of the adolescent—even at the age of twenty-six— as child: a vision not merely romantic (although, confusingly, that too) but in part hostile.

Like Primrose's comments on the nature of youth in *The Vicar of Wakefield*, the narrator's appeals to his readers in *Pendennis* to respond to the essential quality of *youngness* calls attention to the novel's concern with the young as a species—and as a potential threat to the old. The interpolated rhapsodies on youth insist on its nonthreatening, its juvenile, aspects. The concrete imagining of Pen, on the other hand, nervously acknowledges the encroachment of threatening adult qualities—ambition and competitiveness. Thackeray controls the threat through the plot by marrying Pen to a girl who, like Molly Gibson, claims for herself only the power of loving, a girl who may be expected to keep Pen a child as long as possible. Like *Wives and Daughters*, although it concentrates on a male character and employs a radically different perspective, *Pendennis* insists more emphatically than its eighteenth-century predecessors on the desirability of powerlessness in the young. More openly than its predecessors, it conveys the fear behind that insistence.

In this context one may wonder about *Absolute Beginners*, with its location of "divine" power in the young. MacInnes's novel emanates from a period in which sociologists, historians, psychologists, psychoanalysts, and journalists authoritatively described—among other phenomena—the young. By the late 1950s and early 1960s in England, from their varying vantage points, such observers noted that the young had achieved great social power, measurable partly in economic statistics. The young bought things, they created fads that made other people buy things, they generated social institutions. They also claimed loudly their moral, aesthetic, and psychological superiority to their elders: a new development in the history of youth. If individual young people had always treasured in their hearts feelings of superiority, never before had their proclamations been publicly sayable or hearable.

These proclamations were duly reported, if not necessarily believed. Increasing public attention to the young created new grounds for competition. Previous generations had assumed that adults possessed public if not private authority; adolescents could make their claims only in the private realm, only in the context of their lack of money and of social power. Now they had, and were believed to have, both money and power. In counterpoint to the familiar adult promise that when they grew up they would understand, the young suggested that *because* adults had grown up, they could not understand. Excluded from the customs, the music, the argot of their juniors, grown-ups missed a lot.

The sober commentators who described, analyzed, and classified the activities and the inner processes of the young attempted to restore adult control by their aggressive claims of comprehension. As they insisted on how much they understood, they too on occasion conveyed a rather pathetic sense of exclusion. Sociologists and psychologists writing in the 1950s and 1960s about the situation of contemporary youth often plaintively emphasized the fun that adolescents have. "Youth is envied," the British sociologist Cyril Smith wrote, "because life seems so much more fun for the young today, not only in contrast to the life their parents like to think they endured, with the dangers and heartaches of wartime, and the poverty of prewar peacetime, but also as ever in contrast with the lives which the middle-aged are currently experiencing."[22] He elaborated a possible explanation for the "fun."

Youth cultures differ from their parent cultures in industrial societies by placing a far greater value on emotions than upon reason. Feelings are seen to be unique, spontaneous, free, honest and dramatic whereas reason is associated with uniformity, calculation, control, concealment, and routine. British youth culture shares these values, but in an environment notably hostile to them, not only because of the traditional British reserve but also because of our settled ways of doing things. (Pp. 26–27)

By the first-person possessive pronoun, the writer identifies himself with representatives of "settled ways"; but his summary, for all its impersonal passive verbs ("Feelings are seen": a curious locution; "reason is associated") implies a high valuation of that emotional vitality from which his age shuts him out. The reason-feeling dichotomy, like the Victorian opposition of morality and competition, belongs by tradition to the opposition between males and females: as a Steig cartoon in the *New Yorker* puts it, "The female is intuitive. The male reasons." As in *Pendennis*, adolescents retain the childhood association with women. Yet, thought of generically, as Cyril Smith considers them, they also possess a power more readily connected with men. Behind the sociologist's description lurks the suspicion that adolescents have everything.

The more concrete the descriptions, the more emphatically they suggest the felt advantage of the young. Peter Laurie uses the contrast between the frivolous and the sensible (the grasshopper and the ant: or, again by stereotype, the female and the male) to illuminate the adolescent nature. "The distinctive fact about teenagers' behaviour is economic: They spend a lot of money on clothes, records, concerts, make-up, magazines: all things that give immediate pleasure and little lasting use. In contrast, adults spend more on food, rent, washing machines, furniture—the equipment of a stable and continuing existence."[23] The polarities of "immediate pleasure" and "stable . . . existence" suggest, from a moral perspective, adult superiority. Yet our hearts leap at the idea of pleasure. Who thrills to stability? Even a factual account of how teen-agers spend their money hints the ambivalence of adults observing them. To prefer a washing machine to a concert may indicate good sense—but would one wish to confess such a choice? Awareness of the direct appeal of adolescence differentiates much of the "objective" commentary of the mid-twentieth century from that of earlier periods. No longer do the describers and evaluators of youth insist that adults know better.

Of course, as these two examples suggest, acknowledgment of the powerful positive meanings of adolescence coexists with condemnation of youthful superficiality, frivolity (make-up versus food: Laurie), or irrationality (Cyril Smith). Both the positive and the negative views admit (as adult statements in the past less often did) the force associated with youth; and both imply the gap between young and old. Sometimes they convey a notion that responsibility for the chasm dividing youth from age lies with the grown-ups. Thus Frank Musgrove, writing in the early 1960s, observes, "Adolescents whose overt behaviour is suitably non-adult can, however, be made [i.e., manufactured]. They can be excluded from responsible participation in affairs, rewarded for dependency, penalized for inconvenient displays of initiative, and so rendered sufficiently irresponsible to confirm the prevailing teenager-stereotype. They can be made into ineffectual outsiders."[24] Again, like women: treated like women, judged like women, defended, like women, on the ground that their perceived inadequacies derive from social mistreatment. Feminist descriptions of women sometimes resemble Musgrove's account of adolescence. When a feminist writes about women, the stakes are obvious: what is at stake when Musgrove writes about the young? More than two centuries before him, Richard Steele had demonstrated a comparable desire to declare unnatural the "chasm" between young and old—a result of human error; but Steele perceived mistakes and failures on both sides. One important mode of even serious intellectual commentators in the 1960s involved blaming only adults, who were redefined as oppressors. Social-scientific studies of ostentatious objectivity manifest this tendency. John Barron Mays, writing about "teenage culture in contemporary society," betrays considerable anxiety, although his prose virtually eliminates human agents. For abstracted and generalized "youth," in his account, the possessive pronoun is "its."

Probably at no other time in the nation's history has there been so much adverse criticism of youth as there is today, and so little understanding, also, of what really is its role and function in society. So much so, in fact, that there is a very real danger of something like intergenerational alienation developing and spreading in the future. If this should happen, the social consequences will be very serious indeed.[25]

The vague danger ("something like . . . alienation") located "in the future" derives from adult lack of understanding. Later, Mays acknowledges various kinds of teenage alliance ("Beatnik society, teenage cults . . ., artistic Bohemians . . .") and defines their implications: "All seem to be to varying degrees manifestations of a similar rejection of the established way of life, the self-conscious assertion of youth as a self-justifying age-group and a strange mixture of reactive narcissism and nineteenth century romanticism" (p. 23). Young people, in short, reject the ways of their elders: the writer feels their mysterious, threatening power. What is at stake, in these accounts of how society has mistreated the young and then made them objects of disapproval, is different, after all, from the issues implicit in accounts of women's maltreatment. Feminist arguments presenting women as victims argue for restitution on the grounds of justice. Adolescents are seen not only as social victims but as threatening, a source of fear.

The reports of historians suggest reason for the fear. Edward Shorter, writing in the 1970s but looking back over recent decades, examines adolescence in relation to the history of the family. He sees the generational gap as having new meaning in the mid-twentieth century. "Adolescents now soon realize that they are not links in a familial chain stretching across the ages. Who they are and what they become is independent, (at least so they believe) of who their parents are. . . . The chain of generations serves no larger moral purpose for adolescents, and therewith the moral authority of parents over their growing children collapses."[26] That collapse, I would venture, underlies the worry implicit in such works as those by Mays and Laurie. The new development of the 1960s, Shorter asserts, is not the generation gap, not the intense hostility of teen-agers toward their parents, not any change in children's fates. "The new development is that *adolescent* children have begun to manifest a massive uninterest in their parents' values and in their own identities as guardians-apparent of the family line"; the peer group has replaced parents as source and support of youthful values (p. 270). Adolescents now seek "refuge, not in some kind of romantic isolation (the classical historical pattern), but in the company of the youth group" (p. 272).

We need not quarrel about the factuality of these descriptive summaries. Considering them in the context, say, of Kingsley's nineteenth-century sermons or of Dr. Johnson's eighteenth-century account of the antagonism between young and old, we may note, however, both that these descriptions share perceptions and emotions with the past, and that they delineate a further extreme of development. The form of adolescent separatism differs, but the perceived content remains indentical: only now the rejection seems more extreme, more collective, more seriously dangerous. Shorter's "familial chain" evokes both security and bondage, both the desire for continuity and the reasons for youthful defiance. His use of the abrupt verb "collapses" to describe what earlier writers might have called "erosion" of moral authority conveys his powerful response to the phenomenon he describes. Kingsley, a century before, appealed to young people's consciousness of parental moral authority with a desperation suggesting analogous worries about the "collapse" latent in the "massive uninterest" of the young in their parents' values. The solidarity of the youth group may be something new, but the anxiety lest children declare their parents irrelevant sounds familiar.

A final example, from another historian, Harry Hopkins, writing a breezy social history of Britain in the 1940s and 1950s:

In the later Fifties, the "Youth Question" seemed at times to be succeeding to the place occupied by the "Woman Question" in an earlier age. Never had

"Youth"—with the capital "Y"—been so earnestly discussed, so frequently surveyed, so extensively seen *and* heard.... To enter one's teens was to be inducted into an exclusive and privileged order, several millions strong, which those outside it observed with an uncertain mixture of envy, awe, fascination and repulsion.[27]

Not fear, by his account; and he does not identify himself with those observers of a decade earlier. His feelings toward the young, however, provide their own confusions. Inasmuch as youth represents a commercial phenomenon ("The 'sub-teens,' eager pocket-moneyed apprentices, waited impatiently for admission to this booming, neon-lit Teenage Promised Land" [p. 426]), Hopkins feels superior, as though he embodies in contrast the Life of the Mind. Toward some aspects of youth he adopts a neutral tone: "the lack of a firm class sense was one of the most notable things about a great many of the young" (p. 429). But when he comes to the moral life, his attitude approaches reverence. He sees youth as bearing the moral burden of society.

Since few adults—with one part of their lives in the old world and the other in the new—could articulately resolve current confusions, the burden of groping toward a new morality fell upon the young.... What was remarkable and what, as ever, renewed hope for the future, was that they did not lapse into total cynicism and apathy, but retained the confidence to inquire and the will to improvise in the restricted space available. (P. 440)

Hopkins concerns himself with adolescents of the immediate past, not of his own moment; his relation to them, therefore, is not precisely comparable to that of the sociologists describing their perceptions of youth or of the Victorian and the eighteenth-century moralists. Even given this small protective distance, however, his willingness to understand the young as social saviors rather than as outsiders suggests an important mode of confronting teen-agers' collective rejection of their parents' values. One can remove the threat by emphasizing the promise, feeling superior to the young because they spend money mindlessly on records and make-up, yet obsequiously acknowledging their willingness to confront moral issues and begging them to lead the way into the future. Eighteenth- and nineteenth-century thinkers admitted relatively little doubt that leadership should attend seniority, although doubt had intensified by the late nineteenth century; twentieth-century writers sometimes pursue the opposite assumption: they convey misgivings about the kind of leadership grown-ups now offer, and assuage the threatening young. Does youthful power come "straight from mother nature"? Some theoreticians think so, investing the new generation with the force that grown-ups feel deprived of by the sweep of international events, by the pressure of business and professional life, by the overpowering presence of mass media and massive corporations: the ponderous clichés of twentieth-century *anomie*.

Of course, the writers I have quoted hardly "represent" a universal trend even for a single country, a few years. The proliferation of texts about youth precludes confident generalization; indeed, even the less bulky data of earlier centuries include many conflicting responses. In the cacophony of mid-twentieth-century reaction, however, the notes struck by such observers as Cyril Smith and Shorter and Hopkins reverberate frequently and suggest the receding of adult confidence, a corresponding eagerness of youth to fill the moral vacuum, and a half-despairing, half-hopeful adult desire that the young should assume moral responsibilities that their elders have abrogated.

In *Absolute Beginners* as in *The Vicar of Wakefield* and *Pendennis*, the narrative point of view locates crucial issues. Not a father but a son, the nameless narrator speaks consciously for his generation. The gap between author and narrator in this instance, too, creates perplexing problems. The point-of-view character embodies the author's effort to imagine the mind of someone who belongs virtually to a different species. For a grown man to adopt the voice of a teen-ager involves daring comparable to that of a man attempting to evoke the voice of a woman commenting on men. Both exercises compel the author to disclose his fantasies about "the other"—although not necessarily to separate those fantasies from actuality.

The anthropologist Clifford Geertz has written, "There are at least three points where chaos—a tumult of events which lack not just interpretations but *interpretability*—threatens to break in upon man: at the limits of his analytic capacities, at the limits of his powers of endurance, and at the limits of his moral insight."[28] The world of the young, as evoked in *Absolute Beginners,* approaches all three sources of chaos. Although the narrator makes superficial efforts to explain himself and his values to representatives of the grown-up world, he assumes that he and his kind cannot be interpreted by their elders. The potentiality of chaos embodied in the "absolute beginners" constitutes their power: the narrator never defines it in this way, but the novel does. The teen-agers defy analysis by orthodox categories, they challenge their elders' endurance, they operate by a moral scheme so alien that grown-ups cannot penetrate it. Adults may ally themselves with these powerful young; but, in the narrator's view, such alliance implies no understanding. On the other hand, the narrator expounds his own position in terms that make it perfectly comprehensible to the reader. This paradox shapes the novel.

The book opens with the speaker's suggestion that "the whole teen-age epic was tottering to doom" (p. 257). A fourteen-year-old singer has captured popular attention. "'They buy us younger every year,' I cried. 'Why, Little Mr. L's voice hasn't even dropped yet, so who will those tax-payers try to kidnap next?'" (p. 257). The theme of generational antagonism emerges immediately—the relationship between young and old defined by adult exploitation of youth, the youthful sense of moral superiority hinted by the notion of kidnaping associated with Little Laurie's success. But we need not rely on hints: the speaker explicitly states his conviction that he holds moral values wiser and more subtle than those of the Establishment. He takes pornographic photographs, tolerates kinky sex, values jazz partly because it unites practitioners of all forms of conduct in a single clarifying passion: on the whole, he prefers to avoid condemnation, at least of his contemporaries, although he intermittently offers rather penetrating judgments. He enjoys the roles of spectator and commentator; he seeks pleasure rather than profit, profit only as a means to pleasure. Generous to his friends, kind even to his father, eager to enlighten anyone who will listen, full of energy and enthusiasm, he seems an unthreatening figure, despite his ambiguous profession; the reader readily takes his side, and the novel invites just such an old-fashioned response.

The narrator makes many speeches—to the reader and to bystanders—about what he and his kind believe. Above all, they loathe exploitation and boast their ability to outwit exploiters. "To have a job like mine means that I don't belong to [the] great community of the mugs: the vast majority of squares who are exploited" (p. 269). They claim to feel no interest in the Bomb: "No one in the world under twenty is interested in that bomb of yours one little bit. . . . Man, it's only you adult numbers who want to destroy one another. And I must say, sincerely, speaking as what's called a minor, I'd not be sorry if you did: except that you'd probably kill a few millions of us innocent kiddos in the process" (p. 271). National and international politics strike them as grotesquely irrelevant. They justify their irresponsibility by blaming their elders. "'You made us minors with your parliamentary whatsits,' I told her patiently. 'You thought, "That'll keep the little bastards in their places, no legal rights, and so on," and you made us minors. Righty-o. That also freed us from responsibility, didn't it? Because how can you be responsible if you haven't any rights?'" (p. 285). The capacity for casuistry demonstrated in this speech persists. Skillful in self-justification, the narrator converts points of conflict into moral issues and declares his mastery of them. Determined to be "free," a state implying lack of external restriction and acceptance "as a man," he seeks the money that, he appears to believe, virtually defines manhood ("tax-payers" is his chief periphrasis for "adults"), although solvency must combine with self-sufficiency. "If you have loot, and can look after yourself, they treat you as a man, which is what you are" (p. 294). The narrator's father, the novel's chief "mug," proves neither free nor manly; he dies at forty-five, having been treated like an old man by his son apparently for years.

The narrator likes his unthreatening father but not his aggressively sexual mother. The childish, sick father possesses no moral authority. Unlike his son, who claims to understand the world he inhabits, the father understands nothing. Incompetent to deal with his illness, he lets his son lead him to a doctor. The boy indulgently accompanies him to a Gilbert and Sullivan production once a year and takes him for a boating excursion. Since his progenitor challenges him only by occasional conventional political commentary which he easily refutes, he can afford to demonstrate loving tolerance.

The mother, on the other hand, does not need him and declares herself unable to love him. He resents what he sees as her whorishness, her flirtations with her lodgers, her ignoring of his father, her attachment to his half-brother, Vernon; he detests her tendency to exploit others (particularly him) by reducing them to characters in her stories. After a bit of truth telling between them, the mother offers her son a glass of port. He doesn't drink, he says. Don't be a cunt, she says. He drinks the port: the only moment in the narrative when an adult gains ascendancy over him.

The novelistic vision of how an adolescent boy might perceive his parents derives from the social climate evoked by such commentators as Shorter and Hopkins and Cyril Smith, from a situation in which the young reject continuity of values, absorb themselves in a peer-group culture, perceive themselves and are perceived as leading society toward a future governed by a higher morality. The boy's relation to his parents has psychological validity as well: narcissism distorts his vision, enabling him to avoid experiencing in either parent genuine superiority to him. Such denial protects him from awareness of his own insufficiencies, allows him room for growth. Most important, perhaps: the youth's rejection of his parents affirms emotional insubordination and demonstrates the antagonism of generations fundamental to the novel.

Although the idiom of the abundant statements of belief in the narrative (I have quoted some) has the flavor of youth, in content they sound like a grown-up's imagining of the youthful mind. Yet their plausibility and persuasive power generate the novel's moral complexity. Adults within the speaker's world fail to understand him—perhaps because they stand for nothing beyond the money and status that lend them precarious authority: capitalism in this fiction has fallen into disrepute. John Calvin once described the situation of Christian believers as analogous to that of adolescents. "But those are thoroughly founded in the doctrine of Christ, who, although not yet perfect, have so much wisdom and vigor as to choose what is best, and proceed steadily in the right course. Thus the life of believers, longing constantly for their appointed status, is like adolescence."[29] The assumption that "the right course" and the choice of "what is best" lead adolescents to the "appointed status" of adulthood epitomizes securities lost to the twentieth century. Now, on the contrary, we have Erik Erikson observing that psychoanalysis must inquire into "the inner arrest peculiar to adulthood—not merely because of the burden of pervasive immaturities but as a consequence of the adult condition as such—whether 'the times' offer too few final choices of an overdefined kind or too many ill-defined and exchangeable 'roles.' "[30] The "adult condition" embodies arrest rather than progress, making it more difficult than ever to find the right course. Such notions about adulthood shape *Absolute Beginners*, interpretable as a record of adult insecurity, hostility, guilt, and fear, all disguised by an adolescent persona.

"Growing up," as this persona performs it, involves not reconciliation with and acceptance of the adult world, not the confident escape to rural virtue chosen by protagonists of eighteenth-century novels, but an inconclusive and threatening process of realization. The protagonist comes to recognize deeper danger in the world than he has previously acknowledged, to feel more intense antipathy for the "Establishment," to experience the impossibility of both escape and reconciliation. And since adolescence, in this novel, is a public phenomenon, with the narrator explicitly speaking not only for himself but for his kind, the pessimism of this notion of growing up extends beyond the individual instance.

Pessimism belongs to the teen-agers themselves, as rendered here, not only to the adult who has conceived the fiction. Yet as one surmises a punitive element in the plotting of such novels as *The Vicar of Wakefield*, one may posit a similar component in the imagining of this novelistic action. *The Vicar of Wakefield* focuses on a single family. *Pendennis* deals with one young man in a broader social context. *Absolute Beginners* sketches an entire society, from a special point of view, and its important action involves the society at large. The novel's most meaningful event is the riot against blacks in London, which aligns good guys against bad. (The division, incidentally, is not purely generational: four thousand teen-agers reportedly adhere to the wrong side. But since being a teen-ager in the narrator's sense is a matter of style as well as of age, that fact hardly matters. It may indicate the corruptibility even of the young; it does not alter the basic dichotomy.) The novel establishes a clear equation between the beleaguered young, always threatened with exploitation or destruction by elders using money and power as lures and as weapons, and the comparably persecuted Blacks. The narrator treasures his position as outsider. He sees others co-opted by adult society; still he and his innocently corrupt girlfriend and the Lesbian in the basement (in her twenties, but another outsider) and a few others manage their defiant separation from the adult status quo. But as he sees Blacks threatened, attacked, run off the streets, he gets visual evidence of his own precarious situation. Survival, after all, is pretty much a matter of luck.

His father dies and wills him money; he can go anywhere, even to Brazil. He has never left London, and he does not leave now: there is no place to go. He sees an arriving troop of Black immigrants, happy and singing; on this ambiguous note, the novel ends. The Blacks reaffirm the vitality, the capacity for joy, that the protagonist has demonstrated and celebrated throughout. But they are about to enter, all unknowing, a city still torn by racial antagonism. If they allegorize the adolescent situation, the analogy may imply, among other things, the author's consciousness of the degree of unawareness that informs the narrator's utterances, however lofty his claims of understanding. Money from an adult has made his freedom possible—a resolution familiar in eighteenth-century novels. But he, unlike Tom Jones or Roderick Random, has no conception of anything much to do with the money: his imaginative inadequacy, but also a failure of the society. The novel's radical pessimism reflects hostility toward young and old alike: the old have messed up the world, the young cannot improve matters. The antipathy between young and old, like that between white and black, appears to belong to the nature of things; and the vast power of youth, which the narrator blithely affirms, has no effectual force.

"Straight from Mother Nature"

The stylistic richness of the narrative reinforces this point.

Well then, just as I was going to get back into the sausage-machine to re-connect with Oslo, in taxied a plane, quite close to where I was standing, and up went the staircase in the downpour, and out came a score or so of Spades from Africa, holding hand luggage over their heads against the rain. Some had on robes, and some had on tropical suits, and most of them were young like me, maybe kiddos coming here to study, and they came down grinning and chattering, and they all looked so dam pleased to be in England, at the end of their long journey, that I was heartbroken at all the disappointments that were there in store for them. (P. 449)

The comic verve of perspective, the energy of the rapid narrative with its stress on coordinate constructions, the ease of idiom and directness of emotion: all declare the power of youth which the novel has re-created through its prose. But the narrator describes himself as "heart-broken." The scene will end with him declaring his alliance with these men and joining them in their laughter: gestures of marvelous futility.

"Youth has power, a kind of divine power straight from mother nature."

The novel increasingly suggests the source of this power in fantasy, its effective demonstration only in language. A fiction that derives from social assumptions utterly opposed to those of *The Vicar of Wake-field,* relying on a narrative point of view representing an antithetical moral and psychological position, conveys an analogous understanding of the position of the young in relation to the old. The narrator of *Absolute Beginners* has more social freedom and apparent power than George Primrose, but like George he demonstrates the gap between imagination and realization of social force. He can dismiss his conventional elders as "poor old sordids"; George treats them with respect. In his world as well as George's, though, the authority of age, social position, wealth controls significant possibility; the phenomenon of teen-aged pop singers, themselves objects of adult manipulation, does not alter that fundamental fact. The teen-ager's power allows him only to have fun, not to affect the world.

The old deprive the young of power even if they verbally acknowledge the existence of that power. This message, emerging from three novels in three centuries, apparently contradicts the implications of our earlier group of three novels, in which an eighteenth-century heroine generates effectual control through her sexuality, a nine-teenth-century protagonist possesses the rather more ambiguous force of her morality, and only the twentieth-century adolescent heroine proves incapable of effective action on her own behalf. The contradiction, however, is only apparent: both sets of fictions reflect, after all, the same assumptions. Female adolescents, at least in earlier periods, could be allowed some measure of personal power precisely because they utterly lacked social power: they represented no threat. Pendennis possesses just about as much, just about as little, force as Molly Gibson: his innocence, too, gives him a measure of strength. The animus directed against him by the narrator comes from awareness of his potential for operating effectively in the adult male world of competition—the fact that makes him threatening in a way that Molly cannot match.

The difference in atmosphere between the first and the second group of novels derives largely from the difference between an individual and a class perspective. Martha Quest's potential for redemption, her single line of force, stems from her capacity for perception, a gift in no way connected to her age. Nor does her victimization depend on her time of life: adults can feel just as helpless. The young photographer in *Absolute Beginners*, on the other hand, shares the strength and the weakness of his generation. *Absolute Beginners* has more pessimistic implications than *Martha Quest; Pendennis* feels darker than *Wives and Daughters; The Vicar of Wakefield*, gloomier than *Pamela*. The movement from the eighteenth to the twentieth centuries, in the novels treated in this chapter, appears to give the young increasing rather than diminishing power: the protagonist of *Absolute Beginners* certainly has more room than George Primrose. Yet since all three works concern themselves with the prospects of growing up, the photographer actually faces a more limited outlook than does George: adulthood can offer him nothing he wants. The war between the generations reveals the same dynamic over three centuries; the novelists who describe it reveal the same fears; but their hopes and wishes for the young diminish over time.

In the second book of *Gulliver's Travels*, among the benign giant Brobdingnags, Gulliver learns that even this happy race has not avoided "the same Disease, to which the whole Race of Mankind is Subject; the Nobility often contending for Power, the People for Liberty, and the King for absolute Dominion."[31] The disease erupts also as the old contemplate the young—the young contending for liberty, the old for absolute dominion, and both alike seeking power. But in their writing, adults can control reality. They do so partly by their assignments of power.

4

Perplexities of Passion: The Eighteenth Century

In the middle of the eighteenth century, an English clergyman writing a book of advice to the young found himself in difficulties as he tried to bring his treatise to an end.

> I ought now to think of concluding this Paper: But I know not how to give over. I am so much aware of the Inconstancy and Unsteddiness of the human Heart, the Frailty of the best Resolutions, and the most obstinate Virtue we can boast, the fatal Power of Temptation, the terrible Effects of bad Company, and the almost irresistible Force of Example, and withal, the Difficulty of attaining that high Pitch of Virtue necessary to qualify for the Enjoyment of the Christian Salvation, that I tremble to think what Trials you, or any Youth under my care, may have to go through, and of the dreadful Hazard you run in passing through Life.[1]

This anguished vision stresses the weakness of all that lies within—the unsteadiness of the heart, the frailty of virtue—and the energy of what impinges from outside—temptation, bad company, irresistible example. The manual of good advice, a countervailing energy of external virtue, accumulates power from the act of writing: if the author stopped composing, his magic would vanish. Only a constant battery of advice, persuasion, support, warning, denunciation, could strengthen the young against the powerful enemies all face in the corrupting world and in the corruptible psyche. "Alas, my brothers," moaned James Fordyce, author of separate guides for young men and young women, "in how many different directions may the young, the unexperienced, and the heedless, be trained on to destruction! In just as many as there are irregular inclinations to prompt, worthless compan-

89

ions to entice, and dangerous follies to ensnare them."[2] The worthless companions and sinister follies of the world can "entice" and "ensnare," not merely "prompt," the inexperienced youth, but his own "irregular"—that is, sexual—inclinations, peculiarly strong in young men and women, initiate his potential destruction. Lord Kames observed that "Puberty, when new appetites and desires spring up, is the most critical time for education." He also suggested the preferred eighteenth-century mode of dealing with unruly feelings: "Let the animal appetite be retarded as long as possible in both sexes."[3]

Puberty comes upon the growing human being despite all efforts to retard it. In the twentieth century, we claim to welcome and even to admire the advent of acknowledged sexuality in the young, dwell on the psychosocial stage associated with its appetites, call that stage "adolescence," and devote artistic, commercial, and social energy to its celebration. Two hundred years ago, few people spoke of adolescence. Dr. Johnson defined the word as referring to "The age succeeding childhood, and succeeded by puberty." *Puberty*, as we have seen, is "the time of life in which the two sexes begin first to be acquainted." *Youth* is "the part of life succeeding to childhood and adolescence"— in other words, synonymous with *puberty*. The confusion of terminology multiplies in popular usage: *youth* can designate any age from six to twenty-five. One may suspect some effort to blur distinctions, to avert the eyes from the disturbing social and psychological phenomena of the teenage years—of which, however, eighteenth-century adults prove vividly aware. Adolescence presented practical problems precisely because no one had a clear concept of it. Parents, teachers, clergymen apparently expected the young to behave either like children or like adults. In their teen-age years, the young behaved, instead, like adolescents.

We have a good deal of evidence about how youth lived in the minds of those who had survived it two centuries ago. Eighteenth-century commentators thought of youth as a crucial period of ambiguous potential, a necessary turning point at which the individual might establish for a lifetime his or her moral direction and fate. Although didactic writers rarely defined the characteristics of youth as a separate time of life, their comments indicate their awareness of special problems associated with the period following puberty but preceding the full assumption of adult responsibility. And the qualities that they attribute to adolescents indicate some reasons that the young became heroes and heroines for much of the century's fiction and drama.

Preoccupation with power, as we have seen, governs accounts of adolescence through three centuries; writers have found various ways to qualify the power assigned to the young. A look at eighteenth-century accounts of youth can begin to clarify subtler concerns of commentators on adolescence. The next seven chapters of this study move at a more leisurely pace than the preceding ones and consider first major works of the mid-eighteenth century, then writing from later periods in chronological sequence. Although most texts subsume a political understanding of generational dynamics, they also use the subject of youth as a way to consider specific emotional and intellectual issues.

The young, eighteenth-century adults wrote repeatedly, are beings of passion. The consequences of this definition become vivid in imaginative literature. Because of their intense passions, adolescents might be readily perceived as potential victims or as potential heroes and heroines or as both simultaneously. They provided symbolic ways for a writer to assert the value and the limitations of reason as directing force and to muse on the incompatibilities between inner experience and social actuality. As fictional characters and as didactic subjects, adolescents facilitate oblique perspectives on the century's crucial preoccupation with the relation between reason and feeling. In writing about the young, novelists and moralists exposed their ambivalence about the proper place of emotion. Although much eighteenth-century discussion proclaimed the desirability of rational control (and of maturity, adulthood), the vehemence of the proclamations suggests an undertone of doubt. The meaning of this doubt emerges in narratives that attribute to the young the energies of passion. Sometimes passion accounts for weakness (as in the didactic texts quoted thus far), sometimes for strength. And often writers balance uneasily between opposing interpretations.

Youth is a dangerous age: many writers have said so. A commonplace from the French compendium *Sorberiana* (1694) exposes youth's definitive association with passion. Commenting in 1780 on a suggestion she had found there—that human life, like a play, naturally divides into five acts—Hester Lynch Thrale observed that this is one of those views "which seem inherent in every head," appearing clever, when elegantly expressed, merely because they explain to readers their own ideas.[4] Sorbière's version of the ages of man divides the life span into stages beginning with "Innocence" (associated, of course, with infancy and childhood), followed by the "Passions," which belong to adolescence. The individual who survives this anomalous period moves on to the "Understanding or the Sciences," "Honour and Employment," and finally, in old age, to "Piety and Repose."

Another eighteenth-century cliché had it that hierarchy ("subordination," to use Dr. Johnson's reiterated term) formed the foundation of civilization. Order depends upon the fact that the king governs the country, with parliament just beneath him, the rich control the poor, the butler never sits down at the dining room table. (Although all these ideas were being questioned, they remained dominant.) It followed logically that the old should rule the young, the young defer to their elders. Similarly, in the organization of the human mind, reason should govern passion, the principle of energy but also of chaos. On the other hand, minimal reflection leads to recognition of the precariousness with which rational forces establish and maintain control over passion's unruliness. If adolescence belongs to the passions, by definition it threatens all governance; the passions establish their own tyranny. The clergyman William Dodd warned the young to avoid "all those pleasures which are likely to enkindle their passions," explaining that "in their state of life, such Pleasures must be peculiarly dangerous, when reason hath not yet attained its perfect state, and the passions are in full strength and power; willing, as it were, to tyrannize the more, during the minority of Reason their Sovereign."[5] Precisely the aspect of youth that most demands adult guidance guarantees impatience of control.

Given the eighteenth-century assumption that the passions have peculiar power over youth, it becomes provocative to reflect that two of the century's important fictional young people, Clarissa Harlowe and Joseph Andrews, inhabit plots depending on their remarkable dominance over their own passions. Not that either lacks capacity for passionate feeling: Clarissa's disgust for Solmes, the suitor approved by her parents, and her fatal mistake in accepting help from the seducer Lovelace both testify to her sexual awareness, unacknowledged though it is; Joseph's sexuality manifests itself only in relation to Fanny, whom he has long loved, but there becomes sufficiently apparent, although always restrained. But Fielding for comic purposes, Richardson for tragic, imagine youthful protagonists who diverge from the norm in precisely that aspect of character considered to define their time of life: for them, consistently, judgment controls sexuality (although they can and do make mistakes of judgment). Even these atypical fictional characters, however, through the novelistic patterns that contain them, dramatize prevailing eighteenth-century fantasies about the nature and the significance of youth.

The violation of conventional expectation about young men and old generates comic tension and satiric richness in Fielding's *Joseph Andrews* (1742). Joseph has in many respects the poise and self-control of the ideal adult. His mentor, Parson Adams, on the other hand, derives his virtues from his "simplicity": an idealized child. Like the child, he possesses no tolerance for moral ambiguity and little capacity to grasp social complexity. Such summary acknowledges neither Adams's genuine Christian wisdom nor Joseph's need to learn the limits of his own capacities, a realistic adolescent task. Yet to epitomize Joseph in his sexual aspect as the perfect (that is, unreal) adult, effective rider of spirited horses, and Adams in some respects as the perfect child, possessed of adult capacity but doomed to fall off his horse, is to suggest a comic principle of *Joseph Andrews*.

A yet more complicated dynamic of controlled passion, again reflected in violated expectations about the behavior appropriate to various times of life, governs Richardson's *Clarissa* (1747–48). The heroine betrays the uncertainties of her developmental stage in her dictional vacillations, referring to herself sometimes as "woman," sometimes as "child." She resolves the dilemma of whether to be woman or child— the dilemma of what to do with her sexuality—by her death, which also, as other characters within the novel perceive, consolidates her independence and her power. Long before that death, she has confirmed her position as source of spiritual wisdom for her elders: Lovelace's friend Jack Belford accepts her authority almost instantaneously, and others succumb to it sooner or later according to their degree of sinful imperviousness. More and more definitively, Clarissa's essence appears to be virtue, and her transient passion only an accident of her nature. Converting herself into pure spirit, she transcends the threats of her sexuality without ever needing fully to acknowledge them.

Both Joseph and Clarissa figure in novelistic plots that establish abundant external threats to personal integrity. Adolescence, in the received opinion of the eighteenth century, makes itself vulnerable by what the young person lacks as well as by what he or she possesses. The innocent child, amenable to guidance and at least partially immune to corruption because of incomplete sexual development, faces less moral threat than does the teen-ager; the adult, with more highly refined intellectual capacities, possesses resources to combat the menaces of external and internal temptation. "If I can speak experimentally to any moral benefit in growing older," John Aikin writes to his sixteen-year-old son, "it is, that increasing years augment the strength and firmness of the character. This is a part of the natural progress of the human system."[6] The old, strong and firm, can help the young; every youth may profit through wise adult counselors.

Despite the peculiarities of its central character, *Joseph Andrews* belongs to the familiar genre of novels about growing up. If the comic action consists in the unmasking of affectation (often by means of Joseph's and Adams's unconventional reactions to the world), the serious action involves Joseph's maturing on his journey from city to country. Adams functions as guide, philosopher, and friend, source of Christian wisdom and of moral sustenance. Others of Joseph's elders help by sharing exemplary life experience. The morals of their anecdotal tales emphasize another aspect of *Joseph Andrews:* its extraordinary stress on the danger embodied in other people. "Other people" determine reputation, which may support or undermine men and women alike; they sustain the structure of hypocrisy underlying manners and morals; they embody temptation and corruption. Other people make it difficult to remain oneself, even after discovering what that self may be.

Late in the novel, the narrator interpolates an instructive fable about female sexual fears, how they are induced, and what relation they bear to reality—a fable that demonstrates how society externalizes internal threats. Girls, in this story, learn not that they have dangerous passions within, but that they face danger from the world without. At the age of seven or earlier, "miss is instructed by her mother that master is a very monstrous kind of animal, who will, if she suffers him to come too near her, infallibly eat her up, and grind her to pieces."[7] Encouraged in such views by her schoolmistresses and her companions, she flees from males with "dread and abhorrence." When she reaches fourteen or fifteen, however, something new happens. Noticing that young men are beginning to pay attention to her, the girl strives by every conceivable method "to render [herself] so amiable in [the man's] eyes, that he may have no inclination to hurt" her (p. 257). She then discovers that her male counterpart is "all gentleness, softness, kindness, tenderness, fondness" (p. 257). Consequently loving instead of fearing him, she yet retains the impression of her earlier terrors and believes that social disapproval will greet her reversal of feeling. Therefore she counterfeits aversion until finally she imposes on herself to believe that she hates what she loves, never having acknowledged the truth of her feelings.

The comic irony and exaggeration of this account may disguise the truth it contains, but the novel as a whole substantiates the vulnerability of adolescent passion to distortions of social training. Mr. Wilson—

94

a man accidentally encountered by the travelers, ultimately to be revealed as Joseph's father—reports himself victimized by destroyed reputation, lack of adult guidance, and bad company, the active influences operating through his passions (for gambling as well as for women), specifically because of his "early introduction to life, without a guide" (p. 170). Leonora, the Fair Jilt, her story told by another woman, loses as an eighteen-year-old all she wished to gain. For her, as for the typical female victim of social education, feeling has been distorted by responsiveness to social pressure. Dazzled by wealth and fine appearance, she gives up the man who loves her for one who does not, and ends with no one. Both Leonora and Mr. Wilson manifest inner weakness that precipitates their uncomfortable fates, but in both characters pressure from other people encourages the moral flaccidity that makes uprightness a difficult posture. Both, unequipped by early training to withstand the temptation that promises pleasure from indulgence, love what they should fear and are victimized by their own emotional confusion and lack of moral clarity; but they blame their fall on the lures of others and on the absence of wise guidance from their elders.

Other people create dangers yet more powerful than those of temptation. Through most of *Joseph Andrews*, the protagonist experiences others as sources of evil: robbers who strip and beat him, stagecoach passengers unwilling to help, lustful aristocrats who attempt to rape or seduce Fanny. Everywhere he finds corruption: thieves, rapists, misers, hypocrites, lustful women, prideful men. His "growing up" leads him to retreat from the world in order to preserve emotional integrity. Discovering his true parentage, he marries Fanny, buys an "estate," and sequesters himself in an eighteenth-century version of maturity: life controlled by reason rather than by appetite. Growing up in the world implies a corrupting process. Joseph does not avoid that process, like Parson Adams, by fundamental commitment to a world beyond, nor does he escape it, like Mr. Wilson, only after living through it. His control over his own sexuality, that unruly concomitant of adolescence, creates not only the novel's comic *donnée* but its comic resolution. The protagonist moves from the innocence of childhood to the understanding of adulthood with few difficulties of adolescent passion. Adams warns him that sexual desire should play little part in marriage ("all such brutal lusts and affections are to be greatly subdued, if not totally eradicated, before the vessel can be said to be consecrated to honour" [p. 264]); Joseph on his wedding day appears with "eyes sparkl[ing] fire" (p. 296), but he has hitherto kept the fires well banked. Apparently representing no threat to the established order, his dangerous energies contained, he expresses an adult fantasy of the ideal teen-ager, menaced from without but not from within, grateful for help from his elders, able to resolve all problems by shutting out the world, in which exist the evils denied in the youth himself.

Clarissa—surprisingly, considering her sex and the eighteenth-century conventions about it—is more competitive than Joseph; her story dramatizes (among other things) a fantasy of teen-age rebellion and of punitive adult response. The fundamental contest takes place between Clarissa and her siblings, between Clarissa and her parents. Rivalry with her elder sister becomes an explicit theme from the opening of the novel, competition with her brother almost equally open. Her parents, in varying tones of threat and tenderness, proclaim obedience the chief filial virtue; Clarissa insists on her right to choice. Her belief in her capacities leads her to rely on her own efforts to escape the family dilemma, with no help from the wisdom of her elders: she claims independence, and the novelistic action allows only ironic fulfillment of the claim. After her elopement, Clarissa acknowledges that Lovelace "had as great a confidence in my weakness, as I had in my own strength"—and that he was right.[8] Lovelace himself comments on the foolish presumption of girls who trust their own capacities and knowledge of the world: "Silly little rogues! to walk out into bypaths on the strength of their own judgments!" (II, 113). He implies that masculine superiority derives from the greater worldly experience of males, who therefore can trust themselves as young women cannot: they are adults, women remain children. And soon we find Clarissa pleading to him that she is "but a very young creature . . . whose tender years still require the paternal wing" (II, 310); she wishes to recover the status of child since her effort at adulthood has not prospered. Her helplessness is bitterly substantiated in her rape.

Young women, like young men, face the double threat of damage to moral nature and to reputation. Clarissa encounters, in the whorehouse madam Mrs. Sinclair and her crew, monstrous figures who appear able to effect her corruption by sheer physical power; the danger she faces exceeds anything Joseph experiences, and she succumbs to it. Having endured the worst that life can offer, sublimely free of moral responsibility in the immediate situation by virtue of her physical unconsciousness, she converts loss into gain, elevating her "reputation" until she achieves the status of angel—with no further need for help from her elders: thus only she wins "independence." Like Joseph, she has experienced the terror of a world full of malice and guile; she has surmounted all pubertal dilemmas by attaining not adulthood, but death. Her escape from the world, more definitive than Joseph's, has analogous meaning: she, too, rejects her own divided nature, the aspects of that nature particularly conspicuous at her stage of life. Her death (like Joseph's retreat) represents success inasmuch as it declares uncompromised choice: against marriage and the world. Yet the failure implicit in such success lends her fate troubling overtones.

Clarissa's malicious sister, consumed by sexual jealousy, attributes her elopement to lust; twentieth-century readers, less shocked by the idea, take as self-evident the sexual attraction underlying the heroine's semiconscious decision to trust herself to Lovelace. Clarissa, however, for all her minute self-examination, does not accuse herself of passion. Instead she blames herself for pride, a spiritual sin of immense social implications. Her pride consists in her ardent desire "to be considered as an *example*" (II, 378), so powerful in her virtue that she can reform profligate Lovelace, so confident of her integrity that she can risk opprobrium and seduction, demonstrating to others how they might behave. Fundamentally, this pride involves the wish to stand alone, the belief that, despite her tender years, she possesses knowledge, skill, and goodness to guarantee the rightness of her choices. Her proclamations of humility notwithstanding, she retains this desire to the end of her life. Often she reminds her correspondents that "I am a very young creature, you know, . . . to be left to my own conduct in such circumstances as I am in" (IV, 27); she relies heavily on religious consolations; but she does not care to depend on her elders for guidance and help. She has separated herself from her social matrix. One recognizes the nobility of her steadfast course, but also its hubris.

Clarissa's hubris bears a curious relation to that passion which it denies. Unrestrained sexual energy comprises a social sin, from the eighteenth-century point of view, partly because it violates the principle of subordination, by declaring the pre-eminent importance of one's own feelings and of a single other human being and denying the dominance of the larger social network. Clarissa—despite her meticulous and prolonged efforts at reconciliation, despite her concern with reputation, despite her announced dutifulness—fatally denies her subordination to her elders. She cannot survive in the world because she refuses to be guided and governed, since her family propose to guide and govern wrongly. Pattern of purity though she may be, she also thus hints some fundamental force of unruliness: the source of the danger that youth always represents. Joseph, in contrast, is utterly controlled by his commitment to subordination: his horror at

Lady Booby's attempted seduction proves social as well as sexual; his deference to his spiritual father and to his newly discovered natural father remains unfailing.

One may speculate about the degree to which the two fables reveal conflicting assumptions about the sexes. The comic energy in the opening pages of *Joseph Andrews* comes from the incongruity of placing a young man in a sexual situation conventionally associated with young women, and making him respond as one holding female standards of chastity and decorum. The joke turns on the notion that young men and young women are allowed and expected to behave very differently. But Christian morality in fact demands the same premarital control for both sexes (Fielding makes the point again in the voice of Sophia in *Tom Jones*), and Joseph's self-restraint no longer seems ludicrous as the novel continues.

No one rapes Joseph. Granted his lesser trials, however, he demonstrates a psychology comparable to Clarissa's: intense feeling ("O that I could but command my hands to tear my eyes out and my flesh off!" [p. 224]) controlled by intense principle. The difference between the two characters—a difference that helps account for the tragic structure of Clarissa's story, the comic structure of Joseph's—derives importantly from the conventions of their social roles. Joseph, a man though a servant, can act straightforwardly: not only fleeing, again like Sophia, from sexual coercion, but using his strength, intelligence, and good will to make things happen and keep things from happening. Clarissa, a woman though of higher social position, must depend on others, finds limited possibilities for exercising the independence she seeks. Given the rape, death becomes her only resource; but the rape has its own inevitability, dramatizing the failure of all her efforts, all her ingenuity. Even with exceptional gifts of mind and personality, she cannot act effectively—except to become a saint.

To be sure, Lovelace embodies an antagonist of exceptional will and force: with a less formidable opponent, Clarissa might have escaped. (She might, in fact, not have been drawn to him in the first place.) Nonetheless, her victimization makes a statement about her sex not only because it is sexual victimization but because it demonstrates the hopelessness of female efforts at direct counter-action.

Beneath all their differences, however, Joseph and Clarissa as characters reinforce a single point. The tragic fable shows Clarissa ruined by lack of external support and by the evil machinations of other people; the comic one reveals Joseph escaping through the help of his elders (although of course in Fielding's benign universe his native goodness also serves as agent of salvation). Both fables insist that the young need the old.

The English middle classes and aristocracy in the eighteenth century provided little significant occupation for those in their teens or even their early twenties unless a youth intended himself for some vocation pursued through apprenticeship. Universal education did not exist. Although most upper-class boys attended public school, relatively few proceeded to the university; and what limited education girls received was administered, by and large, at home.* No one needed the services of the well-to-do young woman, or of her male equivalent. The girl could occupy herself with paying visits, playing cards, drawing or performing on a musical instrument (not too well, lest she develop a lasting commitment to frivolity), dancing, and flirting; the young man, who possessed the wider social resources of the coffee house, could hunt and fish in the country, talk, drink, and gamble in the city, but he had no customary activity more important than his sisters'.

Society offered, in other words, at least for its more prosperous members, a distinct "psychosocial moratorium"—and worried about its consequences. Lord Kames, for example, observed that "it is not difficult to keep females within bounds; for they are trained to reserve and to suppress their desires." Young men, on the other hand, presented difficulties; one must devise for them strenuous occupation ("hunting or other violent exercise") to keep them busy and leave "no room for wandering thoughts" (p. 249). The danger Lord Kames feared exists within. Another thinker wanted young people taught "to relish the Beauties of Nature" and to understand the natural universe because such a focus of attention would "be a kind of Antidote against the Corruptions of the World":[9] this adviser claimed to dread dangers outside the self. Isaac Watts recommended a more ambitious intellectual program—experiments in natural philosophy, mathematical exercises, speculations in the arts and sciences—for identical reasons: young people "have been often guarded by this Means from the Temptation of nocent Pleasures . . . and many criminal and foolish Scenes of Talk and Action have been prevented by these innocent and

---

* The value of institutional as opposed to home education became a subject for debate in the mid-eighteenth century; the controversy continued well into the next century, particularly intensely with reference to females.

improving Elegancies of Knowledge."[10] A more extreme thinker argued that, between the ages of fourteen and twenty-one, boys should be apprenticed to some business even when there is no financial need; with too much "idle Time on their Hands," young men fall into bad company; "if they were employed in Business, they . . . would be . . . out of the Way of those Rooks that would make a Prey of them."[11] An anonymous woman writer in the *Gentleman's Magazine* actually suggested that even upper-class girls should be apprenticed to some useful trade, because they would thus be less exposed to temptation than they are, for example, at boarding schools, which abound, the writer claimed, in illegitimate pregnancies.[12]

Eighteenth-century commentators on what we would call adolescence almost without exception emphasized its extreme vulnerability. Young women faced two opposed threats: seduction, which would destroy their hope of successful marriage; and social rejection, sometimes precipitated by their apparent sexual knowledgeability (if they showed that they understood a dubious joke, for example, or danced with too much enthusiasm at a social gathering). For young men, the dangers, vaguer and more generalized, amounted to the same thing: bad company of either sex might destroy reputation, weaken character, or cause disastrous physical effects. But the danger embodied in other people as tempters, betrayers, and disapprovers also objectifies evil impulses within the adolescent mind and body. Occasionally a moralist appeared to recognize this direct connection, although in a confused way. Thus James Burgh, advocating Sunday evening lessons in morality for the young, suggested:

The love of life, of riches, of food, of strong liquors, of sleep, of the opposite sex (a subject to be very slightly touched on), of diversions; of finery; the due regulation of each of these is to be pointed out, and the fatal consequences of too great an indulgence of them, as strongly as possible set forth; with cautions against the snares by which young people are first led into sensuality.[13]

Starting with feelings, Burgh ends with "snares"—devices by which the young may be "led" into self-indulgence rather than betraying themselves by their own desires; he does not specify the connection between the two. Moreover, he advocates deliberate obscurity, recommending that one touch only "very slightly" on the most dangerous impulse, the love of the opposite sex, lest mention of the menace intensify it. To locate the forces of evil outside the self simplifies moral responsibility: one responds, ideally, by resisting. But Burgh's view of the evils within suggests a similar mechanism for dealing with them:

to oppose dangerous feelings as though they came from outside, treating them not as parts of the psychic make-up but as alien forces.

A twentieth-century commentator who noted "love of life" in the young would probably praise it. From Burgh's point of view (sanctioned, of course, by orthodox Christianity), love of life like love of food or of the opposite sex reflects weakness and potential evil. All youthful attachments mean danger. That they also mean pleasure or indicate the vitality of those who hold them never emerges from Burgh's remarks or from those of his contemporaries. A visitor at a home containing a gathering of attractive young people confessed that he "could not help discovering by my Looks, the inward Satisfaction I felt, at the Sight of so much *Youth*, and *Beauty*," but he quickly reversed direction: his satisfaction converted itself into "melancholy Reflection, *How many* Dangers it [youth] *was* expos'd *to*, and *how easily it might be* vitiated."[14] Adults accepted as a primary responsibility the task of elucidating the menaces surrounding the young.

Lord Chesterfield—in the letters to his son written when the boy was seventeen, eighteen, nineteen years old—repeatedly specified the perils a young man faces at his entrance into the world (the worst, from his point of view, is ridicule) and reminded his correspondent how fortunate he is to have the advice and guidance of a man so wise in the ways of society as his father. Lord Kames, toward the end of his long treatise on education, concluded that "a young man without experience, is liable to various temptations, partly from his irregular appetites; and without a trusty monitor seldom fails to be led astray" (p. 364). As for the young woman, consider this representative comment:

If I was called upon to write the history of a *woman's* trials and sorrows, I would date it from the moment when nature has pronounced her *marriageable*, and she feels that innocent desire of associating with the other sex, which needs not a blush. If I had a girl of my own, at this *critical* age, I should be full of the keenest apprehensions for her safety; and . . . I should invoke the assistance of some guardian angel, to conduct her through the slippery and dangerous paths.[15]

Lacking a guardian angel, some relative might suffice. After a recital of possible mishaps the adolescent girl faced, one adviser warned her to "tremble at the imaginary danger; learn to distrust your own strength, and depend entirely on the wiser counsel and direction of your aunt."[16] Without the direction of adults, the implicit argument goes—that argument which we have already seen supported in fiction—an adolescent can hardly avoid destruction. Natural feelings cannot be trusted as a guide, nor the power of untried intelligence; the influence of young contemporaries promises only disaster. Groupings of young people can lead to no good:

Thrown together in shoals, into one common reservoir, at a *dangerous age,* when nature bids an unusual fervour rise in their blood, when they feel themselves sprung into a new epoch of existence, actuated with similar feelings and similar desires, and when a restless leisure awakens all the powers of imagination and the senses, they insensibly convey an infection to each other.[17]

Relatively little one can read in the magazines, newspapers, moral essays, books on education, or social history of the eighteenth century would imply, then, anything really desirable about life between the ages of twelve and twenty-five. Advising the young to deny in themselves all impulse—that "unusual fervour" of the blood, emanating from sexual feeling, remains the ultimate source of danger—adults for their part denied the continuance of comparable impulse in themselves and put down any trace of nostalgia for energies now depleted. The ideal adolescent was undistinguishable from someone twice his or her age: a girl under fifteen years old, for example, who "has nothing of the Levity or giddy Airs of the Child about her, but behaves with almost the Decency and Sedateness of a Matron" (p. 145). On the other hand, Watts looked back approvingly on a previous era in which people were treated like children until they were almost thirty years old; he complained about those of the present who "fancy themselves compleat Men and Women at twelve or fifteen; and they accordingly judge and manage for themselves entirely, and too often despite all Advice of their Elders."[18] The assumption of the prerogatives of adulthood without its proprieties aroused the moralist's rage. The young person should act like a grown-up but never claim to be one. Only by incorporating adult counsel, by imitating and deferring to those who have gone before, can the young achieve the calm, the dignity, the true assurance of those who accept their obligations to their society and their God as principles of action. Such acceptance, in the eighteenth-century view, constitutes secure adulthood. It does not belong naturally to youth.

The emphasis in eighteenth-century novels on the external dangers faced by adolescents expresses not only warning but tenderness. The twentieth-century novelist placates the young by saying, "Don't reject us, we're really like you." Goldsmith and Richardson and Fielding say instead, "Don't reject us, you need us, we want to help." Moreover, in the many novels of education that dwell in sympathetic detail on the adolescent struggle toward adulthood, writers reveal ways of valuing youth even as they insist that it must be left behind. Twentieth-century fiction shows adults as potential destroyers of the young. In eighteenth-century novels, one recognizes dangerous adults specifically by their youthful subservience (sometimes with a "grown-up" overlay of hypocrisy) to such sinister passions as lust and avarice. In other words, *bad* grown-ups, not good ones, resemble young people in their susceptibility to feeling. But the principal resources the young marshal against them also derive from passional life. Repeatedly, the century's novels show adolescents responding to crisis on the basis of immediate feeling; and imprudent though such response may be, it testifies to an authenticity that our ancestors, too, admired. Youth must learn, they believed, to control without destroying emotional vitality.

Novels about female adolescence whose heroines follow a less deviant course than Clarissa's demonstrate the point. In the typical arrangement of events, young heroines encounter a frightening world, proclaim their terrors loudly, then conquer them largely by their own efforts. Like Clarissa, they can rarely act directly to fulfill their desires, but they find indirect expedients. Unlike Clarissa, they can accept the necessities of subordination and can deal with their own sexual impulses, usually not altogether conscious. Pamela and Evelina confront their difficulties by "feminine" strategies. Both, for example, use unconsciousness—precipitated by an onrush of emotion—for self-defense. Unlike Clarissa's drugged vulnerability, their fainting at moments of crisis (Pamela when Squire B appears about to rape her, Evelina when she has just rescued an unknown young man from a suicide attempt) dramatizes appealing female weakness and conceals purposefulness. The terror of lost reputation dominates them both, and a quite justified sense of the ever-present danger of seduction or rape. Yet neither *Pamela* nor *Evelina* finally emphasizes the real terror of the world. Both novels provide wise, benevolent adults to advise their heroines (in Pamela's case, at a distance; and of course her parents cannot communicate with her during the period of her greatest crisis); both suggest that marriage will resolve all problems. We see something of Pamela after her marriage, functioning effectively in a social context. Despite her loss of power, she continues to demonstrate a considerable, if disguised, capacity for independent thought and action. Evelina, more passive, nonetheless defends her own convictions through her trying girlhood, relaxing at the end into a new social role.

Both young women are rendered as experiencing internal conflict, including discreetly conveyed clashes between desire and prudence. They fall victim on occasion to their intense fears; they suffer from their ignorance of convention (although neither feels the slightest moral insufficiency). But both achieve precisely what they want—the ambiguous adult status possible for women—without noticeable cost.

These fictional young women fulfill their desires by their own efforts, not by outside help. Evelina's marriage does not depend on her acknowledgment by her aristocratic father, Pamela receives financial benevolence only from her husband. They content themselves with a world composed of good people and bad; apparently they do not compromise their integrity in accepting a varied social context for their anticipated adult life.* Their creators like and value them—and invite readers to feel the same—for their energy, their adaptability, their capacity for feeling, their insistence on remaining themselves. They are eager to grow up, as much as they are allowed to, and eager to conform; they represent no threat to the existent order and are consequently rewarded.

The world through which young male protagonists pass contains more various causes for fear, a fact perhaps suggesting that young men themselves cause more fear in their elders. Youths less conveniently in control of their passions than Joseph Andrews also encounter social complexities, find life less simple than it once appeared, learn a way of being that ensures survival, accomplish, in short, some mode of adulthood; then they, like Joseph, choose seclusion, their mentors' choice as well. (The virtuous if somewhat naïve, Squire Allworthy in *Tom Jones* keeps mainly to Paradise Hall; Roderick Random's father thrives in Brazil, his helpful uncle spends his time at sea.) Avoiding the twin dangers of permanent moral corruption and lost reputation, prospering by the help of others, these lads happily leave their youth behind, along with "the world" as represented by the city, and praise the maturity they have symbolically achieved through marriage. Their experience of danger urges them to seek safety from passion within as well as from evil without—to try to approximate the resolution Joseph achieved.

---

* In a provocative essay about adolescence literal and metaphoric in sentimental novels, G. A. Starr points out that in them heroines tend to come out better than heroes. The female sentimental novel, he argues, "has held out to women the gratifying prospect that their psychological and moral ideals would not unfit them for the world but guarantee their admittance to it on the best possible terms." *Evelina* provides his specific case in point. See " 'Only a Boy': Notes on Sentimental Novels," *Genre* 10 (1977):527.

Such a vision of the course of adolescence enables novelists to criticize society while supporting its professed values. *Roderick Random* (1748) may stand as representative of its kind, its hero a more or less realistic adolescent forced to suppress his "animal appetites" and like Tom Jones to learn prudence in order to win the privileges of adulthood. His world, like Joseph Andrews's, abounds in people with evil intentions toward him or evil effect upon him. His own nature also contains evil. Rich in sadism like all Smollett's novels, *Roderick Random* offers a protagonist who acts out as well as suffers hurtful impulse, although never motivated by sheer malignance.

Like Joseph, Roderick originally lacks middle-class social status; the misfortunes of his upbringing cast him friendless into a hostile environment as soon as he finishes school. Without the leisure of upper-class adolescents, he yet demonstrates their vices, from vanity and narcissism to lust. His uncle accuses him of being interested in pleasure rather than work,[19] but Roderick's irresponsible career in fact reveals a striking absence of pleasure. He indulges his passions, without finding more than fleeting satisfaction. When he, like Joseph and Tom, discovers his rich father, that father comments on his recital of misfortunes by blessing "God for the adversity I had undergone; which, he said, enlarged the understanding, improved the heart, steeled the constitution, and qualified a young man for all the duties and enjoyments of life, much better than any education which affluence could bestow" (p. 516).

Don Rodrigo's opinion on this point may or may not coincide with that of the novel's author; certainly it displays the same punitive energy that one feels in Goldsmith. What Roderick has actually learned from adversity is "the knavery and selfishness of mankind" (p. 593). His education consists in realizing the evil that lies without and passing over that which dwells within, although the reader has been made conscious of both. The novel ends with its assertedly grown-up hero declaring in conventional rhetoric the superiority of adult stability to adolescent tumult. "The impetuous transports of my passion are now settled and mellowed into endearing fondness and tranquillity of love, rooted by that intimate connection and interchange of hearts, which nought but virtuous wedlock can produce" (p. 541). He has been given a good deal of money and seems likely to receive more, since his wife's fortune proves unexpectedly accessible. The book's final words articulate the protagonist's hope that his pregnant wife "will produce something to crown my felicity" (p. 541), and thus confirm his maturity.

At the most obvious level, then, the novel's loose picaresque structure affirms the happy possibility of growing up in the world, discovering a stable adult indentity which controls the passion and avoids the tumult of adolescence. More profoundly, it, like *Joseph Andrews*, declares the *impossibility* of achieving anything valuable without adult help: both mature wisdom and that financial support which symbolizes adult power. Without monetary assistance, Roderick's strenuous attempts to rise in the world and to win Narcissa get him nowhere. Narcissa acknowledges that she loves him, but the lovers cannot marry without aid. Nor can they finally protect themselves against the machinations of self-seeking or malicious others, even against the loss of reputation that would destroy the individual's social existence. Roderick's father and his uncle have apparently achieved prosperity by their own efforts, but no young person in the novel manages a comparable feat. Only through the older generation's beneficence can youth transcend its state of actual or potential victimization to enter the ruling class of adults.

Such male success stories as *Roderick Random* and *Tom Jones*, then, display a slightly different shape from that of their female equivalents, in which young women, using their talents to get what they want, settle at last happily within the social world. But both patterns reveal the same attitudes. Eighteenth-century novelists express their love for adolescence not by wishing that it would last forever but by imagining ways to preserve some of its emotional energy while accepting adult necessities. "The chief purpose of education," Hester Chapone wrote, "should be to moderate and restrain" the passions of youth.[20] In fiction, youthful intensities are readily moderated. Young women, thought in real life to exert more discipline over their emotions than young men could manage, can be allowed in fiction to live in the social world because their proved goodness (as well as their graceful subordination to older husbands) will protect them: for them, finally, society presents few perils since their inner lives betray no sinister forces. (*Clarissa*, of course, implies a less benign view, as its heroine's impulse toward autonomy is severely punished.) To deal imaginatively with less self-controlled males requires different tactics. Boys are asserted to *learn* prudence, triumphing over their lower instincts before they win their brides. But the typical plot of the eighteenth-century novel of male adolescence hints a different truth. The device that in *Joseph Andrews* develops from characterizing the hero as controlling by principle any inconvenient sexuality, that trick of locating continuing danger firmly outside the self, persists in fiction with more realistic heroes, who, having learned their lesson, declare themselves free of conflict and of base impulse by withdrawal. Only the artificial separation of good and evil—good existing in the self, evil finally in the world—substantiates the goal of "maturity" which shapes these plots. Thus the novelist in imagination neutralizes the damaging power of the adolescent boy as of the girl. He also conveys metaphorically, by his stress on the unpredictable dangers of the world and on the youth's need for wise assistance, the conviction that the young man's moral safety remains more precarious than the young woman's.

Clarissa and *Joseph Andrews*, with their odd protagonists, both communicate serious reservations about the demands of social actuality, dramatizing an alternative conformity to Christian standards that makes life in the world impossible. The eighteenth-century novels of adolescence based on more conventional characters also betray doubts about that social conformity that their resolutions through marriage apparently imply. Of course it has long been recognized that Fielding, Richardson, Smollett, Burney function as social critics as well as apologists—but not that their focus on adolescence itself implies this double perspective. Men and women always resent the young for being unlike themselves, value them for representing earlier versions of self, full of possibility. The negative pole of this ambivalence expresses itself, in eighteenth-century fiction, through the unrelenting insistence that girls and boys must grow up; the positive, through the suggestions that they may, in their youth, be morally superior to the society that tries to contain them. Emphasizing the dangers to the young of the world outside, novelists at once criticize that world and insist on the adolescent's necessary dependence on its full members, its adult population. They glorify maturity, as the social mythology of the age glorified it, yet try to imagine a mature mode that neutralizes the threat, without sacrificing the energies, of the dangerous age.

The relation between self and world, between inner experience and external social actuality, involved, in the eighteenth-century view, perplexities yet more intricate than those examined thus far. Moralists' descriptions of youth emphasized the special dominance of the inner life during the teen-age years, and the resultant difficulty for the young of coming to terms with the social world they necessarily inhabit, a difficulty compounded by their relative ignorance of that world. Assuming the desirability as well as the necessity of such coming to terms, they resent the frequent inclination of youth to ignore or defy norms to which right-thinking adults have long since yielded. The passage from Locke cited in my first chapter exemplifies a prevailing attitude. Here it is once more: a description of the fifteen- or sixteen-year-old boy.

What can be hoped from even the most careful and discreet Governour, when neither he has Power to compel, nor his Pupil a disposition to be perswaded; but on the contrary, has the advice of warm Blood, and prevailing Fashion, to hearken to the Temptations of his Companions, just as Wise as himself, rather than to the perswasions of his Tutor, who is now looked on as the Enemy to his Freedom? And when is a Man so like to miscarry, as when at the same time he is both raw and unruly? This is the Season of all his Life, that most requires the Eye and Authority of his Parents, and Friends to govern it. The flexibleness of the former part of a Man's Age, not yet grown up to be headstrong, makes it more governable and safe; and in the after-part, Reason and Foresight begin a little to take place, and mind a Man of his Safety and Improvement.[21]

This evocation establishes the terms for many subsequent accounts. The notion that adolescents cause trouble because they prematurely consider themselves adults, although in fact they desperately need guidance from their elders; the idea that people are more easily dealt with as children, who respond to advice, or as grown-ups, with more highly developed reasoning faculties; the conviction that adolescents prove particularly susceptible to temptation because of their "warm Blood"—these would become the clichés of the age. They apply as readily to young women as to young men. Thus John Gregory, writing more than eighty years after Locke, to a female audience, remarks, "I have insisted the more particularly on this subject of courtship, because it may most readily happen to you at that early period of life when you can have little experience or knowledge of the world, when your passions are warm, and your judgments not arrived at such full maturity as to be able to correct them."[22] Limited knowledge of the world, blazing youthful passion: a bad combination. Because the young know little of the world, they remain peculiarly susceptible to their passions; their susceptibility limits their capacity to attend to the reality outside themselves; no way to break the circle readily presents itself.

The observations by Locke and Gregory betray a crucial fantasy: that vision of untrammeled emotional life that eighteenth-century thinkers both desired and feared, a kind of experience insistently associated with the young. The association suggests the resources as well as the deficiencies of youth and suggests one reason for the ambiguous feelings adults directed toward their juniors.

Even youthful weakness involves great energy. Allusions to warmth, flame, and fire recur with striking frequency in descriptions of the young of both sexes. Adolescent heat rages in vaguely metaphorical blood or more specifically in the passions or imagination.[23] In any case, it threatens "an impetuous conflagration, through the whole extent of their faculties" which may "swallow up, for a time, other views, and other feelings, of high importance." To the young man on fire, "the whole universe beside, with all its interests, shall seem a trifle." (Fordyce, I, 214) "In the warm season of youth," Hannah More observes, "hardly anything is seen in the true point of vision."[24] Lacking true vision, without the capacity to attend to matters of high importance beyond the self, adolescents see only astigmatically. To instruct them about the world does not solve the problem, since such instruction may produce premature cynicism and hypocrisy. To dampen their heat seems scarcely possible. Most moralists in fact evade the puzzle of how to deal with youth, and content themselves by multiplying examples of proper conduct.

The attributed predominance of passion in the young had peculiar importance in a period when the conflict of reason and passion had assumed the place of the medieval psychomachy, the battle of body and soul. Like the earlier symbolic struggle, the relation of these human faculties to one another involved dependence as well as opposition. The passions provide impetus for action; reason supplies guidance—the "card" that helps one steer through passion's "gale." Reason should always dominate passion, as the necessities of the soul should subdue those of the body. But such a *should* implies also the opposite possibility. Passion may take control—may urge the individual toward shipwreck. Potential adolescent tragedy derives from the fact that the passions reach highest intensity before reason has fully developed. The young person exists in precarious imbalance, rich in feeling, poor in the facility to control it.

Adolescents face great risks and great opportunities. With only a few years to set their moral courses, they prove peculiarly susceptible to stimuli from without and from within, a fact defining their special capacity as well as their vulnerability. The line between outside and inside remains blurry for the young, who lack perception to discern the precise outlines of their moral and social environment as well as wisdom to accept benign influence and fortitude to resist malignant pressures and attractions—all these lacks consequent upon the dominance of emotion in youth. The adolescent's adult fate, many eighteenth-century moralists suggest, will depend on his or her youthful intake. William Dodd states more precisely and more emphatically than any of his contemporaries the positive and negative implications of this view. "There is a season," he says, using a familiar metaphor with some uncertainty about whether he's talking about autumn or spring:

—the important season now in your possession,—when a plenteous harvest of useful truths may be gathered; when our passions will readily submit to the government of reason; when right principles may be so fixed in us, as to influence every important action of our future lives. But this season, this seed-time of our hopes, extends neither to the whole, nor to any considerable length of our continuance upon earth: It is limited to a few years of our term; and if throughout these we neglect it, error and ignorance, vice and misery, according to the usual course of things, are entailed upon us; our will becomes our law; our lusts gain a strength which we shall afterwards vainly oppose; wrong inclinations become so confirmed in us, that they defeat all our endeavours to correct them.[25]

The distrust of the psyche that permeates this utterance echoes through the century's thought. A harvest of truths lies ready for gathering in the world; right principles may be fixed within if learned from without. But lusts and wrong inclinations and the will itself (mainly in the sense of "wilfullness") require rigorous control. Only with the help of the aged can youth hope to escape its own limitation, caused by the passions that distort perception and the imagination that substitutes for true vision. Otherwise, adolescents can have only precarious contact with the world outside, dominated as they are by inner forces.

On the other hand, the vitality of the youthful inner life might supply grounds for asserting the superiority of the young to their elders. Passion as energy is the source of action. By its force alone do men and women achieve the extraordinary; they are likely to achieve it in early life. As John Bennet puts it,

the passions were implanted in us by the Deity, as the springs of all our actions.... Amongst these passions, the love of the other sex is infinitely the strongest and the most universal; and by operating at a time of life, when the character and habits are most essentially affected, has given rise to the greatest revolutions in society, and to some of the most extraordinary incidents of common life. (Strictures, p. 59)

110

The paradox of adolescence depends on the identity between the weakness and the strength of the young, whose capacity for intense feeling, even directed toward a single representative of the opposite sex, implies potential for significant action. Hence the anxiety of many moralists lest youth fail to take advantage of its opportunities. Lord Chesterfield reiterates to the point of tedium his conviction that a man will for all his life be what he is at twenty. "For God's sake then reflect," he tells his sixteen-year-old son; and, later the same year, "every week ought to produce fruit or flowers."[26]

The prototypical adolescent who emerges from this advice, description, and warning is a being of tumultuous passions precariously controlled by the alertness of parents and parental surrogates; a being inclined to take messages from within far too seriously and to misjudge stimuli from without; a creature at once terrifying and appealing to grown-ups, in possession of vast energy which may prove destructive or creative. The open fear in this mythic image, fear of the consequences of attending too closely to inner voices, reinforces the cultural assumption that reason should dominate passion, that society's interests must control individual desires. On the other hand, the reiterated conviction of adolescence's special importance hints a counterbelief in (or wish for) passion as power, a source of excitement, stimulation, and effective force.

The emotional complexities of the eighteenth-century image of adolescence readily generate the kind of action that informs fiction: a conflict of values or of energies issuing in external happening. Didactic literature, explaining what adolescents should strive to be, criticizing what they were, revealed also in what compelling forms they inhabited adult consciousness; novels and plays invented plots that drew on the power of those imagined versions of youth.

Adolescent characters in literature dramatize the tension between the self's demands and the world's. The most eloquent statement of the moralists' view of youth occurs in George Lillo's famous play, *The London Merchant*, first published in 1731. Thorowgood, eighteen-year-old George Barnwell's benevolent employer, forgives his apprentice for misdeeds whose nature he does not know, on the stated grounds that the adolescent condition makes consistent virtue more or less impossible.

When we consider the frail condition of humanity [Thorowgood says], it may raise our pity, not our wonder, that youth should go astray when reason, weak at best opposed to inclination, scarce formed and wholly unassisted by ex-

111

perience, faintly contends or willingly becomes the slave of sense. The state of youth is much to be deplored, and the more so because they see it not, being then to danger most exposed when they are least prepared for their defence.[27]

Continuing, Thorowgood warns the young man to "be upon your guard in this gay, thoughtless season of your life; when the sense of pleasure's quick and passion high, the voluptuous appetites raging and fierce demand the strongest curb; take heed of a relapse." George Barnwell, of course, proves unable to use this excellent advice (perhaps he responds instead to the hostility concealed within it); the play ends with him on his way to the gallows for the murder of his uncle. He cannot cope with his unfamiliar and powerful emotions when an older woman sets out to corrupt him; she feels interested in George specifically because his youthful ignorance will prevent his seeing her evil; what makes him attractive also victimizes him. Not many of the century's imaginative works, however, follow the tragic curve implicit in this vision. In the more prevalent comic mode of fiction and drama, youth guarantees triumph. Yet the young people who get their way show themselves, like George Barnwell, controlled by feelings. Their capacity to "win" in a social context demonstrates eighteenth-century duality of feeling about the import of youthful subordination to emotion.

The issue is complicated by the relative absence of change in eighteenth-century novelistic characters. Tom Jones must learn prudence, which will modify and control his expression of his passions, to prove that he has grown up. He simply adds this to his other virtues; he does not alter his nature. In contrast, Pip in *Great Expectations*, roughly a century later, in order to reach maturity has to transform his way of understanding himself and his world. Has to—and *can*: eighteenth-century fictional adolescents appear fixed.

This fact implies a curious relation between adulthood and imagined adolescence. If the youth is already what he will become—Tom Jones ineluctably good, Blifil as unalterably bad—he bears a close resemblance to a hypothetical adult. On the other hand, grown-ups have a stake in declaring the utter difference between maturity and immaturity. Fiction often conveys both apparently incompatible attitudes at once. It may suggest continuity of concern between young and old, so that the young in their perplexities epitomize universal situations at the same time that their mode of dealing with their problems expresses the uniqueness of their adolescent state. The imagined situations of youth provide purified versions of their adult counterparts: the young carry less baggage of convention and obligation. Young people possess the privileged social position of *ingênus,* thus the capacity to shed new light on hidden aspects of society. If adult narrators and adult characters within a fiction use their prerogative of superiority to condescend to youthful ignorance, neither such condescension nor the protectiveness of advice givers conveys the full truth of the adolescent's symbolic role.

The disguises the young discover and use often foretell the strategies of the adult world. The many eighteenth-century novels by women about girls concentrate in particular on acceptable disguises for passion. The inner world of young heroines reveals an ardent life, but the demands of the external world transmute its forms. Young women in fiction appear in some ways to be *born* adult. The lover of a teen-aged heroine, rhapsodizing in her praise, comments, "Ah! how weak is Passion in such a Soul as her's."[28] He means that his beloved acts always by reason or principle, not from feeling; she acts like an ideal grownup. In fact, sixteen-year-old Fanny Meadows experiences intense emotion—pity, sorrow, horror—but she does not dwell on sentiments of love. Female fiction often conveys an impression of emotion oddly deflected. *Evelina* (1778), the most familiar and certainly the best of these novels, provides a seventeen-year-old heroine, newly entered into society, who records the daily fluctuations of her feelings in long letters to her guardian. Although she soon falls in love with Lord Orville, she fails to realize this fact until her correspondent points it out; then she tries to repress the feeling. Her intense emotional experience centers in episodes of embarrassment, her inner life largely responsive to the impression she makes, or believes herself to make, on others, representatives of the social world. She has occasion enough for strong feeling—a man attempts to abduct her, her true father apparently rejects her, a young man with pistols seems to threaten suicide in her presence—and actually has appropriate responses to such episodes; but the emotional weight of the novel lies in the repetitious small events that define social success or failure.

The apparent trivialization of feeling in such a scheme conceals imaginative transformation of the adolescent conflict between internal and external demands. Evelina's vocabulary declares the high importance she assigns to socially induced emotions. Her first encounter with Lord Orville arouses "terror" of "doing something wrong." She imagines that "he must either conclude me a fool, or half mad, for anyone brought up in the great world, and accustomed to its ways, can

113

have no idea of such sort of fears as mine."[29] After a subsequent encounter, she observes, "I am inexpressibly concerned at the thought of his harbouring an opinion that I am bold or impertinent, and I could almost kill myself for having given him the shadow of a reason for so shocking an idea" (p. 72). Again, she feels "inexpressibly distressed" by the notion that Lord Orville might think she has entrusted herself to the protection of caddish Sir Clement Willoughby (p. 96). This terror and distress and inexpressible concern focus mainly on a single man (Evelina uses the language of embarrassment in relation to others, but not with such consistent intensity). Expressing such feelings substitutes for admitting sexual passion; experiencing them replaces conscious experience of their sexual equivalent. To the very end of the novel, Evelina continues to insist that the desire to behave properly motivates her and that she needs the help of those older and wiser (first her guardian, then Lord Orville) to guide her. "Really," she says, "I think there ought to be a book, of the laws and customs â-la-mode, presented to all young people, upon their first introduction into public company" (p. 83). Such a book, she implies, would solve her problems.

This particular form of emotional deflection—substituting concern about social propriety for concern about a man—might encourage Evelina's admirers, too, to celebrate the weakness of passion in such a soul as hers: she dramatizes her effort always to govern herself by reason and principle; her professed values are identical with those of adults, only her lack of adult experience keeping her from flawless behavior. The same description would apply to most adolescent heroines of eighteenth-century fiction by women: they err through inexperience, not through the dominance of passion. They refuse to marry where they do not love, but they do not pursue with force their own desires. What the outer world demands often determines what they demand of themselves—though they may, like Evelina, distinguish between the requirements of true propriety and those of vulgarity and pretension. Yet the energy of feeling that Evelina directs to considering how she affects others reveals her passional nature—a nature in disguise, but the subterranean center of the novel. Evelina evokes interest because of her unaccountable intensities; her embarrassments are the metaphor of her love. Her compromise with the adult world, the world of external social demands, has been made before the action of the novel begins; yet this fiction celebrates the emotional self-absorption and ardency of adolescence even while concealing it. It also, however, justifies the concealments and the deviousness of the adult world, declaring no necessary conflict between youthful emotion and mature conduct. Evelina needs to discover and define her public identity—her roles as daughter and as wife—but she can continue to "be herself," the fable says, regardless of her role. Deeply responsive to events and people, at the mercy of her responses, she industriously accumulates social data to guide her in acceptable behavior; she need learn nothing about acceptable feeling. She embodies the fantasy of having it all ways at once: an adolescent whom adults can instruct, but one already committed to adult principles of behavior.

Tom Jones declares in an altogether different way the conceivable identity as well as divergence of adult and adolescent problems and interests; again, the central issue involves reconciliation of inner and outer pressures. The moral scheme of Fielding's novel depends on the tension between "outside" and "inside" exemplified by the often opposed virtues of prudence and benevolence. Neither virtue belongs exclusively to members of one generation: Squire Allworthy's benevolent impulses prove more fully developed even than Tom's; Blifil manifests his prudence virtually from the time he can speak. The inner glow of benevolence obviously outshines the discreet lamp of prudence, but both qualities prove necessary. Tom, whose moral and emotional growing up coincides almost precisely, in the book's careful chronological development, with his legal coming of age, must learn to take seriously the demands of his social environment as well as those of his nature—a lesson Evelina had learned long before seventeen. Blifil's premature awareness of how to exploit others inhibits his moral growth: he springs full-grown from the heads of the tutor Thwackum and the philosopher Square. Tom's exemplary process of growing through his mistakes, on the other hand, leads him to know that neither his passions nor the demands of others can guide him, although neither can be safely rejected. The Man on the Hill, a recluse whom Tom rescues from attempted violence, offers a paradigm of one kind of youthful experience: led astray by bad company in youth, he narrowly escapes ultimate disaster, and resolves the tensions of conflicting impulse by utter rejection of society. Tom claims that even his limited knowledge of the world reveals the existence of good men and women; the Man on the Hill responds that wider knowledge—adult knowledge—proves the contrary. But such wisdom is not adequate for Tom, who continues to test the thesis by repeated encounters, demonstrating the moral variety of his social universe, until he achieves integrity of relationship and of personality.

The presence in the novel of Squire Western, a man altogether at the mercy of his passions, and of Squire Allworthy, good in impulse but often unable to untangle his perceptions from the deceptions of others, emphasizes the ubiquity of the problems the young man faces. The narrator underlines the point by relating Tom's difficulties also to those of writer and reader. The ideal "historian," he explains, needs, in addition to natural gifts and to the learning obtained from books, another sort of knowledge attainable only through "conversation." "So necessary is this to understanding the characters of men that none are more ignorant of them than those learned pedants whose lives have been entirely consumed in colleges and among books; for however exquisitely human nature may have been described by writers, the true practical system can only be learnt in the world."[30] Like Tom, the aspiring historian must come to know the realm outside himself by living among others, encountering the risks of reality. Yet what he perceives without will depend partly on what he contains within. Blifil's total commitment to self-interest blinds him to the operation of other motives in Tom (IV, 7; p. 243); Jones's veracity keeps him from suspecting that of others (VIII, 7; p. 359). The narrator comments that the capacity for distrust derives either from nature or from long experience; the old, who may possess it, are therefore "apt to despise the understandings of all those who are a little younger than themselves"; the narrator clearly thinks this capacity of dubious value. Every reader has the obligation to assess evoked fictional characters by his or her understanding of the "original book of nature" (VII, 12; p. 319); the quality of that understanding will depend on who the reader is as well as on the experience he or she has undergone. The capacity for distrust presumably would limit fruitful acceptance of the text, as Blifil's distrustfulness limits what he can perceive in the world.

Blifil's lack of the "warm" passions and imagination that characterize Tom, as they mark the archetypal youth evoked by moral commentators, comes to seem a serious deficiency. Sophia's decision to trust her passionate commitment to Tom rather than to follow the worldly and "prudent" course advocated by her aunt signals her depth and courage. Although Tom's passions get him in trouble, they also get him out; his warm responsiveness measures his worth. As a didactic work, in other words, *Tom Jones* does not entirely support the messages of the moralists although it offers a corroborative characterization of its young protagonist. By structure and characterization it suggests not simply that adolescence marks a particularly crucial period of psychic life but that the years of growth epitomize a struggle never resolved or resolvable, the struggle of the individual to come to terms with a world composed of other people—often dangerous other people like Lady Bellaston and Lord Fellamar—without violating a sense of self which partly depends upon the reactions of others: Tom learns who he is partly by learning how he is perceived. Passions and prudence, opposed forces, both help and hinder the protagonist of such struggle. No good advice proves of much use: Squire Allworthy, presumably on his deathbed, tells Tom that he must add prudence and religion to his other virtues, but only the young man's actual confrontations will teach him the proper function and limits of prudence. The old do not necessarily prove wiser than the young; sometimes they are more foolish. The drama of Tom's growth assumes special urgency because his place in the world must be found, he must win his social label; but the psychic drama of self and other, inner and outer, reiterates itself in older characters as well as in Tom's contemporaries. The achievement of a social label only superficially solves problems that plague squires and historians, servants and readers: all who function in the world.

The simplified fictional embodiments of universal dilemmas provided by men and women not yet fully absorbed into society enable adults to imagine resolutions for the experienced incompatibility of self and social world, interior and exterior factuality. By locating the conflict in those declared "immature," novelists, shifting the focus of the moralists, soften implicit social criticism and distance difficulty. As images of effort and fulfillment, the imagined young supply ways of reiterating the rightness of the existing social order while entertaining the fantasy that passion might safely be allowed an important place in the private life.

The ambiguities of adolescent passion, as treated in fictional and didactic texts alike, help to clarify the issues between young and old. If passion located for the eighteenth century both the peculiar strength and the ominous weakness of the young, perception of youthful passion could account equally well for adult feelings of superiority or inferiority to youth. Given these truths, both the force allowed Pamela and the denials of force in *The Vicar of Wakefield* make sense. Pamela embodies, from the point of view of adult society, a "safe" image of youth, her passions indirectly acknowledged but her piety firmly in control. Adults can permit her her moment of power precisely because it will not last. The strivings of youth in *The Vicar* make larger claims: the young tread on their parents' heels. The male aspirations of George and Moses, eager to do and to know, potentially threaten their father's hegemony. The fable that contains them therefore punishes them.

To emphasize the passions of the young reminds grown-ups of what they have that youth lacks—developed reason—as well as of what they lack that youth has. The passional proclivities of youth can focus adult tenderness and rage, the desire to help and to impede, the desire even to imitate or to identify. Passion can signal vulnerability or strength. As a weapon or a weakness of youth, it functions conspicuously in eighteenth-century evocations of intergenerational politics, allowing the expression of ambivalence that later periods would find different ways to render.

5

Annals of Anxiety

Depending on our critical—or political—purposes, we may understand Pamela with equal plausibility as powerful or powerless, as manipulator or as victim. Eighteenth-century didactic works reveal adults' fear of their children (a phenomenon that Dr. Spock recently declared peculiar to the late twentieth century), but they offer as convincing testimony of grown-ups' unquestioning sense of authority and superiority. Such contradictions suggest not only the malleability of texts but the difficulty virtually all adults, in all periods, experience about maintaining a firm, clear, single attitude toward the young, those protean creatures who defy classification and judgment, who in their perplexing combination of resemblance and opposition to their elders inevitably fuel fantasy.

The myth of adolescent power reverses itself into the equally compelling and equally useful myth of adolescent weakness, most readily attached to girls, most emphatically expressed by female writers. By the late eighteenth century, women wrote most of the published novels; they wrote mainly about young women struggling to define themselves and to find mates. In tone and plot structure, these novels duplicate one another, characteristically recording rather haphazard sequences of calamity. Most possess little literary merit; but they offer useful material for a study of adolescence, because they expose with particular clarity the issues that associate themselves with a class deprived of social power yet imagined as rich in personal resource. The passionate proclivities of the young seem especially threatening when they belong to women; so does the will to power. The heroines of many loosely structured late eighteenth-century works manifest both, although, more emphatically even than Pamela or Evelina, they conceal force beneath fear, existing in typical (and externally justified) states of intense anxiety. The ends they seek—independence, control,

119

love—characterize all adolescents—indeed, all human beings. In adolescence, men and women alike first become intensely conscious of and focused on such goals. Women's desires, in a social context that largely prohibited their direct expression (the ideal girl would want marriage but not concern herself with erotic satisfaction), worried moral commentators. Novelists both corroborated and echoed their worries.

Female versions of the picaresque novel of adolescence stress the world's threats more than its possibilities; their happy endings derive less from causal sequence than from fortunate accident. The Gothic fictions of Anne Radcliffe reveal with special clarity a set of issues implicit also in other late-century novels superficially quite different in genre. In the tensions they express, they duplicate a body of late eighteenth-century didactic literature rich in barely acknowledged conflict between perception and prescription.

Prescriptions for girls increasingly emphasize suppression and subordination, epitomized in Hannah More's chilling admonitions:

That bold, independent, enterprising spirit, which is so much admired in boys, should not, when it happens to discover itself in the other sex, be encouraged, but suppressed. Girls should be taught to give up their opinions betimes, and not pertinaciously to carry on a dispute, even if they should know themselves to be in the right. . . . It is of the greatest importance to their future happiness, that they should acquire a submissive temper, and a forbearing spirit: for it is a lesson which the world will not fail to make them frequently practise, when they come abroad into it, and they will not practise it the worse for having learnt it the sooner.[1]

Or, as Lord Kames puts it more precisely, "supposing a young woman perfectly tractable, no means ought to be neglected for making her an useful and agreeable companion in the matrimonial state. To make a good husband, is but one branch of a man's duty; but it is the chief duty of a woman, to make a good wife."[2]

Both these utterances strike a note of practical realism marked in recommendations for young women. For girls, unlike boys, no dichotomy divides the means to earthly and heavenly success. When More speaks of the value for "future happiness" of a submissive temper, she means happiness in the world, but the same temper would help the young woman fulfill her Christian obligations. Kames's notion of "duty" depends on social actuality but derives from Christian tradition. To win her way to a happy marriage defines woman's success; men, on the other hand, craving wealth and power achieved through their own efforts, must as youths be warned not to risk damnation for the sake of immediate reward. To be sure, advice for girls acknowledges that the young may seek to lure attractive men by meretricious or superficial means; but such methods, unlike male strategies of power, will not, advice givers insist, work. Far better cultivate virtues that promise certain reward.

The prescription for girls, in other words, centers on a single simple admonition: Be Good. (In detail, as we shall see, the way to goodness proves far from simple.) The perception that underlies it, or the imagining of the youthful female nature, proves harder to discern. Even the two short passages I have quoted offer evidence of tension. In the Kames sentences, the verb "make" implies effortful creation. The initial hypothesis of "a young woman perfectly tractable" betrays uncertainty (such a woman, only a supposition, may not actually exist), but the moralist rushes ahead to urge his unspecified agent to *make* this woman useful and agreeable—an effort both urgent and difficult, requiring ingenuity in the exploitation of all available means. The woman participates in her own making, apparently converting *herself* into a good wife—yet Kames evidently feels something unnatural about the useful companion, the good wife. Only by effort will the girl become a fully subordinated being.

The More quotation yet more emphatically suggests the energy necessary to hold down female inclinations, as it specifies the enemies of submission: bold spirit, independent opinion. The agent of remaking, mysterious in More as in Kames, must teach girls to give up, not to sustain dispute, because "the world" will in the long run inculcate the same lesson: best learn it early. The capacity to know or to believe rightly has no value in a young woman, whose worth depends on nothing in her nature so much as her capacity to subordinate that nature to others. Although More's advice has at least as much air of authority as Kames's, one may detect or imagine in it also a note of sadness. The author knows what the world offers women; does she recognize the pathos in the fate of girls forced to "acquire" the submissive temper and forbearing spirit which they cannot sufficiently possess without training? The world will "make" its victims submit; the moralist herself submits to its necessities in formulating her doctrine. Like Kames, she imagines insubordinate energies latent in young women; like Kames, she mandates extirpation.

The association of the young with passion and imagination was believed, as we have seen, to create dangers for both sexes. The doctrine of female subordination, however, may have generated—or have de-

121

rived from (impossible to ascertain causality in such matters)—particular uneasiness about the inner life of young women. The threat of seduction only symbolizes a larger, less well-defined threat. In the texts concerned with female education that proliferated late in the eighteenth century, one finds extraordinary stress on the girl's inevitable dependency and on its central importance in her life. Lord Kames warns her to "avoid the intricacies of philosophy and deep reasoning; which would tend to emulation, not to cordiality." "Cordiality," an odd goal for female education, defines the valued aspect of femininity. Prudent education, Kames continues, will make a woman into "a delicious companion to a man of parts and knowledge" (p. 274). He cultivates his intellect; she, her deliciousness. A creature of cordiality, a delicious companion: educators must employ their intellectual resources to reduce female students to beings utterly focused on others, praiseworthy only for what they bring to relationship. The Edgeworths, father and daughter, famous liberal educators writing at the very end of the century, point out that "Women cannot foresee what may be the tastes of the individuals with whom they are to pass their lives. Their own tastes should not therefore be early decided." (Decided by whom? Again, no agent.) The best education would create maximum flexibility, so that "they may attain any talent in perfection" called for by those individuals with whom they share their existence.[3] Such an education, however, requires a complex balancing act. "Her imagination must not be raised above the taste for necessary occupations, or the numerous small, but not trifling pleasures of domestic life: her mind must be enlarged, yet the delicacy of her manners must be preserved"—and so on (II, 550). Nothing to excess: the female meaning of that maxim implies constant check on the life of intellect and imagination which might supply purely private gratification. Nothing to excess, even in the development of talents dedicated to the entertainment of others.

It is perhaps more desirable [Erasmus Darwin writes] that young ladies should play, sing, and dance, only so well as to amuse themselves and their friends, than to practise those arts in so eminent a degree as to astonish the public; because a great apparent attention to trivial accomplishments is liable to give a suspicion, that more valuable acquisitions have been neglected. And, as they consist in an exhibition of the person, they are liable to be attended with vanity, and to extinguish the blush of youthful timidity; which is in young ladies the most powerful of their exterior charms.[4]

On the other hand, Mrs. Thrale, with her customary vigor, complains that "Every Female is harrassed with Masters she disregards, and heaped with Accomplishments which She ought to disdain, when She reflects that her Mother only loads her with Allurements, as a Rustic lays Bird Lime on Twigs, to decoy & catch the unwary Traveller." These reflections come to an unexpected conclusion: "yet is Education at last an admirable Thing, whoever has not been bred to Science, considers his early Life as a Source of future Misery."[5]

This sequence of quotation supplies substance for several sorts of feminist meditation on the hard lot of our ancestors, but my interest at the moment lies in defining one specific mode of perceiving young women. Mrs. Thrale, the only one of these commentators writing in a private rather than a public genre, provides a clue to the others in her clear evocation of the girl as trap (however willing) and in her contrasting hint that education provides a potential resource. Only "Science" rescues one from the misery implicit in misspent youth. Good education generates strength, bad education intensifies weakness, making the girl a passive instrument for the machinations of others, loaded with the allurements that serve her mother's purposes. But why the shift of pronouns in the final clause? In the midst of her reflections on female education, the writer uses a masculine possessive, as though the idea of true learning, even in a negative formulation, naturally associates itself with males. After all, the earlier assertion states that *every* female feels the burden of meretricious manipulation: none escapes. One can hardly take this as a literal assertion, but it delineates the weakness of young women, implicit not in their natures but in their agency. In virtually all pedagogical formulations, girls appear as beings to whom things are done, as objects rather than subjects. Even the kinds of power sometimes invested in them— charm, talent, good disposition—intensify the sense of their weakness, in their assumed necessary subordination. "Every mode which keeps down vanity and keeps back *self*, has at least a moral use," Hannah More writes.[6] To keep back self defines the proper moral goal of young women.

Although all the citations I have offered come from the late years of the eighteenth century, they represent on the whole a conservative body of opinion (Mrs. Thrale defies classification, indiscriminately expressing conservative and radical views alike). Even the most radical proponents of democracy and of women's rights, however, express a view of young women as inevitably weak, in a social if not a personal sense. Mary Wollstonecraft often strikes a note of sadness or uncertainty despite her clear vision of alternative female fates, her vigorous denunciation of the injustice of existing social arrangements. In *Thoughts on the Education of Daughters* (1787), she makes a clear though tentative statement about some differences between girls and women. "When a woman's mind has gained some strength, she will in all probability pay more attention to her actions than a girl can be expected to do; and if she thinks seriously, she will chuse for a companion a man of principle; and this perhaps young people do not sufficiently attend to, or see the necessity of doing."[7] The "perhaps" hints genuine bewilderment. The writer seeks an explanation for the bad marital decisions of young women; she finds it in their inadequacies of perception (what they fail to see) and of attention. Maturing involves the gaining of strength, associated with the adult woman but not with her younger self. For social reasons, youth may provide a "season of gaiety"; certainly adulthood does not.

I have indeed so much compassion for those young females who are entering into the world without fixed principles, that I would fain persuade them to examine a little into the matter. For though in the season of gaiety they may not feel the want of them, in that of distress where will they fly for succour? Even with this support, life is a labour of patience—a conflict; and the utmost we can gain is a small portion of peace, a kind of watchful tranquillity, that is liable to continual interruptions. (P. 135)

This dark view of life does not confine itself explicitly to women; the "we" in the final sentence may refer to humankind in general. Or it may not. The expectation of a season of distress inevitably following that of gaiety appears to be linked with the notion that "young females" have special need for principles as recourse and defence; the terms describing mature existence, with "watchful tranquillity" the best it has to offer, relate more readily to female than to male experience. But the particular vulnerability of the young, in Wollstonecraft's view, characterizes both sexes, and the loss of that vulnerability involves ambiguous gain. The young, for example, have benevolent impulses, but they "afterwards grow selfish; a knowledge of the arts of others, is an excuse to them for practising the same; and because they have been deceived once, or have found objects unworthy of their charity—if any one appeals to their feelings, the formidable word Imposture instantly banishes the compassionate emotions, and silences conscience" (p. 137).

In the dangerous world that Wollstonecraft posits and perceives, feelings form a nexus of weakness. The sequence sketched in the reflections about benevolence embody one paradigm: youthful good feelings yield to unworthy, unattractive impulses of self-protection which block the life of "compassionate emotions" and with it the power of conscience. The warning about the need for principles derives from awareness that the young in their gaiety rely excessively on feeling, which offers no real "support": only principle provides that. And of course anxiety about the tendency of young women to marry the wrong man reflects belief that emotion leads one astray. In *A Vindication of the Rights of Woman* (1792), Wollstonecraft clarifies her conviction that evil forces implicit in the actualities of social organization prevent the good feelings of the young and account for the weakness not merely of young women but of women in general. "The exercise of youthful sympathies forms the moral temperature," she explains. ". . . In youth, the fondest friendships are formed, the genial juices mounting at the same time, kindly mix; or, rather the heart, tempered for the reception of friendship, is accustomed to seek for pleasure in something more noble than the churlish gratification of appetite."[8] This well-tempered heart may, however, lend itself to other uses; Wollstonecraft, too, evokes the passive condition of the marriageable girl, manipulated until she cares only for herself. "Yet, mixing in the giddy circle under restraint, these butterflies long to flutter at large, for the first affection of their souls is their own persons, to which their attention has been called with the most sedulous care whilst they were preparing for the period that decides their fate for life." Wollstonecraft contrasts the pursuit of such "idle routine" with the "dignity" of attachment between the sexes in schools which train young men and young women together for responsible use of their minds (p. 170).

Consistently Wollstonecraft opposes a perceived condition of tyranny by parents and by social forms to an imagined state of freedom in which girls would no longer be "rendered weak and vain, by indolence, and frivolous pursuits" (p. 169). Not nature but nurture, in other words, must bear responsibility for the ignoble state of girls, doomed to passivity by their social setting. The writer's perception of the youthful female condition varies hardly at all from that of more conservative commentators; she differs only in her assignment of responsibility. Such moralists as Hannah More, though they fully acknowledge the complicity of mothers in encouraging the superficiality of their daughters, imply that strong moral fiber in the young will resist contamination; Wollstonecraft suggests the irresistibility of infection emanating from society's fundamental assumptions.

Catherine Macaulay, in her famous *Letters on Education* (1790)—source of some of Wollstonecraft's ideas in *A Vindication*—spends relatively little time considering the situation of young women in particular. The bulk of her advice concerns children; toward the end of the book she veers off into metaphysics. In the central section of the work considering the adolescent years, she vacillates about the matter of sex. Letter XXII of part I asserts "No characteristic Difference in Sex." By an obvious association of ideas, succeeding letters consider "Coquetry" and "Flattery—Chastity—Male Rakes," before returning to the security of "Hints towards the Education of a Prince."[9] The hypothetical subject of education is male, although Macaulay suggests that young men and young women have more in common than statements of the period typically acknowledge, that they share socially defined weakness although immediate conditions intensify it for girls.

More practical than most moralists, Macaulay recognizes the futility of telling a lovely girl that beauty does not matter when everything in the girl's experience assures her that it matters a great deal. The girl advised of the valuelessness of beauty will only think "that we *mean* to keep her in ignorance of her true worth. She will think herself deceived, and she will resent the injury by giving little credit to our precepts, and placing her confidence in those who tickle her ears with lavish panegyric on the captivating graces of her person" (p. 217). Thus a young woman cultivates her vanity. More ominous, "the soothings of flattery never fail to operate on the affections of the heart; and when love creeps into the bosom, the empire of reason is at an end" (p. 218). The astute pedagogue will teach the girl to consider her beauty a power of great magnitude, so that she will become too proud and haughty to yield to love; thus she will gain time "to cultivate that philosophy which, if well understood, is a never failing remedy to human pride" (p. 218). This circuitous procedure assumes that only through a girl's emotions can one hope to reach her. The warnings about novel reading, not explicitly directed toward females, rest on the same assumption. Novels, Macaulay explains, elaborating a point of Dr. Johnson's reiterated by many succeeding moralists, "are all histories of lovers; and love tales are always improper for the ears of youth, whose mind should be ever open to the soft feelings of benevolence, but be kept as long as possible in ignorance of the melting sensations of what is called in pre-eminence 'the tender passion'" (p. 143). The special problem for young women involves the misdirection of feeling toward the self; even love, as Macaulay describes it, serves the primary purpose of narcissistic gratification in a society that allows few other fulfillments for female narcissism. We return thus to female weakness, closely allied to female power. "Suffer them [young women] to idolize their persons, to throw away their life in the pursuit of trifles, and to indulge in the gratification of the meaner passions, and they will heartily join in the sentence of their degradation" (p. 205). The characteristic activity of young women, even for Macaulay, typically involves unworthy goals; responsibility belongs to the elders who "suffer" the girl to behave badly or who, alternately, restrain her. Restraint represents the adolescent female's proper condition.

All these texts purportedly refer to social actuality. Young women exist, they suggest, to be marketed in marriage: a bleak reality. The best deductions of social historians corroborate the economic stringencies of eighteenth-century marriage and the virtual nonexistence of acceptable alternatives for the young woman. Nonetheless, the guides to conduct reflect assumptions about the emotional weakness and passivity of girls as well as observations of the female situation. A final quotation from Hannah More will summarize the view implicit in most moralizing.

Those young women in whom feeling is indulged to the exclusion of reason and examination, are peculiarly liable to be the dupes of prejudice, rash decisions, and false judgment. The understanding having but little power over the will, their affections are not well poized, and their minds are kept in a state ready to be acted upon by the fluctuations of alternate impulses; by sudden and varying impressions; by casual and contradictory circumstances; and by emotions excited by every accident. (*Strictures*, II, 115–16)

The young woman has little power over herself; indeed, hardly any connection with herself. Her moral fate depends upon whether "feeling is indulged" in her—indulged, presumably, by others as well as by some agency of the self. The elements of her psychic make-up— feelings, reason, understanding—will appear as discontinuous entities, subject to external forces. The mind ever "ready to be acted upon" results specifically from the indulgence of feeling; but since much didactic literature associates emotional susceptibility with the state of adolescent females in general, the situation of this particularly vulnerable young woman hardly seems a special case. She represents a sisterhood.

Repeatedly told of her passivity and vulnerability, while exhorted to activity (within strictly defined limits) and strength (of a proper feminine sort), the late eighteenth-century female adolescent faced constant reminders of her social restrictions and frequent suggestions of her fundamental incapacity. The hectoring tone of many moralistic urgencies, by men and women alike, however, may reflect unsureness or

127

uneasiness about the true nature of young womanhood. Thus John Bennett, beginning a series of instructive letters to a girl who has lost her mother by death, defines his purpose: "to rouse young ladies from a vacant or insipid life, into one of usefulness and laudable exertion—to recall them from visionary novels and romances, into solid reading and reflection—and from the criminal absurdities of fashion, to the simplicity of nature and the dignity of virtue."[10] He assumes that only through his intervention will his audience attain "the simplicity of nature." Unnaturalness, then, is easier for a young woman—is in a sense more natural? The question formulates in extreme terms an implication of many moralistic texts. Every one of the passages I have quoted indicates its writer's belief in the urgency of *control* for girls—at the very least, the internal control of principles; more often, the external control of older instructors. The insistent implicit association between young women and the out-of-control speaks of anxiety. Paradoxically, the very fact that girls are early trained to compliant social behavior may heighten uneasiness. If young women do what they have been educated to do, allowing the world to see their training rather than their natures, those natures remain hidden, objects of speculation. Because hidden, perhaps dangerous. The multiplication of prescription for every detail of female behavior suggests the worry that only unremitting efforts at control could prevent eruptions of passion and purpose. The better young women behaved, the more worrisome they might seem: what did their goodness conceal? On the other hand, "bad" behavior also intensified anxiety. Given the social rewards for "goodness," deviations implied overflow from hidden reservoirs of uncontrollable impulse. Late eighteenth-century fiction registers these worries, too, in rather different terms.

"Novels and romances" appear frequently in eighteenth-century references as agents of corruption. By the late century, many novels incorporated awareness of such criticism and made use of the negative images of young womanhood reiterated by the moralizers. Such fiction claimed to share moralists' worries about the dangers of adolescent emotion as well as the didactic purpose of combating such feeling. Novelists, too, could aspire to rescue the young from vacant or insipid lives.

One representative novel, *Memoirs of Emma Courtney* (1796), provides, among other things, a capsule version of the emotional experience of the adolescent girl. At the age of twelve, having been reared tenderly by an aunt and uncle, by the command of my father, I was sent to boarding school.—Ah! never shall I forget the contrast I experienced. I was an alien, and a stranger;—no one loved, caressed, nor cared for me; my actions were all constrained;—I was obliged to sit poring over needle work, and forbidden to prate;—my body was tortured into forms, my mind coerced, and tasks imposed upon me, grammar and French, mere words, that conveyed to me no ideas. I loved my guardians with passion—my tastes were all passions—they tore themselves from my embraces with difficulty. I sat down, after their departure, and wept—bitter tears—sobbed convulsively—my griefs were unheeded, and my sensibility ridiculed.[11]

Although Emma's reminiscences have as their avowed theme the misfortunes generated by her excessive emotionality, the tone of this passage conveys another message. When the speaker reports the ridicule of her sensibility, the ignoring of her griefs, she engages the reader's sympathy. She offers in effect an allegorical account of female adolescence: rejected by her father; "alien, and a stranger" in a world outside her family where she must make her way; constrained, obliged, forbidden, tortured, coerced; full of passion with no return—"no one loved, caressed, nor cared for me." The summary's palpable self-pity does not modify its poignance as a record of the discrepancy between inner and outer experience which marks the adolescent fate. Of course, fiction thrives on feeling; novelistic efforts to discredit life dominated by emotion almost inevitably undercut themselves. The female novel of adolescence in the late eighteenth century frequently proclaims the danger of feeling, only to convey the misery of a situation that demands constraint, offers little opportunity for focused action, and denies the validity of emotional response to limitation and enforced passivity. It thus offers a double message. It corroborates the fear of adolescent female intensity by depicting a girl who exemplifies the moralists' fantasies. It proclaims her mistakes, assigns her a punishing fate. But it also generates sympathy and even admiration for the victim of feeling. The idea of control comes to seem sensible but uninteresting. As the creature of fantasy gets fleshed out, she becomes attractive, not just dangerous; the novel preaches subversive doctrine in the guise of supporting moral platitudes.

The novel-reading or romance-reading girl, a stock character in eighteenth-century fiction and drama, provides an easy comic target, mocked for her alienation from reality. Female authors, however, sometimes make her fill a paradoxical function. Charlotte Lennox's *The Female Quixote* (1752), a work popular throughout the eighteenth century despite its manifest imperfections, simultaneously celebrates and condemns a girl who commits herself to the values of French romances as guiding principles of her life. Relatively early in date, this novel clarifies crucial issues in much later fiction. Arabella epitomizes the nature and function of many novelistic figures more important in the psychological than in the literary history of the past.

The patterns that interest me here emerge with less disguise in second-rate literature than in great works. The books on the *New York Times* best-seller list—their very titles—illuminate our own culture with special sharpness; the popular fiction of the past, more entertaining to talk about than to read, also sheds unexpected light. These books suggest something about us as well as about our ancestors: we may find familiar the shapes of ambivalence in Charlotte Lennox's *The Female Quixote*.

Arabella, as initially presented, has read too many of the wrong books. Her father has reared her in total isolation, having retreated from the world because of "the Baseness and Ingratitude of Mankind."[12] Her mother died at her birth, leaving a large stock of badly translated French romances, purchased "to soften a Solitude which she found very disagreeable" (p. 7). The predictable result of Arabella's solitude and her reading receives lucid summary:

Her Ideas, from the Manner of her Life, and the Objects around her, had taken a romantic Turn; and, supposing Romances were real Pictures of Life, from them she drew all her Notions and Expectations. By them she was taught to believe, that Love was the ruling Principle of the World; that every other Passion was subordinate to this; and that it caused all the Happiness and Miseries of Life. Her Glass, which she often consulted, always shewed her a Form so extremely lovely, that, not finding herself engaged in such Adventures as were common to the Heroines in the Romances she read, she often complained of the Insensibility of Mankind, upon whom her Charms seemed to have so little influence. (P. 7)

This characterization implies the novel's action. The fiction hardly has a plot; instead, it provides a repetitive sequence of events, each episode emphasizing Arabella's mistaken assessment of actuality. Unlike the male Quixote, she cannot travel through the world; doomed to female passivity, she stays home expecting the advent of lovers. An appropriate suitor soon presents himself, but she acknowledges his rightness only after a long sequence of episodes in which she imagines the infatuation of other lovers or demands that men testify to her power by every means short of actually dying for love.

If Emma Courtney's account of boarding-school life allegorizes female adolescence, *The Female Quixote* offers a yet more compelling allegory. As precisely as any other novel in any period, it renders—in slightly indirect terms—the inner experience of the adolescent girl in all its contradictions, uncertainties, and impossibilities. Beneath the surface of its conventional happy ending, it conveys a pessimistic view of the possibility of any girl's getting what she wants. And it clarifies distressingly the timeless issue of the young female's social weakness, as well as her overwhelming wishes.

What do women most desire? The Wife of Bath's tale—and Boccaccio, and many folk tales—answer unequivocally: power. Two passions only control womankind, Pope concluded: love of pleasure, love of sway. Freud confessed an inability to fathom what women want, but many men before him had no difficulty at all with the problem. The meaning of the desire for power, as exemplified in Arabella, modifies usual interpretations of Pope's conclusion, or the Wife's. Arabella's yearning for power, although it expresses abundant hostility, amounts more importantly to a desperate need for some measure of control, over her own life and over other people, in a social context where the forces dominating her allow no scope for independent action or even for significant thought.

Arabella admits in herself little motivation beyond a desire to behave properly. The novel's central comic irony derives from this fact: she actually behaves with wild inappropriateness because her standards come from unacceptable sources. Her nonconformity reflects more complex motivations than she acknowledges. Arabella yearns to make her world more exciting and more meaningful. As she begins to enter the social sphere, she feels its moral inadequacy. The conventional Miss Glanville tells her, after her first encounter with fashionable entertainment, that she has now experienced the best England can offer.

I am of Opinion, replied *Arabella,* that one's Time is far from being well employ'd in the Manner you portion it out: And People who spend theirs in such trifling Amusements, must certainly live to very little Purpose. What room, I pray you, does a Lady give for high and noble Adventures, who consumes her Days in Dressing, Dancing, listening to Songs, and ranging the Walks with People as thoughtless as herself? How mean and contemptible a Figure must a Life spent in such idle Amusements make in History? (P. 279)

Her reactions reveal her narcissim: more even than she wishes to make the world significant, she wants to make her *self* significant. Or,

131

more precisely, she wants a world that allows opportunities for assertion of a youthful female self. She wants to live to some purpose, to make a figure in history; her society denies her that possibility.

The character of this ridiculous girl, alienated from every kind of social actuality, condenses the universal pathos of the adolescent situation. Even at her most foolish, Arabella expresses a longing for moral as well as physical heroism—as when she recommends those "Books from which all useful knowledge may be drawn; which give us the most shining Examples of Generosity, Courage, Virtue, and Love; which regulate our Actions, form our Manners, and inspire us with a noble Desire of emulating those great, heroic, and virtuous Actions, which made those Persons so glorious in their Age, and so worthy imitation in ours" (p. 48). In a poignant moment, after Arabella has offered a bit of penetrating moral commentary, her lover's father "express'd much Admiration of her Wit, telling her, if she had been a Man, she would have made a great Figure in Parliament, and that her Speeches might have come perhaps to be printed in time" (p. 311). The compliment gives her lover great pleasure, although he perceives it as "odd." Its oddity consists in its articulation of the issue hidden just beneath the surface through most of the novel. For a boy with Arabella's gifts of imagination, moral intensity, and verbal expressiveness, the future would open into a prospect of fame, or at least of importance. Such a boy might expect to make a figure in history; at the very least he could anticipate a life lived to public purpose. Arabella's resolute adherence to fantasy reflects her preconscious perception that actuality offers her little. Her singular notions derive from "her Studies, her Retirement, her Ignorance of the World, and her lively Imagination" (p. 323); she willfully preserves her ignorance of the world because only it protects her from society's intolerable restrictions. Observers in all periods have seen adolescents as dreamers, creating for themselves realms closer to the heart's desire. Maturation presumably brings reconciliation to reality. For the adolescent girl in an eighteenth-century context, however, such reconciliation—so the novel suggests—involves intolerable compromise, denial of her most precious capacities. A man may assure her that success would have attended her had she been a man; a man may marry her. What more can she hope for? How can she content herself with hoping for so little?

The Female Quixote also suggests, rather less openly, a more threatening kind of motivation. Early in the novel, Arabella articulates her antagonism to her father on the basis of her romantic models. She resents the very possibility of marrying a man chosen by a parent. The narrator generalizes the opposition of father and daughter: "In those Cases the Remonstrances of a Parent are called Persecutions: obstinate Resistance, Constancy and Courage; and an Aptitude to dislike the Person proposed to them, a noble Freedom of Mind which disdains to love or hate by the Caprice of others" (p. 27). The observation suggests that Arabella appropriates positive moral terminology to justify dubious actions; certainly such a description applies to most of her dealings with men throughout the book. Her most persistent fantasies involve men dying for her sake: pining away from unrequited passion or killing one another in combat or expiring in dangerous exploits undertaken from devotion to her. Her definition of "heroine" emphasizes a woman's utter domination of the men in her life. The longing to control men focuses her desire for power; her attempts at such control invariably involve efforts to prevent males from expressing sexual passion. In one typical scene, she explains that "just Decorum" demands that a lady keep importunate lovers from presuming to declare their passion, however intensely they feel. Sir George argues "that no Man ought to be hated, because he adores a beautiful Object, and consecrates all his Moments to her Service"; and Arabella accepts his point. Adoration meet her approval; revelation of it does not. "Questionless, resumed *Arabella*, he will not be hated, while, out of the Respect and Reverence he bears her, he carefully conceals his Passion from her knowledge; but as soon as ever he breaks through the Bounds, which that Respect prescribes him, and lets her understand his true Sentiments, he has Reason to expect a most rigorous Sentence, since he certainly, by that Presumption, has greatly deserved it" (p. 147). Arabella knows of her lovers' devotion but can deny her knowledge as long as they cooperate by avoiding the explicit; to admit male sexuality (or her own) to consciousness seems intolerably threatening.

Arabella dramatizes typical adolescent emotions: hostility, fear, and attraction toward the opposite sex; uncertainty about the self; dependence on roles generated by fantasy. Her progress toward maturity, symbolized by her willingness to relinquish the values of her books, depends on acceptance of the threat, challenge, promise of a lover. Once she gives up fantasies of hero-lovers, she can respond to the decent man who wants her, since he has perceived her essential decency and her ardor through the protective mask she has elaborately constructed. Two arguments restore her to "normalcy": the way of the world and the demands of morality. First, a sympathetic countess appears to explain that times have changed. (She serves no other function in the plot and vanishes as soon as she has served this one.) "Cus-

133

tom, said the Countess smiling, changes the very Nature of Things, and what was honourable a thousand Years ago, may probably be look'd upon as infamous now" (p. 328). Her arguments make some impression on Arabella, whose desire for decorum exercises great force in her nature. Despite her peculiarities, she feels the need for a common standard; never does she claim the authority of personal opinion. The countess, then, softens her; a clergyman completes the work. Like a psychiatrist, he points out the unnecessary suffering to which Arabella's fantasies give rise: "nothing can hinder you from being the happiest of Mortals, but Want of Power to understand your own Advantages. . . . I see you harrass'd with innumerable Terrors and Perplexities, which never disturb the Peace of Poverty or Ignorance" (pp. 370–71). Then he offers powerful arguments from Christian morality, refuting Arabella's contention that her romances, "if they do not describe real Life, give us an Idea of a better Race of Beings than now inhabit the World" (p. 380). Not better, but worse, replies the doctor, pointing out that the romances encourage two dangerous passions, revenge and love, and lead their readers to a weakened "Sense of our Alliance with all human nature" (p. 381). When Arabella realizes that she runs the danger of harming others by her self-protective indulgences, she announces her reformation. Two pages later, she is married. The novel ends.

The energy of this fable derives not from its coy and whimsical surface but from its essential truth. To translate it into modern psychological terms requires little effort. Although Arabella proclaims that she, like Don Quixote, yearns for more noble human possibility, her goals derive much more specifically from the particulars of her social and sexual position. She does not, as one might anticipate, seek love; she seeks only lovers. Unlike Pamela, she possesses little real power in her adolescent state; she possesses only the power of fantasy. Given that, she can order her lovers about. Without it, she cannot imagine what to do. Unlike Evelina and Sophia Western and, of course, Clarissa, she faces no real danger, no challenge, no opportunity of testing and discovering herself. Fantasy allows her heroism; life does not. Her addiction to romances represents not merely a comic novelistic device but a genuine perception. Arabella, because she is a girl, fears sexuality in herself and others: she wishes to separate herself from her father but needs external sanctions for doing so; she wants to define herself in positive terms but has no social opportunity. Romances resolve her problems by providing ready-made solutions. Since these solutions depend on fantasy, they possess no stability; when Arabella yields them, she has not noticeably grown, except in resignation. Unable to persist in aggressive behavior once forced to recognize its nature, she accepts weakness as her condition and turns herself over to her lover. A sad ending, after all, if a necessary one.

By its central device the novel loudly announces a problem implicit in all eighteenth-century novels (to say nothing of subsequent fiction): what relation does fiction bear to what we call reality? Arabella, supposing "Romances were real Pictures of Life," draws from them "all her Notions and Expectations." If romances do *not* supply real pictures of life, does *The Female Quixote*? Can novels affect readers' notions and expectations appropriately rather than inappropriately? The answer depends partly on a particular novel's readers. Those who respond to the emotional implications of Lennox's novel may come to understand how little adolescent girls can allow themselves to expect. *The Female Quixote* offers a bleak mythology of female adolescence as weakness and deprivation, its only resource the fancy that must ultimately yield to reason's dominion. The novel's loose, repetitive structure reiterates the theme of inconsequentiality. Such structures recur in many of the period's novels by women about girls, providing an arrangement of events peculiarly appropriate to stories of adolescent weakness and frustration. The loose sequence, with little causal connection, little sense of necessity or even control, with endings occurring after an arbitrary number of pages and of happenings, suggests a perception of existential meaninglessness in the adolescent female condition. The fiction covertly undermines its ostensible endorsement of conventional expectations about the growing up of girls. It preaches the principles of rational control with which adults combat the feared irrationality of the young, yet organizes itself with little regard for reason. Such discrepancies doubtless played no part in the work's conscious design; but like other novels of its period, *The Female Quixote* draws on energies more potent than it can acknowledge.

The loose novelistic structure that calls attention to its own lack of rationality marks eighteenth-century novels about other subjects than growing up—notably Laurence Sterne's *Tristram Shandy* (1759–67), a work struggling with the problem of meaninglessness, but one in which no one shows much sign of maturing. The male characters in the novel, except for that perpetual child Uncle Toby, behave like typical adolescents. Tristram's futile efforts to achieve identity, to make connections, to attain a happy ending, duplicate the struggles of novelistic teen-agers—struggles that come to positive fruition in more orthodox eighteenth-century novels than Sterne's and Lennox's. His pervasive impotence represents a nightmare version of the adolescent condition. To link Tristram's fictional experience with that of dozens of adolescents in more conventional, less compelling, novels emphasizes the negative myth sometimes obscured by the successful marriages that end almost all eighteenth-century novels about youth by welcoming the young into adulthood. *Tristram Shandy*, like *The Female Quixote*, may generate in its readers anxiety bred of the tension between conventional expectations and unconventional novelistic structure and content. Such tension implicitly challenges assumptions about social and moral reality. Perhaps human lives assume meaningful shape only because we imagine them so: the idea no longer seems startling. Sterne's adumbration of it, however, has a powerful subversive effect partly because it plays against so many more comforting expectations.

Tristram Shandy, of course, is not "really" about adolescence at all. But even cursory reflection about its iconoclastic form may help us see that late eighteenth-century fiction about the young often supplies only superficial reassurance to conservative adult opinion. Although, unlike *Tristram*, such fiction affirms the possibility of growing up, it often reveals such alarming costs that the possibility comes to mean burden (that burden which Tristram rejects) rather than opportunity. The fiction expresses fears about adulthood while purporting to concentrate on the pre-adult.

How can fiction render the "real world"? The question implies perplexities not only about fiction but about what lies outside the text, about society and experience. The late eighteenth century generated a group of novels explicitly concerned with such perplexities. Ignorance of the realm outside the home, many realized, created problems for young women in particular—for them more than for young men becaue elaborate customs and rituals insulated girls. Novels often reinforced the socially encouraged myth of extreme danger beyond the domestic hearth. In Charlotte Palmer's 1780 novel, *Female Stability*, a mother addresses her teen-aged daughter:

Your own goodness, my Harriet, leads you to imagine dissimulation inhabits not the breast of others: but alas! child, fatal experience will teach you different ideas. Cruelty and baseness are too often disguised under the specious mask of generosity and benevolence; not that I insinuate this is the case with Sir James Thompson, but as your ignorance of men, and the motives from which they act, renders it impossible you should distinguish real worth from the appearance of it, I could not justify to myself my silence.[13]

Arabella, in *The Female Quixote,* found virtue and nobility only in creatures of her fantasy; Harriet's mother suggests that experience would
confirm that benevolence generally depends on illusion. The young
require warning about reality's inferiority to the world of dreams and
of ideals.

In the century's final decade, Robert Bage published a novel entitled
Man As He Is, and followed it four years later with the better-known
Hermsprong; or, Man As He Is Not. Two years after that, in 1798, Mary
Ann Hanway provided a female perspective—and made yet more inclusive titular claims—in *Ellinor; or, The World As It Is.* All three works
involve adolescent characters. Although the eponymous hero of
Hermsprong, an improbably noble Englishman who has avoided corruption by growing up among North American Indians, himself displays no adolescent symptoms (in his twenties, he shows himself spec-
tacularly mature), he falls in love with a teen-aged girl. *Man As He Is*
describes a young man of remarkable passivity, unable to govern himself, ever in need of rescue by women. The preface implies that the
book proposes to educate young women. Many object to novels, this
preface points out, "because novels, as novels, do poison the minds of
young ladies; and young ladies do poison young gentlemen; and so
there is danger of an universal sanies, from this corrupt and corrupting cause. But I humbly opine, that boarding schools, where young
ladies go to learn to dress and behave, and where they do learn to
dress with vanity, and behave with pride, may at least claim an equal
share in this business of corruption."[14] The same animus against females governs the novel's image of the tyrannical mother, frivolous
but demanding, always eager to rebuke her son for real and fancied
misdeeds. The young woman reader may learn from her negative example, or from the positive image of the penniless and virtuous girl
who eventually rescues Sir George, not by active enterprise but by
passive determination. The reader will learn also of the double standard and how it operates: not all male characters resemble Joseph Andrews. " 'Many young men slide in early youth,' said Mr. Lindsay,
'and recover; so may Sir George. It is not the greatest mark of judgment, to decide from first follies, on the character of a man's whole
life' " (III,185). Girls have far less leeway. The reader discovers, in
short, the badness of assertive females, the long-term profitability of
docile virtue, and the limitation of feminine possibility.

In *Man As He Is,* a young man wanders through the world, making
mistakes of considerable moral consequence, but returns at last to the

good girl who awaits him, who, indeed, rescues him from suicidal melancholia, demonstrating her only power in her benevolence. When Mary Ann Hanway invents a plot for the comparable wanderings of a young woman, she allows her heroine no consequential mistakes. She has written her book, she explains, out of her conviction that "the most baneful consequences must result to the rising generation, from reading the monstrous productions that for some years past, have issued from the press, the creation of romantic visionaries."[15] She means, of course, Gothic novels. "By those artful, seductive, inflated descriptions, the young and susceptible heart, is tempted to tread the flowery mazes of *vice*, while the timid imagination is terrified by demoniac incantations!!" (I,iv). Implying her own rigorous adherence to reality and to virtue, she produces four volumes devoid of the supernatural and of attractive forms of vice, but rich in threats and danger.

The plot in its elaborations defies summary. It involves a young girl, seventeen at the beginning of the action, who has spent the preceding five years in a convent. She does not know her parentage or whether her parents still survive. Thrust into the world to make her living, she supports herself as paid companion to the sixteen-year-old daughter of Sir James Lavington. An unexceptionable lover soon presents himself, but she does not love him. Spectacular misfortunes dog her: attempted seduction and rape, vividly destructive calumny, shipwreck and destitution. The benevolent woman who rescues her from the shipwreck and from suicidal despair turns out to be her mother; Sir James, it seems, is her father. Toward the end of volume IV she conveniently falls in love with her lover, supporting the narrator's announced conviction that friendship provides a sounder basis for marriage than passion can. The lover, equally conveniently, inherits a lot of money.

The world as it *is*?

It sounds like a fairy tale, improbable as any Gothic; its exemplary importance depends on its insistence about its own realism. But its picture of the world is very odd.

About 1780, an art historian tells me, English painters began depicting young women in a new way, emphasizing slender, long wrists, frail arms; the scene of a girl fainting became a favorite subject.* *The World As It Is* offers a narrative equivalent for such visual effects. Despite Ellinor's announced aim of independence ("Ellinor never lost sight of her constant end and aim, to live dependent solely on her own talents" [IV,75]), she remains dependent on others. Her reliance

---

*I owe this point to Patricia Crown, of the University of Missouri.

on Sir James (as in some of the fainting scenes) has sexual overtones, almost directly referred to at the point where she discovers his relationship to her: "may I, without a crime, be embraced by that man with whom my soul always sighed to claim relationship?" (IV,272). She needs also the help of older, stronger women. When a benevolent lady rescues her, "the poor invalid threw her arms around her, calling her the preserver of both body and soul, asking if she would be her dear mother; then pausing, cried, 'Ah! no; now I remember I have no parent,—the poor forlorn Ellinor never had one'" (IV,209). The longing for a mother marks the girl's intense need for dependency. She receives significant help also from one of those anomalous independent women who populate late eighteenth-century fiction, Lady John Dareall, whose history begins with an intense childhood companionship with her father. Wonderfully healthy and free-spirited at eighteen, Lady John knows nothing of social restraint and convention. When her parents urge her to marry for money and rank, she responds with an eloquent speech about the necessity of female freedom, but eventually she yields. At this point the narrator expresses explicit disapproval of the character's independence: "she, whom we have seen, was not woman as *she should be,* and by whom the doctrines of passive obedience, and non-recrimination, were never practised" (II,148). How much irony should we discern? At any rate, Lady John defies public opinion to protect and help Ellinor when no one else will offer assistance. Her strength may arouse the admiration of twentieth-century readers, but apparently generates ambivalent responses in earlier observers. Ellinor shows no inclination to imitate her.

The "real world," one would conclude from this novel, contains incredible menaces for the young woman, who must not hope to rescue herself by her own capacities. She needs, until her marriage, the support of parental figures. Although she may manage to earn an independent living, she cannot live an independent life: the forces against her possess far too much power. Her sexual energy increases her danger. Virtue heightens her attractiveness ("the rectitude of her intentions gave a firmness and grace to her whole figure, that struck them with surprise and admiration" [II,75]) and is her most significant resource. Vulnerability is her essence.

The character of Lady John Dareall, Ellinor's announced intent of self-dependence, her refusal to yield at the outset to the convenience of immediate marriage: such elements in the novel suggest a counter-theme to the surface emphasis on frailness and on the impossibilities the world creates for the aspiring female. The fiction has it both ways, elaborating the implications of *Pamela*. It generates titillation and asserts its didactic impeccability by depicting the weakness of the adolescent girl, her need for her elders' help, her control of sexual impulse (she suffers an inconvenient passion for Lady John's son but resolutely suppresses it), her incapacity to accomplish much by herself. It also conveys the covert message that a young woman willing to pay the necessary costs may discover more in herself. The costs diminish if (like Ellinor, unlike Lady John) she disguises her propensities toward independence with frailty, fainting, and loud declarations of need.

The heroine of Anne Radcliffe's variety of Gothic novel bears a strong family resemblance to Ellinor. *The Mysteries of Udolpho* (1794)—action and characters alike—takes on new meaning in the context of the many novels of its own time that never flirt with the supernatural but imagine the adventures and the plight of young women just on the point of entering the social world. Different as they appear—in tone, plot, characterization, and narrative skill—*The Mysteries of Udolpho*, *The Female Quixote*, and *Ellinor* have much in common. They share, in particular, their conceptual dependence on a single difficulty of female adolescence: the lack of outlet, in conventional social circumstances, for a girl's imaginative impulse and energy. Radcliffe's Emily, Lennox's Arabella, Hanway's Ellinor—all yearn, consciously or unconsciously, to *do* something. The authors who invent such characters also must invent extravagant patterns of action to justify, conceal, or fulfill the girls' desires. The satiric context of *The Female Quixote* evades the problem of justification, provides valuable concealment, and allows Arabella to satisfy herself in fantasy if not in fact. The "realism" of *Ellinor* demands other solutions: partial fulfillment, partial justification by necessity (Ellinor must take care of herself because she lacks parents), concealment through personal style. *The Mysteries of Udolpho* finds more complicated solutions and clarifies a host of predecessors.

Emily's asserted attractiveness as a young woman derives mainly from three specified qualities: her great capacity for feeling, her "duty and good sense," and her "noble, though imprudent courage."[16] Duty and good sense mark all young eighteenth-century heroines. Some before Emily demonstrate considerable courage: Clarissa; Sophia Western leaving home alone in the dead of night; even Evelina, although we may mock some of the threats she faces. Emily, however, confronts difficulties of awe-inspiring magnitude and must muster great resources of inner strength and bravery. To characterize her by such traditionally masculine virtues without losing the appeal of youthful femininity requires considerable agility. Perhaps for this reason, Radcliffe emphasizes with special insistence the first of Emily's merits, that gift for feeling appropriate to the girl, asserted in the text to be natural in youth.

Emily's *kind* of feeling belongs to the Romantic sensibility. She shares it with her father, who associates it particularly with his younger days.

"I remember that in my youth this gloom used to call forth to my fancy a thousand fairy visions and romantic images; and I own I am not yet wholly insensible of that high enthusiasm which wakes the poet's dream: I can linger with solemn steps under the deep shades, send forward a transforming eye into the distant obscurity, and listen with thrilling delight to the mystic murmuring of the woods."

"O my dear father," said Emily, while a sudden tear started to her eye, "how exactly you describe what I have felt so often, and which I thought nobody had ever felt but myself!" (I,15)

The quality of the prose hardly invites lavish quotation. The novel's repeated ponderings of the question of sensibility, though, however ponderous, establish an important ideological setting for Emily's bizarre experiences. Her father worries about the dangers of that sensibility "which is continually extracting the excess of misery or delight from every surrounding circumstance." He sees that the world contains more pain than pleasure; consequently "we become the victims of our feelings, unless we can in some degree command them." Understanding that his daughter accepts her susceptibility to suffering as a concomitant of her capacity for pleasure, he yet warns her that happiness will not inhabit a heart "continually alive to minute circumstances" any more than one "dead to feeling." Apathy, however, he considers a vice far more sinister than sensibility (I,82).

Emily shares her capacity for intense feeling with her lover, Valancourt, in whom her father approvingly marks the presence of noble sentiment. Yet the father worries, justly, about how exposure to social corruption will affect the youth. Sensibility makes its possessor vulnerable. The insistence throughout the novel on Emily's exceptional degree of feeling underlines her weakness, the pathos of her ever-intensified victimization. The villain Montoni feels only scorn for what he calls "sentiment," which he, too, associates with weakness and with childishness; his apparent invulnerability through much of the action derives largely from his refusal to allow himself the weakness of feeling.

141

Given a villain with no sensibility and a heroine with lots of it, we may plausibly assign positive value to the way of feeling—and by extension to the weakness associated with it. Emily's weakness justifies her strength. Like generations of future Gothic heroines, she faints and fears and fantasizes, but when absolutely necessary she manages to act effectively—without ever declaring unbecoming self-will or selfish purpose. Early in *Ellinor*, Sir James requests Ellinor to improve the character of his sixteen-year-old daughter; he hopes the new companion will "eradicate that attention to *self* which I see with sorrow is her first consideration" (I,110–11). *The Mysteries of Udolpho* assumes a similar standard. Emily's intense sensibility urges her toward altruism, manifested even in relation to those who, like her aunt, have harmed her: "The sufferings of others, whoever they might be, called forth her ready compassion, which dissipated at once every obscuring cloud to goodness that passion or prejudice might have raised in her mind" (II,284). Her sense of duty stiffens her character, causing her on occasion even to reject the claims of affection—although not without intense struggle that leaves her "with a mind weakened and irresolute, and a frame trembling with illness" (II,189). The trembling frame, like the tear that starts to her eye in conversation with her father, attests her authentic, youthful, weak femininity. Nonetheless, duty and good sense and courage support her, urge her on, enable her at last (like the youthful heroine of *Man As He Is*) to rescue her erring lover by benevolent indulgence.

The fictional action in which she figures resembles that of the other narratives here considered in its tumult of sequential but rarely consequential event, although it differs in its hints of the supernatural (all ultimately rationalized away). Like the other narratives, even more intensely, it suggests an allegorical dimension. The plot embodies a fantastic representation of the adolescent plight, with its sinister parental figures (Emily's true, good parents die early in the novel, leaving her to unrelievedly menacing substitutes), its repeated images of imprisonment, its atmosphere of vague, uncomprehended sexual threat. Recent criticism has explored the affinities of Gothic to female experience. Its association with specifically *adolescent* female experience becomes powerful in *The Mysteries of Udolpho*. The early passage of dialogue between Emily and her father that I have quoted suggests how completely Emily conforms to even a twentieth-century vision of adolescence: the ready tear, the sense that no one has ever felt what she feels, are hallmarks of the condition. But the experience, even more than the psychology, reflects adolescent perceptions. What a fantasy! The cruel stepmother (in this case an aunt), treated with unfailing deference and benevolence by her virtuous niece, victimized by her sexuality and finally getting her comeuppance (she dies miserably); the cruel stepfather, who marries the aunt but lusts for the girl (he claims to want her money), plots against her, imprisons her, threatens her, but comes to a bloody end; the unprotected, vulnerable girl, determined to follow her father's teaching, to be good at all costs, proving herself morally superior to her lover as well as to her persecutors, demonstrating her capacity to relinquish as well as to accept a suitor she loves, thus her transcendence of mere sexuality, mere emotion; but demonstrating also her unusual capacity for feeling of all varieties. The sequence of events, the cast of characters, embody a youthful sense of isolation in the world, of fearful antagonism by the older generation, of hostility toward adults, of moral self-satisfaction, idealism, and superiority. Most of all, they supply objective correlatives for intense anxiety: a dominant emotion of this and the other novels here treated, a feeling characteristically associated by women writers with female adolescence.

"So romantic and improbable, indeed, did her present situation appear to Emily herself, particularly when she compared it with the repose and beauty of her early days, that there were moments when she could almost have believed herself the victim of frightful visions glaring upon a disordered fancy" (II,77). *The Mysteries of Udolpho* objectifies the internal upheaval of adolescence, in contrast with the "repose and beauty" of childhood. Romantic and improbable indeed, its situations provide pretexts for kinds of emotion characteristic of (although not unique to) Emily's time of life. "In the gaiety which surrounded her, Emily vainly tried to participate, her spirits being depressed by the late discoveries, and by the anxiety concerning the fate of Valancourt, that had been occasioned by the description of his manner when he had delivered the ring. She seemed to perceive in it the gloomy wildness of despair; and when she considered to what that despair might have urged him, her heart sank with terror and grief" (II,336). Such affective terminology—"depressed," "anxiety," "despair," "terror," "grief"—marks the entire novel: marks its connection to such fictions as *Evelina*, where the plot invents causes of a different order for depression, anxiety, and terror, but the emotional atmosphere has something in common with the extravagances of *The Mysteries of Udolpho*.

The announced moral of *The Mysteries* emphasizes the vulnerability as well as the ultimate triumph of its heroine: "Oh! useful may it be to have shown, that though the vicious can sometimes pour affliction upon the good, their power is transient and their punishment certain; and that innocence, though oppressed by injustice, shall, supported by patience, finally triumph over misfortune!" (II,344). Most of the novels cited in this chapter lend themselves to similar summary. The single exception, *The Female Quixote*, tells the story of a girl who *wishes* life would present itself in just such patterns. This arrangement of events—affliction poured upon the relatively helpless good, who inevitably win in the end, but not until all appears lost—expresses an emotional tension inherent in the female adolescent situation. The girl trained to goodness, virtually forced to it by lack of any viable social alternative, must believe that virtue will find its reward. But she must also, in all probability, experience her own "goodness"—given its social definitions—as passivity, helplessness, vulnerability. Anxiety therefore characterizes her condition—and becomes, under various disguises, a fictional subject.

The typical disguises involve manipulation of the announced relation to "reality." In *The Female Quixote*, most of the action derives from the fantasies of the heroine—fantasies that express a desperate sense of her literal situation, from which she must escape even at the cost of constant ridicule. In *The Mysteries of Udolpho*, fantasy belongs to the author, whose invention of bizarre "romantic" happenings partly conceals a concern with the emotional realities of female adolescence. Mary Ann Hanway, in *Ellinor*, proclaims her realism but produces a plot adapted from the extremities of romance, justifying the heroine's continuing anxiety by her atypical situation. But all these novels say, in part, the same thing: anxiety and frustration typify the state of female adolescence.

From another point of view, these fictions also justify the apparently different anxieties conveyed by the moralists. If they display, dramatically and insistently, the weakness and vulnerability of young women, they also reveal powerful strategies of survival and potentially of dominance. The taming of Arabella, the subsiding of Ellinor, the domestic resolution of Emily's difficulties do not entirely counteract the impression of the young women's terrific emotional (not specifically sexual) force. The discrepancy between capacity and acceptable opportunity generates emotional difficulties within the novel; the same discrepancy, differently perceived, accounts for the worries of moralists, who, advocating repression and suppression, betray their fear that young women in their natures contain all too much energy needing to be repressed.

The reversibility of eighteenth-century myths of adolescence suggests the perplexity they embody. Adults perceive power in the young and locate weakness in precisely the same characteristics. They understand youth as endangered but also as dangerous. The moral certainties that mark the period conceal emotional uncertainties. Everyone declares manhood, womanhood, adulthood desirable, yet writing in diverse modes hints that everyone envies or fears the young. Although explicit statements of expectation about and for youth convey values often at odds with those of later periods, one need not seek far for evidence of the ambivalence and confusion that we sometimes believe the unique burden of our own time.

6

The Generations: Imagination and Growth (Walter Scott, Jane Austen)

When boyhood advancing into youth required more serious studies and graver cares, a long illness threw me back on the kingdom of fiction, as if it were by a species of fatality.... For several weeks I was confined strictly to my bed, during which time I was not allowed to speak above a whisper, to eat more than a spoonful or two of boiled rice, or to have more covering than one thin counterpane. When the reader is informed that I was at this time a growing youth, with the spirits, appetite, and impatience of fifteen, and suffered, of course, greatly under this severe regimen, which the repeated return of my disorder rendered indispensable, he will not be surprised that I was abandoned to my own discretion, so far as reading (my almost sole amusement) was concerned, and still less so that I abused the indulgence which left my time so much at my own disposal.

There was at this time a circulating library in Edinburgh, ... which, besides containing a most respectable collection of books of every description, was, as might have been expected, peculiarly rich in works of fiction. It exhibited specimens of every kind, from the romances of chivalry and the ponderous folios of Cyrus and Cassandra, down to the most approved works of later times. I was plunged into this great ocean of reading without compass or pilot; and unless when some one had the charity to play at chess with me, I was allowed to do nothing save read from morning to night. I was, in kindness and pity,—which was perhaps erroneous, however natural,—permitted to select my subjects of study at my own pleasure, upon the same principle that the humours of children are indulged to keep them out of mischief. As my taste and appetite were gratified in nothing else, I indemnified myself by becoming a glutton of books.[1]

146

Summarizing an episode of his own adolescence, Sir Walter Scott mingles guilt, self-pity, self-exculpation, and nostalgia. His gluttonous youthful consumption of fiction perhaps foretells his massive adult production; he tells the story while describing his composition of *Waverley*, his first novel. By 1829, when Scott wrote the general preface to a collected edition of his novels with his name prefixed, he had long since won enormous fame for his writing. Yet he needs to apologize: if not, directly, for his writing, at least for his youthful reading, justified by "fatality": by his illness, by his elders' perhaps erroneous indulgence, by his need for gratification. No one helped him, he says, he had no compass or pilot. He could hardly hope to help himself.

The tone of this reminiscence speaks not only of Scott's personal uncertainties but of a widespread anxiety about the place of fiction in adolescent experience, which continued into the nineteenth century. The intense pleasure of literary gluttony for the young in itself generated sufficient cause for guilt in grown-ups looking back at their own youth. Contemplating the reading of their juniors, adults substituted disapproval for guilt. Both reactions hint uneasiness about young people's desire to escape from workaday reality. How does such desire influence the likelihood of their becoming properly functioning adults? What does it mean about their relation to the adult generation that surrounds them?

Such questions, of course, had been asked before. As articulated by Scott and his contemporaries, they reflect the continuing preoccupation, in the early nineteenth century, with the interchange—harmonious and hostile—between generations. The young and the old remain at variance, accurate assignments of power still hard to determine. The eighteenth-century association of youth with passion and imagination continues. But a new note creeps into fictional accounts of how fantasy misleads the young, and a new kind of urgency marks certain moralistic utterances. Adolescent authority enlarges, adult assurance shrinks. Scott's fiction and Jane Austen's, dissimilar in most obvious respects, share a tendency to allow adolescent characters discreet triumphs over their elders. Both novelists also offer, however, abundant compensation for such allowances, thus dramatizing changing forms of ambivalence.

Scott began *Waverley*, he tells us, around the turn of the century, although he completed and published it only in 1814. Its early chapters appear governed by didactic purpose and doctrine appropriate to the eighteenth century. Young Edward Waverley, inadequately controlled by father or uncle, resembles his creator in habit, and Scott describes him in language similar to the account of his own youthful indulgence. "With a desire of amusement, therefore, which better discipline might soon have converted into a thirst for knowledge, young Waverly drove through the sea of books like a vessel without a pilot or a rudder" (I, 22). He likes "romantic fiction," French memoirs as well as romances, Froissart and the Spanish chroniclers "of chivalrous and romantic lore," Northern legend. "And yet, knowing much that is known but to few, Edward Waverley might justly be considered as ignorant, since he knew little of what adds dignity to man, and qualifies him to support and adorn and elevated situation in society" (I, 24). This unambiguous statement foretells a moral tale about disastrous results of ignorance. The consequences, however, prove far more ambiguous than the judgement.

During the early chapters the narrator also describes the kind of novel he does *not* propose to write. He has located the action "sixty years since" rather than calling it "a tale of other days" because the alternative title might have caused "every novel-reader" to anticipate "a castle scarce less than that of Udolpho" (I, 2). This writer, however, intends neither to follow Ann Radcliffe nor Cervantes (and Charlotte Lennox). He proposes to explore the place of imagination and feeling with new kinds of emphasis.

Twentieth-century observers may see in Waverley's character, inasmuch as the story individualizes him, primarily the marks of his stage of life: that idealism and aspiration which nineteenth- and twentieth-century commentators have often found typical of youth. The storyteller, however, insists—at least at the outset—on the definitive effect of fiction on Waverley's consciousness. For a hero involved in so much dramatic action, the young man makes few conscious choices for which he takes responsibility. Things happen *to* him. The chapter entitled "Choice of a Profession" relates his *father's* choice of his profession, a decision precipitated by his aunt's anxiety over his apparent inclination to fall in love with a village girl. Waverley goes to visit the Bradwardine family on his way to his military post because his uncle expects him to. He goes to the Highlands because the opportunity presents itself: a less "romantic" youth would have found such opportunity less appealing. He resigns his commission—an act of great moment—because he feels insulted by his commanding officer. He does not investigate what has happened in order to arrive at a reasoned decision; he proceeds as though compelled. The even more momentous decision to join the Young Pretender's army also comes upon him almost without conscious volition, the result of a friend's manipulation. After fighting and fleeing and spending time in seclusion, having declared himself grown-up, Waverley consciously accepts his responsibilities in going to London for the sake of his uncle, but he then reverts to passivity in deciding to marry Rose Bradwardine, apparently motivated almost entirely by the fact that she cares for him.

If this young man demonstrates idealism and aspiration, he lacks the commitment usually associated with such qualities. Edward Waverley commits himself only to his selfhood. Inasmuch as *Waverley* seriously examines character (and it does so to a qualified extent), it concentrates on this aspect of the adolescent nature: its tendency to convert all experience to self-amplification. From the beginning, we learn of the young man's self-obsession, which enlarges until his blindness to the world outside himself assumes extravagant proportions. He does not really acknowledge the existence of other people as centers of consciousness. He perceives the natural world as a stage drop, a background against which to act and feel; its integrity diminishes in his perception of it. For all the splendors of Scottish scenery and tumultuous event, *Waverley* has an oddly diminished atmosphere. Everything reduces itself to a single adolescent sensibility.

Such intense narcissism must limit the possibility of fruitful relationship. Waverley's first love directs itself toward a girl whom to all intents and purposes he has invented, a local young woman with whom he spends so little time that he can freely create her in fantasy. When his aunt plots to remove him from temptation, the narrator comments that it would have worked equally well to make him pass a whole afternoon with the girl, an event that would presumably force the adolescent dreamer to acknowledge another's reality. He does not fall in love with Rose Bradwardine, precisely because she represents too much of an actual presence, always there, but he happily accepts her deferential treatment. He finds Rose's father ridiculous; he prefers the Highlanders who fit more readily into his literary preconceptions of admirable manhood. And, for that matter, admirable womanhood: Flora, the Highland beauty, appeals to him because of her almost mythic self-presentation as heroine of her people.

In the second half of the novel, events force Waverley to acknowledge serious ways in which other people may impinge upon his life. Those he encounters older than himself sometimes prove manipulative, heartless, or both; the narrator reveals such facts if Waverley fails immediately to recognize them. Thus Fergus, presumably only a few

149

years older than Waverley, politically ambitious, subordinates any real interest in the youth to his plans for using him. Bonnie Prince Charles himself, twenty-five years old, of course has political intents; Waverley characteristically fails to take this into account. Ever blinded by concern with his own dignity and importance, and by his predilection for the "hero of romance" (he sees the prince as one [II, 86]), Waverley continues undiscriminating. When Major Melville points out to him that "the inexperience of youth . . . lays it open to the plans of the more designing and artful," and that Fergus belongs to the latter category, Waverley to the former, the youth reacts with indignation (II, 21). "I detest that cold-blooded, calculating Scotch magistrate," he observes the next day (II, 37). Unable to learn from his wiser elders, unable to discern selfish motivations in those who conform to his fantasy of manliness, Waverley begins to grow only when he spends an extended time with Colonel Talbot, literally his prisoner, but greatly his superior in moral insight, knowledge of the world, and human understanding. The youth's nominal control of the situation disarms him, making him more open to the older man's wisdom. Under the colonel's tutelage, he learns of his own mistakes and of the possibilities of divergent interpretation. He comes to think of his attachment to the Young Pretender's cause as rather less noble than he had supposed, and to realize that he must accept the consequences of a commitment he has made without deliberation or knowledge. When events allow him to escape the scene of battle, he settles contentedly into rural seclusion, avoiding the pressures generated by necessities of practical choice. "It was in many a winter walk by the shores of Ulswater that he acquired a more complete mastery of a spirit, tamed by adversity, than his former experience had given him, and that he felt himself entitled to say firmly, though perhaps with a sigh, that the romance of his life was ended, and that its real history had now commenced" (II, 250).

Subsequent events hardly challenge this smug view. Waverley learns of Rose's endeavors on his behalf and reacts appropriately.

To Rose Bradwardine, then, he owed the life which he now thought he could willingly have laid down to serve her. A little reflection convinced him, however, that to live for her sake was more convenient and agreeable, and that, being possessed of independence, she might share it with him either in foreign countries or in his own. The pleasure of being allied to a man of the baron's high worth, and who was so much valued by his uncle Sir Everard, was also an agreeable consideration, had anything been wanting to recommend the match. (II, 305)

Thus all difficulties smooth out before the young adventurer. He decides to marry, not on the basis of romantic illusion, but on the grounds of practical narcissism. He perceives himself now as in harmonious relation to a man whom he had earlier mentally ridiculed; now, in fact, he appears suddenly to have entered the older generation, showing himself concerned with money ("independence") and alliance, no longer with passionate ideals. If the narrator's tone has its ironies—certainly in the description of Edward's assessment that living for Rose would be "convenient and agreeable," perhaps in the interjection of "thought" in the first sentence, with its implicit qualification of the youth's heroics, again in the pallidness of his calculations about "independence" and "agreeable consideration"—if one feels such irony, it is difficult to know what to do with it. Does the narrator, after all, not quite approve of the young man's "growing up"? Such a question would not occur to the reader of Fielding.

Nothing and no one in his experience criticizes this new version of Edward Waverley. No one points out the costs of his heroics, no one suggests that he should not feel so sure of Rose. He does not grieve for his father, who has died during his northern exploits, or for his other losses, although an agreeable melancholy characterizes his contemplations during his seclusion. When he meets his uncle once more, "The happiness of their meeting was not tarnished by a single word of reproach. On the contrary, whatever pain Sir Everard and Mrs. Rachel had felt during Waverley's perilous engagement with the young Chevalier, it assorted too well with the principles in which they had been brought up to incur reprobation, or even censure" (II, 345). Even his adolescent heroics, in other words, ally him with the older generation. A young man has his fling, learns the limitations of romanticism, accepts the values of his elders, and settles down with a devoted wife as a member of the landed gentry: this summarizes the plot of *Waverley*.

The plot, but not the tone. Although the action suggests orthodox generational hierarchy, *Waverley* does not live in the mind as a work supporting maturity. The vague personal aspiration that marks the adolescent Waverley, his ideal of gallantry, effort, courage without regard for costs—these qualities establish the standards of the novelistic world. Sensible figures like Colonel Melville disappear into the background; sensible figures like Colonel Talbot usefully smooth Waverley's way but engage the narrator's—and the reader's—interest most in their tales of personal distress. Bonnie Prince Charlie—dedicated to a doomed cause, magnanimous, stylish, brave, and gallant under difficulty—epitomizes the value system implicit in the work. The splendid

151

figure of Flora, however implausible, however ridiculous, engages the narrator far more than does good, compliant Rose. The "sensible" grown-ups sound a little sad, a little meager. The narrator's ironic perception focuses on Waverley when he adopts a practical course; by comparison the overt didacticism that questions his earlier romanticism lacks conviction.

All of which brings us back to the question of what the reading of fiction means to the young. The narrator's wise saws in the early part of the novel explicitly dissociate his kind of fiction from the kind that, he suggests, has contaminated Waverley's mind; but covertly this particular work of fiction conveys a different message. Two comments within the text on the nature of the present narrative point to the crucial issues. The first occurs at the end of chapter 5, just before Waverley leaves for Scotland:

I beg pardon, once and for all, of those readers who take up novels merely for amusement, for plaguing them so long with old-fashioned politics, and Whig and Tory, and Hanoverians and Jacobites. The truth is, I cannot promise them that this story shall be intelligible, not to say probable, without it. My plan requires that I should explain the motives on which its action proceeded; and these motives necessarily arose from the feelings, prejudices, and parties of the times. I do not invite my fair readers, whose sex and impatience give them the greatest right to complain of these circumstances, into a flying chariot drawn by hippogriffs, or moved by enchantment. Mine is a humble English post-chaise, drawn upon four wheels, and keeping his Majesty's highway. (I, 42)

This set of claims emphasizes the public and social more than the personal and private. The narrator insists on purposes beyond amusement, on the serious probability of his story, on its mundane realism; he expresses his belief that the motivation of his characters becomes comprehensible only in social terms. The novel he promises bears little relation to the novel we read.

At the end of chapter 41, only a few pages before the end, the narrator describes his accomplishment and apologizes for the huddled-up conclusion so characteristic of Scott's novels:

I must remind my reader of the progress of a stone rolled down hill by an idle truant boy (a pastime at which I was myself expert in my more juvenile years); it moves at first slowly, avoiding by inflection every obstacle of the least importance; but when it has attained its full impulse, and draws near the conclusion of its career, it smokes and thunders down, taking a rood at every spring, clearing hedge and ditch like a Yorkshire huntsman, and becoming most furiously rapid in its course when it is nearest to being consigned to rest forever. Even such is the course of a narrative like that which you are perusing. The earlier events are studiously dwelt upon, that you, kind reader, may be introduced to the character rather by narrative than by the duller medium of direct description, but when the story draws near its close, we hurry over the circumstances, however important, which your imagination must have forestalled, and leave you to suppose those things which it would be abusing your patience to relate at length. (II, 347)

The humble English post-chaise, keeping its steady course down a highway governed by civil law, has turned into a rolling stone, beyond the control of personal or social statute. Emphasis on social actuality has yielded to a claim that the narrator cares mainly about elucidating character. And the narrator's precipitation of the metaphoric stone, his fiction, explicitly connects him with the pastimes of his own youth.

The discrepancies between these two disclaimers indicate what has happened in the course of the narrative. A sober grown-up man controlled it briefly at the outset, stating his superiority to the young, who read too much fiction (*his* fiction will wed itself to truth), to frivolous females, to all who want mere amusement. But the idle truant boy has more imaginative energy. The novelistic impulse comes truly from him, not from that dignified alternate persona who insists on his rectitude. Fiction supports adolescent values, the novel tells us at the beginning: romanticism, commitment to fantasy rather than to reality, emphasis on the personal. *Waverley* itself, a work of fiction, despite its attention to historical authenticity supports exactly such values. Waverley as a grown-up lacks conviction and attractiveness; Waverley as a youth, however misguided, reveals the vitality that makes us interest ourselves in his fate. The subject and the object of the narrative are identical. The announced subject, the inability to make accurate judgment characteristic of a youth too deeply immersed in romantic fiction, coincides with the object that the narrative fulfils. This book, too, teaches its readers to follow personal stars, to glory in chivalry and honor, to reject the cold and common-sensical; and all the while it claims to be teaching something else.

At the heart of *Waverley* lies moral confusion about the proper attitude toward adolescence and toward the imaginative vitality insistently associated with it. As the preceding pages show, the text provides evidence for utterly opposed positions: maturity, politics, common sense supply the proper locus of commitment; youthfulness, the personal, the romantic should engage us. In fact Waverley appears to grow more through his commitment to the world of his imagination than he does through any attempt to follow the sensible course. But the narrator cannot quite allow himself to know this; he can only admit, at most, that his story has got out of control.

The Female Quixote and *The Mysteries of Udolpho*, too, as we have seen, betray ambivalence about the qualities they purport to criticize. Emily must learn to moderate her sensibility, but *Udolpho* invites the reader to admire emotional capacity all the more for its association with short-lived youth; Arabella in the former novel has to give up her romances, but they have made her morally superior to (and more interesting than) most of the women who surround her. *Waverley*, though, demonstrates a new kind of uncertainty. As emphatic as the narrator of *The Female Quixote* in his explanations of exactly why the reading of romance inadequately prepares a youth for the world, Scott's narrator wavers when he describes mature adjustment to the given. Not "bad" men and women but "good" ones—not hypocrites, misers, lechers: just sensible people—appear inadequate, given the challenge of romanticism. Waverley's melancholy and passivity, characteristic of male characters in many early nineteenth-century novels (*Sense and Sensibility*, for example), speak the impossibility of meaningful aggression in a nonheroic context. Bonnie Prince Charlie's wars, like Waverley's books, do not help a young man along ordinary paths; yet most lives fall into such paths.

War, the futile war of a romantic cause against the solid establishment, provides a more comprehensive and dignified emblem of the adolescent condition that does the reading of unrealistic fictions. Unlike the pattern of picaresque wandering characteristic of the eighteenth-century novel, war stresses the perceived aggression in the young man's impulse. Scott both celebrates the doomed cause and stresses its necessary failure, celebrates and punishes the young man's desire to triumph over his father. The conflict with the father takes subtle forms. Waverley's association with the Stuart cause supports his father's political convictions; yet his temporary capacity for forceful activity rebukes and surpasses parental ineffectuality. The blind, dreamlike fashion in which the young man finds his way to the conflict suggests that he is playing out unconscious wishes. His father only talks and plots; young Waverley for a time acts. And wins: his father dies. But then loses: he cannot sustain action, find a continuing outlet, imagine a viable adult life.

The power of *Waverley* as a novel derives largely from its sustained, richly expressed ambivalence. It communicates adult doubt about how to value adolescence and conveys the impossibility of supporting the adolescent vision into grown-up life—with the equal impossibility of finding an adequate alternative. Tom Jones returns to Paradise; Edward Waverley has no comparable option.

Didactic commentary about the imaginative and intellectual situation of the young and about their relation to the old in many respects showed little change in the early years of the nineteenth century. A new emphasis on feeling informed some considerations of youthful development; I will consider that more fully in the next chapter. Occasionally an advisor of youth, or of adults about youth, showed fresh interest in the special psychology of the teen-age years. Isaac Taylor, a thoughtful theorist, makes a point relevant to the issues implicit in *Waverley*: "A child draws its happiness, with very slender aid of external means, from the boundless stores of its own conceptions, and from the rich treasury of its own unspent emotions. A young person, on the contrary, asks large supplies of external excitement, and is ever eagerly in quest of extrinsic means of gratification."[2] The notion that adolescents show a new interest in the world outside themselves differs sharply from the eighteenth-century emphasis on adolescent subjection to inner forces. Not that Taylor failed to recognize the power of the youthful imagination; but he found in the enlargement of interest characteristic of the teen-age years a natural resource to employ against the dangers of inwardness. In another work, he commented:

The picturesque description which led the imagination astray, shall be reduced to its true value, by a glance at the reality; or beauties, which no words can paint, shall fasten upon the delighted recollection. Life, like the landscape, is often distorted thus; and the youthful mind is fired, or disgusted, as the case may be, without real cause. The observation actually made, shall in a short time bring things to their true level; a circumstance of vast importance to our proper action in, and towards them.[3]

He thus summarized the professed purpose of *Waverley*: to recount ways a young man learns to reduce to their true value fantasies inculcated by "picturesque descriptions" which have led his imagination astray.

Taylor's emphasis on words like "true" and "real" speaks of serene faith in the possibility of accurate discrimination and judgment. As a prescriber, he, like the narrator of *Waverley*, recommended adherence to truth. As an observer, on the other hand, he recognized troubling facts about the actualities of youthful life. His effort to reconcile the "real" and the actual gives special interest to his observations. He believed in the value and the urgency of thought. "Thinking, not growth, makes manhood. There are some, who, though they have done growing, are still only boys" (*Teens*, p. 36). Only by thought does one achieve contact with reality; thought belongs to males. Taylor considered the differences between the sexes which imply the desirability of different educations for male and female. "What is proper to male education" must be modified for females, who need luring by emphasis on "the pleasurable associations of intellectual pursuits" and on "pure and agreeable moral sentiments." Boys, on the other hand, can follow thought where it leads, without worrying about moral consequences. Girls have more interest in the concrete and particular than in "abstract principles"; their education should acknowledge this preference (*Household*, pp. 191–92). In other words, the youthful female, restricted by her regard for morality, for pleasure, and for the concrete, can enjoy only a limited relation with the world outside herself. Even the most intelligent and assiduous young woman, who might prove capable of education as arduous as her brothers, should not indulge her desire for it. Boys "must be made to buckle on an armour, and to gird themselves for a conflict, with which it would be not merely useless, but a positive disadvantage to [girls] to have anything to do. No good end can be answered by inuring the female mind to arduous, long-continued, mental exertions" (*Household*, p. 191).

Eighteenth-century thinkers, too, believed in divergent educations corresponding to the divergent fates and assumed natures of male and female. The emphasis on aggression as a male quality worth cultivating, however, strikes a new note. Life is a battle; women have nothing to do with it. Men fight, women please—denying themselves all aggression, having it denied by the world. Hannah More, indomitably continuing into the nineteenth century her advice to young and old, allowed an exemplary character in her didactic novel *Coelebs in Search of a Wife* (1809; a moral work devoid of fictional interest) to reflect on the current education of girls: "The education . . . which now prevails is a Mahometan education. It consists entirely in making woman an object of attraction. There are, however, a few reasonable people left, who, while they retain the object, improve upon the plan. They, too, would make women attractive; but it is by sedulously labouring to make the understanding, the temper, the mind, and the manners of their daughters, as engaging as these Circassian parents endeavour to make the person."[4] The difference between proper and improper education, in other words, depends on the form of attractiveness cultivated, not on any essential divergence of purpose. Girls—their ultimate destinies established, only the specific man who will determine their courses yet to be discovered—should cultivate their minds, emotions, imaginations, conduct, to make all pleasing. Intellectual cultivation for its own sake never appears relevant in considerations of young women.

As for fiction: "[She] lamented that novels, with a very few admirable exceptions, had done infinite mischief, by so completely establishing the omnipotence of love, that the young reader was almost systematically taught an unresisting submission to a feeling, because the feeling was commonly represented as irresistible" (*Coelebs*, p. 131). In the context of a social system that overtly recommends aggression for males, repression for females, the warning takes on new meaning. Girls should not read too much about love, because they must always control and suppress feeling, must subordinate the claims of emotion to those of decorum. Boys must remain wary, because love indulged for its own sake may weaken and divert them from life's battle. Properly directed, on the other hand, love becomes one more form of power, a means to unspecified ends:

To grow up without attachment to the sex is hardly possible. Wherever it occurs, it includes a loss of some of the sweetest sensations which can swell the bosom. To let such attachments be irregular, is to debase those sensations, to the ruin of character and of internal worth. To regulate them is the only chance for good; and if early trained to the support of proper feeling and honourable conduct a great advantage is gained, a power like the fulcrum for which Archimedes longed, when he talked of moving the whole globe. (Taylor, *Teens*, p. 136)

Moralists from Dr. Johnson on worried about fiction's emphasis on love as a danger for young readers. Novelists worried about something else. Waverley does not learn from romances to think himself in love (although his interest in Flora has literary overtones); he learns to value heroic action and the assumptions it implies. The novel-reading fictional heroine, after Arabella, also interests herself more in action than in love. One may wonder whether the moralists' concern with the softer feelings in fact disguises their fear of youthful aggression. Girls, of course, do not present a grave problem. Education can mold them into the proper psychic shapes, protect them from the novels that might distort those shapes. Boys offer more serious threats. If their lives will soon turn into a battle, by puberty their propensities for conflict have become apparent; their combativeness may turn against the older generation. Advisors warn girls, as they have done for centuries, to obey their mothers and treat them with respect; any other course threatens the welfare of the young woman herself. Boys, on the other hand, may challenge their parents in serious ways.

No longer, therefore, account it manly to rebel against your father's commands, to suspect his judgment, or to turn his manners to ridicule; these, or any one of them, mark you as far gone from all that proper feeling, or honourable principle, which promise respectability of character; and you have much to learn, if you do not know this; much to unlearn, if you have habituated yourself to behave thus. Recollect yourself, it cannot be that you are wiser than he; it cannot be that he deserves ill treatment at your hands; it cannot be that ingratitude can be a virtue, or such ingratitude do you honour. I have no hope of you if you hesitate here. The return to proper behaviour may be difficult, but it is indispensable. (Taylor, *Teens*, pp. 70–71)

The bullying, anxious tone betrays awareness of danger. Moralists implicitly resist the idea of adolescent separation from parents. Novel reading and improper education might encourage the development of values opposed to parental ones, thus heightening youthful impulses to resist or to escape. Young women, by and large, had nowhere to escape to: father to husband, one form of supervision to another. Young men might do incalculable things, if not kept firmly in line. Didactic texts reveal none of the novelists' ambivalence about the desirability of growing up, but they locate precisely the same issues— aggression, insubordination—dramatized in fiction.

Waverley, as a youthful male character, finds little significant opposition from his elders. His commanding officer stands almost alone in imposing adult standards of discipline and duty; Major Melville briefly fills a comparable function. But his father dies, his uncle never opposes him, the Baron of Bradwardine feels delighted to welcome him as son-in-law. His experience of the world does not lead him to great respect for grown-ups; he neither threatens nor is threatened by them to any great extent. As a novel concerned with youthful romanticism, *Waverley* evades direct consideration of what such romanticism means in the world of adult functioning, except inasmuch as the narrator's uneasy moralizing brings up the question. Yet that question belongs inherently to the subject. The implications of youthful commitment to fantasy rather than to actuality as they bear on the relations between young and old make that commitment problematic. If belief in the world evoked by fiction did not threaten effective functioning in the world controlled by adults, no one would bother to talk about it.

Scott's most distinguished novelistic contemporary, Jane Austen, confronted the issue squarely. In her consideration of the girl who has read too many Gothic novels, Austen investigates the relation between excessive belief in an unreal world and acceptance of the orthodox hierarchy of generations. Although the moralists imply that girls never importantly defy their elders—unless they take the dreadful way of illicit love and end in disease and desolation—Austen raises the possibility of ambiguous and concealed but nonetheless meaningful defiance. *Northanger Abbey* suggests by its tone far less seriousness than do the sonorities of *Waverley*, but it engages more profoundly a crucial social issue.

Henry Tilney's reasons for prosposing to Catherine Morland closely resemble Waverley's motives for wooing Rose Bradwardine:

Though Henry was now sincerely attached to her, though he felt and delighted in all the excellencies of her character and truly loved her society, I must confess that his affection originated in nothing better than gratitude, or, in other words, that a persuasion of her partiality for him had been the only cause of giving her a serious thought. It is a new circumstance in romance, I acknowledge, and dreadfully derogatory of an heroine's dignity; but if it be as new in common life, the credit of a wild imagination will at least be all my own.[5]

From the beginning to the end of *Northanger Abbey*, the narrator keeps always before the reader's consciousness the difference between "an heroine," a conventional female creation of literary fantasy, and the particular creation Catherine Morland. Catherine's ordinariness, her conformity to what girls do and feel "in common life," constitutes her essence, by the narrator's repeated assertion. If her lover's grounds for proposing deprive Catherine of dignity, so do many other events of the narrative. Dignity, we come to feel, matters little. When Waverley decides to bestow himself on Rose, his own lack of awareness, combined with the narrator's uneasy ironies, makes it difficult to know what attitude one should adopt toward him. Austen's narrator, on the other hand, implicitly specifies what attitude she expects and encourages. Her own amused superiority does not preclude a sense of universal participation in human foibles; she has been from the beginning on the side of "realism"; idiosyncrasies, failures of dignity, make people appealing to one another, she suggests. Her tone implies that Henry does not know quite why he is proposing—he appreciates Catherine's good principles, he thinks—but the narrator knows, smiles, and approves. The "heroine" of romance (and the hero of *Waverley*) seem stiff and uninteresting in comparison to the flawed human beings Austen depicts.

159

Like the speaker in *Waverley*, the storyteller of *Northanger Abbey* calls frequent attention to the kind of narrative here under construction and to the influence of fiction on the adolescent mind. As for the influence of her own fiction—that remains an issue for the reader. Several characters in *Northanger Abbey* are defined by their reading and their reaction to it. Narcissistic John Thorpe cannot tell one author from another and does not scruple to offer ferocious negative judgments of books he has not read. His literary judgment precisely delineates his procedures in relation to people, about whom he offers equally cavalier and self-serving positive or negative pronouncements. Henry Tilney claims to have read everything—more novels than Catherine or his sister, history as well—and to be able to judge. No one challenges the claim, and Catherine readily accepts him as her moral arbiter: a man, he knows the world, she believes. Catherine and Isabella share an exclusive taste for Gothic romance. For Isabella, such reading appears to be entirely a matter of fashion; like her other experience, her literary experience fails to sink in. Catherine, on the other hand, takes literature and life seriously—too seriously for her own good, it seems at first; but she has her reward.

From the novel's first sentence, the narrator repeatedly calls attention to her own purpose of offering an anti-romance. "No one who had ever seen Catherine Morland in her infancy, would have supposed her born to be an heroine," the book starts. It then explains in lucid detail Catherine's differences from the conventional heroine and her justification for providing the center of interest in a work of fiction. "Her heart was affectionate, her disposition cheerful and open, without conceit or affectation of any kind—her manners just removed from the awkwardness and shyness of a girl; her person pleasing, and, when in good looks, pretty—and her mind about as ignorant and uninformed as the female mind at seventeen usually is" (p. 18). The narrator insistently stresses her own realism: Catherine's virtues exemplify those really possible in the world; her defects belong to her age and situation. Her ignorance and lack of information, however, prove useful. "She was heartily ashamed of her ignorance. A misplaced shame. Where people wish to attach, they should always be ignorant. To come with a well-informed mind, is to come with an inability of administering to the vanity of others, which a sensible person would always wish to avoid. A woman especially, if she have the misfortune of knowing any thing, should conceal it as well as she can" (pp. 110–11). The matter-of-fact tone, the insistence on an informing knowledge of actuality, the refusal to offer explicit judgment, the construction of a "should" based on that knowledge of actuality rather than on any ideal—these aspects of the "sensible person" as narrator precisely locate the advice being offered within the social universe to which Catherine must belong, however she may long to participate instead in a realm of romance. The narrator's ironies at the expense of the social world do not qualify her insistence on the need to live in it. Catherine herself does not reject actuality, she only fails to know it. As she learns more, she accepts the actual, capable of criticizing individual people or actions but uncritical of the great scheme of things. That's the kind of heroine she is.

That's the kind she is, but what does she *mean*? In a famous passage early in *Northanger Abbey*, the narrator—unlike her equivalent in Scott—explicitly defends the moral value of novels.

There seems almost a general wish of decrying the capacity and undervaluing the labour of the novelist, and of slighting the performances which have only genius, wit, and taste to recommend them.... "And what are you reading, Miss_____?" "Oh! it is only a novel!" replies the young lady; while she lays down her book with affected indifference, or momentary shame.—"It is only Cecilia, or Camilla, or Belinda;" or, in short, only some work in which the greatest powers of the mind are displayed, in which the most thorough knowledge of human nature, the happiest delineation of its varieties, the liveliest effusions of wit and humour are conveyed to the world in the best chosen language. (Pp. 37–38).

Knowledge of human nature—to say nothing of wit and humor—marks *Northanger Abbey*. Its moral implications, however, have subversive undertones.

The concluding clauses of the novel call particular attention to the generational issue: "I leave it to be settled by whomsoever it may concern, whether the tendency of this work be altogether to recommend parental tyranny, or reward filial disobedience" (p. 252). Establishing several parental figures, and several modes of conflict with them, the novel proceeds by a rhythm of generational interchange corresponding to the action's spatial shifts. The opening summary of Catherine's childhood and early adolescence in Fullerton defines her relationship with her own parents. Although both, by the narrator's account, exemplify admirable qualities, the mother of ten children can give little attention to any one of them. Catherine consequently prefers "cricket, base ball, riding on horseback, and running about the country, at the age of fourteen, to books—or at least books of information" (p. 15). A tomboy as well as a romantic ("from fifteen to seventeen she was in training for a heroine" [p. 15]), she expresses in both roles unconscious defiance of maternal values and expectations—a point made vivid at the novel's conclusion, with its stress on Mrs. Morland's contrasting commitment to common sense and domesticity. During the trip to Bath, Mr. and Mrs. Allen fill parental roles, their inadequacy making itself apparent even to naïve Catherine. Mrs. Allen, with genuine interest only in clothes, can neither focus nor sustain attention on other matters; although sensible enough, Mr. Allen, like other adult males in Austen's work, absents himself psychically or physically from Catherine and her problems. Later, at Northanger Abbey, Catherine endures the dominance of formidable General Tilney, at once ingratiating and tyrannical. The heroine finds happiness after her ignominious return to Fullerton when her lover arrives, having defied his father; but the young people must wait to marry until Henry wins paternal consent.

Of the cast of parental characters, only General Tilney possesses obvious direct importance for the novel's action. Yet Catherine's relations with each parental figure direct her growth. Despite the signs of independence implicit in her roaming about the countryside, her reading of romances, in Bath she seems at the mercy of circumstance. Henry Tilney invites her to dance; that fact alone makes him fascinating. Isabella Thorpe offers friendship; no penetration into the other girl's character impedes Catherine's acceptance. John Thorpe insists on wooing her; she has too much self-doubt, too little experience, to acknowledge even to herself his inability to please her. But she learns to value Henry for better reasons, to reject Isabella and John on the basis of their conduct. Her reproach to Mrs. Allen for failing to warn her about the impropriety of excursions with John signals her increasing awareness. Mr. Allen's comment has alerted her to the issue; she feels relieved by his approbation of her behavior "and truly rejoiced to be preserved by his advice from the danger of falling into such an error herself" (p. 105). But she also feels conscious that Mrs. Allen has failed in her obligation, and she feels able to say so. Her declared dependence coexists with her realization that she has not received advice she needed; in the future, she will make more independent decisions.

Soon she finds herself inhabiting General Tilney's establishment, where she must yield to the vagaries of a man whom at first she feels obliged to believe flawless because of her attachment to his children. She expresses her anger at him in her fantasy of his responsibility for his wife's death; eventually she allows herself to know that anger directly. Her moral superiority to her friends' father becomes apparent finally even to her; by the time he drives her away, she does not doubt his wrongness. She can feel no such conviction about her mother's gentler sway, enforcing the doctrine of useful work without repining, as General Tilney supports the gospel of self-interest. Although Catherine has learned, and the reader with her, the possible corruption of the grown-up world, she has little effective recourse against it, and even less against adult moralism, which must also be combated for the sake of self-realization.

Catherine's commitment to fantasy derived from Gothic romance gives way to an increasing desire and capacity for understanding the actual. Her elders, on the other hand, remain ruled by fantasy. In the parental figures she depicts in detail, Austen reveals significant separation from important truths of experience. Mrs. Allen consistently ignores the essential for the nonessential, remaining blind to the feelings or the needs of others because of her preoccupation with a fantasy world dominated by patterns of muslin. General Tilney, locked in a dream of his own importance, proves equally out of touch with reality, unable to distinguish John Thorpe's visions of grandeur of squalor from the facts to which they obliquely refer. Even Mrs. Morland, an admirable representative of middle-class female values, inhabits a world of her own: her theories about what is wrong with her daughter derive not from perception but from a set of ideas and assumptions altogether unrelated to the immediate situation. Catherine, on the other hand, having used her derivative fantasies to express hostility and rebellious impulse (a crucially important function), surmounts her need for them. By the novel's end, she knows what she really wants; the admirable moral qualities that Henry has perceived in her all along are now less obscured by inexperience and uncertainty.

Another parody of Gothic romance from the same period, Eaton Barrett's *The Heroine* (1813), a work in the tradition of *The Female Quixote*, illuminates the special importance of Austen's contrast of generations. A lively and entertaining work, heavily reliant on farce, *The Heroine* supplies as central character fifteen-year-old Cherry Wilkinson, who, believing herself to be Cherubina de Willoughby, engages in a series of Quixotic adventures in pursuit of her true inheritance. Interested in adventure more than love, she acquires a set of loyal followers, as well as a dangerous suitor, defends a ruined castle as her family seat, appears in public in the guise of romantic heroine. Finally an attack of brain fever and the advice of a good clergyman teach her the error of her ways; she accepts her mundane position in life and a stable suitor.

This novel, too, expresses abundant hostility toward parents. Cherry actually confines her father in a madhouse; she convinces herself that he has usurped the parental function and she cannot tolerate being his child. She encounters in a dungeon an enormously fat, loathsome personage with a toad in her bosom who declares herself Cherry's mother. The resulting conflict between duty and inclination causes Cherry to decide that she will "make a suitable provision" for her mother but never "sleep under the same roof with—(ye powers of filial love forgive me!) such a living mountain of human horror."[6] But Cherry is mistaken in both instances—she rejects her father only because she does not believe in his paternity; the mother she loathes is not her mother—and utterly wrong, as she abjectly confesses, in allowing herself to be seduced by romance. In *Northanger Abbey*, Catherine employs her fantasies to express her feelings, grows through them, and rejects them; only once does someone else need to tell her of her mistake. Cherry uses romance to separate herself from reality ("Oh, could I only lock myself into a room, with heaps of romances, and shut out all the world for ever!" [II, 216]); she requires enlightenment by others; her indulgence in fantasy, although it has allowed her to claim active independence, facilitates no growth and eventuates in her total submission to the judgment of others. Her father has no faults beyond his inability to cope with her; her challenge to received opinion meets utter defeat. Her involvement with romance emphasizes the stereotypical young person's incapacity to understand the world without guidance from her elders.

Catherine, too, displays incapacity and needs guidance, but the fable that reveals her nature emphasizes her ability to use what experience she has, an ability greater than that of many of her elders. The conjunctions of old and young through which the action progresses convey the dangerous message that value does not inhere automatically in maturity or conventionality. Austen, in short, uses the assumed conflict of generations as she uses the convention of parodying Gothic romance: to explore the ambiguities and the potentialities of growth.

Catherine Morland, like Taylor's prototypical teen-ager, attends for the first time, in the course of the novel, to a world outside herself. As naïve observer and participant, she both provides satiric focus ("the emperor isn't wearing any clothes") and serves as satiric target. More worldly men and women strive to control her discourse. Henry tells her what she should say at a dance, Isabella tries to educate her in the language of social hypocrisy, John bullies her with his linguistic extravagances. She feels puzzled, and says so, by the emptiness, exaggeration, or mere conventionality of acceptable talk. Her innocence and openness protect and sustain her; they win her a husband and keep her from corruption. Finally her mother recommends an essay in a collection called *The Mirrour*, metaphorically advocating the traditional female recourse of self-disciplining self-contemplation. Catherine does not read the essay, does not focus on herself; she remains interested in what lies outside. If she has seen the outside realm through a haze of illusion derived from unrealistic literature, she has nonetheless perceived such essential truths as the General's tyranny. And she has revealed herself authentically: the truth of her feeling has attracted the most eligible man around.

In making Catherine so successful, and successful in these terms, Austen, like Scott, suggests that the young have something the old lack. Modifying the admirable moral standards of her upbringing by the emotional values of her reading, Catherine surpasses her elders. She makes herself ridiculous but finds a woman's devious modes of independence; she gets her man. Yet readers often feel vaguely disappointed by the implications of getting such a man: a determined mentor whose superiority to Catherine neither he nor she doubts. (His vulnerability to a young woman willing to reveal her affection for him may suggest insecurity—but he does not know that.) Like Waverley's entrance into adulthood, though for different reasons, Catherine's feels less than triumphant—less unambiguously valued than Evelina's, less enthusiastically greeted than Pamela's. Pamela gives up sexual power in her marriage but gains the social status she wants. Catherine relinquishes little power, but her special attractiveness—her innocence, vitality, directness—will surely yield to the demands of an adult social world. Less dependent than Waverley on romantic illusion, less openly self-concerned than he in choosing a mate, Catherine, too, shrinks in doing what the moralists know she should do. If she has metaphorically triumphed over her elders by being right, they win in the long run by being adult: they will turn her into one of them.

Unlike Scott's narrator, Austen's never loses control. When, at the very end of *Northanger Abbey*, she marries off Eleanor Tilney to a young man not previously present in the novelistic action, she remarks that "the rules of composition forbid the introduction of a character not connected with my fable" (p. 251) and takes care of the problem by observing that the gentleman in question had left behind at the Abbey the laundry list that earlier tempted Catherine to believe she had discovered a momentous manuscript. The playful aggressiveness of this little joke (aggressiveness directed at the reader), with its implicit mockery of "rules of composition," marks the storyteller's assurance: she can play with details of plot because she has the deeper action so firmly under control. *Northanger Abbey* conveys a consistent message, although not one for which the narrator takes explicit responsibility. From start to finish it dramatizes the necessity for a young woman to discover her self independently of her elders. *The Mysteries of Udolpho* offers a concealed fable of independence; Catherine Morland uses it in her struggles for her own autonomy. She relinquishes her attachment to Gothic fiction only as she replaces it with an increasingly lucid sense of self and of others. She can absolve General Tilney of the charge of murdering his wife and realize how he suppresses his children; she can love and cooperate with her mother, yet know that mother to be wrong in assessment and judgment. For girls, too, life is conflict—conflict concealed.

As Catherine's reading indirectly helps her to assert herself, so *Northanger Abbey*, with its fable of imaginative growth, may teach the reader necessities of self-assertion as well as their futility. *Waverley* in many ways resembles the kind of fiction it purports to challenge; *Northanger Abbey* declares its utter dissimilarity to romantic fantasy. But like the "unrealistic" literature it mocks, it may help adolescents escape restrictions imposed from above even while comforting adults by reaffirming their control of the world.

7

The Generations:
Submerged Conflict
(Walter Scott, Jane Austen)

Rob Roy, Sir Walter Scott's dashing Highland outlaw, acknowledges only one worry: the future of his two teen-aged sons. A dialogue between him and the Lowland businessman Nicol Jarvie inaugurates the subject. Jarvie reproaches Rob for not having educated the boys properly.

"They are as ignorant as the kyloes ye used to drive to market, or the very English churls that ye sauld them to, and can no naething whatever to purpose."

"Umph!" answered Rob; "Hamish can bring doun a black-cock when he's on the wing wi' a single bullet, and Rob can drive a dirk through a twa-inch board."

"Sae muckle the waur for them cousin! Sae muckle the waur for them baith!" answered the Glasgow merchant, in a tone of great decision; "an they ken naething better than that, they had better no ken that neither. Tell me yoursell, Rob, what has a' this cutting, and stabbing, and shooting, and driving of dirks, whether through human flesh or fir deals, dune for yoursell?"[1]

Direct aggression, Jarvie suggests, gets one nowhere. When he subsequently volunteers to take the boys as apprentices in the weaving trade, Rob reacts with ferocious rage to the idea of his sons as weavers. Later in the evening, however, talking alone with his young friend Francis Osbaldistone, he admits his concern. " 'But ae thing bides wi' me o' what Nicol said. I'm vexed for the bairns; I'm vexed when I think o' Hamish and Robert living their father's life.' And yielding to despondence on account of his sons, which he felt not upon his own, the father rested his head upon his hand" (VIII, 269). Frank in turn offers help in converting the lads to respectable citizens, by using his own father's connections to get them into the foreign service. The idea brings a tear to Rob Roy's eye; it appears to tempt him. By morning, however, he has changed his mind, explaining that King James needs every man he can get: the lads must follow in their father's footsteps, fighting for the pretender to the English throne.

Scott, in other words, is still at it, now exploring more fully the relations of fathers and sons. He and Austen do not long content themselves with mere hints about the losses of turning from youngster to grown-up, but neither do they commit themselves to unambiguous value judgments. Instead, both look into the perplexities of the generations. They can admit that fathers and sons, even mothers and daughters, may resent and fear one another, and they can imagine what happens as a result. What happens does not promise happy endings. Scott's notorious difficulty in concluding his narratives and Austen's predictable marriages hint similar doubts, reservations, and ambivalences. The problem is not, as in Smollett or Fielding, that the social world implies corruption. The process of growing up itself, it seems, involves so much compromise that one must at least wonder what the future can possibly hold for young folk newly converted into solid citizens.

The relations of fathers and sons supply the central subject of *Rob Roy*, despite a title that promises a straightforward novel of adventure. The situation between Rob and his sons parallels, in reverse, that between Francis Osbaldistone and his father. The senior Osbaldistone has devoted his life to business; he, too, wants his son to follow him. Rob's horror at the notion of weaver sons duplicates Mr. Osbaldistone's emotion at the possibility of his son as a poet. Rob's response to the suggestion that his sons might profit from a different sort of education echoes the reaction of Frank's father to the notion that the youth might attend Oxford or Cambridge or spend time on the Continent broadening his knowledge. Both parents find it intolerable to imagine their offspring following some course radically different from their own. Mr. Osbaldistone will disinherit Frank if he refuses to comply; Rob Roy cannot even imagine filial insubordination. Nor can he imagine choosing for his boys the respectability he himself has rejected, though he knows the costs of the rejection.

Frank sympathizes with Rob's feelings as a father; neither he nor the reader knows anything about the sons' emotions. About Frank's feelings, on the other hand, we know enough to realize the dimensions of the gap between generations. *Rob Roy* suggests that sons cannot want for themselves what their fathers want for them, but also that the discrepancy may mysteriously disappear with time. It does not specify how one should feel about or judge either discrepancy or disappearance. Frank cares about Rob's emotion because he thinks the outlaw wishes for his sons a new kind of life—a wish that would reveal the possibility of amicable divergence between the courses of sons and fathers. When Rob turns out not to want anything of the sort, Frank loses interest. He does not recognize that the outlaw has revealed conflicting emotions rather like his own, that the dilemmas of fathers and of sons resemble one another. *Rob Roy* enforces this recognition on the reader.

Young Osbaldistone's situation and psychology take conventional forms. Returning, at the age of twenty, from an apprenticeship to a mercantile enterprise in Bordeaux, Frank faces paternal wrath. He has announced, in a long and carefully calculated letter, his disinclination to follow a merchant's career. He does not understand his father's hopes and plans for him; he knows only the absolute necessity of free choice for himself.

His father pays little attention to his desire. "All of this signifies nothing, Frank; you have been throwing away your time like a boy, and in future you must live like a man" (VII, 16). Living like a man, of course, implies living like one's father. When the older man discovers that his son has wasted time writing verses, his anger mounts. The boy's suggestions about a possible scheme of action—travel, university, the army—meet only disapproval. Mr. Osbaldistone points out the economic sanctions at his disposal, threatens to disinherit his son in favor of a nephew, and (rather implausibly) sends Frank off to the north of England to see for himself the six cousins from whom his successor may be chosen. The youth finds himself on the verge of adulthood without a profession, on ambiguous terms with his father, not knowing what may happen next: a typical adolescent situation.

Francis Osbaldistone as an old man narrates the experience of his youth. He purports to write for the benefit of a contemporary, to report his Highland adventures. Only occasionally does he sound like age contemplating youth; more often he identifies with the feelings of the boy. A rare instance of retrospective meditation opens the third chapter, as Frank sets out on his northern trip. The chapter begins with four lines from a song of John Gay's, an account of a rudderless

169

boat. The narrator explains that his use of such quotation is intended "to seduce your continued attention by powers of composition of stronger attraction than my own"; then he elucidates the specific allusion.

No schoolboy, who, betwixt frolic and defiance, has executed a similar rash attempt, could feel himself, when adrift in a strong current, in a situation more awkward than mine when I found myself driving, without a compass, on the ocean of human life. There had been such unexpected ease in the manner in which my father slipt a knot, usually esteemed the strongest which binds society together, and suffered me to depart as a sort of outcast from his family, that it strangely lessened the confidence in my own personal accomplishments which had hitherto sustained me. (VII, 31)

As in Scott's accounts of sailing on the ocean of reading without compass or rudder, this summary carries an undertone of exhilaration. The speaker soon acknowledges the fact: "In the mean while, I was lord of my person, and experienced that feeling of independence which the youthful bosom receives with a thrilling mixture of pleasure and apprehension" (VII, 33). Lessened confidence, but thrilling independence; loss of the secure father-son tie, but also of its restrictiveness: Francis balances against the positive and negative pulls of separation.

The importance of *Rob Roy* as a narrative of adolescence, however, depends less on its direct evocation of adolescent psychology than on its invention of a suggestive pattern of action. If the plot proves minimally satisfactory in manipulating the material of adventure, it brilliantly evokes the problems of youth. Its important happenings derive mainly from two characters, both realistically implausible, both epitomizing adolescent fantasy. Diana Vernon, the eighteen-year-old heroine, and Rob Roy himself both seem figments of adolescent imagination. As Frank remembers them, they provide objective correlatives of his youthful inner condition, and they help him to resolve its perplexities.

The vigor of the language evoking Die Vernon suggests the narrator's enthusiasm, and Scott's, for a hermaphroditic female. She presents no sexual threat. On the contrary, she repeatedly suggests that Frank think of her as a man. Young and "exquisitely beautiful" (VII, 72), she offers Frank immediate confidence and treats him with a frankness unprecedented in his experience of women. He considers her openness a tribute to his own attractiveness and promptly falls in love with her, despite his resolution to consider her as a companion rather than an intimate. (Secret restrictions, she early tells him, make marriage impossible for them.) As he comes to know her better, he discovers her entirely masculine values. Educated like a man—science, history, classics, and more—she emphasizes her masculine accomplishment. She treasures not female knickknacks but emblems of male valor: an ancestor's sword, a coat of mail, the hood and bells of a favorite falcon, a light fowlingpiece. And she lists as the first of her three great grievances being born female: "In the first place I am a girl, and not a young fellow, and would be shut up in a mad-house if I did half the things that I have a mind to; and that, if I had your happy prerogative of acting as you list, would make all the world mad with imitating and applauding me" (VII, 128). Utterly committed to the Pretender's cause, she lives by the standards of chivalry: loyalty, courage, gallantry. She differs from Waverley, for example, in her capacity for utter devotion and self-subordination but not at all in her value system.

In emphasizing Die's total acceptance of a masculine system, I do not mean to deprecate her charm. Compared with Rose Bradwardine, compared even with Rowena and Rebecca of *Ivanhoe,* she manifests an altogether appealing vitality. Jeannie Deans (*Heart of Midlothian*) has something in common with her—but Jeannie is already middle-aged, and pretty asexual herself. Die Vernon appears to capture the narrator's imagination specifically *because* she manifests so few conventional characteristics of her sex (an occasional tear, an occasional admission of weakness—but Rob Roy himself sheds a tear) and because she hardly presents herself as a sexual being. The sexual potency of adolescence, which makes this time of life often a dangerous object for adults even to contemplate, disappears in this imagining of a young woman full of energy and appeal but devoid of sexuality. The difficulty for the male adolescent of coming to terms with his own passions and with those of the opposite sex disappears as well. Frank faces hardships and threats on his journey to maturity (if that phrase accurately describes the metaphorical journey he takes), but he avoids the most ominous threat of all. He proves his own courage, loyalty, and gallantry; he does not have to prove his sexual capacity.

The male adolescent invariably encounters two challenging varieties of "otherness," two opposites to himself: the female and the adult. If Die Vernon represents the de-fanged female, Rob Roy embodies the de-clawed adult: member of the older generation, father of teen-aged sons, but in values and assumptions virtually identical to the romantic side of Frank. He, like Die, adheres to the Pretender's cause, a loyalty

171

Frank does not share; but the specific cause hardly matters, except for purposes of superficial adventure. Far more important is the chivalrous code Rob lives out, with a wider sphere of action than Die's. He specializes in daring exploits, hairs-breadth escapes; his followers would die for him; Frank comes to trust him as a kind of magical guardian, an attractive, dashing, powerful alternative to the business-like, cool father who demands his son's loyalty to the cause not of a hopeless claim to the throne but of a promising business enterprise. Die resembles a marvelous, affectionate teen-aged boy; so does Rob Roy. After a moment of minor disillusionment, Frank acknowledges, "I felt the childishness of my own conduct, and the superior manliness of Miss Vernon's" (VII, 220); he might often have had similar feelings about Rob Roy—given a rather simplistic definition of "manliness." Nicol Jarvie says to Frank, "I maun hear naething about honour,—we ken naething here but about credit. Honour is a homicide and a blood-spiller, that gangs about making frays in the street; but Credit is a decent, honest man that sits at hame and makes the pat play" (VIII, 110). There speaks the voice of the adult as "other," the voice in effect of Frank's father, opposed to open aggression, supporting its mercantile disguises. Rob Roy stands unequivocally for honor, happy to risk frays in the street, bored with the idea of sitting at home. He can exploit a grandiose rhetoric of self-justification, but his gusto for the life of honor does not derive from his sense of being abused, it emanates from his essential self.

Rob Roy, in short, perpetuates and justifies the idealism, the rashness, the rebellion of youth. His role as outlaw emblemizes Frank's situation at the beginning of the narrative: outside civilized society, outside the family, refusing to conform to the assumptions of business mentality, feeling his superiority to the world that rejects him and his inadequacy to the demands that face him. Rob Roy, a Robin Hood fantasy figure, shows that such a situation, such feelings, can equip a man for triumphant action. Die imagines that, given the status of man, she would make all the world imitate and applaud her; Rob *is* the man whom many imitate and applaud (although lesser beings reproach and combat him).

Given these two powerful characters at the heart of the action, much of *Rob Roy* amounts to an elaborate playing out of adolescent fantasy. In this aspect the novel suggests, more clearly than *Waverley*, the superiority of unconventional, romantic young folk to their workaday elders. But, like *Waverley*, *Rob Roy* has other aspects as well. Before turning to the ways the narrative resolves the conflicts it has depicted, let us give more thought to Jane Austen's modes of confronting generational conflict.

Consider, in this context, a summary of *Persuasion*, Austen's last completed novel. A nineteen-year-old girl loves and is loved by a young man with his fortune still to make. Her father and her main female advisor join to oppose the match. Accepting their prudential arguments, the girl remains unmarried until, eight years later, her lover reappears, they reach an understanding, and she welcomes his renewed proposal. Even then, she believes herself right in having yielded to an older woman's judgment, although she would not, she says, herself offer similar advice in a comparable situation.

This plot hinges on generational conflict, but the assignment of values suggests a complicated system of assumptions. Anne Elliott, the protagonist of *Persuasion*, with a more highly developed moral sensibility than her advisor, Lady Russell, paradoxically attests her worth by yielding to the persuasion of a moral inferior. The principles that govern her at twenty-seven reverse those appropriate for nineteen. As a girl, she declares her virtue by accepting the hegemony of even misguided elders; as a woman, she must assert her independence. If conflict between the young and the old seems inevitable here, too, one does not immediately know what hierarchy of values governs it.

Not all Austen's young people demonstrate the moral perceptiveness of Anne Elliott. At one point in *Mansfield Park*, Julia Bertram finds herself forced to accompany an older woman in whom she feels no interest. The narrator summarizes, "The politeness which she had been brought up to practise as a duty, made it impossible for her to escape; while the want of that higher species of self-command, that just consideration of others, that knowledge of her own heart, that principle of right which had not formed any essential part of her education, made her miserable under it."[2] Anne Elliott's superiority consists in her possession of the qualities Julia lacks. The heroines of *Northanger Abbey, Sense and Sensibility, Emma, Pride and Prejudice, Mansfield Park*—all have or develop self-command, self-knowledge, consideration of others, right principle which converts politeness to an expression of feeling rather than duty. The terms comprise a familiar moral litany. Yet each novel contains at least one unworthy female contemporary of the heroine—frivolous, insensitive, or foolish. Virtue does not necessarily inhere in adolescents, nor do we know where it comes from. The quotation from *Mansfield Park* implies that Julia's inadequacies derive from poor education, but the diversity of siblings in

173

Austen's novels allows no such facile interpretation. Elinor Dashwood and Marianne, daughters of the same mother, embody opposite moral positions; the Bennet sister, the Bertram brothers, the Price children— all exemplify the problematics of pedagogy. Bad training does not guarantee moral insufficiency; Austen's novels never directly describe a "good" education.

Within the confines of the fictional world, assertions of causality abound; characters readily and insistently explain actions in terms of hidden or apparent causes. Charlotte Lucas marries Mr. Collins *because* at her age she could hardly hope to do better; Emma is spoiled, according to Knightley, *because* she has always been the cleverest in her family; Lydia Bennet elopes with Wickham *because* her undisciplined upbringing has left her responsive only to impulse. Occasionally, however, a narrator raises questions about such impositions of logic on the social universe. Sensible Elinor Dashwood, for instance, blames Edward Ferrars's peculiarities on his mother: the narrator comments, "it was happy for her that he had a mother whose character was so imperfectly known to her, as to be the general excuse for everything strange on the part of her son."[3] Ignorance, fantasy, and wish contribute heavily to the structures of causality erected by the actors in Austen's dramas. The reader in turn can manufacture comparable structures on similar grounds, or on the grounds of knowledge the novel has supplied, or on the basis of his or her understanding of how things work in the world of direct experience; in crucial instances Austen herself (or her narrator) supplies no adequate causal explanations. The characters exemplifying adolescent moral excellence by and large comprise such instances. Often the novels suggest a general association between adolescence and a disposition to folly. At nineteen (and yet more at fifteen or sixteen), little can be expected of anyone. Edward Ferrars, for instance, may be forgiven his youthful infatuation with Lucy Steele; but four more years, "years, which if rationally spent, give such improvement to the understanding, must have opened his eyes to her defects of education" (*SS*, p. 140). Elinor similarly counts on time to improve the quality of her seventeen-year-old sister's thought and perception, finding foolish romanticism appropriate to her age but much inferior to opinions settled "on the reasonable basis of common sense and observation" (*SS*, p. 56). But though the novels reiterate the view of folly as adolescent norm, they depict youthful characters who evade it, making mistakes of judgment and action but possessing even in girlhood the essential virtue of right feeling.

For such virtue the parental generation can rarely claim responsibility. Austen's fictional mothers and aunts seldom offer much to admire. They bear a comfortable relation to the society they inhabit and support that society's assumption that young women exist to marry and young men to be married: "a single man in possession of a good fortune, must be in want of a wife."[4] They understand the social connection of love and money and feel no shame at attempting to further prosperous matches for young people they care about. Even the sentimental mother of *Sense and Sensibility* allows her fantasy to play about a young man eligible because wealthy, although she professes not to care about money; and that man has a mother whose protectiveness merges with social and financial ambition. Mrs. Bennet worries about money and status, not about feeling; so does Lady Catherine de Bourgh. The selfish and superficial Aunt Norris fills an equivalent role in *Mansfield Park; Emma* provides the background figure of Mrs. Churchill to exemplify the same attitude. Fathers as well as mothers may concern themselves with wealth and status; those in *Northanger Abbey* and *Persuasion*, exemplars of capitalistic morality and of triumphant narcissism, actively interfere with the course of young love. More characteristically, fathers absent themselves, literally or metaphorically. Mr. Bennet avoids his family's central concerns in *Pride and Prejudice* until events demand his participation; even then, others serve as agents of rescue for erring Lydia. He wishes to be left alone in his library, aware of his younger daughters' inadequacies, reluctant to involve himself in remedying them. Although he supports Elizabeth in her rejection of Mr. Collins, he provides little help. Sir Thomas Bertram in *Mansfield Park* exemplifies sound principles and good sense, but his prolonged absence expresses his psychic distance from his family. Emma's father focuses her loving attention but supplies no guidance, enclosed in infantile self-concern. By their embodiment of meretricious values or their failure actively to represent sound ones, fathers as well as mothers in these novels impede their daughters' progress toward maturity.

The admirable daughters, then, owe relatively little that we can see to their parents. Unlike their mothers, they do not consciously pursue marriage as life's goal. Only Emma explicitly declares her intent of remaining unmarried, but even those who recognize their emotional entanglement with a man (Fanny Price, Elinor Dashwood, Catherine Morland) seek other modes of personal fulfillment first: imaginative excitement in Catherine's case, service to others for Fanny and Elinor. These heroines feel more or less surprised when they discover their reward in a man. Their less admirable contemporaries—Harriet Smith, the Bertram sisters—pursue marriage with single-minded purpose, but this fact helps to measure their moral insufficiency. Unlike their fathers, however, the adolescent heroines do not separate themselves from their social context; they live by its rules without allowing those rules to corrupt the heart.

The gap between the generations does not manifest itself in the same way, let me say again, for all young people and all adults. Some of the young prove prematurely corrupt, some merely silly; a few grown-ups (the Bennet sisters' sensible aunt, Knightley in *Emma*) possess moral clarity and integrity. Moreover, the measure of the admirable involves more than moral criteria. Jane Bennet, Elizabeth's elder sister, excels her in altruism but interests the reader far less; she marries a less complicated, less compelling, and less wealthy young man than her sister wins. Elizabeth has more vitality, courage, and charm— qualities she shares with other youthful Austen heroines, and qualities associated particularly with the young in these novels, rarely granted to adults, and never explained by any explicit sequence of causality. The novels provide means of defining what makes these heroines good and attractive, but not of altogether accounting for how they got that way.

Perhaps the responsiveness that generates moral capacity and marks energetic involvement in life amounts to a native gift that cannot guarantee moral achievement but alone makes it possible. Bad environment, bad education may threaten the individual's development; but, given the will to self awareness, she can triumph over such obstacles. The action of Austen novels acknowledges in detail the necessities of social actuality, but the "good" characters do not simply sink into compromise. Their marriages, by no means the goal of their previous existence, testify to their ability to live within the system but also to their capacity for self-definition; their submerged conflicts with their elders have the same double meaning. It all sounds very cheerful. Like the glorification of adolescence in *Rob Roy*, however, the cheerfulness contains some qualification.

The idea that self-sustenance depends on innate and mysterious power which allows its possessor to grow through experience links Austen with her "Romantic" contemporaries. Eighteenth-century novels, especially novels about women, explained youthful virtue as largely the consequence of adult guidance. The picaresque tradition generated a literature about young male wanderers who achieve adulthood as a result of painful experience; such young men clearly possess a natural goodness that needs only appropriate channels for expression. But Tom Jones and Roderick Random, as we have seen, need adult mentors in order to learn. Young women in eighteenth-century novels, although they too grow through experience, do not enlarge the moral perceptions acquired through early adult instruction. Pamela's goodness, derived from good parents, remains undeviating; Evelina's depends on her training by a virtuous clergyman. She learns more about the world and its demands but never alters her judgments: although she acquires new reasons for disliking the cad Willoughby, she has known enough to disapprove of him from the beginning. Camilla, the youthful heroine of Fanny Burney's third novel, gets in trouble whenever she attempts independent action and learns to rely always on adult advice. Clarissa differs from her fictional sisters in her utter rejection of what her elders have to offer, but in fact her experience substantiates her parents' rightness in disapproving of Lovelace (although not, of course, their advocacy of Solmes) and corroborates the moral doctrine she learned at her grandmother's knee. Although the twentieth-century reader may recognize Clarissa's inadequate self-knowledge, Richardson supplied little evidence that self-awareness, in Austen's complicated sense, concerned him as a central moral issue.

The flourishing phenomenon of advice literature in itself implies the view of publishers and readers as well as of writers that adults have something of value to offer the young. Even at the very end of the century, John Aikin wrote a two-volume collection of letters to his son based on the assumption that a young person's moral growth depends on incorporating the ideas of the previous generation. He dealt with landscape gardening, ruins, the ancients and the moderns, the nature of truth—everything that crossed his mind. A doctor himself, he wanted to instruct a teen-aged boy who planned to enter the church; his awareness that the young will not necessarily listen to the old only intensified his determination. Thus he commented that parental advice about marriage has "peculiar propriety" because the advisors possess experience unavailable to their offspring. On the other hand, such advice may have little effect, for "passion commonly takes the affair under its management, and excludes reason from her share of the deliberation." Such a conclusion, however, did not long deter him: youthful passion, he felt, will yield to wisdom properly delivered. "I am inclined to think," he concluded, "that the neglect with which admonitions on this head are treated, is not unfrequently owing to the manner in which they are given, which is often too general, too formal, and with too little accommodation to the feelings of young persons."[5] He could not accept the implications of his own perception: in effect he denied what he had just affirmed.

Parents, this stress on advice giving implies, bear absolute responsibility for the moral welfare of their children. Even Mary Wollstonecraft seems inclined to think so, suggesting that children end up "neither wise nor virtuous" because their parents have mistakenly tried to protect them. She believed in the value of self-knowledge and of knowledge of others, both derived—as Jane Austen thought, too—only from experience; but unlike Austen she declared parents responsible for their offspring's inadequacies of experience.[6]

An early nineteenth-century review of a work by Elizabeth Hamilton (*Letters Addressed to the Daughter of a Nobleman*) observed—with incalculable proportions of naïveté and irony—that "the rising generation ought to be much better than that which is passing away, since so many more endeavours have been made to promote their improvement." A view of the young as ideal passive recipients of moral instruction still prevailed. "Youth is not the season for discussion and examination," the review continues; "and therefore the object should be rather to store than critically to exercise the mind."[7] So books of advice multiplied, for parents and children alike. Parents received repeated warnings about their immense responsibility: "the mistakes and follies of those to whom the nurture of youth is committed, even of such as are on the whole truly respectable, leave ill impressions which are not easily worn out, and have been productive of great and lasting evils."[8] The young, ever subject to emotional blackmail, were reminded of a parent's anxious feelings "on the occasion of a beloved son's first removing from the safe shelter of the parental roof" as justification for a three-volume discourse on religion and manners;[9] their emotional obligations are insistently reiterated. A wish to prolong the subservience of young to old echoes through many moral utterances of the early nineteenth century as of the century preceding. And such utterances characteristically emphasize the notion that feeling provides an undependable guide to action. Submission to one's own feelings, as opposed to submission to the presumably rational guidance of adults, will lead the young astray.

One does not expect opposition to feeling as a literary theme in the first quarter of the nineteenth century, and a counterstrain indeed developed, in reflective prose as well as in fiction and poetry. Isaac Taylor, who spoke also for the opposite point of view, in *Home Education* raised the possibility that "the unwarped reason" of youth might

178

rightly, although not without danger, resist the imposition of "preju-dices . . . authoritatively forced upon the young" under the guise of rationality.[10] In *The Friend*, Coleridge provided a full statement of the doctrine that the insight of the young might exceed that of the old. Those who have had "some intercourse with nature," he explained, even if educated under the prevailing system, "when they pass from the seclusion and constraint of early study, bring with them into the new scene of the world, much of the pure sensibility which is the spring of all that is greatly good in thought and action." The danger such young people face in the world, he continued, is not "the seduc-tion of its passions, but of its opinions." They will find about them many eager to function as guides but offering "little else than variety of danger"; far more dependable is the steady "inward impulse" of the youth whose environment has enabled his "speculative opinions" to "spring out of [his] early feelings."[11] Feelings, in other words, generate wisdom; other claims to authority remain suspect.

Well into the nineteenth century, such authors as Mary Brunton continued to flourish, their novels bearing titles like *Self-Control* and *Discipline* (Jane Austen described *Self-Control* as "an excellently-meant, elegantly-written Work, without anything of Nature or Probability in it").[12] But from the late eighteenth century on, many works of fiction covertly or openly declared the high value of youthful feeling, even when such feeling generated insubordination. Hermsprong, for in-stance, in Robert Bage's novel, courts teen-aged Caroline Campinet, daughter of an irascible and unreasonable father, partly by urging her to disobey that father and follow her own sense of right. When she returns to her parent, she receives a reproachful letter from Herms-prong which causes her "to doubt whether the step she had lately taken, was as meritorious as she wished to have thought it."[13] Only when she learns the moral limits of filial obedience does she become worthy of her suitor, whom she ultimately marries with paternal ap-proval, the novelist hedging his bets at the last minute. One readily deduces the hopeful message that natural goodness will lead the young to embrace truth and justice, while their elders linger in a mo-rass of conventional expediency.

Jane Austen's work does not fit readily into a context of novels based on the assumed virtue of youthful feeling any more than it be-longs to the line of fiction in which young characters learn to wel-come their elders' guidance. Unlike much minor fiction of her period, Austen's novels rarely offer explicit advice to their readers, and nei-ther the advice-book tradition which warns that the young must pro-

179

tect their intuitive resources nor that which tells youth to heed the wisdom of age accounts for her fiction's implicit moral doctrine. If Austen learned something of technique from Fanny Burney and Maria Edgeworth, she did not learn from them any relevant theory of the relation of generations. Yet the context supplied by all these works nonetheless helps to clarify her achievement.

Advice flourishes on simplification. To recognize the complexity of choice makes it difficult to offer prescriptions; it should not surprise us that early nineteenth-century moralists had to see things in one clear-cut way or another in order to exhort. Novelists who believed that they might inculcate morality by injunction likewise adopted blinkered vision, at least so long as they wrote in the didactic strain. (Their emotional messages, as we have seen, sometimes contradicted their announced doctrine.) But the virtual unanimity of the eighteenth century was beginning to break down. Anyone who read Coleridge *and* Hannah More could hardly fail to realize that their incompatibilities implied vexing questions about how one should think and feel about the young.

Jane Austen does not reconcile warring opposites, but neither does she exist outside them. To extract doctrines from her fiction would be irrelevant, but it is not irrelevant to note that her fictions imply ideas. As many critics have observed, with many shades of meaning, Austen writes as a moralist. The traces of other people's ideas take new shapes in her writing.

The problem of how novels inculcate morality attracted the attention of at least one literary critic among Austen's contemporaries, an anonymous commentator in *Blackwood's Magazine* who explains that novels, however virtuous their intent, necessarily fail to engage the will and therefore cannot achieve true moral effects. "Mastery over our feelings is gained by exerting the will in the course of our personal experience; but, in reading a novel, the will remains totally inactive."[14] The assumption that only through exercise of the will can one achieve moral advancement characterizes much eighteenth- and nineteenth-century thought; it probably does not characterize Austen, who relies instead on the unstated conviction implicit in *Northanger Abbey*: significant growth takes place through involvement of the imagination. Both the content and the fictional structures of her novels reiterate that "mastery over our feelings" involves more than will. The novels accept the eighteenth-century notion that emotional mastery represents a crucial moral achievement, but they also acknowledge that feelings can serve as moral guides, that one should respond to, reveal, and grow through one's emotions. Austen characters suffer as often for denial of feeling as for indulgence. To achieve the proper emotional balance represents a crucial moral task, and a task of special immediacy for the young, traditional victims of their own emotions. Austen's protagonists fulfill the task—but not by exercising their wills. The *Blackwood's* writer scorns the overt didacticism of much early nineteenth-century fiction; Austen provides an alternative. But her vision of how the young grow has its dark side. The world they inhabit allows no simple flowering.

Most readers have felt the somber aspects of *Mansfield Park*, generally acknowledged the most puzzling of Austen's novels. Although the theme of generational conflict seems less conspicuous here than in other Austen works, it draws together many of the book's emotional strands.

Alone among Austen's heroines, Fanny Price lacks both self-confidence and assertive force; she lacks, in fact the kind of attractiveness the others display. But she possesses considerable powers of passive resistance, through which she substantiates her moral superiority to most of those around her. The moral opposites of the novel—which hardly sound like opposites—are "selfishness" and "tranquillity"; both words recur frequently. "Tranquillity" reflects and encourages lack of selfishness; it represents an ideal condition of living with others. Although Fanny yearns for this state as her native air, she rarely achieves it for long, as other people's selfishness creates endless obstacles. In the two events that most vividly threaten her tranquillity, the excursion into amateur theatricals and the visit to Portsmouth, she discovers the limits of passivity as self-defense. Both episodes provide abundant displays of self-interest. The others contend over the choice of a play; Fanny watches and listens, "not unamused to observe the selfishness which, more or less disguised, seemed to govern them all, and wondering how it would end" (*MP*, p. 131). It ends, of course, badly, with Fanny herself at least apparently implicated: she cannot entirely retain the role of outsider, first inflicted, then chosen. The visit to her family involves her among noisier and more blatant clashes of selfishness, the domestic chaos echoing the disorder of opposed private interests. Fanny acts to moderate the discord: important self-assertion. Her *learning*, unlike that of most Austen heroines, involves coming to understand her responsibility to act in relation to others without their direct request, to trust her feelings and act on them. For this learning she does not depend on Edmund, whom she considers the source of her previous knowledge of right principle. Indeed, Edmund himself—unlike Austen's other lover-mentors—makes mistakes, misled, as he explains, by fantasy: "it had been the creature of my own imagination, not Miss Crawford, that I had been too apt to dwell on for many months past" (*MP*, p. 458).

Imagination's propensity to re-create the world to its liking, as Dr. Johnson had pointed out, represents a constant moral danger. Austen, who understood imagination as a means of growth, also saw its pitfalls. All her novels contain characters whose moral failures derive from inward-turned imagination—what we now often call *fantasy*. Amateur theatricals provide an obvious symbol of fantasy's power; both Henry and Mary Crawford openly regret the loss of their theatrical fantasy-world. The Bertram sisters also rely on fantasy; their education has failed to instruct them in "self-knowledge, generosity, and humility" (*MP*, p. 19), which depend on awareness of others. Their marriages and love affairs reflect their capacity to ignore reality's incorrigible unpleasantness for dreams of social power or romantic freedom. Aunt Norris inhabits a realm of her own creation and tries to impose it on others. Similarly, in other novels, Emma's fantasies lead to Harriet's disillusion and her own; Elizabeth Bennet reconstructs Darcy's character on the basis of her "prejudice," which generates its own fantasies; Marianne Dashwood perceives her experience as romance. Such characters' moral education teaches them about reality, the only source of tranquillity; selfishness both generates and is supported by private fantasy. Fanny, less susceptible than others to the temptations of self-romanticizing, must yet learn how properly to assess her own importance, given as she is to underestimate rather than to overestimate her place in the scheme of things. ("I can never be important to anyone," she observes [p. 26], to be rebuked by Edmund.)

Fanny's capacity for this significant learning marks her specialness, as her sister Susan's eagerness to learn marks hers. In different ways from *Northanger Abbey*, *Mansfield Park* dwells on the problem of what enables some to grow, while others remain immobile. Both the novel's narrator and, finally, Sir Thomas Bertram attribute the Bertram sisters' deficiencies to adult failures in their upbringing. Edmund blames Mary's moral inadequacies on corrupting influences in her environment. On the other hand, the clumsily integrated Portsmouth episode provides the younger Price boys and Betsy, the youngest girl, as evidence of the damaging effects of environment, but also presents Susan Price to demonstrate that the naturally good may escape corruption.

182

Fanny ponders at length the mystery of Susan. "Her greatest wonder on the subject soon became—not that Susan should have been provoked into disrespect and impatience against her better knowledge—but that so much better knowledge, so many good notions, should have been hers at all; and that, brought up in the midst of negligence and error, she should have formed such proper opinions of what ought to be—she, who had no cousin Edmund to direct her thoughts or fix her principles" (pp. 397–98). Once more, the novel demonstrates in the structure of its plot—the good progressing through increasing self-knowledge to their reward, the misguided suffering the consequences of their selfish separation from reality—the mystery and the high importance of human capacity for goodness.

In evoking this mystery, *Mansfield Park*, too, relies on the conflict of generations, emphasizing that virtue is not distributed on the basis of seniority. Aunt Norris helps to make Fanny's life miserable by her aggressive selfishness, Lady Bertram's passive selfishness provides no succor, Fanny fears Sir Thomas as his children do. The reader feels conscious of Fanny's moral superiority, in action and in feeling, to her elders; but not until her refusal of Henry Crawford does she come into direct conflict with parental figures other than Aunt Norris. The issue of marriage has special symbolic importance for generational conflict. As John Aikin had pointed out, parents necessarily have first-hand experience of the institution which their children necessarily lack; parents therefore draw on powerful sanctions in asserting their authority. On the other hand, marriage for the young represents adolescent escape from parental supervision; youthful lovers thus often feel powerfully impelled to defy their elders at this point. The most significant, sometimes the *only* significant choice available to a woman, the selection of a life partner may provide her single moment of independence—unless she allows her father to pre-empt it. Austen's juvenile fictions reiterate with crude and insistent, although ostensibly comic, emphasis the theme of parental tyranny and youthful defiance, both focused on issues of young love. Defiance mutes itself in the mature novels, but even meek Fanny Price, bathed in tears at the very thought of displeasing Sir Thomas, feels no doubt of her absolute right to determine her own marital destiny or at least to reject a man of whom she disapproves. Julia Bertram claims a similar right, on different grounds. Fanny knows the correctness of her moral judgment; Julia knows her will to social power. Julia—unlike Anne Elliott in *Persuasion*—asserts her prerogative to choose; Fanny, only her need to refuse. Both demonstrate the strength of youthful will; and Fanny, like the other heroines, embodies the possible superiority of youthful discernment to that of the old and experienced.

Such embodiment implies no ideological program, no specific recommendations about conduct. Austen's heroines guide themselves by principled morality and function as ethical Christians, but the novels do not finally suggest that morality, in the sense that matters most to Jane Austen, can be taught at all—although it can be learned. Good conduct and politeness are matters for teaching; "right principle," though teachers may inculcate it, develops often without conscious instruction: in Susan Price, for example, in Anne Elliott, in Elinor Dashwood. The action of Austen's novels, the patterns of aspiration, conflict, reward, and nemesis, reiterate the value of capacity to learn through experience. The middle-aged, in these books, seldom possess it: if Mr. Bennet briefly sees the error of his ways, he does not alter his life as a result; Sir Thomas learns to regret the past and change his personal style, but he is unique in Austen's novels; no middle-aged woman in Austen's fiction changes in any significant respect at all.

So the young provide—as they often do in fiction of every period— the nexus of social hope. They epitomize as characters a truth of possibility, although the novels they inhabit also carefully reiterate alternative possibilities. The "realism" of Austen's fiction depends partly on its refusal merely to accept the limitations of assumed social actuality. Meticulous in its rendition of speech and custom, it depicts with equal exactitude different modes of human development and dramatizes their implications. Constructing plots that turn on moral conflicts between accurate young and muddled old, yet basing those plots on mores that assume the authority of society's elders, Austen expands her readers' perceptions. Her mode of fictional embodiment enlarges the meaning of generational conflict, placing it in the context of a poetics as well as of a morality of personal growth. The idea of growth shapes the novelistic structures: Catherine moves from the restriction of a mind shaped by fanciful reading to the freedom of real relationship; Fanny proceeds from moral and psychological confinement to an enlarged life which she has earned by her comprehension of it. Imagination must join with will, may sometimes even replace will, as means of education. People—especially young people—learn by exploring possibilities never realized in actuality, by attending to their own inner life, and by rigorous investigation of the relation of inner and outer. Fantasy, the undisciplined production of the mind, separates from reality those who indulge in it; the more valuable forms of imagination, involving the capacity to enlarge experience by conjuring up alternatives to the given, involve, in Austen's world, a discipline that returns one to the real. The fictions instruct their readers by inviting their imaginative participation in social and psychological dilemmas involving moral as well as emotional issues. They manipulate their characters in comparable ways, demonstrating how imagination provides the means of change: through the romances Catherine uses as guides to conduct before rejecting them as inadequate moral mentors; through Fanny's sympathetic and increasingly disciplined imaginative identification with the needs of others.

In all respects, Jane Austen appears to believe, the young prove more educable than the old, and often possessed of more accurate intuition. On the other hand, the moral point of *Persuasion* is reiterated in other novels: the young who understand their own necessarily inadequate knowledge of the world must assume and defer to the wisdom of their elders; willingness to do so defines their educability. Adults, however, seldom justify their trust. Adult modes of dealing with experience often involve hardened commitment to alienating fantasy and such fantasy finds abundant social support.

Some young people—the Bertram sisters, John Thorpe in *Northanger Abbey*—indulge in the sort of fantasy that will turn them into just such adults; others accept the rigorous task of training the imagination for growth rather than for restriction. The reader has the same alternatives, warned by the text of the dangers of false attributions of causality, selfish acceptance of limited goals, but also offered examples of the growth that derives less from conscious will than from unconscious capacity and depends on the ability to acknowledge the limits of a single sensibility as means of grasping reality. Like Dr. Johnson, Austen acknowledges the imagination's danger; like Wordsworth, she recognizes its moral potential. Her characters achieve happy or unhappy fates largely on the basis of their use of imagination. Fanny Price, in many ways old before her time, gets what she has always wanted and settles into a state of uninterrupted tranquillity: an emphatically happy ending.

And yet, and yet . . . The harsh exclusions of the concluding action and the insistent ironies of the narrator's tone make the ending of *Mansfield Park* far from euphoric. Mansfield Park regroups its forces by shutting out the sources of disturbance: sex and aggression. Erring Maria must live in exile with angry Aunt Norris, the two of them constituting one another's punishment. Henry and Mary Crawford must remain in London where they belong, remain in "the world," source of all corruption, with their energy, vanity, and sexiness. The elder Bertram son, Tom, tamed by illness, can stay at the Park, and fourteen-year-old Susan Price, eager to serve, and of course Fanny and Edmund, ever decorous, ever appropriate. Mary Crawford attracted Edmund by her vitality; his clearly sexual response long overpowers even his moral convictions. His attraction to Fanny is of another order. He feels for her

a regard founded on the most endearing claims of innocence and helplessness, and completed by every recommendation of growing worth. . . . Loving, guiding, protecting her, as he had been doing ever since her being ten years old, her mind in so great a degree formed by his care, and her comfort depending on his kindness, an object to him of such close and peculiar interest, *dearer by all his own importance with her* than any one else at Mansfield, what was there now to add, but that he should learn to prefer soft light eyes to sparkling dark ones. (P. 460)

This detailed description of essentially parental feeling also reveals (in the phrase I have italicized) Edmund's narcissism: like Henry Tilney, he values a girl because she values him. The account avoids suggesting that Edmund recognizes anything of Fanny's individuality beyond her devotion to him. He sees her as a narcissistic extension, not as a sexual object; she sees him as a mentor. No conspicuous passion here. (Henry, on the other hand, had loved her "rationally, as well as passionately" [p. 469].)

Edmund's learning to prefer light eyes to dark ones adumbrates the general changing of minds at the end of *Mansfield Park*. Sir Thomas decides that Mrs. Norris is impossible, that Yates is not so bad, that he hopes for a marriage between Edmund and Fanny, the same connection he had earlier feared. Lady Bertram decides that Susan's indispensability exceeds Fanny's. Maria and Henry learn to hate one another, Tom Bertram becomes "what he ought to be" (p. 462). The narrator comments that "the cure of unconquerable passions, and the transfer of unchanging attachments, must vary much as to time in different people" (p. 470). Ideas like "unconquerable" and "unchanging" constitute agreeable fictions; the observation colors the later assertion that "the happiness of the married cousins must appear as secure as earthly happiness can be" (p. 473). The verb can bear considerable ironic weight, as can the narrator's assertion at the beginning of the final chapter: "Let other pens dwell on guilt and misery. I quit such odious subjects as soon as I can, impatient to restore every body, not greatly in fault themselves, to tolerable comfort, and to have done with all the rest" (p. 460). The happy ending, in other words, depends on narrative contrivance. As for the realm of human experience to which the narrative alludes—in that realm, people regularly change their minds, re-creating reality to meet immediate emotional needs. So adults live, and adolescents as well.

At the novel's end, Edmund and Fanny have been unambiguously welcomed into the adult world. By comparison, Tom, the twenty-six-year-old elder son ("useful to his father" [p. 462]) and Yates, the new son-in-law ("disposed to look up to him and be guided" [p. 462]), appear to continue their adolescent status. Perhaps their probationary roles reflect a fear that they may still embody dangerous passions. Edmund and Fanny have purged themselves of passion. They live close to the senior Bertrams, seeing them every day: good daughter, good son, therefore good grown-ups.

Sex and aggression pushed aside, the need for separation denied: the comforting fantasy resolves problems adolescents present to adults. Yet the narrator has called so much attention to the ways fantasy operates that it is hard to feel quite comfortable with this resolution. If the novel has demonstrated the enlargements of imagination, it has also shown the distortions; and every reader is implicated. Are concepts of secure earthly happiness, of familial harmony, of adulthood itself, agreeable fictions like the notion of unconquerable passion?

At any rate, *Mansfield Park* makes it clear that social order depends on exclusion, that dangerous energies must be shut out, that the young person of relatively low vitality will win adult approval, that happy endings rely heavily on denial.

Rob Roy suggests a similar perception. At the end of the novel, Frank Osbaldistone, without further discussion, agrees to follow whatever path his father chooses for him. The narrator conveys this fact in a dependent clause: "It so chanced that, instead of commanding me to the desk, as I fully expected, having intimated my willingness to comply with his wishes, however they might destine me, I received his directions to go down to Osbaldistone Hall" (VIII, 305). Frank's feelings have not changed. He alludes to the conflict of desire between himself and his father only once more, in terms that make this fact clear: "he was very desirous to see me 'settled in life,' as he called it; and he was sensible that, in joining him with heart and hand in his commercial labours, I had sacrificed my own inclinations" (VIII, 341). The reporter of his own past does not elucidate the reason for such a sacrifice.

The opening of the narrative, on the other hand, offers two discussions of mercantile reality which might rationalize Frank's ultimate compliance. He apologizes retrospectively for his opposition to his father on grounds of his lack of maturity, therefore of a capacity to understand actuality.

It may, I hope be some palliative for the resistance which, on this occasion, I offered to my father's wishes, that I did not fully understand upon what they were founded, or how deeply his happiness was involved in them. Imagining myself certain of a large succession in future, and ample maintenance in the mean while, it never occurred to me that it might be necessary, in order to secure these blessings, to submit to labour and limitations unpleasant to my taste and temper. (VII, 11)

The other argument for the commercial way takes an opposite tack:

Yet in the fluctuations of mercantile speculation there is something captivating to the adventurer, even independent of the hope of gain. He who embarks on that fickle sea requires to possess the skill of the pilot and the fortitude of the navigator; and after all may be wrecked and lost, unless the gales of fortune breathe in his favour. This mixture of necessary attention and inevitable hazard,—the frequent and awful uncertainity whether prudence shall overcome fortune, or fortune baffle the schemes of prudence,—affords full occupation for the powers, as well as for the feelings of the mind, and trade has all the fascination of gambling without its moral guilt. (VII, 5)

Both mature prudence and youthful adventurousness, in short, justify the life of buying and selling.

It comes as a shock to find the uncharted sea metaphor, previously describing a youth's immersion in books, applied now to commercial enterprise. In these reflections Frank tries retrospectively to understand and justify his father's character. He does so by asserting an identity of impulse between father and self: wandering around the Highlands with an outlaw or making a business decision, it's all the same. Conversely, the asserted necessity of submitting to unpleasant labor and limitations suggests that sons should adopt the same course of self-denial and repression as middle-class fathers. Both comments implicitly declare an identity between generations, either of "youthful" or of "mature" values. Frank's "learning," through the action related in *Rob Roy*, leads him to assign the highest importance to such identity.

Throughout the events the novel reports, Frank, like an Austen heroine, appears to owe nothing to heredity and little to the guidance of his elders. His proclaimed interests, assumptions, and convictions differ sharply from his father's. Equanimity and remoteness mark the older man's demeanor; the son considers himself a being of passionate intensity. Mr. Osbaldistone betrays no feeling at the idea of disinheriting his son, acknowledges no emotional stake in the youth's following his path. When Frank returns from the Highlands, his father embraces him tenderly and says, "My dear, dear son!" (VIII, 290). This unique moment of revealed feeling alone substantiates the emotional bond between father and son. Yet that bond, based on no likeness of taste, conviction, or experience, determines the novel's outcome.

The life of the imagination, in Austen's novels, means the inner life. In Scott, that life becomes externalized. Frank's imaginative experience consists in doing things: watching to see who meets Diana Vernon at night, keeping appointments with mysterious figures, riding into the Highlands, fighting an abortive, and finally a conclusive, duel. By doing things he learns not to do them, to convince himself that sitting at a desk "affords full occupation for the powers, as well as for the feelings of the mind," to submit willingly to the unpleasant.

As for that yet more romantic adolescent, Diana Vernon—she, it turns out, has all along guided herself by absolute subordination to her father, the unknown, ominous presence in the library at night, her domineering companion in the Highlands, a man referred to mainly as "His Excellency." He determines the course she must follow; her air of freedom and frankness is only a mask to face the world. When her father dies, she is "placed" in a convent, her "sexlessness" thus finding an appropriate harbor. From this convent, Frank removes her. His father approves of the match because "so dutiful a daughter cannot but prove a good wife" (VIII, 341). By implication, the wife's course, too, depends on total subordination. At any rate, we hear nothing of Diana's response to Frank's wooing, nothing of her independent impulse. She becomes Frank's adjunct. Like him, she apparently has learned through her romantic youth the necessity of relinquishing or suppressing romantic impulse.

The old conquer, in short, and should. Yet, like *Waverley, Rob Roy* betrays some uneasiness about this point. The novel does not end properly. In the last few pages, all Frank's cousins come to hasty ends (so that he can inherit the estate), Die's father succumbs, Frank's father gives permission for the marriage, Rob Roy's subsequent life is summarized. The final sentences, in brackets, read, "Here the original

189

manuscript ends somewhat abruptly. I have reason to think that what followed related to private affairs" (VIII, 342). In other words, the novelist can find no appropriate conclusion. He has just summed up Rob Roy as "possessed of many qualities, both of head and heart, which would have graced a less equivocal profession than that to which his fate condemned him." The assertion that Rob's fate, rather than his nature, condemned him to his profession evades the issues the novel has explored; but the concluding reference to Rob in itself recalls the importance of those issues. To insist on acting out the impulses of feeling and fancy dooms one to the equivocal; yet how much more appealing Rob seems than the old servant Andrew, utterly unequivocal in values, only waiting for Frank to grow up. ("I'm sure ye'll be a credit to your friends if ye live to saw out your wild aits, and get some mair sense and steadiness" [VIII, 164].) Andrew prophesies accurately: Frank will be a solid citizen, Rob can only live precariously. But the fiction mobilizes the reader's sympathy and identification not with the canny servant but with the daring outlaw.

Rob, too, needs to declare a community of interest between young and old. In the sequence quoted at the beginning of this chapter, he insists that his sons must follow his way, however dubious; he decides, in other words, precisely what Frank decides, from the opposite side of the generation gap. The novel makes such decisions feel like necessities, not triumphs: not really happy endings. Imaginative exploration may take place in the world, but it leads the young to submit to rather than to surpass their elders. The tone of this conservative message, corresponding to implications of Austen's more confined fictions, foretells the melancholy that marks much Victorian fiction of adolescence.

8

Us or Them: Some Victorians

According to the dominant cultural myth of Victorian England, society depended on the family: strong father, noble mother, happy children. The existence of *un*happy children outraged such writers as Dickens partly because of the prevalent assumption that childhood should be a state of bliss. Philippe Ariès, suggesting that to every period of history there corresponds "a privileged age and a particular division of human life," argues that in the nineteenth century the crucial age was childhood; in the twentieth, adolescence.[1] The nineteenth century, however, did not lack adolescents. How did the Victorians respond to that anomalous time between the virtuous childhood of natural innocence and the virtuous adulthood of moral achievement?

The nineteenth-century English father brooding about the recent marriage of his twenty-year-old daughter wrote in tones veering from sentimentality to strained irony. He allowed himself outbursts of slightly disguised rage at "this tyranny of youth! The world is all for it—all joys but money-getting are for young men and maidens. Beauty, poetry, love, day-dreaming—how absurd are we to talk of what they alone understand, and which is theirs only!" The young couple, the writer complained, eagerly embark upon their new stage of life, without realizing that they push Papa to a new stage as well: "his *last*."[2] Such an open acknowledgment of the real issues between the middle-aged and their successors—young people have all the fun, and, far worse, they outlive us—was almost as rare in 1862 as it is today. More typically, then as now, commentators concealed profound fears behind superficial ones or demonstrated an emotional identification with the young which obscures the fundamental fact of their inexorable succession. Victorians made room for adolescence, recent social historians have explained, for clear economic and social reasons. Society, fearing the radical impulses of the young, as manifested, for exam-

191

ple, in the Chartist movement, wished to segregate them from adult life; new ideas about individual freedom, encouraging youthful romanticism, began to flourish in the late eighteenth century as capitalistic morality triumphed; overcrowding in English professions by the third decade of the nineteenth century justified the lengthening of the educational process that kept middle-class young people from full parity.[3] Such theories help account for what happened; they do not explain the complexities of feeling that emerge as novels and essays consider the uncomfortable relation between youth, the time of self-exploration, and adulthood with its commitment to marriage and family.

Adulthood meant both self-discipline and the training of experience. Urging young people to grow up, didactic writers made sharp distinctions between boys and girls. Adolescent women tend to fall into extremes, they claimed: of frivolity, of pseudo-masculine claims to independence, of self-abnegation. The girl's weaknesses may derive, male commentators often suggested, from her sex; only stern discipline will combat them. Or, as women writers typically argued, the weaknesses may stem from the social conditions under which she lives. At any rate, the "girl's emotions lie near the surface; they are easily called out, and as easily calmed."[4] Her school training makes her "priggish, conceited, one-sided, superficial, and either languid or full of partisan tendencies."[5] Open competition is likely to "derange" her nerve-centers, which manifest "a state of greater instability [than boys'], by reason of the development of her reproductive functions."[6] Even if she aspires to virtue, she will cultivate masochism, "self-denial," believing the ideal life to "consist in an exaggeration of the passive, instead of the active, virtues."[7] More typically, she deviates from an obsessive concern with fashion only to seek "frantic independence," in Dinah Mulock's phrase. Mulock sees the woman's common alternatives as "foolish aping of men's manners, habits, and costumes" or "frivolous laziness, worse than womanish inanity," and sees both as equally destructive.[8] Like the male commentators I have just quoted, she perceives the young woman of whom she writes a distinctly *other*. The female adolescent emerges as an alien creature, a scapegoat enabling her critics to assert by implication their own superior seriousness.

Penelope Holland, young wife of a clergyman, in writing anonymously of "Our Offence, Our Defence, and Our Petition" (1869), exemplifies the complexity of a woman's views about younger women. Despite her use of the first-person plural pronoun, she effects an emotional separation between herself and those she describes. Explicitly and implicitly she raises familiar feminist issues: male control of all avenues of possibility, the absence of choice in female experience—both urgent problems for adolescent girls full of vague aspiration, like the young in all ages. But she also perceives in young women the potential weakness of all women writ large: from this she must separate herself. We now believe young people to embody qualities and values peculiar to their state; for our forebears, female young people in particular demonstrated what might be feared in the next generation of mothers. A sort of psychological Darwinism pervades utterances about adolescence: the asserted decadence of youth may interfere with the orderly evolution of the race.

Noting that "pulpit and press" denounce contemporary young women, Holland does not attempt to rescue them from denunciation, only to explain their folly: "there is scarcely any alternative for a girl in fashionable society, between reckless dissipation and convent life."[9] She sketches a representative seventeen-year-old girl, "by nature intelligent, high-spirited, and warmhearted," a newspaper reader and sermon hearer who wishes to remedy some of the world's wrongs, "to have a post assigned her in the battlefield of life": a metaphor with masculine associations so strong as to suggest the futility of the attempt (p. 324). The detailed account of the girl's specific frustrations in seeking meaningful possibilities of action concludes with her efforts of self-education, highly reminiscent of George Eliot's Maggie Tulliver in *The Mill on the Floss*. Only success at balls, however, wins social approval. "Compelled to live" her self-indulgent life, she finds her conscience deadened, herself falling away from her "girlish ideal." The solution for her problem, Holland argues, lies in the establishment of a "ladies' college" which by unspecified means would provide young women with opportunities for "the service of their God and of their fellowcreatures," releasing them "from their present bondage of idle selfishness" (p. 331).

The imagined girl in her frivolous life "sees some of her friends saved all this degradation by a happy marriage, and wishes to change her lot for one in which she might have some object to live for beyond herself, some purpose in life not wholly selfish. Hence proceed many unhappy marriages, when the bride only flies to marriage to save her from the insipid uselessness of her life. Hence also many mercenary marriages which often tempt girls by offering them a larger sphere of action" (p. 326). If adolescence, as society shapes it for women, forces them to stasis rather than action, so, more emphatically, does marriage, the word itself structurally paralleled to the abstract noun "useless-ness" (one flies to marriage to escape uselessness), a "lot" rather than a relationship, a temptation because of the kind of "sphere" it provides. A woman may "have" an object or purpose in life: she does not *develop* goals. The suspicion that "sphere" rather than "action" is the opera-tive word in the sentence about mercenary marriages is confirmed by the sentence immediately following: "We think if men oftener had themselves the chance of winning power, wealth, independence, and rank, by a flattering word or an expressive smile, we should hear few-er hard words on the subject" (p. 326). Although power and indepen-dence may make action possible, the grammatical ordering of the group of nouns suggests that they represent possessions more than opportunities. As Holland enlarges upon the situation of the unmar-ried woman, she makes explicit what has been implicit all along: "Treated up to the very confines of middle life as if still a child, with no more liberty or independence than at sixteen" (p. 326). Regardless of age, a woman remains an adolescent until she marries. Allowed to *have* but not to *do*, she is denied the possibility of growth.

Holland's fierce moralism derives from defensiveness about her own intellectual activity as well as from willingness to take young ladies more seriously as human beings than "society" takes them; she observes that the world considers it "a very black crime" that a young woman should "do profitable work with her brains" (p. 329). By both echoing and explaining the denunciations of press and pulpit, she jus-tifies her own difference from the frivolous while she expresses her understanding of them. This particular kind of self-implication in the issues discussed belongs only to a woman—indeed, only to an upper-class woman struggling to deal with her own intellectual capacities. But all writers about adolescence are implicated in their subject if sim-ply by the fact that they have survived their teens. Most, in the nine-teenth century, attempted to deny this self-implication.

The Victorian moralists on adolescence implicitly claimed their utter transcendence of adolescent dilemmas. Their authoritative public voices appropriated the language of official morality to assert that young people embody alien and dangerous impulses that by their very existence threaten the social order. Although one may sympathize with the plight of young women, one must fear the consequences of their self-indulgence. Frivolous or saintly, seeking marriage or inde-pendence, the Victorian girl embodied for those commenting on her a force to be controlled or repressed.

The novels of this period depict young women with characteristics comparable to those rendered by the moralists, but convey sharply different attitudes. If for social commentators, the adolescent constitutes "the other," for novelists he or she becomes a version of the self. The Brontës, Eliot, Dickens, moralists all on frequent occasion, nonetheless revealed toward adolescence in their fictions a predominant wistful identification. Like Penelope Holland, they often perceived the young woman as victim; she therefore allowed them to express awareness of the self's vulnerability and pleasure in the possibility of transcending weakness. Adolescence, like childhood, was something adults had lost. Victorian novelists understood it as the time of life when everyone— even women—can make the greatest claims on the world (although the world is unlikely to fulfill those claims). For the static view of adolescence implied by moralistic accounts they substituted stress on change and understood this time of life in ways more congruent with twentieth-century psychological theory, as one of crucial transition.

In life, it goes without saying, every adult feels toward adolescents some ambivalent combination of the two attitudes I have opposed to one another: sympathetic identification and pained or angry rejection. One can attempt to resolve such feelings by urging the adolescent to leave adolescence behind as fast as possible: a common Victorian solution, despite the fact that adolescence as a kind of holding period was an adult invention. Novelists agreed with moralists that young people must grow up, but expressed the sadness of that necessity even more emphatically than had earlier writers of fiction.

When George Eliot, in *The Mill on the Floss* (1860), tried to examine the shift from childhood to adulthood, she ended by drowning her central characters—a resolution unsatisfactory to generations of readers, made only rhetorically acceptable in the text, but inevitable because of the unresolvable nature of the characters' problems. From my immediate point of view, the novel's special interest derives from its systematic attempt to compare male and female moral development in adolescence, and from the light it sheds, in particular, on attitudes toward young women. Although Tom and Maggie Tulliver are vividly individualized, they also reveal, as Eliot takes pains to point out, characteristics peculiar to their genders. Both concern themselves with *winning* and *losing*, the structural polarities of this novel as of Penelope Holland's reflections, but more variously defined.

The material stakes for competition include not only money and the possessions it buys, but also husbands and wives. "We don't ask what a woman does, we ask whom she belongs to," Wakem explains to his son;[10] conversely, the imagined gossip of St. Ogg's, given that Maggie had married Stephen, would exculpate her because she had won both a trousseau and a prosperous only son. Tom, accepting materialistic criteria, believes the world his oyster, as two chapter titles suggest (III, 5: "Tom Applies His Knife to the Oyster"; VI, 5: "Showing That Tom Had Opened the Oyster"). He formulates his ultimate ambition at the age of sixteen: "he was thinking that he would buy his father's mill and land again when he was rich enough, and improve the house and live there; he should prefer it to any smarter, newer place, and he could keep as many horses and dogs as he liked" (II, 335).

This plan reflects an adolescent fantasy of possession and power and glory with no awareness of costs. Its imaginative and moral level exemplify that of most of the novel's nominal adults. Characters who share Tom's view of winning—Mr. and Mrs. Tulliver, her sisters, their husbands, Wakem, Stephen—define the ideological and moral extreme that the society of *The Mill on the Floss* accepts as norm. Against this norm Maggie struggles; her difficulties, despite her utter lack of frivolity, parallel those outlined by Holland for the upper-class girl. Her situation in life precludes obvious self-determination; she must depend on men; all her experience directs her, classically, toward preoccupation with the inner life, the locus of her selfhood.

But the crude contrast thus implied between Tom and Maggie by no means adequately suggests the moral complexity of this novel. Tom, too, has a moral life. The same question affects boy and girl alike: given the alternatives of winning and losing, how can an adolescent win? Winning implies competition as well as gain, in an arena shaped by adult assumptions and standards, and it implies a locatable and acceptable shared system of values. The adolescent can win only conditionally as long as he or she remains adolescent. A young woman may use her sexual power to attract a man; a young man by energy and will gets ahead in the world. To consolidate their gains, each must accept some stable self-definition, discover who he or she is willing to be. The adolescent wins, in other words, by ceasing to be adolescent: so the action of *The Mill on the Floss* suggests.

The implications of this fact differ as dramatically for Tom and Maggie as do their achieved definitions of "winning." Tom finds self-definition easy, but his oyster proves tasteless; Maggie commits herself to a whole series of passionate self-definitions and achieves nothing more than eyes of intense life in a weary face. Tom's primitive but vigorous morality gives him a premature sense of self. He never feels himself to have done wrong; Maggie forever wishes she had done something different. When Maggie appeals to her own more inclusive morality of feeling against his moral rigidity, he points out that his conduct, unlike hers, justifies his principles. As a grown man, twenty-three years old, he responds to Maggie's claim that feelings account for her actions by boasting that he himself has consistently suppressed feelings, finding his comfort in doing his duty. He will not allow the disgraced Maggie under his roof: "the world shall know that *I* feel the difference between right and wrong" (II, 291). This belief in the absolute and immediate distinction between right and wrong derives, the narrator suggests, from Tom's limited vision; more specifically, from his early commitment to an externally authorized code of rules. "Adulthood," for Tom, depends on mere chronology, which confirms in him an identity established in early adolescence. When he goes to work at sixteen, he has already stopped growing, psychologically and morally.

Maggie's constant wish to have done something different, on the other hand, urges her toward moral experimentation controlled by her powerful desire for goodness and her enlarging awareness of others' needs. Her Victorian progress from self-will to self-sacrifice wavers when challenged by Stephen Guest, the charming, wealthy young man who loves her but is engaged to her cousin Lucy. Rescued by a dream from subsequent moral and physical drift, Maggie arrives at a first halting statement of the principled position to which she will adhere until her death. Controlled by a vision of justice, the favorite virtue of philosophers, she refuses to complete her elopement with Stephen, although she has allowed him to lure her into a prolonged boat trip. (Since the excursion has lasted overnight, it destroys Maggie's reputation.) She defines justice in relation to "the heart's need," a formulation of principle dependent on her belief in the sacredness of ties of loyalty. She relies, in crisis, on all that her "past life has made dear and holy" (II, 284); although Stephen reproaches her with the inadequacy of a woman's love in comparison with a man's, she remains faithful to her vision until the end.

But that end expresses the inconceivability of adulthood—like adolescence a socially defined state—for Maggie. Having achieved a principled morality, she must live in utter isolation. The good clergyman who tries to help her admits defeat: he cannot find for her a viable way of life in her own community. She has not "grown up" in any way her society can understand; her death asserts the impossibility of her life.

Paradoxically, *The Mill on the Floss* reveals both more ardent optimism and more profound pessimism about the possibilities for female adolescents than emerge from the writings of Penelope Holland and her like. Recognizing the same social realities that lead Holland to deny that young women can choose or act, Eliot imagines a character whose determination creates the opportunity for inner change, which depends less on circumstance than on the capacity to respond to even the circumstance of limitation. However mysterious the sources of such a capacity, its power manifests itself unmistakably: Maggie's eyes of intense life declare her energy. Compared to Holland's seventeen-year-old, Eliot's heroine achieves moral triumph.

On the other hand, she drowns; Holland's young woman only marries—at worst a metaphorical drowning. Holland, like the other moralists, holds an ideal of adulthood; her anger at the restriction of female opportunity feeds on faith in some conceivable alternative. A comparable vision appeared no more available to George Eliot in *The Mill on the Floss* than to her protagonist Maggie. To be sure, in other novels Eliot provided wise and fulfilled adults: the Garths in *Middlemarch*, for example, with their informed acceptance of painful reality—an ideal of sorts, but not one the young would rush to embrace. Dorothea Brooke marries, survives to participate in adult life; so, imagined by other women, do Cathy Linton (whom we leave, in *Wuthering Heights*, on the point of marriage), and Jane Eyre, and even Charlotte Brontë's staunch Shirley. Yet the atmosphere of compromise surrounding these marriages in novels of female experience suggests, more ambiguously than does *The Mill on the Floss*, comparable doubts about the relation between female existence and self-fulfillment. Adolescent girls must grow up or die; both fates have dark and bright aspects.

Does adult male life provide more obvious satisfactions? Victorian didactic prose did not take up the question. Conveying the view that adulthood, for men, means civilization, such prose expressed outrage and concealed admiration for the barbarism of the young. Aggression by now had become an open preoccupation of many moralists. Adolescent boys, like their female counterparts, tend toward excess, but in different areas. Development from infancy to manhood recapitulates racial evolution. Boys may appear miniature adults, "but watch them by themselves, and you will see that, at home and school alike, they possess many of the noblest virtues, many of the meanest vices of a less civilized age." No instances of noble virtue emerged from the anonymous essayist's subsequent reflections, but he detailed the male adolescent "vices" noted by many commentators. "They are apt to be selfish and violent; to feel at times a positive pleasure in giving pain and annoyance to others; to abuse physical strength to the torment of their weaker companions."[11] Such moral defects differ from those attributed to girls specifically in their relation to adult life. Most observers noted, with varying degrees of approval, the extreme competitiveness of adolescent boys and the establishment in school of hierarchies of strength, patterns of dominance and submission. One must regret the "pain" and "torment" involved, but critics appear to have felt it inevitable: one of them noted "the innate, we had almost said the mysterious, tendency to abuse personal strength and size, to torment, tease, and tyrannize over the younger and weaker" (p. 405). And this "tendency" bears some clear relation to the spirit of "generous emulation" which the moralist praised in public schools, explicitly contrasting it with the petty rivalries of young women. Call it tyranny or emulation, the will to compete and to triumph foretells success in the world of business and politics; the boy even in his flaws is making himself a man to reckon with, unlike the girl, whose inadequacies will make her an inadequate woman. The critic who commented on the mysterious tendency to tyrannize observed also boys' necessary moral difference from females: "Be they never so good, they will not sacrifice themselves for others as their mothers do; they will have, at best, an inordinate respect for personal strength and agility; they will often take a provokingly distorted view of the actions and motives of their elders" (p. 405). This statement of negative qualities contains an undertone of respect—or perhaps of envy. Boys are distinctly other than, even alien from, men, more primitive, less civilized. Grown-up men try to civilize them—but preferably without destroying their primitive energy, energy being, as the Scottish author Samuel Smiles explained in *Self-Help*, the most crucial single requirement for success.[12] Misuse of energy creates the weaknesses of adolescent boys, criticized as harshly as their female counterparts, but with some lurking awareness of their potential for triumphant adulthood. Girls, in contrast, seem potentially as well as actually negligible. It all sounds very familiar.

No one appears to have worried about the relations of mothers and daughters; many writers concerned themselves with fathers and sons. The British journalist and reformer William Cobbett, in 1829, confessed his motivation for striving to improve his own children: "I could not be *sure* that my children would love me as they loved their own lives; but I was, at any rate, resolved to deserve such love at their hands; and, in possession of that, I felt that I could set calamity, of whatever description, at defiance."[13] From wish to fantasy is an easy step: Cobbett's moralizing hints his conviction that the young *must* love him. Herbert Spencer justified his doctrine of the "discipline of natural consequences" partly on the ground that it prevents those horrifying "mutual exasperations and estrangements" between father and son that other modes of discipline may encourage.[14] Some moralists tried to bludgeon the young into compliance: Charles Kingsley, for instance, announced that "a disobedient, self-willed son, who is seeking his own credit and not his father's, his own pleasure and not his parent's comfort; a son who is impatient of being kept in order and advised, who despises his parent's counsel, and will have none of his reproof"—such a son must prove incapable of grasping or accepting the truths of Christianity, deprived of salvation by self-will.[15]

Many writers berated the young for qualities that alarmed moralists perceived as foretelling the nation's fall. An anonymous piece called "Our Modern Youth," published in *Fraser's Magazine* in 1863, provides an illuminating counterpart for Penelope Holland's essay on young women. The 1863 polemicist, certainly male, concerns himself with boys and girls alike, reserving a particularly ferocious salvo for the follies of current feminism. His treatment of adolescent males, however, articulates with special intensity and clarity the fears of his generation about their successors.

The essay begins by declaring "the deep national importance of the mental condition of the rising generation."[16] Acknowledging the widespread interest in educational issues, the commentator argues that it has obscured facts about the actual state of the young. Their great sin is "self-assurance. Afraid of nothing, abashed at nothing, astonished at nothing, they are ever comfortably assured of their own perfect competence to do or say the right thing in any given position" (p. 115). The writer's outrage suggests his fear. Adults, his implicit argument goes, win the right to self-confidence by arduous effort and achievement. To precede achievement by confidence devalues the rewards of maturity. The young now *take* rather than *win* grown-up privilege.

Moreover, they claim equality. Democracy both causes and reflects the assertiveness of youth; America shows England's evils in intensified form.

The parental rule is more relaxed than among ourselves, the spirit of independence and the arrogant tone more marked among the young. It is asserted that public opinion operates to narrow the exercise of the most legitimate authority to such a degree that the discipline necessary for education is almost abandoned, and a mother has been known to say that she *dared* not punish her child. Every youth feels that independence will soon be within his grasp and exults in the almost boundless field open to his energies. His ignorance and inexperience may naturally seem no obstacles, when the constitution of his country considers such drawbacks no impediment to the possession of the most serious political privileges. (P. 124)

The point—the underlying fear—becomes clearer a few sentences further on: "Where go-ahead is the ruling principle of life, those who have most energy for the race and most prospect of distancing others will necessarily hold the first rank; and these must be the young, the men of action, as opposed to the men of thought and experience" (pp. 124–25). The older man who prefers not to be distanced must shift the ground of competition, claiming, as this essayist explicitly does, his own moral superiority, wisdom, and perception. Yet "these gray-hearted boys," as he calls them in a moment of open anger at their lack of sensibility, their failure of feeling, arrogantly claim a triumph which may in fact be real (p. 119).

What the essayist attributes to America he sees all around him: the key words ("independence," "arrogance," "energies," "ignorance") echo through the essay, defining the power of the young. The spatial metaphors in the passage on America emphasize the writer's sense of chaos. The exercise of legitimate authority—adult authority—*narrows*, while the youth finds a "boundless field," discovering "no obstacles" in what should constitute serious impediments. Young people, in this version of things, get ever more of what they want; adults, ever less. Nor does the commentator know what to do about this state of affairs. After a penultimate paragraph of questions implying almost total despair, the essay ends in uncertainty: "it is not too soon to seek around us for some methods of dealing with the young which shall look a little deeper than those now in vogue into principles of human nature and the best interests of society" (p. 129). The unsureness of vocabulary (what kinds of *methods* might "look a little deeper"?), the vagueness of allusion, the tentativeness of advocated action all reinforce the feeling that this article has dramatized as well as partially described a clash between young and old in which sureness and victory belong to the young.

Woman writers who discussed the prototypical girl confidently asserted her eagerness to reform, given the opportunity. The cause of evil lies without; the will to change inheres in the young woman. Even male writers less certain than Penelope Holland of society's responsibility for female frivolity tacitly assumed that a young woman properly instructed would be capable of reform. The adult world that instructs and summons her embodies wisdom and privilege as well as

201

sobriety; if the promise it holds forth is, as Holland argued, partly illusory (women being urged toward adulthood but never fully admitted to its rights), the idea of adulthood still exerts a powerful pull on the girl.

The boy, moralists suggested, is different, his defiance of "mature" standards issuing from profound causes. To him, too, his elders offered the command, "Grow up! Be like us!"; they felt eager to neutralize his threat by welcoming him among them. Moralists admired as well as feared the force of male adolescence. They directly acknowledged no corresponding part of themselves; on the other hand, whether they raged or persuaded, they implied the promise of social and professional position which would provide new forms of power. Writers on education in particular assumed that ambition motivates young men to convert school's crude competition into sophisticated adult analogues, a progress that constitutes civilization.

The contrast we have seen between sober journalistic views of young men and young women conforms to what we know already about the comparative positions of men and women a bit more than a century ago. Thinking back to Tom Tulliver, however, we may recall that his ascent to adulthood, although more "successful" than Maggie's, brings him few rewards. His financial prosperity intensifies his self-esteem, yet his life seems devoid of deep satisfaction. Direct social commentary of the Victorian period confirms a sense of absolute division between the fates of young men and young women and between the feelings of adults toward each of the sexes. Fiction, despite its social realism, sometimes suggests, on the contrary, that youthful male and female experience bear a close resemblance to one another. Novels assign to the two genders comparable psychic outcomes and convey congruent attitudes toward them. Emotional danger and psychic cost assume different forms yet weigh equally on both sexes. Long before Richard Feverel loses his bride, he discovers the virtual impossibility of living with her a responsible adult life—not because of her weaknesses, but because of his utter lack of readiness for adulthood. David Copperfield marries a child and learns the frustration of attempting to conduct professional and domestic affairs without really growing up. He declares his desire for adulthood, at the novel's end he has married the right woman, yet an elegiac tone dominates the final summary of his success. For what "really growing up" means, to Feverel and Copperfield and many other male fictional protagonists, is not what one would assume from reading tracts on education or morals. It has little to do with career or competition, but involves primarily what David Copperfield calls the "discipline of the heart"—Maggie Tulliver's discipline.

Moralists and educational theorists made a sharp, usually explicit, distinction between the proper concerns of the two sexes. Principle and feeling belong to women, who may (and should) help men to achieve them, too. In nineteenth-century novels, however, the struggle to use feeling properly and to achieve steady principle creates the chief problems of adolescent males. Pip, in *Great Expectations*, defines himself initially, as the title suggests, in terms of what he is to be given: wealth, social position, Estella to love. As painfully as Maggie, though by a different process, he learns to attend to "the heart's need" and to accept the ultimate authority of old ties. Like Maggie, he must give up all he wants, or believes he wants. He does not drown at the end; in fact, in the second version of the ending, he expects to be united with Estella. Yet the first ending, which declares the impossibility of the union, more logically concludes the narrative. Even if the marriage took place, the chastening process that Pip has undergone has left him so straitened, so diminished in aspiration and in self-esteem, so unable to grow up in any full sense, though forced to abandon childish illusions, that one cannot anticipate much joy in it. Here we see an imagined version of precisely the education the *Fraser's Magazine* moralist would recommend for "Our Modern Youth," the reverse of that state of affairs he described in America: the "almost boundless field" that seems open to Pip at the beginning narrows until he finds impediment everywhere. In every moral respect, his education effects improvement: Pip at the end has grown more attractive, more wise, more sensitive than he was in early adolescence. Yet the feeling of loss dominates over the perception of gain. The gap between great expectations and diminished actuality reveals itself gradually; we recognize the moral insufficiency of the expectations, find something familiar in the actuality, know the necessity of coming to terms with the everyday, but continue to wish that life might be otherwise.

Such a wish reflects the longing to hold onto the sense of high possibility uniquely associated with adolescence. As certainly as *Wuthering Heights* expresses the conflict between the gratifications of adolescent narcissism and those of mature relationship, *Great Expectations* articulates the tension between the pleasures of adolescent fantasy and the more dubious satisfactions of adult realism. In neither case can any simple resolution dismiss the problem: if we applaud Cathy Linton for her painful discovery of Hareton's virtues and of her need for him, we continue to feel far more involved with her mother's fate; we approve of Pip in his final renunciations and acceptances, yet identify more passionately with his younger, grandiose self. Catherine and Heathcliff mistreat the gentler folk who surround them; we conventionally disapprove, while thrilling to this evidence of the overriding force of a grand passion. Pip mistreats that infinitely virtuous natural man, Joe, and calls the reader's attention to his moral failure. We take the point, we know already how unlikely Pip is to find the road paved with gold and Estella at his side, we know that the moral worth of Joe and Biddy far exceeds that of Miss Havisham and Estella; yet we want, at some profound level, just what Pip wants. On such emotional conflicts does the nineteenth-century novel of adolescence turn, forcing adult readers to acknowledge in themselves the survival of ancient impulse. A century earlier, novels reported their protagonists' straightforward (although sometimes impeded) progress toward the adult place in the world established by marriage and by the social definition of clear heredity, occupation, or alliance. By the twentieth century, adolescents in fiction could claim moral superiority to the corrupt adult society around them. Although that society might defeat them, readers and characters need feel no uncertainty about where true value lies. Eliot and Dickens, a hundred years ago, both demonstrated clear awareness of society's corruptions without accepting the corollary that adolescence should triumph. The wisdom their protagonists acquire in transcending their adolescent state does not enable them to lead viable lives; neither does it enable them to avoid, or even consciously to wish to avoid, the responsibilities of adulthood. Eliot and Dickens, consequently, like Scott, and for some of the same reasons, had trouble with their endings. Their readers re-experience in their novels of youth some of life's most profound conflicts, and the impossibility of resolving them. "It was an uncomfortable consideration," Pip remarks, "on a twenty-first birthday, that coming of age at all seemed hardly worthwhile in such a guarded and suspicious world as [Jaggers] made of it."[17] The worth of "coming of age" remains ambiguous to the end of *Great Expectations*.

Pip's effort to discover his identity originally assumes forms comparable to those familiar from the eighteenth-century novel. Like Tom Jones, he takes for granted the need to function in the world, believing that possession of wealth and other concomitants of the gentleman will ensure success. Unlike Maggie Tulliver, he does not seek to define himself through moral achievement, which is, rather, thrust upon him. As his assumptions and expectations begin to totter, he finds it necessary to re-assess his brief history. This process differs from Maggie's eventual coming to terms with her past specifically in his conscious realization that a personal history consists not only in a set of experiences but in a set of interpretations, infinitely alterable. Pip has manufactured his versions of reality out of slight materials; he comes to recognize it as a construction comparable to the grotesque setting Miss Havisham has made for herself. "As I looked round . . . at the stopped clock, and at the withered articles of bridal dress upon the table and the ground, and her own awful figure with its ghostly reflection . . . , I saw in everything the construction that my mind had come to, repeated and thrown back to me" (V, 322). Miss Havisham's construction determines the possibilities of her adult life; so does Pip's. When he finally realizes the utter "simplicity and fidelity" that Joe and Biddy represent, he realizes also his "own worthless conduct to them" and concludes, "I could never, never, never undo what I had done" (V, 344). He can change his mind, and does, but not his past action. To recognize the ineluctability of conduct marks an important stage of his moral development.

Like Maggie, as I have said, Pip comes to realize the heart's importance; like Maggie, he finds the realization of little use in the world; like Maggie, he has no viable model of adulthood. The lovable adults, here as in other Dickens novels, are children at heart: Joe, all generous feeling, but perceived even by a very young Pip as essentially a fellow child; Mr. Pocket, incompetent to deal with economic facts; even Magwitch, whose view of the world manifests the child's incapacity to incorporate complexity. Miss Havisham herself, living in her own "construction," epitomizes the refusal to grow up. At the other extreme, having totally repressed the child within, Mrs. Joe and Mr. Jaggers embody successful adult dominance. With Pip, the reader wonders at their power; but one cannot wish Pip to imitate them. The schizophrenic Wemmick, child at home, Jaggers-like at work, has found a more attractive solution to life's problems, but he hardly supplies a model. Pip, like Tom Tulliver, is reduced to commitment to work, but without Tom's sense of a goal to be won. His role as onlooker at the happy marriages of others cannot resolve his problems; his love for Estella seems only clinging fantasy. He has come to know the value of love and of relationship without finding object for his own emotional capacity; Maggie, with her deep devotion to Tom consummated in her death, in this respect proves more fortunate than Pip. Although society allows the young man far more opportunity than his female counterpart, the male adolescent entering adulthood, in this and other nineteenth-century novels, finds no happier life than does the young woman. Even Tom Brown, that hearty specimen of idealized British youth, embarks on marriage, at the conclusion of Thomas Hughes's *Tom Brown at Oxford* (1857), with a pervasive, emphasized, unexplained sense of sadness. Something goes wrong, these novelists suggest, as adolescence ends.

Of course, young men and women are not rendered as experiencing the same difficulties in the same way. Looking at Pip with the perspective established by the journalists and moralizers, one can find the predictable male traits. His competitiveness and desire to triumph manifest themselves at home in his attitude toward Trabb's boy, later in his obsessive contests with Bentley Drummle and in his self-display at Jaggers's dinner table. He seeks satisfaction mainly in the world outside—not, like Maggie, within. His mind focuses on the future. He values physical strength and prowess, he assumes the subordination even while feeling the power of women, he overflows with energy. His assumptions and his purposes differ from Maggie's; he comes to the doctrine of benevolence by the road of insistent self-assertion, self-absorption, self-display, rather than, like Maggie, through the temptations of self-sacrifice and of submission.

Yet the fact remains: whether they depict male or female adolescence, the novelists of the nineteenth century often reveal a conviction that growing up is regrettable as well as necessary, involving a discipline of the heart with all the rigorous implications of the abstract noun, a discipline that restrains, restricts, subordinates, punishes, controls the life of feeling; that implies loss. Moralists express anger at the reprehensible aspects of adolescence; novelists stress the sadness of relinquishment. Both sorts of writer share a set of established moral assumptions, agreeing in what they value, differing in ways of relating value to feeling. The difference seems natural enough: the generalizing moralist who perceives a character from outside must have a different perspective from the novelist who imagines a character's inner reality. The novelist recalls and fantasizes what it feels like to be adolescent; the moralist comments on the social significance of adolescent action and inaction.

On the other hand, in a period when Ruskin and Mill alike testified, from opposite ideological positions, to the profound differences between the social experiences of men and of women, it is surprising to discover that important male novelists who dealt with male adolescence (Dickens, Meredith, Butler) and important female novelists of female adolescence (Charlotte and Emily Brontë, Gaskell, Eliot) evoked similar kinds of private experience. And it is surprising, too, that the adolescents described by moralists and journalists seem so consistently "bad," by the official standards of the age, when fictional adolescents of both sexes, usually "good" in impulse, at any rate learn to practice and to value the kind of goodness that Victorian public utterances associate with female morality and sensibility.

This summary, however, returns us to the paradox articulated earlier: such learning involves growing up, involves necessary loss. What of adolescents who refuse to pay the price?

"No story is the same to us after a lapse of time—or rather, we who read it are no longer the same interpreters."[18]

In *The Mill on the Floss*, Eliot offered a version of her own girlhood experience. Maggie Tulliver corresponds at many points to Mary Ann Evans; the novelist looks back on her own story after a lapse of time and reinterprets it in fictional terms. No wonder the reader feels her sympathetic identification with the central character.

Three years before *The Mill on the Floss*, however, Eliot had published *Adam Bede* (1859), with its study of an adolescent girl gone wrong. Hetty Sorrel, seduced by Arthur Donnithorne, bears and murders her illegitimate child at the age of eighteen. She escapes the gallows at the last possible moment, is transported instead, and dies offstage without further exploration of her character. Her seducer, just turned twenty-one, also manifests an adolescent sensibility. He, too, disappears from the scene after Hetty's pardon, although he returns briefly, eight years later, to attest his repentance and suffering. This tale of the young counterpoints the novel's other story, of Adam Bede and Dinah Morris. Chronologically, psychically, and morally adult from the outset, these two concern themselves with the welfare of others, learn more of the world's suffering, but need mainly to learn only their feeling for one another. Maggie Tulliver in her youth discovers the meaning and power of interhuman bonds; she cannot live. Hetty Sorrel discovers nothing beyond her own suffering; she cannot live either. The transition from adolescence to adulthood once more constitutes an insoluble problem.

The narrator of *Adam Bede* does not approve of Hetty. Insistently described by analogy to appealing small animals and birds, the girl has few definitely human qualities. She cares only for herself. For several years she has functioned as a member of the Poyser household, yet she shows no feeling for the family's children or adults, no maternal instincts, no desire for fellowship. Her infatuation with Arthur only manifests her vanity—she sees in him an opportunity to rise in the world, to acquire more pretty things to set off her beauty. She has no sense of moral consequence and only a rudimentary awareness of physical consequence. Little from outside herself can penetrate her almost impregnable narcissism. She troubles herself more about her earrings than about her relationships, although she worries about the opinion of others when she faces the danger of social shame.

But she's very pretty, this girl.

I might mention all the divine charms of a bright spring day; but if you had never in your life utterly forgotten yourself in straining your eyes after the mounting lark, or in wandering through the still lanes when the fresh-opened blossoms fill them with a sacred silent beauty like that of fretted aisles, where would be the use of my descriptive catalogue? I could never make you know what I meant by a bright spring day. Hetty's was a spring-tide beauty; it was the beauty of young frisking things, round-limbed, gamboling, circumventing you by a false air of innocence,—the innocence of a young star-browed calf, for example, that, being inclined for a promenade out of bounds, leads you a severe steeple-chase over hedge and ditch, and only comes to a stand in the middle of a bog. (I, i, 119)

The ambiguity of this evocation pervades the entire account of Hetty. On the one hand, she has "divine charms," capable of making the sensitive forget themselves, possessed of mysterious power to elevate the soul by sheer beauty. She attracts Adam, to whom she means everything good; she encourages in him, by her very existence, the capacity for selfless devotion that defines his moral grandeur. On the other hand, her beauty conveys "a false air of innocence." Its falsity, as the metaphor elaborates itself, apparently derives from lack of moral signification. "Guilt" and "innocence" are equally irrelevant to a calf, following out animal inclinations until it and its pursuer alike come to a stop in a bog. One may condemn a girl for having no more moral nature than a calf—but can one properly condemn anyone for his or her nature? Animal amorality constitutes Hetty's essence. It brings its own punishment, in this narrative, but it contains no possibility for education.

And education is always Eliot's subject.

Victorian pronouncements on pedagogy display impressive faith in the force of intellectual and moral environment. Bad environments produce bad women: "Within the walls of their house of discipline girls learn to grasp after show and pomp; and, as women can rarely *acquire* these for themselves, they are taught to look at marriage as the means of making their fortune. Thus their education is but a training for somewhat in prospect; they are taught to live upon expectancy; they are to fit themselves to catch at the straw, and wait upon the wheel of fortune."[19] Hetty has learned precisely these lessons—but from what environment? Mrs. Poyser encourages no frivolity. Her strict though affectionate guidance inculcates industry, discipline, self-subordination—none of which Hetty manifests. From the point of view of the novel, grasping after show and pomp, living upon expectancy, eagerness to catch at straws appear to belong naturally to youth. Bessy Cranage, whom we first encounter as she listens to Dinah's preaching, manifests the same qualities. Dinah turns to her because her "bonny youth and evident vanity had touched her with pity"; she urges the girl to accept Christ. "You think of ear-rings and fine gowns and caps, and you never think of the Saviour who died to save your precious soul" (I, i, 139). Bessy, sobbing, wrenches the earrings from her ears; but she soon relapses. Her suggestibility makes her undergo several moral revolutions, but her essential values resemble Hetty's. Mrs. Poyser's rebukes to the other girls working in her household suggest that they, too, share the same assumptions.

None of the others, however, meets so dark a fate as Hetty's. For that fate her "spring-tide beauty" appears to bear responsibility. The narrator emphasizes this beauty with almost vindictive force, explaining Hetty's pleasure in the idea that people like to look at her, tracing how her fantasy attributes ever greater power to her own attractiveness. Youth by its nature tends toward narcissism, the narrator says, and toward dependence on fantasy. Hetty's lover resembles her in his unaware narcissism, focused on his self-perceived moral excellence rather than on his physical presence. "His own approbation was necessary to him, and it was not an approbation to be enjoyed quite gratuitously; it must be won by a fair amount of merit. He had never yet forfeited that approbation, and he had considerable reliance on his own virtues" (I, i, 180–81). Needing the approval of others as well as of himself, he takes the easy way to get it. His social position makes all easy for him; his circumstances have never imposed stringent moral demands. He lacks the self-control and the perceptiveness to avoid the self-indulgence of a liaison with Hetty, lacks the moral courage to confess to his mentor or to persist in the affair, lacks the responsibility to keep track of her welfare after he leaves her. He interests the narrator far less than Hetty does; his psychology never becomes the subject for penetrating analysis. Enough to perceive him as Hetty's counterpart in youth as well as in character.

The affair originates specifically in the participants' youth. Its simplicity derives from lack of consciousness. Like peaches or brooks, without even animal awareness, the lovers come together, wishing for nothing, knowing nothing, beyond their entwining. But lack of consciousness also creates the danger that attends this mingling.

Poor things! It was a pity they were not in that golden age of childhood when they would have stood face to face, eyeing each other with timid liking, then given each other a little butterfly kiss, and toddled off to play together. Arthur would have gone home to his silk-curtained cot, and Hetty to her home-spun pillow, and both would have slept without dreams, and tomorrow would have been a life hardly conscious of a yesterday. (I, i, 190)

Childhood unconsciousness implies no sinister possibility because its possessors lack sexual maturity. The butterfly kiss of toddlers arouses no further impulse; the kiss of adolescents awakens uncontrollable longings. Childish unconsciousness, adult sexuality: the concatenation sounds familiar. It had defined the nature of adolescence for moralists a century before George Eliot—but those moralists revealed quite different feelings about this combination of capacities and incapacities.

Hetty's beauty protects her from other people's moral demands. The narrator generalizes that all men respond to beauty as equivalent to goodness. They look at a lovely woman and conclude that she will dote on her children, that anything wrong in her marriage must be her husband's fault. People who love peaches, the narrator adds, don't remember the stone "and sometimes jar their teeth terribly against it" (I, i, 225). This return to the peach metaphor which has earlier evoked the ease of young love (I, i, 193) jars the reader, too; the comparisons of Hetty to birds and butterflies, puppies, kittens, sprites, water nymphs, flowers, and fruit take on increasingly sinister overtones. Still, men cannot find fault with her. The impossibility, for most observers, of judging the girl by standards applicable to other mortals means that she endures no external moral discipline, no need to conform to social laws that dissolve in her radiance. Even the narrator claims to feel her enchantment.

But Hetty's loveliness, the novel implies, dehumanizes her. Her ignorance belongs naturally to youth; her beauty preserves ignorance beyond the normal stage of enlightenment. Her life has taught her neither of the world's evil nor of possible self-enlargement through the experience of others. The text repeatedly refers to the narrowness of her thoughts, her mind, her feelings, her imagination, to the shallowness of her roots. She lacks all capacity for enlargement but must yet, like all Eliot's characters, bear responsibility for her actions.

The story of Adam and Dinah frames that of Hetty and Arthur; field and frame frequently intersect. At the novel's opening, we encounter Adam at work, speaking for the value of dedication to work; at the end, we see him in the context of familial devotion and harmony. Work and love, classic prerequisites of maturity. Hetty can achieve neither. Girlish "passion and vanity" make up what passes for love in her life (I,ii, 43); although her passion briefly humanizes her, allowing her to respond momentarily to Adam's devotion, it never flowers into grown-up love. Work represents to her only an imposition. She has no more capacity for or knowledge of the possibility of devotion to a task than of devotion to a man. Doomed to perpetual miseries of adolescence, she comes, under Dinah's tutoring, to some participation in Christian faith, but one can hardly believe that it goes deep. Arthur has slightly more capacity; he goes off to make his life as a soldier and appears to immerse himself in tasks at hand. He feels retrospective awareness of and remorse for the suffering he has caused, but no mature love replaces the immature one. Dinah and Adam start and end as grown-ups; Hetty and Arthur begin and finish as adolescents. No one crosses the gap between.

Altogether unambiguous in moral attitude, the novel unmistakably endorses the grown-ups and criticizes the immature. Its sympathies, however, seem rather more complex than its endorsements. If *Adam Bede* condemns Hetty for her severe moral inadequacies, it also conveys a perception of her as victim as well as villain: victim of her youth and beauty and of the excessively high value assigned these qualities by others.

The imagery of birds and small animals, fruit and flowers both conveys Hetty's lack of human responsibility and hints her helplessness. Dinah suffers no equivalent helplessness—but Dinah exists in a very different relation to the rest of the world. *Giving* and *taking* represent structural polarities for this novel, too. Dinah wants only to give; Hetty, only to take. When they encounter one another in Hetty's prison cell, "The two pale faces were looking at each other: one with a wild hard despair in it, the other full of sad, yearning love" (I,ii, 230). Hetty's despair reflects her perception that the world has given her nothing she desires. She has been given a child; she has destroyed it. Dinah's yearning love expresses her will to relate, to help, to give. Even Dinah, however, eventually has to restrict her desires: she can no longer preach, given a decision of the church's governing body. She has never acknowledged any personal gratification from her preaching, she willingly relinquishes the activity in favor of working with individuals. Her happiness depends on not admitting personal wants, although she finally confesses, fearfully, her desire for Adam. He, too, restricts his wants. He yearns for Hetty, then for Dinah, but not for power, wealth, prestige. Personal advancement comes to him, but he does not seek it. Another apparent moral of the novel: one protects oneself by limiting one's wants.

Adolescents always *want*, and they always want much they can never get. In all historical periods, representations of this time of life rest on this assumption. What Hetty and Arthur want may be judged meretricious; yet one feels the pathos of frustrated wanting. "Poor things!" the narrator says: poor things, not children nor yet adults, caught between, painfully ignorant of the laws of consequence but subject to them, accustomed to nourish themselves by the easy approval of their social worlds and unprepared for more difficult forms of relationship. They merit our disapproval, but also our pity. And the mature lovers who know how little they dare want—do not they also deserve pity? Once more in *Adam Bede*, although good adults take up all the novel's moral space, subterranean echoes speak of the high cost of growing up. No better alternative exists in the world; those who accept maturity's obligations and restrictions win applause and satisfaction, but not without the undertone of sadness.

Hetty Sorrel does not read novels. Consequently she does not know what to expect of life, and she expects wonderful things. "It was as if she had been wooed by a river-god [Arthur too has his inhuman aspects], who might any time take her to his wondrous halls below a watery heaven. There was no knowing what would come, since this strange entrancing delight had come." If she read novels, she would understand reality better. "Hetty had never read a novel; if she had ever seen one, I think the words would have been too hard for her; how then could she find a shape for her expectations?" (I,i, 198–99). George Eliot's characters often reveal only constricted expectations. Reading her novels, we discover that no river gods exist, that if one came he would prove unsatisfactory, that only the young believe in or hope for such things, that such belief, such hope, constitute their possibility and their doom.

Concern about what the young may imagine and want for themselves preoccupied many Victorian thinkers of a much lower order than George Eliot. One of the period's most popular novels, Charlotte Yonge's *The Daisy Chain*, appeared only a year before *Adam Bede*. A narrative of family life, it concentrates on the development of a group of adolescents and provides a kind of feminine counterpart of *Tom*

Brown's Schooldays, a book dominated by its central perception of life as an arena for manly struggle. The important characters of *The Daisy Chain* include young men as well as young women, but the value system derives from "feminine" rather than "masculine" Christianity. Every significant piece of action illuminates the danger of ambition, for boys and girls alike. The most talented boy in the family gives up his aspirations in order to become a missionary; the next most talented chooses to be a country doctor. The gifted girl stops studying Greek and rejects the idea of marriage for the sake of devoting herself to her father. (The mother of the family dies in an accident early in the novel, thus intensifying the burden of guilt and obligation on the surviving children.) Dwelling in detail on various manifestations of adolescence, the fiction conveys a view of this time of life as the ideal moment for discipline, particularly self-discipline. It acknowledges the impulse toward idealism in the young and suggests that only this impulse deserves gratification.

Early in *The Daisy Chain,* the mother makes explicit the theme of the entire action. " 'I dare say it is very good for us not to have our ambition gratified,' said her mother. 'There are so many troubles worse than these failures, that it only shows how happy we are that we should take them so much to heart. . . . I often think there is more fear for Norman. I dread his talent and success being snares.' "[20] The effort to discover what is "good" for them (as opposed to what they *want*) comes to control all the children. Ethel's struggle over Greek characterizes the book's mode of reflection. "When she went to bed, she tried to work out the question in her own mind, whether her eagerness for classical learning was a wrong sort of ambition, to know what other girls did not, and whether it was right to crave for more knowledge than was thought advisable for her. She only bewildered herself, and went to sleep before she had settled anything, but that she knew she must make all give way to papa first" (p. 164). Earlier, in response to Ethel's suggestion that she inherits her heedlessness from their heedless father, her sister—articulating a subtheme of the novel— points out that "it is more a woman's work than a man's to be careful" (p. 124). Both sexes, however, must avoid self-gratification at all costs.

The young enjoy themselves perhaps more in *Tom Brown,* but this world of male values also implies resolute self-suppression. "And so, wearily and little by little, but surely and steadily on the whole, was brought home to the young boy, for the first time, the meaning of his life: that it was no fool's or sluggard's paradise into which he had wandered by chance, but a battle-field ordained from of old, where there are no spectators, but the youngest must take his side, and the stakes are life and death."[21] Again: "After all, what would life be without fighting, I should like to know? From the cradle to the grave, fighting, rightly understood, is the business, the real, highest, honestest business of every son of man. Every one who is worth his salt has his enemies, who must be beaten" (p. 312). Life as struggle: such a perception of the world, in popular fiction, controls "good" adolescents, trained to consider not what they want but what they owe—to parents, schools, church, society. Adults presumably learn to want only what they should have. Ambition is focused want. Victorian moralists attempted to encourage ardent effort in the young—the kind of effort suggested by Yonge and Hughes—while discouraging ambition. "I must ask you to start with the assumption," one educational theorist wrote, "that in a true education goodness is the end aimed at, while the intellect and the physical powers come in for their share of attention,—the former because character can certainly be molded through it, the latter because we have no right to ill-treat our own bodies" (Lyttleton, p. 5). "The true end of intellectual education," Dorothea Beale explained, is "the elevation, the discipline of the moral nature."[22] This emphasis on subordination and discipline—the subordination not only of impulse but of physicality and intellectuality— implies the rejection of worldy ambition, although the social environment might encourage it. William Johnston wrote, in a work entitled *England As It Is, Political, Social, and Industrial, in the Middle of the Nineteenth Century*:

In the present state of society, education is so much more diffused [than fifty years ago], and the candidates for preferment are so much more numerous, that it is idle to delude young people with the notion that if they mind their learning they will obtain power and prosperity. Besides, we should consider that these motives are not noble enough, and that they induce young people to set up in their own minds standards of success which they are but too prone to erect for themselves, without any suggestion.[23]

But he added, "We cannot, however, disguise from ourselves that the rush for education in these days is like that of the commercialists to California—it is all for gold. To get on in life, and to make the most of life in the most rapid way, is the uppermost idea in the minds even of boys" (II, 132).

The dichotomy between Christian principle and capitalistic practice has long been manifest—particularly conspicuous among the Victorians, with their professions of piety. The dealt with the incompatibility between ideals and actuality partly, as many commentators have noted, by making women the guardians of goodness and allowing men free range in the marketplace. For the young, however, such a solution seemed inadequate: one could hardly say out loud that boys should seek power and prosperity, leaving virtue to their sisters. Johnston's apparent contempt for those who wish "to get on in life, and to make the most of life in the most rapid way" coexists with his realization of the impracticality of worldly self-advancement as a goal: the world does not provide enough room for everyone. This perception led him to the notion that desire for self-advancement represents an insufficiently noble goal in life. The vision of institutionalized nobility, of moral elevation inculcated like mathematics, reflects a fantasy of reconciliation. Properly taught, properly disciplined, perhaps the young can preserve the energy of fighters and direct that energy to social improvement; perhaps they can make life better.

But even such hearty novelists as Hughes and Yonge hinted in their fiction an awareness of goodness's psychic penalties. In an editorial for the first issue of a magazine intended for the young, Yonge wrote, "It has been said that everyone forms their character between the ages of fifteen and twenty-five, and this magazine is meant to be in some degree a help to those who are thus forming it."[24] She thus inaugurated a straightforward, unconflicted endeavor to improve by restricting the character of late adolescents. *The Daisy Chain*, on the other hand, displays conflict and hints costs.

Anthony Trollope does not come readily to mind as a novelist of adolescence. His overriding concern with how things happen in the social world, his endless fascination with the manipulations of power imply his concentration on the adults who possess, or can possess, social force. Yet reflections on adolescence recur in several of his works. They emphasize how the young relate to social actualities, at what cost they participate in the arrangements of their society, at what cost they exclude themselves. In *The Bertrams* (1859), Trollope examined ambition, in young men and young women alike; in *The Small House at Allingham* (1864), he looked into self-sacrifice. Without the ostentatious moral claims of such writers as Yonge and Hughes, with a commitment to the detail of middle-class life unlike Eliot or Dickens, with a greater air of disengagement, he conveys again the message moralists implicitly deny: that adolescents lose by growing up. They also lose by refusing to grow up.

Trollope assumed differences between the sexes which affect their relative times of maturity. Boys, in the view frequently expressed in the fiction, may postpone the time of growing up.

There are men who are old at one-and-twenty,—are quite fit for Parliament, the magistrate's bench, the care of a wife, and even for that much sterner duty, the care of a balance at the bankers; but there are others who at that age are still boys,—whose inner persons and characters have not begun to clothe themselves with the "toga virilis." I am not sure that those whose boyhoods are so protracted have the worst of it, if in this hurrying and competitive age they can be saved from being absolutely trampled in the dust before they are able to do a little trampling on their own account. Fruit that grows ripe the quickest is not the sweetest; nor when housed and garnered will it keep the longest.[25]

Girls, on the other hand, must often hasten on their maturity. "There is nothing among the wonders of womanhood more wonderful than this, that the young mind and young heart—hearts and minds young as youth can make them, and in their natures as gay,—can assume the gravity and discretion of threescore years and maintain it successfully before all comers. And this is done, not as a lesson that has been taught, but as the result of an instinct implanted from the birth" (OF, p. 163). Yet girls, the narrator speculates, are happiest in their youth, and boys achieve their greatest happiness only as grown men.

There is great doubt as to what may be the most enviable time of life with a man. I am inclined to think that it is at that period when his children have all been born but have not yet begun to go astray or to vex him with disappointment; when his own pecuniary prospects are settled, and he knows pretty well what his tether will allow him; when the appetite is still good and the digestive organs at their full power. . . . As regards men, this, I think, is the happiest time of life; but who shall answer the question as regards women? In this respect their lot is more liable to disappointment. With the choicest flowers that blow the sweetest aroma of their perfection lasts but for a moment. The hour that sees them at their fullest glory sees also the beginning of their fall. (OF, p. 528)

This sequence of didactic quotations establishes the ideological context for Trollope's fictional treatments of the young. The controlling assumptions of these utterances derive from melancholy awareness of social actuality. Competition governs the world: trample or be trampled. The youth who postpones participation may preserve qualities of private rather than of public worth: sweetness and integrity. Gaiety belongs inherently to the young; girls learn to relinquish it for the sake of survival. Women exist to be seen; their "glory" depends on their youth and defines the range of their power. The happiness of men seems equally precarious although less clearly limited. Gaiety and glory will vanish soon; the evocation of "the most enviable time of life" suggests that manhood teaches its possessor to value inadequate substitutes. The necessity, the discipline, the sorrow of maturity; the preciousness and the precariousness of youth: such associations dominate these passages. *The Bertrams* pairs at the outset two young men, a "winner" and a "loser." Arthur Wilkinson, son of a clergyman, has achieved, after strenuous effort, only a second-class degree at Oxford; his friend George Bertram, reared by a rich uncle, wins a double first. To George the world appears rich in possibility; Arthur must embrace the destiny of country clergyman. When his father dies, leaving Arthur the sole support of his mother and sisters, he takes a living with the provision that his mother shall enjoy most of its income; thus he cuts himself off from any hope of marrying. The world in effect deprives Arthur of most of his adolescence, demanding of him the responsibility, sobriety, and limited hopes of an adult. George, on the other hand, free to indulge in boundless fantasy, can take his time deciding on his own version of manhood.

Paired with these young men—not, for a long time, mated to them, or what would we do for a plot?—are two correspondingly opposed young women: Adela Gauntlet, rural, good, retiring, devoted; and Caroline Waddington, glamorous and ambitious. In due time, Adela and Arthur marry and live happily ever after, rewarded by their virtue, by abundant children, and by an unpretentious, comfortable life. Eventually Caroline and George also come together—but not until Caroline has made for herself a disastrous first match, ended by her husband's suicide.

The narrator summarizes the married life of the Bertrams: "Their house is childless, and very, very quiet, but they are not unhappy."[26] This summary may sufficiently suggest that the plot of *The Bertrams* does not follow an altogether predictable path. One might expect a simple reversal: that the "loser" turns into the winner at last. In a sense, precisely that happens: plodding Arthur achieves more solid happiness, more personal satisfaction, than does dazzling George. But the action conveys more complicated implications than such a description of it indicates.

Those implications by this time must sound familiar. The happiness Arthur achieves inheres in his goodness, his choice of a good wife, and his acceptance of a limited life; his story tells of narrowed hopes and aspirations. Conversely, George receives punishment not for his initial success but for his hope of more. The final words of the novel make the point explicit: "Reader, can you call to mind what was the plan of life which Caroline Waddington had formed in the boldness of her young heart? Can you remember the aspirations of George Bertram, as he sat upon the Mount of Olives, watching the stones of the temple over against him?" (II, 374). Aspiration belongs to adolescence; further experience chastens it. The youth who extends his adolescence, as many youths do, thus extends his happiness, which consists in the sense of potential. But potential disappears as life continues. Before the novel's end, George's talents seem as empty as his dreams. Adulthood implies not having what you want.

Not that the narrative reveals anything much wrong with George's youthful wants in themselves. He does not yearn to make money; he thinks of moneymaking as "but a disagreeable means to a desirable end." As for the end: "Two ends appeared to him to be desirable. But which of the two was the most desirable—that to him was the difficult question. To do good to others, and to have his own name in men's mouths—these were the fitting objects of a man's life" (I, 68). Unlike his worldly father, George thinks about his own capacities and how best he can use them, not about how he can get the most with the least effort. Nor are Caroline's ambitions meretricious. She has high hopes which she does not propose to allow love to interfere with; she wishes to marry a man who will make a figure in the world, and to gain vicarious satisfaction by helping her husband's achievement. She remarks to George, "It is useless for a woman to think of her future; she can do so little towards planning it, or bringing about her plans" (I, 159). But the narrative makes clear her special gifts.

We will say, then, that she was perhaps even more remarkable for her strength of mind than for her beauty of person. At present, she was a girl of twenty, and hardly knew her own power; but the time was to come when she should use it. She was possessed of a stubborn, enduring, manly will; capable of conquering much, and not to be conquered easily. She had a mind which, if rightly directed, might achieve great and good things, but of which it might be predicted that it would certainly achieve something. (I, 127)

Why, in the moral logic of the novel, must these two dramatically fail in the attainment of their ambitions? By the time George wins Caroline, she has suffered so greatly that she has lost most of the vitality and purpose that first attracted him. By the time she marries him, she no longer feels much capacity to enjoy herself. His professional aspirations have disappeared or have become irrelevant. The atmosphere of compromise suffuses his life as well as Arthur's; George, too, must learn the incompatibility of reality and dreams. As an account of adolescence yielding to adulthood, this reiterates the moralist's fearful message that adolescents must be tamed. It also clarifies the implications of that message by indicating its social concomitants. The advice to narrow oneself reflects skepticism about the existing society considerably more intense than that implied by the eighteenth-century novels that place their heroes finally in rural seclusion, away from the corruption of cities. Now no meaningful seclusion appears possible; relative isolation like Arthur's suffuses itself with consciousness of what has been relinquished to gain it. Tom Jones will probably not reflect about how much happier his life might prove had he in fact joined the army or remained in London.

Arthur may never allow himself conscious repining, but he vividly knows the alternatives to his own fate. His choice, forced upon him, does not represent willed rejection. Men like George, saddened and enlightened by their youthful experience, may work in the city without defilement, but they cannot hope to fulfill their brightest aspirations. The character who from adolescence dedicates himself wholeheartedly to such fulfillment, Henry Harcourt, ends in suicide. The aspirations, the idealism of the young can flourish only before their possessors participate in the world of adult struggle. Maturity implies sadness because it involves living in a realm with few compensations for the dreams it nullifies.

The subject of adolescence, particularly for writers of fiction, lends itself to reflection on society, indeed almost demands such reflection. The transition from adolescence to adulthood, in all cultures, involves movement from the position of social outsider, not yet admitted to the rights and privileges of the powerful, to that of social participant. Adults traditionally train the young in order to prepare them for such participation. If the fully privileged members of a society doubt the value of what they can offer the young, their advice must have a certain hollowness—or, at the very least, the melancholy of Victorian fiction. What can the grown-up world provide to compensate for what the young give up in entering it? Very little, these novelists suggest.

Moralists sound less depressed partly because they largely avoid the matter of "the world." They can advise transcendence, warning against the dangers of ambition, advocating commitment to higher things; or, like Samuel Smiles, they can enthusiastically recommend energy, striving, cheerfulness directed toward self-advancement, without ever contemplating precisely what "self-advancement" might mean. The more detailed imaginings of novelists permit no such avoidance.

Novelists of any period might promulgate the message implicit in *The Bertrams*, that worldly ambition offers no guarantee of happiness; in any era, we would expect a fictional character like Pip to learn the inconsequence of his great expectations, and would anticipate Hetty's reaping the penalties of her indiscretion. The tendency of Victorian novelists to suggest also the futility of extreme virtue has more troubling implications. Maggie's fate, some critics have thought, reveals George Eliot's failure of imagination; it does not derive from a necessity of character or plot. It may, however, derive from a necessity of cultural imagination. In the eighteenth century, Clarissa had to die, given her sexual impurity, however inadvertent. But her death partakes of triumph, and the slow process of her dying enables her to assert her moral ascendancy, acknowledged by all about her. Fielding's grown-up Amelia suffers in Griselda-like fashion, but wins the reward of her nobility—worldly reward, and psychological as well. Maggie finds no reward. Neither does Trollope's Lily Dale, a figure allowing the novelist to study a type of orthodox female nobility. The moral weight of *The Small House at Allingham* lies on her side; the fiction allows no question about her essential superiority to the worldly suitor who wins her love and breaks her heart. But her lifelong commitment to futile love and fidelity does not win the admiration of those about her; it does no good to her or to anyone else; it guarantees the continued unhappiness of her more worthy lover as well as of her mother and her uncle. If it generates a kind of happiness for Lily herself, we are made to feel the perversity of such satisfaction. Lily's commitment to love without return derives from her adolescent idealism, solidified into a rigid mold for her future life. Her fate, like that of John Eames, her good and devoted admirer, has a significant connection to her psychological age.

In this novel as in *The Bertrams*, Trollope reflects explicitly on certain concomitants of adolescence. In several works of fiction, he repeats his observation that women mature more rapidly than men. The conflict between the generations, as Trollope presents it, derives specifically from social function; *The Small House at Allingham* indicates that social function can be a complicated matter. John Eames and Adolphus Crosbie alike work as clerks. The narrator stresses this correspondence of roles—and stresses also the absolute difference of the two men's stances toward the world. The role of clerk has utterly opposed meanings to its two practitioners. Crosbie has dedicated himself long since to his own advancement; his immediate post provides preliminary means to a glorious end. Eames has no clear commitment of any kind, except his largely unarticulated love for Lily. He belongs to the class that Trollope labels "hobbledehoy":

Such young men are often awkward, ungainly, and not yet formed in their gait; they straggle with their limbs, and are shy; words do not come to them with ease, when words are required, among any but their accustomed associates. Social meetings are periods of penance to them, and any appearance in public will unnerve them. They go about much alone, and blush when women speak to them. In truth, they are not as yet men, whatever the number may be of their years; and, as they are no longer boys, the world has found for them the ungraceful name of hobbledehoy.[27]

After this precise summary of the adolescent male condition, the narrator makes explicit his own preference for slow maturing and elaborates an analogy between the adolescent and the fruit that ripens naturally, as opposed to the forced product exemplified by such men as Adolphus Crosbie. Trollope then adds an emphatic declaration of the hobbledehoy's imaginative vigor. Despite his uneasiness with real woman, the hobbledehoy triumphs among the beauties of his imagination, conquering "through the force of his wit and the sweetness of his voice," winning the rewards of Don Juan without the great lover's heartlessness (*SHA*, I, 36). He spends much of his time in solitude, indulging his fantasies, practising his oratory, and thus preparing himself for the future. "Thus he feeds an imagination for which those who know him give him but scanty credit, and unconsciously prepares himself for that latter ripening, if only the ungenial shade will some day cease to interpose itself" (I, 37).

This emphasis on the youthful imagination sounds familiar from the eighteenth century; but in the Victorian image of youth, the power of fancy directs its possessor toward goodness, not toward unruliness. John's imagination focuses on conquest without aggression. In actual life, he behaves well. In a mild way he sows his wild oats, with no ill consequences for anyone. He displays his courage and idealism by physically attacking Lily's betrayer—without doing any lasting damage. He saves the life of an agricultural nobleman and sustains with dignity and grace the resulting patronage. Eventually he gets promoted; a good career opens up before him; the narrator declares him to have matured. Nonetheless, he cannot win Lily. His dreams have concentrated on her without preparing him for anything in the real world; they prepare him only for the further dreams with which he will presumably compensate throughout his adult life for the lack of erotic satisfaction its reality supplies. Imagination helps to make him "good," but goodness guarantees no rewards.

Lily, John's female counterpart, exemplifies another version of the adolescent imagination. The narrator goes out of his way to suggest that her betrothal signals her growing up, as it indicated commitment to the appearances of maturity for Augusta in *Doctor Thorne*.

And now Lily Dale was engaged to be married, and the days of her playfulness were over. It sounds sad, this sentence against her, but I fear that it must be regarded as true. And when I think that it is true,—when I see that the sportiveness and kitten-like gambols of girlhood should be over, and generally are over, when a girl has given her troth, it becomes a matter of regret to me that the feminine world should be in such a hurry after matrimony. (I, 58)

The same speaker, of course, commented that the hobbledehoy's prolonged ripening produced sweeter fruit than the forced maturing of more sophisticated types: he declares explicitly his preference for youth prolonged, though not the grounds for such preference that emerge in the course of the novel. Loss of playfulness may be sad enough in itself; even sadder are the penalties of life in the world.

Committed to his imagination, incompetent to perform the manipulations required for social success, John Eames fails to achieve his love. Lily suffers more total failure: her entanglement in the creations of her fancy prevents her from choosing the proper love in the first place, from understanding the man she has committed herself to, from engaging further in the life of the world once he has failed her. She may desist from kittenlike gambols, but she never gets beyond her emotional adolescence in *The Small House at Allingham*. Isolated in her dream of utter devotion, she shows not the slightest likelihood of ever violating that isolation. To live the life of imagination implies in her no violation of social decorum: on the contrary. She behaves throughout with utter propriety and nobility—but she cuts herself off from every chance of a full life.

Like John's central fantasy, Lily's involves conquest. The aggressive component of her vision emerges distinctly when she believes her dream realized. "I don't think that a man ever has the same positive and complete satisfaction in knowing that he is loved, which a girl feels. You are my bird that I have shot with my own gun; and the assurance of my success is sufficient for my happiness" (I, 138). A few pages later, the narrator underlines the implications of this striking metaphor: "I will not deny that she had some feeling of triumphant satisfaction in the knowledge that she was envied. . . . As she herself had said, he was her bird, the spoil of her own gun, the product of such capacity as she had in her, on which she was to live, and, if possible, to thrive during the remainder of her life" (I, 145). Being loved rather than loving comprises the girl's triumph; she says so herself. She likes poetry and moonlight, she realizes, "because I longed to be loved." When her lover adds, "And to love," she readily agrees, but immediately adds that her true delight consists in the recipient's role, which she equates with having shot the bird (I, 103). One feels a certain sympathy with Crosbie when he registers in himself a "calf-like feeling": "He did not like to be presented, even to the world of Allingham, as a victim caught for the sacrifice, and bound with ribbon for the altar" (I, 99). Bird or calf, the destined victim escapes—leaving the victor to declare to herself the "duty" of continuing to love. Crosbie leaves her for a richer woman. "Morning and night she prayed for him, and daily, almost hour by hour, she assured herself that it was still her duty to love him. It was hard, this duty of loving, without any power of expressing such love. But still she would do her duty" (II, 3).

The narrator does not explicitly comment on the sources of this perverse sense of duty, but his analysis of John Eames's psychology seems apropos. We see in Lily the same retreat from ordinary kinds of relationship, the same reliance on self-constructed, self-sustained fantasy, the same substitution of imagination for actuality. Everyone feels irritated with her, no one can do anything about her bizarre commitment. Unable to sustain the oddly aggressive satisfaction of being loved, she preserves another form of aggression—one, incidentally, related to her mother's determined "nobility"—in her insistence on loving without return or immediate purpose. If it does no one else any good, it at least preserves her adolescent grandiosity, her special sense of self.

At the novel's end, John Eames embarks upon his manhood, with no promise of gratification in it. The final words of the narrative, however, concern Adolphus Crosbie, that "adult," worldly, knowing young man, whose life has become misery because of his practical, loveless, bitter marriage. Two mature lovers appear to have found happiness in the subplot, but their sensible course fails to interest us much or, apparently, to occupy the narrator deeply. Too reasonable for misery or ecstasy, Bell Dale and Dr. Crofts will have a contented life, not a romantic one. Lily's intensities preclude mere contentment. Her irritating wrong-headedness declares her superiority to the resignation that marks most adult lives. The novel does not endorse her course, but it accords her significance for following it.

The fates of the two who prolong their adolescences, Lily Dale and John Eames, exemplify characteristic Victorian novelistic outcomes. Such resolutions proclaim the emotional grandeur and the worldly inadequacy of youth; they imply for adults no superior wisdom except that of compromise. The degree to which grown-up storytellers identify with their juniors, instead of preserving the distance necessary for the moralist's praise or blame, marks an apparent decline of social confidence. Although Trollope's narrators, like Dickens's and Eliot's, often adopt a superior tone to comment on some specific idiosyncrasy of the young, on the whole their voices suggest weariness and melancholy over worldly actuality, rather than confidence in the value of what adults know and do that adolescents cannot. Inasmuch as the novelists perceive, or would like to perceive, their youthful characters as versions of themselves, they identify with the role of outsider. Outsiders, as imagined in these fictions, need not possess moral superiority to those accepted as full members of society. They are not nineteenth-century versions of Holden Caulfield, conveying rage at social corruption. Incontestably, however, they demonstrate emotional superiority to their elders. Even Hetty Sorrel, for all her inadequacies, shows herself richer in energy than those older and wiser than she. Narrow in sympathy, benighted in perception, wrong in judgment, she yet possesses the beautiful natural vitality of butterfly or bird. Such vitality hardly deserves praise, since it belongs automatically to a specific time of life. But it calls forth nostalgia and longing; so do the ridiculous idealism of Lily Dale, the self-dramatizing fantasy of George Bertram.

The adolescent characters of eighteenth-century fiction often imply, through their imagined courses of action, substantial social criticism. Maggie Tulliver also in her being expresses such criticism; Hetty Sorrel's plight and Lily Dale's comment on the inequity of existing social arrangements. But on the whole, late nineteenth-century fictional adolescents convey mainly sadness. Their creators apparently accept as necessities civilization's discontents; they understand adolescence as a brief period of evasion.

When considered in comparison with the novels of Scott and Austen, or of the eighteenth century, Victorian fiction suggests a comprehensible progression in attitudes toward adolescence. The cautiousness of writers who protected their heroes from corruption by consigning them to a country estate gives way to the ambivalence of early nineteenth-century novelists who assess youthful protagonists against the moral flaccidity of some adults, the moral realism of others. To grow up involves a large gamble: the world contains few adults of continuing integrity. Marriage and business alike threaten the energy and imagination for which adolescence leaves room; the straitening of maturity constricts many out of real existence. For Dickens and Eliot and Trollope, ambivalence has yielded to pessimism. The transition from adolescence to maturity now seems virtually impossible; no one grows up with impunity. On the other hand, no viable alternative presents itself. Dickens's lovable eccentrics can hardly supply models for youth. Lily Dale dramatizes her girlhood idealism into later years, but the perversity of such a solution manifests itself to everyone. Adam Bede offers much to admire, but he has relinquished, if he ever had it, the passionate intensity of the young.

Victorian didactic writers, for all their harshness, help to explain the perception of loss that dominates the novelists. Their eighteenth-century precursors had stressed the need to control and guide the young, and the need for the young to accept control and guidance in order to develop safely to the next stage of life. The Victorians display considerable anxiety over the qualities that might provide impetus for development. When they scold girls for frivolity or, alternately, for impulses toward "self-dependence"; when they castigate boys for excessive ambition or competitiveness, they in effect criticize the values of their own adult society. What's wrong with young people is that they resemble older ones. To lose the innocence of childhood implies automatic moral regression, in the apparent view of most commentators. Experience rarely means something good. Although a gambit like Kingsley's evocation of wonderful British mothers, wives, and aunts intimates that grown-ups may be admirable, the bulk of didactic writing implies without acknowledging that the fall from infantile innocence, like the expulsion from Eden, should provoke mourning. If only boys would not worry about winning, if only girls would avoid asserting themselves, as sexual objects or as thinking entities! Although nominally the moralists urge everyone toward maturity, their fear of youthful aggression makes them overvalue the relative passivity of childhood.

Novelists rarely esteem passivity. (The passive heroes of the early nineteenth century are ambiguously valued by their creators.) Identifying with the young, Victorian writers of fiction dramatize emotional consequences of adolescents' perception that the parental generation

225

does not really want them to grow up—not if growing up involves passionate aggression or passionate love or any other troubling variety of passion. Maggie Tulliver and Pip and John Eames perceive an adult world with no room for them unless they shrink.

The lessening faith in the possibilities of adult life helps to account for the different shape of eighteenth- and nineteenth-century novelistic plots centered on the young. Lily Dale's stubbornness differs dramatically from Clarissa's. Clarissa's inevitable progress toward death depends not only on her hubris but on her resolute adherence to Christian values long assumed to be the foundation of responsible adult life. Even as she dramatizes her uniqueness, she declares her participation in an ancient community. Lily, on the other hand, although she can call on a hallowed tradition of romantic love to sanction her conduct, in her intransigence speaks essentially for herself and her time of life, not for the real or professed standards of her community. In fact, she ironically repudiates the community's standards by exaggerating them: her pointless devotion mocks the familiar ideal of woman as heroic self-sacrificer. The endings of *Great Expectations*, *The Mill on the Floss*, *The Bertrams*, would have been unimaginable a century earlier. With the perceived possibilities of life, those of fiction change.

Yet the change in attitude amounts to hardly more than a gradual shift of emphasis. Tension between generations, adult fear of youthful sexuality and aggression, anxiety about the loss of passional energy in moving from youth to maturity—these issues recur from *Pamela* to *The Bertrams*: and after. As the nineteenth century drew toward a close, however, England had partly lost the context of social and moral assumptions that once contained and controlled such tension, fear, and anxiety. Valuing innocence over experience, yet understanding the distortions implicit in efforts to preserve innocence, thinkers about youth had reached a logical impasse.

In all the fiction, all the didactic commentary thus far considered, no one has yet articulated a clear, inclusive concept of adolescence. John Locke's description of male youth comes close, but like other educators and moralists of the eighteenth and nineteenth centuries, he assumes that young people violating adult standards deviate from a norm, not that they define one. Trollope's definition of the "hobbledehoy" amounts to an evocation of adolescence; but it refers, we are told, only to a small minority, a special subclass within the category of young men. Lacking a concept, observers would necessarily perceive adolescent behavior as anomalous, would necessarily urge the young to act grown-up or to remain children. When, just after the turn of the twentieth century, the American psychologist G. Stanley Hall resurrected the notion of adolescence and subjected it to exhaustive analysis, he resolved the nineteenth-century impasse and established a direction for the next several decades.

9

Heroes: The Early Twentieth Century

Adolescents have always existed, but the myth of adolescence has thrived most richly since G. Stanley Hall invented it. In 1904, Hall—president of Clark University and professor of psychology and pedagogy—published his massive two-volume work entitled *Adolescence: Its Psychology and Its Relations to Physiology, Anthropology, Sociology, Sex, Crime, Religion, and Education.* Even this exhaustive title hardly suggests the scope of the book's concerns, which include also morality and literature. Hall takes all learning to be his province and relates all to the great subject of adolescence. His work proved to be enormously influential, directly and indirectly. An American book, it quickly acquired an international audience. It inaugurated a period, still continuing, in which the adolescent assumed a place of pivotal importance in sociological, psychological, and literary thought and in the popular imagination as well.

Midway through the first volume, in a chapter called "Diseases of Body and Mind," Hall lists a few psychic traits of puberty, with a promise to mention more later. They include "inner absorption and reverie,"[1] a state analogous to that of the indulger in drugs and intoxicants ("This preliminary expatiation of the soul over a vast realm, actual and possible, of life and mind, somewhere within which it will lay down the limits of its personality, is good for the strong and healthful" [I, 312]); an efflorescence of imagination; a tendency to self-criticism and oversensitive conscience ("The slightest hint or frown of disapproval by others causes depression" [I, 315]); "overassertion of individuality" ("His ego must be magnified and all in the new envi-

228

ronment subordinated to it" [I, 315]); heavy reliance on imitation; a dramatic stance toward life; indulgence in "folly"; "a new speech consciousness," producing either a more lavish flow of language or intensified concealment and reticence (I, 318); "the dominance of sentiment over thought" (I, 318). These characteristics of the teen-age psyche belong, in Hall's expressed view, to the realm of pathology; he perceives in them seeds of psychic distress. Yet even these definitions of weakness, often offered in a tone of benevolent condescension, betray also the writer's intense, rather wistful, admiration for the beings he so exhaustively describes.

To read Hall's *Adolescence* for tone as well as content, seeking evidence of the feelings that underlie its ideas, reveals emotional patterns comparable to those apparent in much twentieth-century fiction. The author's alternations between expressed superiority and inferiority to the youngsters he purports to analyze recapitulate the extremes of utterances on adolescence from the eighteenth century to the present. In his demonstrated capacity to classify, summarize, understand, the psychologist controls his subject. Inasmuch as he speaks with the voice of an intellectual, in other words, he conveys benign authority over those incapable, by virtue of youth and inexperience, of understanding the phenomenology of their life. But the voice of the feeler contradicts that of the thinker. Adolescents have all the emotional advantage. One may declare "the dominance of sentiment over thought" a weakness and demonstrate its dangerous consequences, but by the turn of the twentieth century, eighteenth-century certainties no longer survive. The dominance of passion signaled clear and present danger in an earlier period; one might acknowledge passion's fruitful force, but always feel the need for its rational control. Hall pays lip service to the same necessity.

One need accept in detail none of the current theories of the nature of genius to understand that it largely consists of keeping alive and duly domesticating by culture the exuberant psychic faculties, of which this is the nascent period, and that just as domestic animals and plants easily revert to wildness, so our faculties if not duly recomposed and harmonized to the new and higher life of altruism must retrograde. (I, 309)

The spirit of the Victorian breathes through the glib reference to the higher life, the valuation of composure and harmony, the insistence on an order of subordination. But the association between the exuberant psychic faculties of youth and the essence of genius marks a new stress on the importance of adolescent energies. The young person must learn to domesticate as well as to sustain these energies, but to exalt their significance implies that the commentator will condone failures of domestication if they imply preservation of vitality.

Youthful dements wrestle with great problems and ideas; their delusions are of royalty, celestial and infernal beings, telepathy, hypnotism, spiritism, great inventions, the highest themes of politics and religion, but their powers are inadequate and they grow mentally dizzy, confused and incoherent. . . .
In many of the rich clinical details which Kraepelin has so admirably gathered, it is easy to see the germs of genius of many kinds, for this is the crude ore of which the great productions of art, invention, heroism, and moral and religious reform would be made if the processes of elaboration and the supreme Greek virtue of temperance or avoidance of excess were adequate. The soil is always rich to profusion, insemination abundant, choice exotics and all the flora of culture strike root, but weeds are rank and choke them, and decay may be the direct resultant of superfetation. (I, 310–11)

Each sentence provides a double view of adolescent imbalance: positive potential, inadequate control. In every statement, however, the positive conveys more conviction than its qualification. Compared with the grandeur of youthful imaginings and conceptions—and of youthful willingness to wrestle with them—inadequate powers hardly matter. The potential of great accomplishment captures the imagination far more than does the warning about the need for "adequate" temperance. And the powerful image of superfetation (fertilization of an ovum in the uterus of an already pregnant woman), suggesting extraordinary generativity and fecundity, in its positive implications far outweighs the negative burden of the weeds and decay that "may" result. Who would not risk a few weeds for richness, insemination, exotica, and cultivated flowers? As this example suggests, even Hall's accounts of youthful pathology acknowledge the possibilities of this period of development, possibilities stronger within the youthful mind than in the consciousness of observers, but real for the latter, too. "The youth's powers are now tested, and who knows but he may become the greatest among men? The whole soul is now protensive, and there is no life but in the realm of the possible, for the real is not yet" (I, 316). The list of "psychic traits" delineates specific loci of potentiality. In willingness to risk folly, in burgeoning imagination, in sensitivity to speech, in dramatic experimentation, and the rest lie the possible sources of the young person's ultimate power. Because "the real is not yet" for the young (in Hall's point of view; others might argue that the young inevitably collide with reality), not only can they imagine everything for themselves, the observer can also partake in the nebulous glories of their possibility.

Hall's specific reasons for admiring youth resemble those deducible from the adolescent heroes in fiction of the past three centuries. The young possess passion, imagination, and vitality. So their elders have long seen them. No one before Hall, however, had devoted such meticulous attention to locating the manifestations of these characteristics. In a chapter called "Feelings and Psychic Evolution," for example, he comments on the "instability and fluctuation" apparent in youthful feeling (II, 75). The next fourteen pages list traits that display themselves alternatively: energetic action versus torpor, elation versus depression, self-affirmation versus self-abasement, selfishness and altruism, good and bad conduct, and so on, all described with concrete detail and rhetorical elaboration. Each pair of opposites, each side of each opposition, demonstrates adolescent wonderfulness.

To have a good time is felt to be an inalienable right. The joys of life are never felt with so keen a relish; youth lives for pleasure, whether of an epicurean or an esthetic type. It must and ought to enjoy life without alloy. Every day seems to bring passionate love of just being alive, and the genius for extracting pleasure and gratification from everything is never so great. But this, too, reacts into pain and disphoria, as surely as the thesis of the Hegelian logic passes over to its antithesis. Young people weep and sigh, they know not why; depressive are almost as characteristic as expansive states of consciousness. (II, 77)

The word "genius," frequently recurring, reveals Hall's bias. The young person's capacity for gaining pleasure constitutes not merely a "gift," it displays genius: giftedness beyond common possibility, awesome specialness. The young feel their "inalienable right" to a good time, and the writer shares their feeling: youth "ought to enjoy life without alloy." The capacity for pain also merits admiration; it, too, testifies the intensity of adolescent consciousness.

Hall justifies his high valuation of intensity partly by examining its public manifestations in chapters on "Adolescent Love" (more poignant, more devoted, more powerful than grown-up love), "The Adolescent Psychology of Conversion" (youthful sensitivity to religious feeling may promise a vitalization of Christianity), and "Social Instincts and Institutions" (the altruism of the young has important social possibilities). More fully and explicitly than any of his predecessors—and this fact defines one aspect of his importance—Hall relates his interest in adolescence to his concern with the state of his society. Adolescents, he believes, embody the powers that civilized adults lack; adolescents foretell the future possibilities of the race. The first view has greater force; it lurks just beneath the surface even when not openly stated. It finds vivid expression in the context of the discussion of feelings.

In our day and civilization, the hot life of feeling is remote and decadent. Culture represses, and intellect saps the root.... The life of feeling has its prime in youth, and we are prematurely old and too often senile in heart.... Our sensibilities are refined, but our perspective is narrow, our experiences serene and regular, we are protected, our very philosophy as well as our religion suppresses and looks with some contempt even upon enthusiasm in matters of the cold reason. We have experienced no soul-quaking reconstruction of our souls like Paul, Augustine, or Luther, we are anemic and more prone to deny than to believe, to speculate than to do, and we turn to novels and the theater for catharsis of our emotions.... What we have felt is second-hand, bookish, shopworn, and the heart is parched and bankrupt. (II, 59)

The first-person pronoun identifies grown-ups, the "prematurely old," cut off from the emotional energy of youth, for which "the hot life of feeling" can take control. The self-abasement of this summary, the anger and despair, strike a startling note. In his contempt for the second-hand and bookish, his assertion that culture represses and civilization saps, the writer undermines his own attempts at objectivity, rationality, inclusiveness. Speculation, in this summary, becomes inferior to doing, the life of the mind inferior to that of the emotions, the old inferior to the young. Looking at adolescents, we see what we have lost; we envy and admire. Hall draws his readers into that "we," his condemnation of emotional sterility including the entire adult civilized world. He abandons adult prerogatives to embrace the traditional adolescent position of outsider. He can admire and envy, he can berate himself and his kind, but he cannot participate: he feels excluded, as in earlier centuries the young were excluded, from the real action. He sees the young as virtually a unique species, appropriate subjects for wonder and awe.

The attitude which perceives adolescents as intimately involved with the fates of their elders offers greater hope. The crucial importance of adolescence, in this view, involves its promise for mankind. "It is the most critical stage of life, because failure to mount almost always means retrogression, degeneracy, or fall. One may be in all respects better or worse, but can never be the same. The old level is left forever. Perhaps the myth of Adam and Eden describes this epoch. The consciousness of childhood is molted, and a new, larger, better consciousness must be developed." (II, 72). The association to Eden is curious. Does Hall wish to suggest that adolescents must reject knowledge of good and evil in order to avoid the fall, that they must endeavor to preserve their innocence? How might Adam have "mounted"? Or does the writer allude to the paradox of the fortunate fall, the notion that the expulsion from Eden inaugurated human accomplishment and growth? At any rate, he here suggests a view that he soon articulates more clearly: that the lives of adolescents are "an open sesame to the history of the race" (II, 100). In the imagination of the young exists the possibility for universal development.

Youth seeks to be, know, get, feel all that is highest, greatest, and best in man's estate, circumnutating in widening sweeps before it finds the right object upon which to climb . . . It is the glorious dawn of imagination, which supplements individual limitations and expands the soul toward the dimensions of the race. (II, 302)

Poetry's "very highest function" would be to describe the "new inner dawn" which marks adolescence (II, 302); the literature of adolescence has vast importance for adults. "To rightly draw the lessons of this age not only saves us from waste ineffable of this rich but crude area of experience, but makes maturity saner and more complete" (I, 589). Hall's ever more extravagant assertions of adolescence's immense social importance culminate in his claim that understanding of youth provides the key to progress:

Youth, when properly understood, will seem to be not only the revealer of the past but of the future, for it is dimly prophetic of that best part of history which is not yet written because it has not yet transpired, of the best literature the only criterion of which is that it helps to an ever more complete maturity, and of better social organizations, which, like everything else, are those that best serve youth. The belief that progressive ephebic needs will be met is the chief resource against pessimism in the modern world, for there is no better standard of the true worth of every human institution. (II, 448)

The pedagogic relation usually implies control of the young by the old, who try more or less conscientiously to inculcate beliefs and knowledge. Hall's concern with educational practice dominates large sections of his book. But the quotations in my last paragraph suggest his problem as an educator. If youth holds the secret of progress, if maturity must have the lessons of youth in order to achieve sanity, if the best literature (which "helps to an ever more complete maturity") must wait upon the revelations of youth—if one believes all this, the traditional pedagogic relation reverses itself. Youth can teach maturity; has maturity anything to teach youth? "Our problem as teachers is how to conserve all the freshness of life now nearing its culminating point, and not how the sad wisdom of years can be effected in the earliest twenties" (II, 538). The teacher must seek ways of preserving youth's vitality; of revealing to the young the importance of knowledge, not inflicting knowledge upon them; of infusing the wisdom taught in schools with that "passion for the ideal" (II, 548) which marks its intended recipients. The thinker's goal is to sustain youth in his charges for as long as possible. Genius itself, we finally learn, amounts to prolonged adolescence:

Gifted people seem to conserve their youth and to be all the more children, and perhaps especially all the more intensely adolescents, because of their gifts, and it is certainly one of the marks of genius that the plasticity and spontaneity of adolescence persists into maturity. Sometimes even its passions, reveries, and hoydenish freaks continue. (I, 547)

Christianity's supremacy as a religion derives from its emphasis on the spiritual stage of youth, "glorifying adolescence and glorified by it, and calculated to retain and conserve youth before the decline of the highest powers of the soul in maturity and age" (II, 361). Women, whom Hall idealizes (his treatment of women deserves special attention to itself), manifest endless adolescence:

woman at her best never outgrows adolescence as man does, but lingers in, magnifies and glorifies this culminating stage of life with its all-sided interests, its convertibility of emotions, its enthusiasm, and zest for all that is good, beautiful, true, and heroic. This constitutes her freshness and charm, even in age, and makes her by nature more humanistic than man, more sympathetic and appreciative. (II, 624)

What one would glorify, one labels adolescent—although such a label also guarantees the superior authority of the labeler.

Rarely does Hall's language sound like a scientist. He writes more often as celebrant. To define adolescence clearly as a special life stage, it seems, is to privilege it. Youth, understood as youth, cannot be held to the responsibilities of adulthood or to the restrictions of childhood; Hall makes no attempt to locate responsibilities or restrictions appropriate to youth's special state. Concentrating on the psychology of adolescence, he emphasizes conflicts and possibilities. His moralizing tone rebukes the old more often than the young, though he inveighs against the sin of masturbation and other forms of indulgence for youth. The protectiveness of the eighteenth-century moralist merges with the existential insecurities of twentieth-century man to create a large space for a group that previously had no "official" space at all.

It is a curious phenomenon, Hall's book: almost fourteen hundred pages of biological, anthropological, sociological, psychological, theological, and literary data, purporting to offer an exhaustive examination of adolescence as a phenomenon, and gradually converting it into a standard of value. Such a resolution may derive from the writer's despair with existent culture and society, but this hypothesis makes it no less curious. How strange to confront adult emotional and social malaise by offering as salvation the powers of a group for whom "there is no life but in the realm of the possible, for the real is not yet"! Hall has all the capacities of an eminent practitioner of his profession in the early 1900s. He assembles an enormous mass of accurate and plausible objective material. We can hardly fail to recognize the young people he describes; our eighteenth-century ancestors would recognize them, too. They would not, however, have agreed that the meeting of "ephebic needs" is the best "standard of the true worth of every human institution." Youth must meet the standards of age, past generations believed—not without acknowledging the losses implicit in such conformity. Hall, on the other hand, yearns that age might hold onto youth's values, that the real might merge with the possible. He wishes, as we all wish, to have everything; and he codifies that wish into hopeful prescriptions for the preservation of adolescence.

I don't mean to sound patronizing, or not *only* patronizing. One may condescend to Hall for his extraordinary anxiety about masturbation, or for his serene assertions that the ideal woman actively enjoys her menstrual flow and feels sad each time it ends, but one cannot simply condescend to him for his glorification of adolescence. In his effort to imagine ways of incorporating the values of the young into the experience of the old, he displays a revolutionary spirit of intellectual experimentation. To say that emotion suffuses and directs his intellectual endeavors amounts to valuing him by his own terms. His open acknowledgment of the emotional response generated in adults by adolescence—rage and despair over the impoverishment of their own lives, envy at the vitality and intensity of the young, longing to retain what proves so evanescent in individual history—represents something new in intellectual and social history: something new, lasting, and important. We still live with its consequences.

After the turn of the twentieth century, adolescent protagonists in fiction assume a new aspect: more aggressive, more complicated in feeling, more *significant*. Their nineteenth-century predecessors, often orphans, conduct conflicts with their elders in discreet fashion. If Maggie Tulliver disagrees intensely with her mother, she never assumes her right to open defiance for the sake of self-gratification. Her principles may lead her in a different direction, she will steadfastly follow them, but she will challenge her mother only from necessity. Even Molly Gibson, of *Wives and Daughters,* with a meretricious stepmother as focus for antagonism, avoids open conflict as much as she can. In the nineteenth century, male and female characters alike often learn through experience the rightness of the elders with whom they initially disagree; if they continue to perceive wrongness, that wrongness (of Mrs. Reed in *Jane Eyre,* for example) assumes such flagrant forms that no reader of the time could dispute their judgment. Adolescents in these novels face the task of growing up, which means, almost always, conforming. A narrator might convey the melancholy of conformity, a novelistic action might suggest means of evading it, but in the last century no one imagined the possibility of preserving adolescent values unchanged into adulthood.

The feeling Stanley Hall manifested in his study of adolescence belongs to his period in history. In the early twentieth century, comparable feelings reveal themselves also in fiction—not because novelists knew directly of Hall's work, but because society and social assumption had changed. A genius, Hall maintained, manages to preserve much of the feeling of his or her adolescence. Perhaps the proposition could be reversed: might one assume that to preserve the feelings of adolescence implies genius? Novelists began to celebrate characters who refused to conform, and novels explored the psychology of such refusals.

The new space opened up by Hall's investigation, the new sense of entitlement associated with the young, implied new heroic possibilities. No longer would novels of adolescence automatically fall into the pattern of novels of education. Tom Jones needs to learn prudence in order to come into his inheritance; Stephen Dedalus would destroy his identity by learning anything of the sort. Adolescents, in twentieth-century mythology, are trailblazers; the trails they mark may prove too perilous for ordinary, grown-up mortals, but everyone can admire their progress.

Even writers conservative in technique and assumption, by comparison with the great experimenters of the early twentieth century, show themselves fascinated in new ways by the young as subjects. Arnold Bennett, for instance, in two novels published before the First World War approached the problem of youthful female insubordination. First he drew back from it, then he followed it to a logical conclusion. *Hilda Lessways* (1911) imagines the life of a young woman whose inner life leads her to vague new aspirations and defiances. Her hopes find no fulfillment in the course of the novel, but her character demands admiration. Five years later, in *The Lion's Share*, Bennett faced his subject more squarely. Again he settled for a somewhat evasive ending, but before reaching it, he created an up-to-date adolescent heroine.

Hilda Lessways has a widowed mother of impeccable goodness whom she finds intolerably irritating. On the second page of Bennett's novel, the mother asks where she's going as she mounts the stairs. Hilda replies, "Upstairs." Hardly the stuff of crisis, one might think, but twenty-year-old Hilda feels it as such.

"If I stayed down, she wouldn't like it," Hilda complained fiercely within herself, "and if I keep away she doesn't like that either! That's mother all over!"

She went to her bedroom. And into the soft, controlled shutting of the door she put more exasperated vehemence than would have sufficed to bang it off its hinges.[2]

The material of drama, in *Hilda Lessways*, inheres in just such episodes. The objective significance of events bears an inverse ratio to their internal importance. Hilda leads a restricted life and feels intensely about it at every moment. As her life becomes more compelling—the plot gradually accumulates its dramatic happenings—her responses seem less violent: it is as though she requires a stable quotient of emotion.

Hilda's central problem, at the beginning, is her age.

She was a woman, but she could not realize that she was a woman. . . . She was in trouble; the trouble grew daily more and more tragic; and the trouble was that she wanted she knew not what. If her mother had said to her squarely, "Tell me what it is will make you a bit more contented, and you shall have it even if it kills me!" Hilda could only have answered with the fervour of despair, "I don't know! I don't know!" (P. 5)

Not knowing what she wants, she cannot feel herself adult. "Soon, soon, she would be 'over twenty-one'! And she was not yet born! That was it! She was not yet born! If the passionate strength of desire could have done the miracle time would have stood still in the heavens while Hilda sought the way of life" (p. 9).

The girl's confusion about identity and possibility dominates her through most of the novel, although she acts often with remarkable force and decisiveness, differing from her contemporaries in her capacity for effective and often unconventional action. The mother whom she makes into an antagonist in fact offers little opposition. Hilda gets herself a job, in the office of a new newspaper; she stays at the office late at night in the company of men and glories in her own daring. When her mother goes to London for a few days, leaving her behind, Hilda enjoys her solitude and independence. Because of her inadequately understood inner needs, she fails to respond immediately to a telegram informing her of her mother's illness. By the time she reaches London, her mother has died.

In a nineteenth-century novel, such an event would generate sufficient guilt to fuel the rest of the action. Hilda indeed feels guilty but also relieved, although she never openly acknowledges the latter fact. Her guilt fails to paralyze her; she proceeds toward constructing an independent and interesting life. Unlike a nineteenth-century heroine, she does not marry the man who truly attracts her; she marries, without external compulsion, the man with whom she has worked. He, it turns out, has another wife. Without undue distress, Hilda leaves him, returning to solidify her relation with the man she really likes better. At the novel's end, however, she has discovered her pregnancy: she cannot marry the man she loves; she does not know how she will deal with the coming child; the action concludes with her life in disarray, its psychic issues unresolved. The last sentence reads, "And the invincible vague hope of youth, and the irrepressible consciousness of power, were almost ready to flame up afresh, contrary to all reason, and irradiate her starless soul" (p. 533).

One would hardly call Hilda a chronological adolescent at this point, in her early twenties, pregnant, her social identity established by marriage although currently in question once more. Psychically, however, she remains what she was. Much earlier, before her mother's death, she has arrived in her own parlor to meet her mother and another older woman. "She was tingling with keen, rosy life, and with the sense of youthful power. She had the deep, unconscious conviction of the superiority of youth to age" (pp. 116–117). The narrator appears to share the conviction. As Hilda commits herself to her disastrous marriage, refusing to feel frightened by its unknown possibilities, the narrator comments, "With all her innocence and ignorance and impulsiveness and weakness, she had behind her the unique and priceless force of her youth. She was young, and she put her trust in life" (p. 383).

The survival of this force in Hilda entirely defines her status as heroine. By conventional standards, she does not behave well. She unreasonably disapproves of her mother and torments her in small ways; she considers her own gratification the highest good; she shows little perceptiveness in her choice of a husband and little scrupulosity in her willingness to lure another man into marriage without telling him her situation. She does not accomplish much, as she herself recognizes: "She had had money, freedom, and ambition, and somehow, through ignorance or through lack of imagination or opportunity, had been unable to employ them. She had never known what she wanted. The vision had never been clear" (p. 416). Her adolescent uncertainty, in other words, has prevented her from mustering sufficient clarity to achieve what lay within her power. But her adolescent ardency compensates. The sense of power, the capacity to trust life, the energy to keep trying, the endless interest in her own sensations: these make Hilda worthy of attention, although unattractive traits accompany them.

To accord a young woman the freedom and power implicit in Hilda's sense of herself would consitute a remarkably daring novelistic enterprise, and Bennett draws back from it. His depiction of Hilda includes a contradictory set of impulses leading her toward total subordination to a powerful male. "She knew that she would yield to him. She desired to yield to him. Her mind was full of sensuous images based on the abdication of her will in favour of his" (p. 378). In her imagination, the language of power sometimes oddly turns on itself.

Of herself she thought, with new agitations: "I am innocent now! I am ignorant now! I am a girl now! But one day I shall be so no longer. One day I shall be a woman. One day I shall be in the power and possession of some man—if not this man, then some other. Everything happens; and this will happen!" And the hazardous strangeness of life enchanted her. (P. 218)

Her dream of maturity turns into a fantasy of submission, a fantasy that excites her with its promise of something new, remarkable, grown-up. A late-twentieth-century reader may feel the inauthenticity of such a characterization. It fits implausibly with the rest of Hilda; it speaks less of her imagination than of her creator's—an imagination not unlike G. Stanley Hall's, with its romantic fantasies of the "womanly."

Again attempting to evoke an adolescent female sensibility, in *The Lion's Share*, Bennett risks a more uncompromising characterization, this time betraying occasional discomfort through anomalies of tone. Audrey Moze, nineteen at the novel's opening, has wealth and independence, her parents having been conveniently disposed of in the initial chapters. Still alive in the beginning, those parents provide only obstacles to Audrey's dreams. The first paragraph exposes her fantasy "that she was rather like an animal in captivity," an idea that gives her "bitter pleasure," though the narrator comments that "it was not at all original."[3] Feeling her father and mother as captors, she plots an escape: in the initial paragraph she has just stolen money from her father's safe to facilitate her getaway. Although she has sufficient practical intelligence to understand the necessity of money, "She had none of the preoccupations caused by the paraphernalia of existence. She scarcely knew what it was to own. She was aware only of her body and her soul. Beyond these her possessions were so few, so mean, so unimportant, that she might have carried them to the grave and into heaven without protest from the authorities earthly or celestial" (p. 11). This description, also from the opening page, emphasizes Audrey's utter difference from the grown-ups who surround her. Archetypal adolescent, archetypal outsider, she shares no values with her parents. The novel endorses her position almost abjectly, allowing her freedom to live out her fantasies, power to reshape the world to her liking, indulgence for the dreams that belong to her time of life.

While her parents live, Audrey can declare openly (although not directly to them) her contempt for and defiance of them. She complains that her father is "mad about me and men. He never looks at me without thinking of all the boys in the district," and that "he ought to keep me in the china cupboard" (p. 20). She feels "outraged by the hateful hypocrisy of persons over fifty" (p. 22). She claims the status of a woman, objecting that her father acknowledges her womanhood in his fears about her sexuality, yet denies her the freedom of that condition (p. 24). When her parents die, she proposes to begin real life in Paris but announces, "I'm not silly enough to go to Paris as a girl. I've had more than enough of being a girl" (p. 62). In France, pretending widowhood, she indulges all her desires. The language that evokes her suggests total approval: "Audrey ate and drank with gusto, with innocence, with the intensest love of life. And she was the most beautiful and touching sight in the café-restaurant" (p. 87). Her youth, the novel explains repeatedly, gives her the capacity to touch and manipulate the emotions of all who come in contact with her. Unlike Hilda, she fantasizes dominion, not subordination. Men fall at her feet; she assumes that they belong there. She chooses between the wealthy fatherly figure and the youthful musical genius (his genius a little problematic, but his success undeniable); she chooses against the responsibilities of political commitment, in favor of her own pleasure.

The narrator's occasional ironies suggest reservations about this mode of conducting life. Consider, for example, a passage about Audrey's responses after the musician Musa has broken his arm playing tennis. She considers herself responsible because she has refused to play with him; if she had been his partner, she believes, nothing would have happened. She perceives herself as very important indeed:

Audrey was troubled. As suited her age and condition, she was apt to feel the responsibility of the whole universe. She knew that she was responsible for Musa's accident, and now she was beginning to be aware that she was responsible for his future as well. . . . She saw him listless and vanquished in the basket-chair; and she perceived that only a strongly influential and determined woman, such as herself, could save him from disaster. No man could do it. (P. 127)

A comic perception of disproportion governs this summary: perhaps we should not after all take Audrey quite seriously. More profound grounds for criticism emerge:

She was intensely and calmly happy. No thought of the past nor of the future, nor of what was going on in other parts of the earth's surface could in the slightest degree impair her happiness. She had done nothing herself, she had neither earned money nor created any of the objects which adorned her; nor was she capable of doing the one or the other. Yet she felt proud as well as happy, because she was young and superbly healthy, and not unattractive. These were her high virtues. And her attitude was so right that nobody would have disagreed with her. (P. 146)

The passage locates a basis for moral disapproval of this heroine, yet its final sentence withdraws all disapproval. That sentence, too, reverberates with irony, directed at the universal assumption of youth's authority, when such authority rests only on the evanescent foundation of age, health, attractiveness.

Yet the narrator, perceiving the fatuousness of adolescence worship, participates in it; his capacity for irony is intermittent. When Audrey

241

notes the wistful glance of the rich older man who wishes to marry her,

It gave her the positive assurance of a fact which marvellously enheartens young girls of about Audrey's years,—to wit, that they have a mysterious power surpassing the power of age, knowledge, wisdom, or wealth, that they influence and decide the course of history, and are the sole true mistresses of the world. Whence the mysterious power sprang she did not exactly know, but she surmised—rightly—that it was connected with her youth, with a dimple, with the incredibly soft down on her cheek. (P. 392)

If the narrating voice hints some doubt about this "fact," it does not discount the degree to which Audrey's conviction operates to make it effectively true. The voice conveys anger as it recounts the girl's tyrannies, her unawareness, her assurance of her own centrality in the universe—anger and bewilderment, but also resignation. The absolute power of youth defies established moral categories, but one cannot dismiss it for that reason. Quite simply, it *is*.

The novel's title alludes to Audrey's expressed determination to have everything. "I want everything, and I'm going to get it—or have a good try for it. . . . I want to have a husband and a house and a family, and a cause too. That'll be just about everything, won't it? And if you imagine I can't look after all of them at once, all I can say is I don't agree with you" (p. 386). At the end two older women describe Audrey in revealing terms:

"Yes," said Miss Ingate, "she wants the lion's share of it, that's what she wants. No mistake. But of course she's young." "I was never young like that." "Neither was I! Neither was I!" Miss Ingate asseverated. "But something vehy, vehy strange has come over the world, if you ask me." (P. 426)

Audrey's nature, in other words, embodies a social as well as an individual phenomenon, a manifestation at which the old can only wonder—and applaud. The novelist himself, compelled by his own imaginings to accept the supremacy of a power based on nothing more permanent than a stage of psychic development, fantasizes the possibility of this stage preserved far beyond its normal chronological limitation: Audrey, too, is married, in her twenties, but retains the enormous, unchallengeable prerogatives, of glorified adolescence.

Bennett's novels feel dated now partly because of the embarrassing explicitness of their assumptions. The interest in youthful protagonists has burgeoned since Bennett's time, but who would now say out loud that chronological age in itself justifies moral shoddiness and unrelieved self-interest? Youth gives Hilda and Audrey confidence (although it also causes turmoil); confidence gives them strength, they need no further resource. When an older woman says, "I was never young like that," she calls attention to the narrative's *donnée:* youth now means something new. The excess of meaning attached to it in Bennett's mythology can shape his fictions—the curve of action in *The Lion's Share* duplicates that of idealized adolescence: release, developed capacity, ascendance—but proves finally too simplified to satisfy.

Yet Bennett's glorifications of adolescence expose ideas important also in the work of novelists of more subtle imagination. To claim power is to have it, his novels say. Not quite so easily as all that, other novelists respond: but writers of such stature as Joyce and Lawrence explore the same conviction.

A sense of alienation dominates Bennett's relation to his material. Both his ironies and his extravagant praise declare his conviction that he himself cannot share the force that the young contain. The role of outsider, for Bennett as for Stanley Hall, belongs to the representative of civilization rather than to the youthful barbarian who defies restriction. James Joyce and D. H. Lawrence, on the other hand, in the early years of the twentieth century expressed in fiction a degree of identification with youthful heroes surpassing that of their Victorian counterparts. The Victorians wrote as adults looking back on their own adolescence and nostalgically aware of the impossibility of preserving the temporary. Joyce and Lawrence, in their autobiographical early novels, wrote as though from deep inside the experience of adolescence. Although the authority of their phrasing declares their adult distance, although they achieved ironic or pitying or critical perceptions of their protagonists, they also identified profoundly with the suffering and the heroism of characters who assert their genius in refusing to yield to the values of the adult world. Joyce and Lawrence wrote of young men who justify their claim of specialness by their roles as artists—roles that, given their youth, exist mainly in potential, but that nonetheless provide authority. These novelists imagined (or remembered) adolescents imagining themselves as powerful, despite their adolescent experience of youth's familiar impediments.

Lawrence's *Sons and Lovers* (1913)—its action beginning before Paul Morel's birth but concentrating on his adolescence—explores in particular, as its title suggests, the problem of relationship. In *Adolescence,* Hall touches on some kinds of difficulty the young experience in interchanges with others: the trials of youthful love, the stresses of excessive sensitivity, the tension between desire to assert the self and desire to sacrifice it to an ideal. Lawrence penetrates more deeply the perplexities of a gifted youth torn between his need to rely on others for sustenance and his drive toward independence, between loving and fearful impulse, between reverence for and terror of women.

Like Hilda Lessways, like most fictional and all real adolescents, Paul must discover who he is and what he wants. The narrative of his effort to form his identity examines the impetus and the obstacles provided by other people. Its intensity and its wavering alike derive from identification between the narrative voice and the sensibility it describes. It treats with utter seriousness the problems of a young man confronting the world. Unlike eighteenth- and nineteenth-century novels of youth, which conclude in marriage, *Sons and Lovers*, like *Portrait of the Artist* and the two Bennett novels, concludes with its central character affirming the adolescent condition of isolation. (Audrey, at the end of *The Lion's Share*, has married, but she explicitly declares her intent to preserve significant experience separate from her husband.) Not intimacy but independence marks the qualified success of these characters, who prolong their youth rather than relinquish it.

Paul Morel must separate himself from his mother. He tries to do so verbally by insisting on the necessary gap between generations:

> "You're old, mother, and we're young." He only meant that the interests of her age were not the interests of his. But he realized the moment he had spoken that he had said the wrong thing.
> "Yes, I know it well—I am old. And therefore I may stand aside; I have nothing more to do with you. You only want me to wait on you—the rest is for Miriam."
> He could not bear it. Instinctively he realized that he was life to her. And, after all, she was the chief thing to him, the only supreme thing.
> "You know it isn't, mother, you know it isn't!"[4]

Paul is twenty-one years old when this bit of dialogue occurs. He seems much younger, with his feeling that his mother represents the only supreme thing; the interchange reveals his incapacity to oppose the maternal will which has formed his nature and his fate. His effort to differentiate himself founders on his mother's bitter specificity. His verbal response ("You know it isn't") syntactically refers to his mother's final comment, "the rest is for Miriam." He explicitly denies, in other words, the reality of commitment to a woman of his own generation; the love he declares belongs to his past.

His mother affirms him, as he affirms her. Unlike Bennett's protagonists, Paul cannot contest her authority, although he readily (and largely offstage) announces his utter independence from his father. The symbiotic relationship surviving from infancy assumes new forms in his adolescence, centering increasingly on his capacity for accomplishment.

> Mrs. Morel clung now to Paul. He was quiet and not brilliant. But still he stuck to his painting, and still he stuck to his mother. Everything he did was for her. She waited for his coming home in the evening, and then she unburdened herself of all she had pondered, or of all that had occurred to her during the day. He sat and listened with his earnestness. The two shared lives. (P. 114)

A sense of physicality controls the language of clinging and sticking and unburdening, until Paul's earnestness, evoked in the odd prepositional phrase, seems itself a physical substance, and the sharing of lives suggests two people crouched over a single dish of ice cream.

The theme of Paul's obsessive closeness to his mother hardly requires elucidation, so loudly does it dominate the novel. It contributes to the ambiguity of Paul's characterization and to the ambiguity with which we perceive the two young women in his life. To what extent does Paul function as hero of this fictional action? Are we to admire him, to pity him, or to condemn him; or does the novel demand all three responses?

Paul kills his mother at last, literally. Riddled with cancer, she refuses to yield. His entanglement with her survives. "Sometimes they looked in each other's eyes. Then they almost seemed to make an agreement. It was almost as if he were agreeing to die also. But she did not consent to die; she would not" (p. 392). He gives her an overdose of morphia, to which she succumbs only after hours of resistance. He thinks of smothering her, because the person in the bed does not resemble his mother. Finally she dies.

> He kneeled down, and put his face to hers and his arms round her:
> "My love—my love—oh, my love!" he whispered again. "My love—oh, my love!" (P. 398)

Looking at her some hours later, he sees her "like a girl asleep and dreaming of her love" (p. 399). He contemplates the physical details before him; then "he bent and kissed her passionately." His father refuses to confront the reality of death. At the funeral, the father declares that he has always done his best for his wife. "And that was how he tried to dismiss her. He never thought of her personally. Ev-

erything deep in him he denied. Paul hated his father for sitting senti-
mentalizing over her. He knew he would do it in the public-houses"
(p. 401).

The sexual overtones of Pauls's responses contrast sharply with the
father's asexual self-justifications, and the cavalier condemnation of
the older man's reaction appears to issue from his son's psyche, not
from the narrator's consciousness. Or can one discover any difference
between the two? Repeatedly, the narrator speaks for Paul. The first
three sentences just quoted, in the voice of the narrator, convey the
same hatred that the fourth sentence attributes to Paul, but the earlier
sentences do not clearly locate the emotion. The narrating consciousness participates in rather than understands the protagonist's involvements. No reservation about his contemptuous dismissal of Walter
Morel qualifies Paul's judgment, which stands as the book's definitive
statement about the father.

Mrs. Morel's death does not free her son. The physical language that
has described their relationship continues, to suggest the young man's
drift toward dissolution. "Paul felt crumpled up and lonely. His mother had really supported his life. He had loved her; they two had, in
fact, faced the world together. Now she was gone, and for ever behind
him was the gap in life, the tear in the veil, through which his life
seemed to drift slowly, as if he were drawn towards death" (p. 407).
His passivity, which has allowed him to accept his mother's control,
continues: "He wanted someone of their own free initiative to help
him." "Someone": another woman. To resolve his relation with his
mother, he must settle his connections with Miriam and Clara. The
account of how he does so draws to a knot another skein of the novel's
complexities.

Miriam represents spirit to Paul; Clara embodies flesh. Such dicho-
tomizing characterizes the adolescent mind, which deals with new
perceptions of the world's intricacies by isolating them into their components. To deal with one thing at a time presents fewer difficulties
than confronting experience's ambiguous multiplicities. Paul displays
in convincing detail the marks of the adolescent; one might take Hall's
list of psychic traits (inner absorption, efflorescence of imagination,
overassertion, speech consciousness, dominant feeling, and the rest)
and find each realized in Paul. His youth accounts for much of his
personality, although the novel differentiates him sharply from other
adolescents in his own family, his older and his younger brothers and
his sister. One can at least dimly imagine the possibility that he might
grow out of some passionate peculiarities.

The reason such imagining remains dim and uncertain involves, once more, the uncertainties of the narrative voice. If the narrator's judgment of Walter Morel appears identical to Paul's, so, at times, does his judgment of Miriam and Clara: a fact that generates confusion about the narrative thrust. One can more readily accept Miriam's "spirituality" as a phenomenon of Paul's perception than believe in her asserted incompleteness as an objective fact.

Often Paul "hates" Miriam. On one occasion he offers an explanation for his feeling. Many dramatic moments of their relationship have centered on Miriam's passionate love of flowers. Now she fondles daffodils, asking him to concur about their magnificence (he will agree only that "they're pretty"), smelling them and kissing them.

"You're always begging things to love you," he said, "as if you were a beggar for love. Even the flowers, you have to fawn on them—"
Rhythmically, Miriam was swaying and stroking the flower with her mouth, inhaling the scent which ever after made her shudder as it came to her nostrils.
"You don't want to love—your eternal and abnormal craving is to be loved. You aren't positive, you're negative. You absorb, absorb, absorb, as if you must fill yourself up with love, because you've got a shortage somewhere." (P. 219)

Although the reader, too, may feel something creepy about Miriam's way of relating to the natural world, Paul's response has creepy aspects as well. His condemnation clearly reflects his own anxieties, his sense of inadequacy as a giver of love, rather than any real perception of Miriam, who manifestly gives rather than takes in dealing with unsentient nature. I say "clearly"; but one cannot feel sure how clear it is to the narrator, who often participates in Paul's hatred without providing objective grounds for it.

The "grounds" consist in a series of dubious judgments.

With Miriam he was always on the high plane of abstraction, when his natural fire of love was transmitted into the fine stream of thought. She would have it so. If he were jolly and, as she put it, flippant, she waited till he came back to her, till the change had taken place in him again, and he was wrestling with his own soul, frowning, passionate in his desire for understanding. And in this passion for understanding her soul lay close to his; she had him all to herself. But he must be made abstract first. (P. 173)

That final, crucial indictment of Miriam issues from the presiding voice of the novel, which also asserts, earlier, "She did not fit in with the others; she could very rarely get into human relations with anyone: so her friend, her companion, her lover, was Nature" (p. 165).

247

Such summaries support Paul's view: Miriam wishes to be loved by, given to by, nature; she cannot value the mundane and physical, she can value only the spiritual; she prefers pain to pleasure; she lives most richly in the abstract.

The artificiality and implausibility of this account supply a basis for questioning it, but the novel itself also offers glimpses of Miriam that suggest quite another interpretation, "She wondered what he was thinking of as he stood suspended. His thick hair was tumbled over his forehead. Why might she not push it back for him, and remove the marks of Beatrice's comb? Why might she not press his body with her two hands. It looked so firm, and every whit living. And he would let other girls, why not her?" (p. 207). Again: "Her free, fine curls tickled his face. He started as if they had been red hot, shuddering. . . . She was coloured like a pomegranate for richness. His breath came short as he watched her. Suddenly she looked up at him. Her dark eyes were naked with their love, afraid, and yearning" (p. 208). She has reason for fear. Paul bullies and tyrannizes over her, as teacher and as lover. She does not expect an easy life if she joins herself to him, and one can hardly disagree. The two sequences I have just quoted suggest her rich physicality—unawakened, to be sure—and the degree to which Paul denies it, and her. Such accounts raise the possibility that Paul's aggressive characterization of Miriam as life rejecting, nonphysical, serves his own psychic purposes but utterly distorts her reality.

To perceive how adolescents work out their natures and roles by creative distortion would supply a compelling basis for a novelistic action. Inasmuch as *Sons and Lovers* rests on such a perception, it has remarkable psychological power. But the novel wavers between understanding Paul's psychological and moral inadequacies and endorsing them. Paul sees himself, at the novel's end, as tragically, heroically, alone. If those adverbs belong also to the narrator's evaluation, they raise questions about the degree to which that narrator has identified himself with the adolescent sensibility that he purports to describe.

The account of Clara raises similar issues. It serves Paul's purposes to understand her as a woman of deep physical nature, able to gratify his sexuality and to initiate him into a life of sexual possibility. The corollary of this understanding, in Paul's formulation, involves Clara's lack of intellectual and spiritual capacity to fulfill his most profound needs. Moreover, Clara, too, arouses his fear of being possessed. "You've never given me yourself," Clara complains (p. 363); her desire to *have* him parallels the compulsion Mrs. Morel has asserted in Miriam. Talking with Clara's husband, however, Paul asserts that Clara really wants her spouse: " 'That's how women are with me,' said Paul. 'They want me like mad, but they don't want to belong to me. And she *belonged* to you all the time. I knew' " (p. 404). So in effect he gives her back to Dawes, asserting her essential status as a possession, thus rejecting whatever claim she might have made to owning him. Clara feels, as well she might, angry. "He was a mean fellow, after all, to take what he wanted and then give her back." But the narrator justifies Paul: "She did not remember that she herself had had what she wanted, and really, at the bottom of her heart, wished to be given back" (p. 407). The lack of conviction in that final assertion, its offhand air of confidence slightly obscuring its thinness, creates pallid justification. It again suggests that the narrator endorses Paul's system of thought, a system perhaps excusable in youth but meretricious when sustained into nominal maturity.

Many readers before me have noted the anomalies in the accounts of Paul's woman friends. I wish not simply to berate Lawrence—entertaining though that exercise is—but to wonder about the relation between the uncertainties of moral viewpoint and the particular subject matter of *Sons and Lovers*. The novel resolves itself in an alternation of passivity and grandiosity characteristic of Paul and not commented on by the narrator. First comes the final renunciation of Miriam: she wants him to take her, he wants her to take him, they cannot resolve the impasse. Paul, however, has the last word:

She could not take him and relieve him of the responsibility of himself. She could only sacrifice herself to him—sacrifice herself every day, gladly. And that he did not want. He wanted her to hold him and say, with joy and authority: "Stop all this restlessness and beating against death. You are mine for a mate." She had not the strength. Or was it a mate she wanted? or did she want a Christ in him? (P. 418)

This summary presents Paul's point of view—shocking in its self-justification and its contempt for the other. His desire to lose responsibility for himself dramatizes his extreme passivity and his capacity to elevate passivity into virtue; "sacrifice," in contrast, he perceives as weakness. His demand that the woman assume the active role issues finally in his scornful speculation that since Miriam lacks the "strength" to take him, she must want not a man but a version of godhead.

Nothing in the text encourages an alternative interpretation of the Paul-Miriam interchange. Nothing suggests any criticism of Paul's enormous narcissism. The grandiosity of his final vision ("Whatever spot he stood on, there he stood alone. From his breast, from his mouth, sprang the endless space, and it was there behind him, everywhere" [p. 419]) likewise stands without criticism. He thinks of his mother, imagines her as his only source of sustenance, then declares his capacity to go on alone: "But no, he would not give in. Turning sharply, he walked towards the city's gold phosphorescence. His fists were shut, his mouth set fast. He would not take that direction, to the darkness, to follow her. He walked towards the faintly humming, glowing town, quickly" (p. 420). So the novel ends, with the promise of an unknown future, the isolated protagonist refusing to yield to the demands of others, setting out to confront the unknown world, determined to live, to strive, to win.

Paradise Lost also ends with its central human characters setting forth into an unknown world, not without a sense of possibility. But Adam and Eve have been firmly located in a moral context; we know the meaning of their situation, of their losses, and of what lies before them. No such precise knowledge informs our perception of Paul Morel, whose moral context remains indeterminant and changeable. Adolescence *means* possibility: so writers in all centuries have felt. Not until G. Stanley Hall's century have novelists sustained a fantasy of preserving its values and its indeterminacy. Dicken's narrators convey regret for the loss of youth, but they do not imagine an alternative; the marriage that ends a Victorian novel may not prove happy, but it feels necessary. Lawrence acknowledges no necessary fate. Writing an autobiographical fiction, therefore deeply identified with his protagonist's experience, he achieves for his narrator no clear moral point of view apart from that of the central character. Paul Morel perceives, as young men and women customarily perceive, a world of sharply etched distinctions; the narrator, most of the time, sees it the same way. And all the reader's information—the data of Miriam's sensuality, the evidence of Paul's myopia—comes necessarily from the same narrator: the novel provides the wherewithal to judge its inadequacies. But it does not integrate its perceptions. The narrator has moments of clear separation from the central character, moments of understanding and judgment, but *only* moments. Much of the time, he sees little more than Paul Morel sees and lacks moral perspective to comprehend from other viewpoints than that of the magnified adolescent ego that subordinates all to itself. Paul's narcissism dominates *Sons and Lovers* in ways damaging to fictional clarity and authority although rich in emotional energy.

Sons and Lovers belongs to a richer fictional universe than do Bennett's novels. Although Bennett's narrator as well as Lawrence's betrays an uneasy relation to his material, the uneasiness reflects a different problem. Bennett offers fictional substantiation of theoretical convictions about youth in the modern world; hence his thinness. Lawrence transforms his own intensely felt experience. Probably neither man read Stanley Hall's magnum opus. The contemplation of Hall, Bennett, and Lawrence together, however, dramatizes what they share: an attitude finding diverse embodiments in the first quarter of the twentieth century. Suddenly the young had new psychological rights, new authority. A new mythology developed around this vision, a mythology articulated at various levels. Hall wrote a quarter of a century after Charles Kingsley; he sounds as though he inhabited a different galaxy. *Sons and Lovers* appeared roughly half a century after *Great Expectations*; it reflects the revolutionary assumption that the young will chasten rather than be chastened by their elders. As Miss Ingate observes in *The Lion's Share*, "Something vehy, vehy strange has come over the world."

The problematic relation between "artist" and "young man" dominates James Joyce's *Portrait of the Artist As a Young Man* (1916), a novel in obvious ways dissimilar to Lawrence's, yet sharing with it important assumptions and perplexities derived from those assumptions. Stephen Dedalus's youth makes him the target for gentle mockery of a sort absent from *Sons and Lovers*. Yet it also makes him heroic. More dramatically than Paul Morel, because more consciously and purposefully, Stephen embraces an adolescent self-definition as isolate, rebel, outsider. His sense of specialness begins early and steadily intensifies. In seeking his identity, he seeks his freedom, which he apparently understands as the absence of ties. He sees the fate of those born in Ireland as controlled by "nets": "When the soul of a man is born in this country there are nets flung at it to hold it back from flight. You talk to me of nationality, language, religion. I shall try to fly by those nets."[5] Nets, as George Eliot often reminds her readers, may imply connection, linkages among human beings. Stephen willingly relinquishes his connection in order to avoid entanglement; indeed, he perceives no positive possibilities in the idea of nets. In his odyssey toward freedom, he makes mistakes of perception, understanding, and action, all targets for the novel's obvious ironies—ironies that do not, however, challenge Stephen's nature and cherished assumptions. At the end of his school career, the boy wins thirty-three pounds in prize money. He spends it on self-indulgence, heightens his efforts at self-discipline, and attempts to cement his relations with other members of his family.

He bought presents for everyone, overhauled his room, wrote out resolutions, marshalled his books up and down their shelves, pored upon all kinds of price lists, drew up a form of commonwealth for the household by which every member of it held some office, opened a loan bank for his family and pressed loans on willing borrowers so that he might have the pleasure of making out receipts and reckoning the interests on the sums lent. When he could do no more he drove up and down the city in trams. Then the season of pleasure came to an end. The pot of pink enamel paint gave out and the wainscot of his bedroom remained with its unfinished and illplastered coat. (Pp. 97–98)

The pellmell list of activities evokes the comedy and the pathos of the situation: comedy in the projector's unconsidered boyish enthusiasm, pathos in the impossibility of success for his undertaking. The culminating action of riding up and down in trams epitomizes the boy's undirected and futile energy; the grotesqueness of pink enamel paint, the discordance between its suggestion of superficial prettiness and the reality of ill-plastered walls, sum up the impossibilities of Stephen's hopes. Stephen's own retrospective judgment, extravagantly somber, recognizes the facts implicit in the narrator's ironic conjunctions. "How foolish his aim had been! He had tried to build a breakwater of order and elegance against the sordid tide of life without him and to dam up, by rules of conduct and active interests and new filial relations, the powerful recurrence of the tides within him. Useless" (p. 98). Stephen's judgment characteristically exaggerates the significance of what he does and suffers; one prefers the narrator's faint amusement. The storyteller's superiority in experience to his subject emerges in that capacity for amusement. The grandiosity of Stephen's boyish schemes yields to more complicated forms of grandiosity. His understanding of the world outside himself continues to partake of imaginative distortion, to attract the ironic perception of the narrator. Paul Morel divides women into beings of flesh and of spirit and so demonstrates an adolescent habit of mind upon which *Sons and Lovers* fails to comment. Stephen's equally categorical divisions of experience display themselves in his alternation between endeavors at total goodness and indulgence of full corruption. His inability to imagine or to exist comfortably in a middle state derives from his youthful intensity of thought and feeling.

The text leaves little doubt about how to evaluate his vacillations: as characteristic of his age, as matters for indulgent understanding, but also as inappropriate responses to realities. Stephen's corruption involves exaggeration of what lies within as well as without himself. "Beside the savage desire within him to realize the enormities which he brooded on nothing was sacred. He bore cynically with the shameful details of his secret riots in which he exulted to defile with patience whatever image had attracted his eyes. By day and by night he moved among distorted images of the outer world" (pp. 98–99). His fantasies of goodness imply equally unrealistic comprehension of social and psychological possibility: "He would love his neighbour. He would love God Who had made and loved him. He would kneel and pray with others and be happy. . . . It was easy to be good. God's yoke was sweet and light" (p. 143). The two modes of imaginative transformation comment on one another, the childlike simplicities of the language of "goodness" emphasizing the linguistic heightening ("savage desire," "enormities," "exulted to defile") of the sense of personal evil. Both varieties of moral fantasy yield to a dull acceptance of physical actuality: watery tea, yellow dripping, pawntickets, enameled basin; his mother washing his neck and urging him to "Dry yourself and hurry out for the love of goodness" (p. 175), a phrase ironically recalling his earlier obsession with the minutiae of virtue. In the artful narrative, the sequence (indulgence in evil, indulgence in good, indulgence in disgust, Stephen's response to the physical summed up as "an ache of loathing and bitterness" [p. 175]) by its unemphatic sequentiality comments on the moral vacillations of a youth not yet aware of his true commitments.

Stephen's sense of specialness seems at the outset merely characteristic of childhood and adolescence, but its ontological status becomes more ambiguous: perhaps, finally, a registration of reality rather than an index of fantasy. More and more firmly, the youth rejects the significance of everything external to him. His theory of art constitutes a mode of separation from his companions and his environment. Explaining it to Lynch, he becomes in the process increasingly isolated. He starts with the basket on a butcher boy's head, elucidates its *integritas*. "Bull's eye!" Lynch comments; Stephen hardly notices. On he goes, to *consonantia* ("Bull's eye again!") and *claritas*. His comrade says nothing to this last elaboration; all the better, from Stephen's point of view. "Stephen paused and, though his companion did not speak, felt that his words had called up around them a thoughtenchanted silence" (p. 213). Although Lynch responds enough to fuel the continuing monologue, his irrelevance to Stephen's intellectual and emotional experience becomes increasingly apparent. Lost in his theory, Stephen need not notice the falling rain, the people around him, the realities of his existence. Finally Lynch complains about the weather ("What do you mean . . . by prating about beauty and the imagination in this miserable Godforsaken island" [p. 215]) and calls Stephen's attention to the presence of the young woman who interests him. Now the young artist loses his rhapsodic isolation. "His mind, emptied of theory and courage, lapsed back into a listless peace" (p. 216).

The association between theory and courage belongs peculiarly to Stephen, for whom indulgence in the abstract—that mode of intellectual play which Paul Morel hated Miriam for allowing herself—supplies a saving resource. His courage consists in his willingness to separate himself from his kind, to embrace alienation and suffer its consequences. The novel provides no clear basis for evaluating this commitment in its protagonist. Other people criticize: Cranly suggests to him the terror of loneliness; his mother prays "that I may learn in my own life and away from home and friends what the heart is and what it feels" (p. 252). Stephen interprets Cranly as fearing his own loneliness and dismisses his mother's prayer as irrelevant. No narrative shift in tone, no ironic conjunction, directs the reader. Stephen, in his journal, manifests a capacity to mock some of his own posturing, but by no means all. He understands himself as in revolt, and understands the revolt as heroic. An adolescent stance—the artist's as well?

The romantic view of the artist emphasizes the alienation attending the role of creative soul in modern society. The artist as heroic outsider perceives the evils of a society in which he cannot participate, blessed and cursed as he is with the mission of showing his culture its own lineaments. So Stephen comprehends himself: "I go to encounter for the millionth time the reality of experience and to forge in the smithy of my soul the uncreated conscience of my race" (pp. 252–53). He has cut himself off from the real father whose storytelling opened the novel, and embraces instead the mythological father of his imagination.

Imagination gives him a great resource against and for the world. If he exaggerates its power, perhaps such heightening itself declares his fundamental identity as artist, an identity intensifying all the traits of the adolescent as Hall described them and as we have seen them ever since. Stephen yields nothing of his youthful romanticism, he grows out of nothing. Instead, he grows more fully into a self of boyish ardency, boyish self-absorption, boyish conviction of infinite possibility. He refuses to grow up. Should we deplore or applaud? The text encourages an interpretation congruent with Hall's theory that genius depends upon preservation of adolescence—encourages this interpretation at least by supplying no clear evidence against it. Stephen's villanelle leaves something to be desired as poetry, but who would expect a young artist to write like a mature one? His theory of poetry sounds like the product of a mind removed from daily actualities, but that hardly discredits it as aesthetics. Those in the novel's world who demonstrate no enthusiasm for the theory can claim little attention on their own merits; their implicit criticism therefore lacks authority. The young man displays a disturbing degree of separation from human contact and uses his linguistic power to intensify that separation; but perhaps he thereby creates for himself the artist's necessary conditions. The writing in Stephen's journal at the novel's end includes jejune, self-loving, and mawkish passages: necessary experimentation for the budding artist? His willingness to risk the embarrassing, his insistence on holding onto just those aspects of adolescence that grown-ups most want the young to relinquish, may mark his genius.

Stephen identifies himself with Icarus as well as with Daedalus and ignores the moral of the legend about flying too near the sun. Such blindness to the warnings of myth—to the wisdom of the race—marks adolescent hubris. Like Paul Morel, Stephen Dedalus is a self-centered monster; like *Sons and Lovers, Portrait of the Artist* does not openly acknowledge this fact. Readers who find these young men detestable may thus declare their own philistinism; those who would warn Stephen against hubris undervalue heroic risk. The artist as hero has a long history; the adolescent as fully valued hero, a short one. Stephen Dedalus, the artist in potential, as a fictional character makes a claim for adolescent absolutism, alienation, contempt for the established, as artistry's inner conditions. The text mocks him for his mistakes, occasionally for his presumption, but not for these qualities. Because Stephen's devotion to the idea of his own greatness merges with his devotion to "art," his character justifies what previous generations had perceived as the flaws of adolescence. Paul Morel at the end of *Sons and Lovers* has learned, precariously, that he can survive without his mother and that he prefers living to dying. Stephen Dedalus at the end of *Portrait of the Artist* has learned that he can reject his mother, his church, and his country. Both young men go toward indeterminate

255

futures. The indeterminacy that, according to recent psychologists, marks the adolescent moratorium constitutes the resolution of these fictional actions. Adolescence emblemizes many of the values clustered under the label of "modernism." Its heroes refuse to surpass their youthful condition; instead, heroes and novelists alike give signs of believing that this condition itself surpasses maturity.

10

Guilt and Responsibility: The 1950s and the 1960s

In youth the tables of childhood dependence begin slowly to turn: no longer is it merely for the old to teach the young the meaning of life, whether individual or collective. It is the young who, by their responses and actions, tell the old whether life as represented by the old and as presented to the young has meaning; and it is the young who carry in them the power to confirm those who confirm them and, joining the issues, to renew and to regenerate, or to reform and to rebel.[1]

Like G. Stanley Hall before him, Erik Erikson elucidated the perplexities the young present to the old; he, too, has emphasized the portentousness of adolescence as a developmental stage. Erikson wrote the words above in 1961. A year later, Anthony Burgess published *A Clockwork Orange*. Its adolescent protagonist, speaking a bizarre but comprehensible lingo, comments on the adult view of the young:

And there was a bolshy big article on Modern Youth (meaning me, so I gave the old bow, grinning like bezoomny) by some very clever bald chelloveck. . . . This learned veck said the usual veshches, about no parental discipline, as he called it, and the shortage of real horrorshow teachers who would lambast bloody beggary out of their innocent poops and make them go boohoohoo for mercy. All this was gloopy and made me smeck, but it was like nice to go on knowing one was making the news all the time, o my brothers. Every day there was something about Modern Youth, but the best veshch they ever had in the old gazetta was by some starry pop in a doggy collar who said that in his considered opinion and he was govoreeting as a man of Bog IT WAS THE DEVIL THAT WAS ABROAD and was like ferreting his way into like young innocent flesh, and it was the adult world that could take the responsibility for this with their wars and bombs and nonsense. So that was all right. So he

257

knew what he talked of, being a Godman. So we young innocent malchicks could take no blame. Right right right.[2]

This commentary in its eloquent contempt evokes an unnerving futuristic world in which the young refuse to confirm anything for their elders, considering themselves self-generated and unique.

The novel's concern with social regimentation and freedom, its use of a pseudo-Russian dialect, its stress on public decisions as determinants of private fates: such elements invite the reader to understand it as a political fable. To contemplate it as a late-twentieth-century myth of adolescence, however, reveals other aspects of the narrative. Its vivid expression of adult ambivalence toward the young combines with adult self-castigation. Alex, the fifteen-year-old protagonist (seventeen by the end), finds no virtue in his elders, and little in the novel counters his view. Although P. R. Deltoid, his "Post-Corrective Adviser," seems decent enough and even mildly perceptive (unique among the book's adults in his capacity at least dimly to comprehend adolescent psychology), his utter ineffectuality suggests the bankruptcy of the values that *A Clockwork Orange* implicitly supports yet deprives of vitality. Alex's mother and father have nothing to offer him. He pities them for their lives of dreary, dutiful work, but finds in them no vestige of integrity. Bewildered, they indulge their sociopathic son and ignore his activities; but when he ends up in prison, they readily substitute in his room and in their lives a more conventional older man who will play the filial role in comprehensible fashion. The prison chaplain appears to have homosexual inclinations; he lacks moral courage and understanding of the doctrine he professes. Other adults manifest brutality or total self-interest or both. This nightmare of the future provides images of utterly hollow adulthood to counter its construction of youth brimming with energy and depraved purpose.

Alex, a lad who finds the Crucifixion exciting because he imagines helping to pound in the nails, understands badness as self-assertion. "Badness is of the self . . . and that self is made by old Bog or God and is his great pride and rodosty" (p. 40). He thus stands for a value more strongly realized than any other in this fiction. Moreover, the action finally endorses it. In the grips of a totalitarian government, Alex suffers the brainwashing that makes him definitively "good," reduced to helpless nausea at the thought of sex or violence, groveling before those who would attack him. But an implausible huddled-up sequence of events rescues him; he returns to his violent fantasies, with every prospect of realizing them soon once more in action.

He also asserts finally his utter dominance over his parents:

I shut my glazzies tight in like pain and said: "Go away now. I'll think about coming back. But things will have to be very different."
"Yes, son," said my pee. "Anything you say."
"You'll have to make up your mind," I said, "who's to be boss."
"Owwwwww," my mum went on.
"Very good, son," said my papapa. "Things will be as you like. Only get well." (P. 174)

Alex understands the conflict of generations. When a group of old men attack him, he explains: "It was old age having a go at youth, that's what it was" (p. 144). The antagonism of youth and age constitutes for Alex an absolute moral fact. Except for his one remark about the course of modern history, he interprets his experience as a function of "us against them," "us" defined entirely by youth. When he discovers that two of his erstwhile henchmen have joined the police, his astonishment reflects his belief in the dichotomy between young and old. "'You're too young,' I said. 'Much too young'" (p. 148). "Was young," one policeman responds. "That's what we was, young droogie. And you it was that was always the youngest. And here now we are" (p. 148). He, too, accepts age as a symbolic definition of moral position. Alex, by remaining "the youngest," remains a potential victim of those who declare themselves adult (his former cronies beat him almost to death). Only his restored capacity for violence protects him; only by the potential of physical power can he bully his parents. Lacking the possibility for violent aggression, he experiences himself as utterly helpless. In his previous encounter with his parents, he has burst into tears and regressed to maudlin self-pity: "I've suffered and suffered and suffered and everybody wants me to go on suffering. I know" (p. 137).

As the product of an adult sensibility, this fable of generational conflict has disturbing implications. It expresses the fear and rage of grown-ups toward those who refuse to join them: fear in the vision of uncontrolled youth terrorizing cities and nations, unwilling to acknowledge adult authority, thus depriving that authority of consequence; rage in the fantasy of absolute adult control over youthful minds and hearts through a technology of moral rehabilitation. If Alex and his cronies reduce their elders to helpless terror, making them cower in their homes after dark, those grown-ups can retaliate by eliminating in their victims the very capacity for violence. The counterpoint eloquently conveys the potential emotional devastation of the opposition between young and old.

But it draws back from fully rendering the devastation and the anger and fear behind it; it does not allow the repressive grown-ups to triumph. Benevolent adults finally restore Alex to his full capacity for violence. In the novel's political logic—its logic of public politics—the denouement makes sense: however evil Alex's impulse and action, his right to choice demands acknowledgment. Inasmuch as the fiction concerns *private* politics, on the other hand, it evades resolution. *A Clockwork Orange* concludes with an image of Alex listening to his favorite symphonic work, Beethoven's Ninth. "When it came to the Scherzo I could viddy myself very clear running and running on like very light and mysterious nogas [feet], carving the whole litso [face] of the creeching [screaming] world with my cut-throat britva [razor]" (p. 179). The imaginative connection of music with violence has dominated Alex's sensibility; he loses his capacity to enjoy music when he loses his will to destruction. The ambiguous vision of him using great music to stimulate fantasies of mayhem expresses the acceptance of youth-as-it-is by the novel's most effective adults and suggests the author's conviction, or wish, or fear, that the young must have things their own way.

As far back at least as *Tom Jones*, novelists have hinted analogies between large and small bodies politic. The threat of a usurper disappears in *Tom Jones*; the kingdom's order restores itself, and the miniature kingdom of Paradise Hall also returns to serenity. The Vicar of Wakefield's little republic faces the threat of anarchy but re-establishes good government at last. In the twentieth century, the political analogy no longer has such reassuring implications. We inhabit, and have for decades inhabited, a world that assumes neither the stability nor the uprightness of existing governments. If the role of father continues to parallel that of king, or president, or dictator, none of those elevated figures now possesses the enduring authority once implicit in them: the analogy currently adumbrates precariousness. Youth has, Erikson maintains, the power to confirm, therefore also, implicitly, the power to refuse confirmation: the strength of the electorate, of the discontented masses. The nuclear family is dying out: we hear that as often as we hear of the death of the novel. If family and novel and society stubbornly survive, they do so under threat of devastation from within.

The relation between large political units and small ones has provided a consistent subject for Erik Erikson, who, as the title of his best-known book (*Childhood and Society*) indicates, interests himself in the interplay of individual and social world. Unlike Hall, Erikson obviously knows the pitfalls of romanticizing; he neither castigates adults nor glorifies adolescents as openly as his predecessor. And his mode of thinking acknowledges historical reality in ways that Hall did not. Through the 1950s and 1960s, Erikson published a series of works investigating the significance of adolescence as well as of childhood in various social contexts. More precisely than Anthony Burgess, he perceives specific psychological stresses of adolescence as reflecting social and political equivalents. He expresses neither the terror and guilt deducible from Burgess nor the faith in the adolescent's salvationary force discernible in Hall; he stresses the literal rather than the metaphoric link between young people and their political and social environment. The human being, he says, is "at all times an organism, an ego, and a member of a society"; and again, "there is no individual anxiety which does not reflect a latent concern common to the immediate and extended group."[3] The orderly set of definitions—biological, psychological, social—in fact implies a chaotic reality, in which national pathology generates individual counterparts.

Adolescence, in Erikson's view, involves warfare, internal and external. He speaks of the "physiological revolution" associated with puberty; he points out that "adolescents have to refight many of the battles of earlier years," and that in order to do so they create artificial "adversaries," making "perfectly well-meaning people" play these roles (*C & S*, p. 261). Their central struggle concerns the forging of an identity, to use Erikson's often-repeated metaphor. But "identity," in his view, involves more than the individual. "It is the ideological outlook of a society that speaks most clearly to the adolescent who is eager to be affirmed by his peers, and is ready to be confirmed by rituals, creeds, and programs which at the same time define what is evil, uncanny, and inimical" (p. 263). "American youth can gain the full measure of its identity and of its vitality only by being fully aware of autocratic trends in this and in any other land as they repeatedly emerge from changing history" (p. 323). "'Bosses' and 'machines' . . . present to the emancipated generations, to the generations with tentative identities, the ideal of an autocracy of irresponsibility" (p. 322). Erikson's most positive and most negative visions of possibility for the adolescent focus on how society encourages and shapes him or her. Despite the young person's powerful will toward autonomy, his or her

261

destiny will depend on the kind of "affirmation" and "confirmation" provided by the environment. The tentativeness implicit in the adolescent condition makes youth vulnerable to ideological certainty; "an autocracy of irresponsibility," offered as an ideal, will exercise compelling force because it associates sureness (everyone's doing it) with ease (everyone's doing what comes naturally). The fate of whole generations of adolescents teeters on their society's largely unspoken commitments. "I have nothing to offer except a way of looking at things," Erikson says (p. 403). His way of looking has profoundly influenced current thought; it has also—as he would readily acknowledge—been influenced by the contemporary scene. Yet much in his message sounds more optimistic than most public utterances. He relies heavily on a soothing moral vocabulary, words in the passages already quoted like "confirm," "renew," "regenerate," "vitality," "ideal"; words like "loyalty," "confidence," "courage," "energy," "trust," "discipline." Even their negative counterparts, which also appear, contribute to the atmosphere of positive expectation which informs Erikson's writing. He believes in clarity, in the possibility of moral distinctions, in a universal dynamic of growth which society may thwart or distort but which contains regenerative force. His case histories, miniature or extended, and his examples from imaginative literature reiterate his faith in moral clarity and in the potential power of individuals. *Young Man Luther* (1958) provides a detailed instance of his capacity to illuminate a life by his understanding of psychological law.

Young Martin Luther, suffering a prolonged identity crisis, exemplifies the difficulty and the power of the adolescent state. In his "psychobiography," Erikson frequently articulates his own general principles.

I have called the major crisis of adolescence the *identity crisis*; it occurs in that period of the life cycle when each youth must forge for himself some central perspective and direction, some working unity, out of the effective remnants of his childhood and the hopes of his anticipated adulthood; he must detect some meaningful resemblance between what he has come to see in himself and what his sharpened awareness tells him others judge and expect him to be.[4]

Erikson never forgets that Luther represents the special, gifted individual for whom the patterns of development assume special forms; but Erikson understands those special forms as variations on a common theme. Thus Luther feels with particular intensity the adolescent need to reject what has earlier had importance for him (aspects of the internalized father), the need to attach himself to convictions that will help him discover his selfhood. Acts of repudiation and devotion raise questions of choice, unavoidable for the young.

The introspective late adolescent, trying to free himself from parents who made and partially determined him, and trying also to face membership in wider institutions, which he has not as yet made his own, often has a hard time convincing himself that he has *chosen* his past and is the chooser of his future. Moved by his ravenous sexuality, his commanding aggressive power, and his encompassing intellect, he is tempted to make premature choices, or to drift passively. (P. 113)

Luther's particular choices centered on his religious commitments. Erikson returns to his theme of how society determines the form of individual identities with his view of how the religious movements of Luther's time contributed to "the sense of identity of an age." "The particular Christian combination of a Higher Identity in the form of a Personal Maker of an absolutist moral bent and a father figure who became more human in heaven as he became more totalitarian on earth was, we suggest, gradually robbing medieval man of just that existential identity which religion owed him" (p. 177). Luther, therefore, inasmuch as he shifted a pattern of religious belief, contributed to resolving the identity problems of his contemporaries as well as of himself. Perhaps equally important, from Erikson's point of view: Luther embodied the grandest possibilities of adolescence, providing an example for our time as well as a catalyst for his own. In most men, according to Erikson's scheme, the "integrity crisis" is the final stage of psychic development. It emerges as "a life-long and chronic crisis in a *homo religiosus*. . . . This short cut between the youthful crisis of identity and the mature one of integrity makes the religionist's problem of individual identity the same as the problem of existential identity. To some extent this problem is only an exaggeration of an abortive trait not uncommon in late adolescence" (p. 261). Luther's "specialness," in other words, intensifies a quality inherent in the adolescent state.

Like Hall's view, this belief in the potentiality of adolescence hints the possibility of elevating the young to social heroes. Erikson does nothing so simple. Both heroism and victimization, he believes, depend on the state of society. Hall sees adolescents as potential rescuers of a decadent society; Erikson understands more vividly how social

decadence impinges on the young. Thus he forgives youth its twentieth-century excesses:

in a time of rapid change, be it the disintegration of the old or the advancement of the new, the meaning of confirmation changes. . . . Today this problem faces us most painfully on that frontier where leaderless and unguided
youth attempts to confirm itself in sporadic riots and other excesses which
offer to those who have temporarily lost, or never had, meaningful confirmation in the approved ways of their fathers, an identity based on a defiant
testing of what is most marginal to the adult world. (P. 114)

The lack of leaders and guides accounts for riotous activity; the young,
in this account, bear little responsibility for their own actions.

Erikson would not, of course, quite say so; he would perhaps not
acknowledge the implication. But his emphasis on the interchange between society and the individual has the effect, finally, of removing
the onus for reprehensible action from the performers of such action.
("We young innocent malchicks could take no blame. Right right
right.") Luther's extraordinary achievement declares his extraordinary
nature; his inadequacies derive from his history. The young, poised
between childhood and adulthood, bear the burdens of both: the
weight of their own pasts, the weight of parental (paternal, really, in
Erikson's mythology) failure. Erikson conveys compassionate understanding for the weaknesses and failures of human beings at every
stage in the life cycle; and he conveys consistent hope. His developmental view implies the possibility of change and growth at any age;
his optimistic assessment of the potential of middle age, even old age,
foretold a new attitude among professional commentators on the nature of internal process. Yet the special quality of adolescence compels him to unusual tolerance. That specialness, as he perceives it,
consists in the "betweenness" of the stage, its looking forward and
backward; in its unique energy and ambition; and in the sense of potential connected with it—all aspects of adolescence likewise compelling for commentators in preceding historical periods.

Erikson's vocabulary and sentence structure declare his high regard
for balance, mastery, and ethical commitment.

The evidence in young lives of the search for something and somebody to be
true to is seen in a variety of pursuits more or less santioned by society. It is
often hidden in a bewildering combination of shifting devotion and sudden
perversity, sometimes more devotedly perverse, sometimes more perversely
devoted. Yet, in all youth's seeming shiftiness, a seeking after some durability

in change can be detected, whether in the accuracy of scientific and technical method or in the sincerity of conviction; in the veracity of historical and fictional accounts or the fairness of the rules of the game; in the authenticity of artistic production (and the high fidelity of reproduction) or in the genuineness of personalities and the reliability of commitments. This search is easily misunderstood, and often it is only dimly perceived by the individual himself, because youth, always set to grasp both diversity in principle and principle in diversity, must often test extremes before settling on a considered course. ("Youth," p. 14)

The preponderant abstractions belong to moral rather than to psychoanalytic discourse; they indicate the goal of growth. One grows into goodness, into moral strength and control; one grows by active experiment. Youth, in the paragraph's implicit metaphor, engages in an arduous quest, searching, seeking, grasping, testing in an effort to find the proper "course." Adult activity, expressed only in the passive voice, involves seeing, detecting, and misunderstanding; the passive constructions universalize the action of observation but also make that action less important than its object. The sentence structure, however, suggests another expression of adult energy, in its insistent establishment of balanced opposition. "And" and "or" control the syntax, setting up significant pairings (something and somebody, devotion and perversity, accuracy of method or sincerity of conviction, the veracity of the written or the fairness of the unwritten, diversity in principle and principle in diversity . . .). Most of those pairings at first glance yoke unlikeness: devotion seems the opposite of perversity, scientific method bears no obvious relation to sincere conviction. As they multiply, however, they reveal hidden affinities, emphasized by Erikson's characteristic word play. "Sometimes more devotedly perverse, sometimes more perversely devoted": perversity and devotion can modify one another; the distance between them dwindles. "The high fidelity of reproduction," in the context of a discussion of adolescent capacity for fidelity, metaphorically links the technological to the moral, helping to substantiate a connection between integrity of method, however technical, and that of conviction. The activity of seeing and detecting as exemplified in the writing becomes a powerful ordering force, a mode of moral as well as of physical perception, the ideal goal of the adolescent quest.

A strong emphasis on balance and control marks Erikson's characteristic sentence structure, as the previous quotations, chosen for other reasons, attest. Exemplifying the mastery of maturity, this structure

265

reminds us that Erikson does not in any simple sense identify with youth, nor does his tone betray wistfulness. If he acknowledges the power of adolescence, he knows the need to surmount its hurdles. He recognizes that important figures in ideological history have never resolved their adolescent conflicts:

Is it not probable and in fact demonstrable that among the most passionate ideologists there are unreconstructed adolescents, transmitting to their ideas the proud moment of their transient ego recovery, of their temporary victory over the forces of existence and history, but also the pathology of their deepest isolation, the defensiveness of their forever adolescing egos—and their fear of the calm of adulthood? ("Youth," p. 25)

The recognition does not imply endorsement; the observer understands the weakness as well as the strength of the preserved adolescent position. The imperative of growth supersedes all lesser imperatives; arrested development constitutes failure.

Erikson's style, with its balanced constructions, its moral abstractions, its insistent word play, calls attention to its own control and to the writer's power—a power that the educated middle classes have assigned, in the twentieth century, to members of his and allied professions, the "knowers" of human complexity. Alex, in *A Clockwork Orange*, can mock those who "explain" youth; Doris Lessing's Martha Quest speaks of the novels that might make one conclude "that everyone (no less) suffered adolescence like a disease," and registers her feeling that only their perception of adolescence as pathology gives novelists something to write about: "and here she suffered a twisting spasm of spite against those cold-minded mentors who so persistently analyzed her state, and in so many volumes."[5] The analysis in novels and in newspapers derives indirectly from such writers as Erikson. Erikson cannot, of course, be held responsible for dilutions and perversions of his doctrine. I am not, in any case, at the moment interested in doctrine at all: I am interested not in Erikson's "way of looking" important though that is, but in his way of speaking. That way of speaking arrogates perception. The analyst acknowledges, even emphasizes, the possibility of misunderstanding, of dim or false perception, but such mistakes never belong to him. Nor does tentativeness mark his assertions, even about the perplexing. "The puzzle, we must grant throughout, is in the essence of the phenomenon. For the unity of the personality must be unique to be united, and the functioning of each new generation unpredictable to fulfill its function" ("Youth,"

p. 9). Such sentences depend on rhetorical parallelism and balance rather than on substantive content. But their tone expresses absolute authority. If the speaker "grants" that the puzzle is in the essence of the phenomenon, he allows that puzzle no power to perplex: unpredictability and uniqueness (a special form of unpredictability) become part of the case he wishes to prove, become further counters in the structure of comprehended development.

The combination of authoritative tone and meticulous attention to the individual phenomena of adolescence (everything is understood) with the assignment of vast force ("his ravenous sexuality, his commanding aggressive power, and his encompassing intellect . . .") to this time of life makes a peculiar combination. The force of adolescence, as Erikson understands it, consists both in its nature—sexuality, power, intellect—and in its social role: to confirm or refuse to confirm the meaning of life as defined by the old. The dominance of adulthood depends on adult capacity to incorporate any act of youthful rebellion, any eruption of the unforeseen, into a structure of understanding. The grown-up writer thus asserts victory in every controlled sentence, even while celebrating the world-changing possibilities of adolescent energy. This new embodiment of the eighteenth-century opposition between youthful passion and adult reason differs from the old in its refusal to establish moral imperatives for the young to defy. To understand rather than to rebuke adolescent extravagance involves, perhaps, a more secure form of dominance: it is, in any case, a characteristic form of the late twentieth century.

Fiction writers, however, have seen disturbing possibilities in this ideology of understanding, imagining counterideologies it might generate. If adults define their function as comprehension rather than, as in the eighteenth century, guidance, the young may feel free of restraint. *A Clockwork Orange*, a fable of the 1960s, spells out this eventuality. Alex falls victim to professionals' precise understanding of his psychology and to the manipulations such understanding generates. But the grown-ups' concern with understanding and manipulation and countermanipulation testifies, from his point of view, to their moral barrenness: they stand only for the will to control. His will not to be controlled, his determination to declare his own power and his elders' lack of significant moral meaning (they provide nothing to confirm or to reject)—that will finally triumphs. And, given the environment's moral sterility, Alex's defiant selfhood seems the best thing going. As an imagining of the future, the novel comments on per-

267

ceived potentialities of the present: the potential of moral vacuity deriving from the ideology of insight, and the possibility of uncontrolled aggression rushing to fill the vacuum.

To suggest any connection between the persuasive wisdom of Erik Erikson, whose compassionate comprehension has moved as well as enlightened his contemporaries, and the psychological technologists of *A Clockwork Orange* has an aspect of perversity: the differences, far more apparent than the similarities, are crucial. The point is that even Erikson, with his moral clarity and emphasis, exposes in his written accounts of adolescence the outlines of a system of thought which can rationalize and intensify tension between the old and the young, the old now standing for the power of mind, the young for the power of mindlessness, the antipathy between them intensified by the implicit claim of dominance in understanding. More clearly than our predecessors, we understand that we, as adults, define the shape of the society which we feel largely helpless to change, a society we have inherited as well as created but for which, in the eyes of the young, we bear responsibility. And, as the dangerous aspects of our society become increasingly apparent, we feel, the young encourage us to feel, guilt for what we pass on to them. In the past, written texts suggest, adults attempted to arouse guilt in the young; now the pattern has partly reversed itself. Erikson's language speaks of traditional values, but his description of actuality emphasizes how, in the present, "society" helps to generate and to intensify the problems of the young.

Hall's close attention to adolescence led him to celebration; he declared the young to contain the promise of salvation and thus expressed his unease with the condition of the world ruled by his peers. Re-creating the adolescent as hero, he opened the possibility of reverse education, the young instructing the old. More than half a century later, the state of things in the world of adult affairs has worsened, but faith in the possibility of salvation has also diminished. Erikson, too, admires the energy of youth, but with less hopefulness than Hall. Inhabiting a world in which few believe that human purpose or will materially affects history, he preaches a doctrine of responsibility. His authoritative prose poises hope against despair: hope in awareness as a force of change, despair at the burden of the past. Adults bear guilt for the state of affairs and responsibility to alter it; the young are what we have made them. If they have more immediate personal power than their progenitors, they still cannot surmount—or can surmount only with great difficulty—the limitations of their culture, *our* culture. Grown-ups have the power of comprehension, the weakness of guilt. Adolescents have neither: more free as well as more energetic than their elders, they reproach but cannot save us.

The sense of guilt implicit in even the most "objective" analysis of social reality in the 1950s and 1960s registers in fiction as well. Earlier in the century, Stephen Dedalus and Paul Morel grow in proud solitude, glorying in their isolation, defining themselves as artists set apart from the rest of the world. More recent imaginative writing evokes a class of youthful outsiders, criticizing by their very existence a society that they have rejected as surely as it has rejected them. They facilitate fictional exploration of adult social guilt, through the fantasy of beings who do not participate in it. On the other hand, the rebellious young, in typical midcentury fiction, also reflect in distorted form the moral consequences of the society they reject. Alex and his cohorts, in the futuristic intensifications of A Clockwork Orange, exemplify this trend, illustrating the imaginative identification of adolescent and outlaw. Alan Sillitoe's well-known short story, "The Loneliness of the Long-Distance Runner," embodies the myth in more realistic terms.

The protagonist and narrator of the story, a lad named Smith, meditates on life and ethics while confined in a Borstal prison for theft. He sees his experience as "war between me and them."[6] "Them," from his point of view, means mainly the law-abiding middle class; his mother, like him, hates policemen. But the young of the lower class differ from their elders in their active defiance of laws they despise. Adolescents steal and deceive and are punished, their imprisonment a testimony to their virtue. "I remember when I was fourteen and I went out into the country with three of my cousins, all about the same age, who later went to different Borstals, and then to different regiments, from which they soon deserted, and then to different gaols where they still are as far as I know" (p. 15). Like being in the army, being in jail amounts to a rite of passage. The boys desert the army; they cannot so readily escape jail. The story examines the modes of escape and defiance they find.

Joyce and Lawrence portrayed their young artists with sufficient complexity to create problems of evaluation for the reader. Sillitoe's portrayal of the youth as criminal leaves little room for ambiguity. Smith asserts his ethical superiority to his elders and social betters, and nothing in the story challenges his case.

I'm a human being and I've got thoughts and secrets and bloody life inside me that he [the governor of the Borstal] doesn't know is there, and he'll never know what's there because he's stupid. I suppose you'll laugh at this, me saying the governor's a stupid bastard when I know hardly how to write and he can read and write and add-up like a professor. But what I say is true right enough. He's stupid, and I'm not, because I can see further into the likes of him than he can see into the likes of me. Admitted, we're both cunning, but I'm more cunning and I'll win in the end even if I die in gaol at eighty-two, because I'll have more fun and fire out of my life than he'll ever get out of his. He's read a thousand books I suppose, and for all I know he might even have written a few, but I know for a dead cert, as sure as I'm sitting here, that what I'm scribbling down is worth a million to what he could ever scribble down. I don't care what anybody says, but that's the truth and can't be denied. I know when he talks to me and I look into his army mug that I'm alive and he's dead. He's as dead as a doornail. If he ran ten yards he'd drop dead. If he got ten yards into what goes on in my guts he'd drop dead as well—with surprise. At the moment it's dead blokes like him as have the whip-hand over blokes like me, and I'm almost dead sure it'll always be like that, but even so, by Christ, I'd rather be like I am—always on the run and breaking into shops for a packet of fags and a jar of jam—than have the whip-hand over somebody else and be dead from the toenails up. Maybe as soon as you get the whip-hand over somebody you do go dead. . . . [A]nother thing people like the governor will never understand is that I *am* honest, that I've never been anything else but honest, and that I'll always be honest. Sounds funny. But it's true because I know what honest means according to me and he only knows what it means according to him. (Pp. 12–13)

Smith's values, and those of the story, emerge clearly in this sequence. He stands for life as opposed to death, for greater as opposed to lesser cunning, for true honesty, integrity, "fun and fire." These virtues belong partly to his class—the socially oppressed—but more significantly to his age. His father, representative of lower-class manhood, has died abjectly, victim of economic exploitation. His mother spends happily but shows no capacity to get money; she supports her son in his ways of understanding the world but does not exemplify equivalent capacities to his. Smith's youth is his power. He can run fast, with heavy symbolic weight attached to the gift that expresses not only his will to escape restriction but his physical superiority to his elders. Those elders wish to use him, to subvert him into their system, but he cannot be subverted: he escapes corruption not by running but by refusing to run, losing the race he could easily have won, because, like Stephen Dedalus, he will not serve.

Stephen's escape depends on evasion—flying by the nets that would entrap him; Smith's, on direct opposition. He defines himself, as the long quotation indicates, entirely in opposition: all his values are comparative. "We're both cunning, but I'm more cunning." And he sees authority as the source of corruption: "Maybe as soon as you get the whip-hand over somebody you do go dead." The sentence epitomizes the adolescent's resentful perception of adults, a perception in earlier fiction characteristically suppressed or disguised. Smith's fictional world, however, corresponds in many respects to a literal society in which sociologists studying working-class adolescents can remark, "even in more favourable circumstances than apply to these young people the period of adolescence in our culture almost inevitably involves frustration, dissatisfaction, uncertainty and even for some a degree of paranoia."[7] The law-abiding young workers they analyze share some of Smith's attitudes: "Arising from their feeling that they are under attack and that something like a 'cold war' exists between the generations has come some disenchantment with adults, particularly with those in positions of authority" (p. 214). This pallid formulation hardly conveys the rage and energy that pervade Smith's utterances, but it suggests the degree to which adults in the 1960s assumed not only the hostility but the "disenchantment" of the young: not the antagonism that, as Dr. Johnson perceived, has always existed between the generations, but a new hostility containing aggressive judgment— adults are not *good* enough, not as good as they claim, not good enough to have the right of control they exercise.

Like *A Clockwork Orange*, like much fiction of adolescence, "The Loneliness of the Long-Distance Runner" feeds on the emotional energies of the author's double identification. Imaginatively participating in the adolescent experience, he enjoys the force and suffers the impotence of youth. His position as adult, writer behind the narrator, is harder to define. What does it mean for an adult to imagine in such detail an indictment of this kind? He cannot altogether separate himself from the class of adults, yet he sees adults, by and large, as monsters. And he knows that they run things: they will defeat lawless youth, leaving it only the luxury of its moral superiority. From the adult point of view, the fable suggests guilt (why else describe grown-ups as so *bad?*) and perhaps anger (what punitive fantasies lurk behind the accounts of repression?). Or perhaps alienation: lack of connection to the adult society the writer necessarily inhabits. But to feel cut off from one's kind in itself implies guilt and anger, somewhat differently focused.

Dual identification belongs to the mode of fiction about youth: Fielding took pleasure in Tom Jones's energy and lawlessness while speaking in the voice of the wise, knowing, civilized adult; but if he understood and even vicariously participated in Tom's rebellion, he accepted no responsibility for adult corruption. Bad grown-ups abound in his narrative: money-grubbing, lecherous, corrupt. But the adult middle class is not the object of wholesale indictment. Squire Allworthy exists: not a norm, to be sure, but an ideal. Tom, more essentially virtuous than most of his elders, nevertheless can never attain, without growing up, the stature of an Allworthy. Victorian fictional adolescents have to grow up, too; Stephen Dedalus and Paul Morel, later versions of the type, evade some of life's necessities only by their claim as artists. By the 1960s, such a solution no longer seems available to important British writers: the ideas that Erikson so forcefully expounded have revealed their dark underside. If the young, who require confirmation by their elders, demonstrate their inability to accept the code of civilized society, the fault must lie not in them but in those who have failed to provide acceptable values. The interaction of young and old proceeds, we believe in the twentieth century, by circular paths. The anger of youth against age finds instant counterpart in the rage of age against youth; the failures of the young perpetuate those of their elders. Creators of fiction about puberty, by the 1960s, rarely imagined flying by the nets. Nor could they accept, in their imaginative work, the necessities of adulthood. The new pattern worked out in the fiction of the 1960s (not, of course, the only pattern: older arrangements also persist) involves a circle of rage, guilt, and futility, in which the young hopelessly imitate the old even as they attempt to escape. Sillitoe's Smith, insisting on his absolute difference from the bourgeois adults he despises, reflects and parodies their values. The governor of the Borstal exemplifies the competitive orientation of capitalistic society. A devotee of winning, he preaches "hard honest work and . . . good athletics" (p. 9). Like the other inhabitants of a world of schoolmasters, warders, businessmen, and aristocrats, he exemplifies the potency of cunning. "Cunning is what counts in this life," Smith observes, adding, "I'm telling you straight: they're cunning, and I'm cunning" (p. 7). They're cunning, and he's cunning; they believe in honest work and athletics, and so does he; they want to win, and he wants victory even more intensely. If he shifts the meaning of such terms as "honest" or "winning," his emendations belong to a strategy of combat. The conventional grown-ups use their moral vocabulary as bludgeons; he bludgeons back. In a perverse sense he finds in the society he defies precisely the confirmation he needs. The law of each man for himself governs conformists and nonconformists alike.

Smith's claim of moral superiority to the representatives of law and order rests partly on the superior integrity of his commitment to the values proclaimed alike (with different meanings) by "In-laws" and "Out-laws." Unlike the Governor, Smith knows what he believes. The authorities think their honesty should govern; hence they build Borstals. Smith comments, "if I had the whip-hand I wouldn't even bother to build a place like this to put all the cops, governors, posh whores, penpushers, army officers, Members of Parliament in; no, I'd stick them up against a wall and let them have it, like they'd have done with blokes like us years ago, that is, if they'd ever known what it means to be honest, which they don't and never will so help me God Almighty" (p. 14). When the authorities hold out the promise that Smith may become a professional runner if he wins the Borstal cup, he finds himself possessed by a fantasy: "running and beating everybody in the world . . ., when suddenly: CRACK! CRACK!—bullets that can go faster than any man running, coming from a copper's rifle planted in a tree, winged me and split my gizzard in spite of my perfect running, and down I fell" (p. 35). He has integrity, but "they" have power; he projects the rage of his "honesty" onto them and envisions their destructiveness as the counterpart of his own.

Only in fantasy do "they" shoot Smith; in actuality they lock him up. But in imagining bullets splitting his gizzard, he may accurately convey feelings adults only partly conceal. As in *A Clockwork Orange*, adults in Sillitoe's story stand in a punitive relation to the young. (Smith's parents feel themselves to be on the same side as he—his mother never pays income tax, his father has refused hospitalization for terminal cancer—but they have less importance in his life than those he opposes.) To identify with adolescents implies identifying with victims; to identify with adults means declaring oneself an oppressor. The oppressors win. Smith explains that he has given his story to a pal who will never betray him, with directions to publish it if its author ends up imprisoned once more; the public existence of the text thus declares the confinement of its writer. If he "wins" in his own terms, by preserving his spiritual integrity, one feels the hollowness of the victory—as well as its reality.

The paradoxical relation between the text as emblem of confinement and as declaration of freedom (the writer as metaphorical runner . . .), the story's acknowledgment of opposed points of view about the same experience, rescues it, precariously, from sentimentality. Nothing in the narrative implies positive valuation of the way of conformity, but the "adult" system manifests its power. Sillitoe's story resembles Burgess's novel also in its perception of the relations between young and old as political, involving manipulations and pre-emptions of power. Novelists two centuries earlier had perceived the component of power in generational interchanges, but their fables imply orderly succession from generation to generation. The Vicar's children must live in subjection to him to the time they marry, but in due course they will succeed to the perquisites of established places. Sillitoe's fable, like Burgess's, implies circularity. Smith imagines himself in jail at eighty; the reader readily shares his vision. Alex will win and lose, win and lose, but one would not prophesy that he will become, literally or metaphorically, a policeman. Social power, in these narratives, implies tyranny; the purer power of Smith's running implies futility (no place to run to, no way to win). The anger of old against young, young against old, remains virtually unmodified by affection or by moral commitment. Neither Smith nor Alex will paint or write, as artist, however alienated, making contributions to the society from which they stand apart. (Smith has presumably written one narrative, but he does not imagine himself as artist.) Their heroism inheres in their refusal to achieve. Unlike Morel and Dedalus, they function as antiheroes, voices of disaffection, expressing not the rich potential of adolescence (what Hall perceived as equivalent to genius) but the imagined anger of youth as a class and the slightly disguised anger of the adults who do the imagining.

The criminal adolescent supplies a forceful image of the young as ferocious critics of the world they are expected to enter, the world that should confirm them. Less violent embodiments can serve the same function. *The Prime of Miss Jean Brodie*, Muriel Spark's ironic fantasy of education, establishes, in more "realistic" terms than *A Clockwork Orange*, a political context for its action, which takes place in England in the 1930s. Miss Brodie, the eccentric, charismatic teacher who shapes the destinies of several girl pupils, finds Mussolini's fascism attractive. References to international politics permeate the text, which describes a political system smaller but hardly less intense than Mussolini's.

The narrative relies heavily on repetitive allusion, building effects by slow accretion. It supplies glimpses of Miss Brodie's pupils at several stages of development, prepubertal to adult, with stress on the crucial years of sexual awakening. The Brodie group have won fame in their school for well-defined characteristics about which we read early and often. Mary is famous for her stupidity, Rose for sex, Sandy for her vowel sounds. Such definitions represent attempts by the rest of the school to come to terms with Miss Brodie's group. Thus the world deals with the young—by labeling, classifying. Spark's novel derives its structure and its meaning from the girls' progress toward simultaneous confirmation and evasion of classifications.

The men in this narrative serve as conveniences for the girls and women; boys appear as speechless louts, leaning on their bicycles. The female world, populated mainly by adolescents (although Miss Brodie towers over them), differs sharply from the male world of Smith or Alex. It substitutes private fantasy for overt competition; the girls appear to specialize in compliance rather than in rebellion. None follows a criminal course; a little illicit sex comprises their furthest excursion into the extralegal. Miss Brodie resembles her charges in her reliance on a created internal reality closer to the heart's desire than is the world without. She teaches them to focus on higher things, to specialize in "dedication," to think about Pavlova and avoid team spirit. Their most self-indulgent fantasies, unlike Smith's or Alex's, involve not violence but love: if adventure, adventure shared with a dashing man and interesting mainly by virtue of his involvement. Their public activities, performed largely in school uniform, involve tea parties, music lessons, at worst a carefully shepherded excursion through Edinburgh's slums: a far cry from Alex's mayhem or Smith's running and stealing.

Despite the disjunctions between the male texts and this female one, however, all three share twentieth-century fantasies about adolescence. *The Prime of Miss Jean Brodie*, indeed, makes such fantasies part of its subject. Miss Brodie organizes her life around visions of vicarious fulfillment through her charges. She identifies with them partly because she has not grown emotionally beyond adolescence herself. Although she fills a powerful adult role, schoolteacher, she works by means traditional to the youthful victim: deviousness, disguise, "acting out." She believes herself more powerful than she proves, as she comes to experience the obscure rebellion of her adolescent pupils. Sandy, grown-up, betrays her, thus dramatizing the treachery of a literal adult toward a metaphorical adolescent as well as the escape of a literal adolescent—the girl she was—from the tyranny of Miss Brodie in the guise of adult. The dark implications of Spark's fable reverberate as disturbingly as those of Burgess's and Sillitoe's more melodramatic narratives.

Five years before the first publication of *The Prime of Miss Jean Brodie* in 1961, *Encounter* magazine printed three adjoining articles on "The Younger Generation." The first of these, a largely statistical survey entitled "The Facts of Young Life," describes in detail, with lavish percentages, how England's young spend their time: working at jobs that provide money for self-indulgence, ardently consuming goods and services intended for their entertainment (make-up, "frivolous" clothes, records, movies), rejecting youth clubs and courses organized for them by their elders (they enroll, the article reports, but never come), scorning the politics and religion of their parents' generation, "going out" several nights a week. The comparison between generations, implicit throughout, becomes increasingly explicit toward the essay's end:

> As far as older people are concerned the main social purposes of going to the pictures, looking at the television, or reading seem to be three: to kill time, to prevent other people talking to them, and to equip themselves with the same stock of conversational trivia that others have and thus make possible fairly amiable contacts with them on a completely impersonal level.
>
> Young people have no particular need of these three services. The bulk of them seem to be essentially gregarious and they read and go to the pictures in order to know what's going on on a level of real sociability, to find out what they ought to be doing in order to register progress in their growing up, and, above all, how to deal with the opposite sex.[8]

In the context of an analysis at every stage meticulously documented and supported, these assertions of what "seems to be" the case among the young and the old have a startling effect. The author, Mark Abrams, gives no clue about the source of his conclusions. His contempt for the "older people" who, he believes, wish to avoid real contact with others and who organize their lives to prevent authentic encounters emerges as vividly as his relative respect for the "essentially gregarious" young, capable of "real sociability," eager to learn and to grow. A few paragraphs later, he reaches his rather unexpected conclusion: "The portrait of modern British youth which emerges from this account of its work and leisure may not be altogether pleasing to its elders. If so, they might remember that adult society usually gets the adolescents it deserves; they can be grateful that more young people do not realize that they often fail to get the adults they deserve" (p. 42). The non sequitur (surely if the young embody what adults deserve, the converse must follow) underlines the commentator's bias. His statistics have created a picture of the young as involved with trivia, as unambitious, unconcerned with any context larger than immediate personal relations. Nothing in those statistics points to adult responsibility for this state of affairs; the conclusion comes from somewhere else. At a much lower intellectual level, it reflects assumptions more carefully worked out by Erikson.

Nothing in this essay—neither its tone nor its content—indicates directly the jockeying for power between generations which fictional evocations suggest. But belief in the moral superiority and the social irresponsibility of the young provides the raw material for much fiction about power. An article paired with this one, Martha Gellhorn's "So Awful to Be Young," also avoids overt expression of anger; indeed, it explicitly identifies, in quite different terms, the emotion felt by each generation toward the other: "The young are young and won't stay that way. Their elders will never understand them, but may feel pity. No doubt, one day these young will look back on their gay, mad youth in the Espresso bars of London and tell the new young what they have missed. The young will never understand them, but may feel pity."[9] "Pity," however, hardly evokes the complexities of emotional response in this observer's account of teen-age life in London's espresso bars. Setting out "full of expectations and ignorance" (p. 42), she finds little joy, much protestation of joyfulness among the young. Bad food, lukewarm coffee, young people "with empty faces and blind eyes" (p. 46), vacuous statements about aspirin or about the Christian Union or about nothing at all ("I dint say nuthin to him but he said . . ." [p. 46]), dubious interior decoration: Gellhorn admires little that she sees or hears. At best, "charm," the "agreeably bogus," one remarkably beautiful girl telling a story about a chicken and a window:

At the end of my visit in this strange country, I had found one enviable inhabitant, for surely it would be heaven to be a tiny Chinese-Javanese-Siamese beauty, with tiny square feet and a face to break the heart and a laugh like that, and sit in an Espresso bar of an evening telling one's boon companions about chickens and windows. Failing that, however, the young can have it, it's all theirs. (P. 47)

The nature of "it" has not become altogether clear. Behind the dismissal, behind the superiority of the writer with confidence in the superior elegance and force of her own speech, the superior value of her own taste, lies bewilderment, a palpable suspicion of something yet hidden, something to account for the fact that these young people for all their vacuity believe themselves happy, feel themselves entertained. The observer declares her superiority in her ironic tourist's stance—the superiority not only of observation but of a possessed culture. Mark Abrams has his statistics to support him; Martha Gellhorn has her style. But both betray suspicion that the young, however measured, observed, and explained, know something they do not know.

Such journalistic assessments seem a far cry from *The Prime of Miss Jean Brodie*, whose adolescent characters resemble neither the working-class youth Abrams describes nor the coffee-bar habitués that preoccupy Gellhorn. The suspicion of an undefinable superiority in the young may account for the fictional development that allows Alex to triumph and leaves Smith's fantasies essentially unchallenged; it coexists with the guilt that Abrams records directly and Sillitoe and Burgess slightly more deviously, the sense that youthful failings derive from adult insufficiencies. And that dreadful suspicion becomes in a different way the subject of *Miss Jean Brodie*. Even the career of Mary Macgregor, "the last member of the set, whose fame rested on her being a silent lump, a nobody whom everybody could blame," provides a microcosmic account of how a victim can triumph (although, like Clarissa Harlow, she must die in the process) by generating unease in her oppressors.[10] Alive, Mary focuses everyone's hostility, preserves group spirit by providing a target for all. Sandy retreats in fright from the temptation to be nice to Mary, "since by this action she would separate herself, and be lonely, and blameable in a more dreadful way than Mary who, although officially the faulty one, was at least inside Miss Brodie's category of heroines in the making" (p. 38). Dead, Mary arouses everyone's guilt. When something goes wrong, the other girls wonder whether they shouldn't have been nicer to Mary; Miss Brodie wonders whether Mary perhaps betrayed her.

The other girls live to evade Miss Brodie, to escape a social organism so tight, so compellingly governed, that one might think its compulsions unavoidable. Sandy's early perception ("She perceived herself, the absent Jenny, the ever-blamed Mary, Rose, Eunice and Monica, all in a frightening little moment, in unified compliance to the destiny of Miss Brodie, as if God had willed them to birth for that purpose" [p. 38]) emphasizes the ineluctability of Miss Brodie's power; Sandy's slightly later awareness "that the Brodie set was Miss Brodie's fascisti" (p. 40) translates the metaphysical perception into political terms. Such emphatic summaries of Miss Brodie's absolute government underline the significance of her pupils' escape: the escape of young people determined to live their own lives despite their apparent compliance to adult authority. They exist in total subservience to Miss Brodie's will; then, somehow, they all get out from under. Sandy's story, the account of a character by no means entirely sympathetic, supplies evidence for the internal mechanisms by which escape is effected. Like much twentieth-century fiction, *The Prime of Miss Jean Brodie* parodies the satisfactions provided by earlier novels. Its dry tone discourages excessive response; it offers no really agreeable characters to indulge the reader's sentimentalities. Miss Brodie, compelling in her peculiarities, appealing in her romanticisms, gradually reveals the fascism that justifies Sandy's betrayal. As for Sandy, whose point of view frequently controls the narrative—Sandy, with her tiny eyes and her destiny, remains too calculating to be lovable. No character in the fiction is allowed detailed emotional gratification or full expressivity. In the background, Rose proceeds to her sensible marriage; in the foreground, Sandy becomes a nun, Miss Brodie's lover marries another (but we learn little of her reaction), Mary runs back and forth in a hotel fire and dies. Frustrated expectation governs characters and reader alike.

The powerful intergenerational dynamic between Sandy and Miss Brodie emphasizes the stature of these two as worthy antagonists, worthy allies. They share the same reflectiveness, the same tendency to organize their experience into mythic patterns, and, most crucially, the same will to control. Miss Brodie, the adult authority figure, appears at the outset to have all the advantages: the absoluteness of her convictions, the reassuring finality of her interpretations, the security of her position as possessor and transmitter of knowledge. Under her tutelage, little girls acquire her attitudes and convictions; they rest in the comfort of her assurance and experience their superiority to more ordinary students in the certainties of their beliefs: "team spirit" is bad, Pavlova is good, one must prefer "classical" to "modern" education regardless of individual gifts or propensities. If Eunice rebels against that last dictum, because she wants time for her gymnastics, Miss Brodie simply concurs in the rebellion, making that, too, her own. For children, for adolescents, one can hardly imagine escape from a system so absolute, an authority so relentless.

But Sandy learns not only from what Miss Brodie says but from what she *is*, and she uses her learning to declare her independence. Her tiny eyes focus sharply on Miss Brodie and Miss Brodie's doing, and the teacher cannot control the girl's power simply by labeling it "insight." Miss Brodie has erotic fantasies about Teddy Lloyd, the one-armed art teacher; she works out a plan for sexy Rose to sleep with Mr. Lloyd and for insightful Sandy to tell her about it.

There was no pressing hurry in the matter, for Miss Brodie liked to take her leisure over the unfolding of her plans, most of her joy deriving from the preparation, and moreover, even if these plans were as clear to her own mind as they were to Sandy's, the girls were too young. . . . But in fact the art master's interest in Rose was simply a professional one, she was a good model; Rose had an instinct to be satisfied with this role, and in the event it was Sandy who slept with Teddy Lloyd and Rose who carried back the information. (Pp. 134–35)

When Miss Brodie finds out about the episode, Sandy inquires blandly what difference it makes who sleeps with the art master; but of course she knows. Miss Brodie's gratification comes from bringing things to pass; Sandy's comes, it sometimes seems, from frustrating others' plans.

Miss Brodie turns her fantasies into verbal manipulations; Sandy follows a more inward way. Her perpetual inner drama places her in literary settings with literary companions—Allan Breck, Mr. Rochester—or converts real-life figures into their romance equivalents (the policewoman who has questioned Rose, for example). Her outer life contrasts with her inner one, in which she fills the role of romantic heroine. Externally, her stature, in girlhood, derives from her ability to control others by her imagination and "insight." She "sees" that Miss Brodie has a lover and proceeds accordingly; she tells her companion to withhold information from the teacher; she looks at Mr. Lloyd with her insolent stare, and he promptly takes her to bed; she becomes "deeply absorbed in his mind, from which she extracted, among other things, his religion as a pith from a husk" (p. 151). That religion, Roman Catholicism, makes her a nun; yet in her seclusion she continues to exercise power, the power of her mysterious being, clutching the bars, writing her book, never revealing herself. Miss Brodie, on the other hand, finally stands utterly revealed to her: hence the "betrayal." After learning that the teacher has persuaded a girl to fight for Franco and thus sent her to her death, Sandy lets the headmistress know about Miss Brodie's fascist politics, supplying the data to justify the teacher's dismissal. "If you did not betray us it is impossible that you could have been betrayed by us," Sandy writes the bewildered teacher (p. 154). Miss Brodie's betrayal consists in her use of her power to bad ends; Sandy, using her power to "put a stop to Miss Brodie," believes in the goodness of her own betrayal.

Miss Brodie and Sandy resemble one another in their concern with power and their skill at manipulation, their mastery of the politics of a small group. They differ most profoundly in outlook because of their difference in generation. Miss Brodie, to put it crudely, stands for stasis; the young embody change. When Miss Brodie, in her middle-aged prime, becomes erotically interested in an art teacher and a music teacher, she revises her account of the dead lover from her past to assimilate him to her present: she cannot allow, in her own mythology, for any essential shift. Her definitions of the girls by instinct or insight or stupidity amount to attempts to hold them steady within her comprehension. They, on the other hand, insist on growing, on passing outside the limitations of her understanding of them. The structure and style of the novel, introducing information almost as an aside, elaborating it much later, offering the same fact to the reader's attention repeatedly—the structure and style emphasize repetition and change as modes of growth. The representative of adult authority attempts to hold back the young; the young insist on progressing in their own way. Miss Brodie offers abundant "confirmation" of their identities; indeed, she eagerly creates identities for them. But only stupid Mary lives contentedly within her definition; and even Mary manages, unpredictably, to die. Miss Brodie's bewilderment—who could have betrayed me? why should anyone have wanted to? what are those young folk really up to?—echoes that of adult observers unable to understand what the young want, what they're doing; and the response Sandy offers—it's all your fault—parodies the explanation popular through the 1960s. What the young do is their elders' fault: and mutual resentment continues.

"At that age [about nineteen] behavior of older people seems, more often than not, entirely meaningless.[11] To believe in the arbitrariness of grown-up conduct provides a splendid defense for the young. Nicholas Jenkins, narrator of Anthony Powell's twelve-volume *A Dance to the Music of Time,* readily discusses what appears to him incomprehensible, although sometimes the mysterious behavior of his elders impinges forcefully on his life. On the whole, though, *A Question of Upbringing,* the narrative of Jenkins's adolescence, imagines the world of the young as subjectively self-contained, if also significantly reflective of the codes and conduct of the mature. Nothing much happens in the novel—nothing equivalent to the bizarre events of *A Clockwork Orange* or *The Prime of Miss Jean Brodie,* no inner drama so well defined as that of "The Loneliness of the Long-Distance Runner." Unlike these other works, the book records no emphatic conflict of value between a young person and an older authority figure. A headmaster suspects two boys of smoking and subjects them to minor persecution, a boy plays a trick on the headmaster: that's about it. Nicholas does not seriously fall in love, find a profession, define his nature, or triumph over anyone. The novel opens with one inconclusive encounter between Nicholas and Uncle Giles; it closes with another. But this twentieth-century fiction, depicting the process of growth as one of intensifying political awareness, focuses with peculiar intensity on the delicacies of power relationships. The politics of adolescence, as imagined here, involves not open conflict with the old but preparation for replacing them. No Squire Allsworthy exemplifies the benevolent potential of adulthood; the grown-up world provides neither admirable models nor horrors to be avoided. Yet, however irrelevant that world seems to the young, they will grow into its shapes. The unemphatic tone of *A Question of Upbringing* disguises a vision at least as bleak as that of other mid-twentieth-century works, a vision of various realms of action all controlled by power politics that participants may or may not grasp. Perception provides possibilities of dominance; such perception rarely inheres in the young, whose relative innocence enables them to proceed unknowing through civilization's minefields.

Nicholas Jenkins emphasizes the differences in perception between his adult and his adolescent self. What he does not know, as a youth, mostly involves the laws of social intercourse and of feeling. "Clearly some complicated process of sorting-out was in progress among those who surrounded me: though only years later did I become aware how early such voluntary segregations begin to develop; and of how they continue throughout life" (p. 69). ". . . A figure whose origins and demeanor suggested enigmas that I could not, in those days, even attempt to fathom" (p. 81). "At that age I was not yet old enough to be aware of the immense rage that can be secreted in the human heart by cumulative minor irritation" (p. 141). "I did not know in those days that it was impossible to convince egoists of Monsieur Dubuisson's calibre that everyone does not look on the world as if it were arranged with them . . . at its centre" (p. 145). None of these pieces of missing knowledge—and the novel alludes to many more of a similar sort—promises much pleasure in itself. Awareness about the complexities of social segregation, of origin and demeanor, of human rage and egotism brings its possessor the security of understanding aspects of a complicated and largely threatening social universe—a universe with little more reassuring knowledge to offer. Tom Jones learns the range of human badness and goodness, the spectrum from greed to benevolence, from lustful indulgence to convenience; he can thus choose goodness. Nicholas Jenkins recognizes no comparable choice. He encounters, in this chronicle of his youth, no one strikingly bad, no one remarkably good; moral categories do not occur to him. The relevant categories make social and psychological discriminations, helping their users proceed warily. Awareness and wariness, derived from the same linguistic root, imply one another in Jenkins's learning. He looks back on his adolescent years with apparent wonder that he managed to proceed unscathed with so little knowledge. Not only to proceed, but to grow. Despite its lack of manifest drama, *A Question of Upbringing,* too, reports the consolidation of an identity. Between his first and his second encounter with Uncle Giles, Nicholas Jenkins has discovered himself. The unexpected visit from his uncle at his school, early in the novel, fills Nicholas with unrest.

On the whole it could not be said that one felt better for Uncle Giles's visit.
... He was a relation: a being who had in him perhaps some of the same essence that went towards forming oneself as a separate entity. Would one's adult days be spent in worrying about the Trust? What was he going to do at Reading? Did he manage to have quite a lot of fun, or did he live in perpetual hell? These were things to be considered. (P. 25)

The impersonal passive construction of the final sentence, the impersonal third-person pronoun substituting for the first person throughout: these syntactical maneuvers reflect the distancing effort of a lad disturbed by possible connections between himself and an enigmatic adult. Understanding his own nature no better than he understands Uncle Giles's, he fears a connection whose meaning he cannot comprehend. If Uncle Giles lives in hell, perhaps he will, too; if constant worry about financial minutiae characterizes the life of one adult, it may define a necessary parameter of maturity. The mystery of "essence" and "entity" compels and eludes the young observer.

The smoking episode when Uncle Giles visits Nicholas and Stringham in their room epitomizes the perplexities of adult-adolescent relationship at this stage in Jenkins's development. The grown man infringes the taboo against smoking despite the fact that Nicholas immediately warns him of the rule and explains the danger that the housemaster, smelling smoke, will think the boys have sinned. Uncle Giles cannot grasp the situation, although he endorses the rule with sanctimonious utterances about the danger of youthful indulgence. Unquestionably in the wrong, he yet insists on an adult posture— which instead puts the boys at an obscure moral disadvantage. "Uncle Giles straightened his back and squared his shoulders. One had the impression that he was well aware that young people of the day could scarcely attempt to compete with the rigorous standards that had governed his own youth" (pp. 18-19). By the time he extinguishes his cigarette, smoke permeates the room; the headmaster, as a result, indeed believes the boys have broken the rule; when Nicholas attempts to write Uncle Giles for confirmation of their innocence, he meets no response, his letter is finally returned; the headmaster makes his students' lives deliberately uncomfortable to express his disapproval.

The fable expresses the impossibilities of the adolescent position. Nicholas merges with his uncle in the headmaster's perception: precisely the merging Nicholas fears. He can establish no unambiguous separate identity; his word requires adult confirmation. Subject to adult rule, adult suspicions, adult power, he experiences helplessness. His friend Stringham, more knowing than he, succeeds by devious means in making Uncle Giles put out the cigarette (too late); Nicholas himself, in his innocence talking straightforwardly of prohibitions and necessities, meets no success. He neither knows his own "entity" nor the power manipulations by which grown-ups operate. The episode reveals the experienced and witnessed ineffectuality of a boy just beyond childhood—an ineffectuality even exceeding the spectacular futility of Uncle Giles's every maneuver. Because Uncle Giles belongs to the upper ranks of the hierarchy of age, he possesses power altogether unrelated to his human worth.

At the novel's end, Nicholas, two or three years older (more knowing, more powerful), in effect ends his relations with Stringham, who demonstrates his own primary concern with social and sexual matters quite alien to his friend. Left at loose ends after Stringham breaks an appointment, Jenkins decides to meet Uncle Giles at the Soho restaurant the older man frequents. He finds the place uninviting, interpreting its appearance in relation to his own rupture with Stringham: "The immense depression of this soiled, claret-coloured exterior certainly seemed to meet the case; for there is always something solemn about change, even when accepted." Inside sits Uncle Giles, unsurprised to see his nephew. "It had not occurred to him that I should do otherwise than come straight up to London, so soon as informed that there was an opportunity to see him again. He put his book face-downwards on the tablecloth. I saw that it was called *Some Things That Matter*. We discussed the Trust until it was time to catch my train" (p. 230).

This final paragraph of the novel shows Nicholas more fully in control of himself and his situation than he proved earlier in the narrative. Uncle Giles has not changed, still obliviously self-concerned, obsessed with his relation to the Trust. Nicholas, on the other hand, has changed quite a lot. Now his ironic tone (in noting the title of his uncle's book, for example), his confident use of "I," his assertion of awareness (he understands what Uncle Giles is about: at the moment, not only in retrospect) mark his possession of himself as entity. If he indulges his uncle by discussing the Trust, he also sets his own limits on the discussion, which ends at his convenience. The beginnings of his maturing have brought him no particular happiness; yet the perceptible advance in consciousness and control marks the "happy ending" of this first in a long sequence of novels.

The subsequent novels report more confirmations than surprises. Events may astonish characters and readers; character, it seems, takes shape in adolescence—or perhaps before: perhaps it only becomes apparent in adolescence. Nicholas's role as watcher, the role of the narrator, derives not from mere convention but from the nature that *A Question of Upbringing* shows consolidating itself. The process by which he separates himself securely from Uncle Giles divides him also from other people. If he grows through encounters—and the book emphasizes encounter far more than event—they promote not intimacy but distance. At first he understands virtually nothing about others or about himself. He associates with Templer and Stringham because he rather vaguely likes them, but has no grasp of their natures; he finds Widmerpool ludicrous because others do so. The rearrangement of his school alliances constitutes the novel's plot. Templer and Stringham both find places in the adult world, pursuing directions Jenkins has neither the wish nor the capacity to follow: Templer turns into a vulgar young businessman; Stringham involves himself in aristocratic society. Their personalities remain mysterious: Jenkins glimpses ambiguities and paradoxes emblemized by the curious episode in which Stringham precipitates the mistaken arrest of their housemaster, thus generating for Jenkins a characteristic sequence of questions. "Why, for example, should Stringham, singularly good-natured, have chosen to persecute Le Bas in this manner? Was it a matter for regret or congratulation: had it, indeed, any meaning at all?" (p. 70). Neither motive nor meaning reveals itself to the observer; earlier, immediately after the arrest, he has watched Stringham singing a hymn as part of a congregation: "He looked grave, lost in thought, almost seraphic: a carved figure symbolizing some virtue like Resignation or Self-sacrifice" (p. 50). The discrepancy between appearance and action, like the mysteries of motivation and signification, remains impenetrable. Through such puzzlings Nicholas discovers himself, by learning what interests him. He does not, however, arrive at any articulated comprehension of his schoolfellows; he arrives only at partings from them.

Widmerpool emerges more sharply than either of the men Jenkins likes better. Earnest and ridiculous as glimpsed at school, he retains both qualities when Jenkins encounters him again during a summer in France arranged "partly as a solution to that urgent problem—inviting one's own as much as other people's attention—of the disposal of the body of one of those uneasy, stranded beings, no longer a boy and hardly yet a man" (p. 72). The stay in France, in other words, represents a way of dealing with the troublesome phenomenon of adolescence by getting its victim out of the way. Like Templer and Stringham, Widmerpool proves in some ways more grown-up than Jenkins. He has clear vocational plans (and feels shocked by Jenkins's utter lack of long-range purpose); he articulates the adult wisdom that controls the entire sequence of novels: "Brains and hard work are of very little avail, Jenkins, unless you know the right people" (p. 135). The ambiguities of "knowing" will preoccupy Jenkins throughout his recorded career. One receives brains as a gift and can work hard by will; knowing the right people—meeting them, engaging their interest, understanding them well enough to make use of them—comprises a complicated challenge. The "knowing" necessary for exploitation, Widmerpool's kind, does not necessarily coincide with the "knowing" of the observer-writer, Jenkins. Jenkins watches in fascination as two Scandinavians, grown men, feud; Widmerpool sets out, rather successfully, to reconcile them. His success does not significantly qualify Jenkins's unreasoned sense of superiority to him, nor is it likely to modify the reader's more or less amused perception of his gracelessness and of something morally distasteful about him, a perception derived, of course, from the narrator's. Yet Widmerpool exemplifies the strength of adolescent will focused on the necessity to assert power in an adult world. Like Stringham and Templer, although in a mode different from theirs, he understands realities of power which Jenkins has yet to grasp.

In the society Powell depicts, as all these instances suggest, growing up depends crucially on knowledge—on awareness and its corollary wariness. Even the burgeoning sexuality of adolescence proves for Jenkins more importantly a matter of knowledge than of experience. When he dances with Lady McReith, a fellow guest at the Templers', he finds the experience "intoxicating" but immediately translates it into terms larger than those of immediate emotion. "The revelation was something far more universal in implication than a mere sense of physical attraction toward Lady McReith. It was realization, in a moment of time, not only of her own possibilities, far from inconsiderable ones, but also of other possibilities that life might hold; and my chief emotion was surprise" (p. 92). He realizes also that Peter Templer already knows what he has first discovered. "Keen awareness of Peter's point of view on the subject followed logically on a better apprehension of the elements that went towards forming Lady McReith as a personality" (p. 92). Awareness, logic, and apprehension control the potential terrors of physical awakening, converted, like most of the novel's happenings, into social and intellectual terms. Similarly, Jean Templer's behavior at a dance has the effect for Jenkins of "precipitating acquaintance with a whole series of emotions and apprehensions, the earliest of numberless similar ones in due course to be undergone" (p. 93). The curious distance of the formulation strikes the novel's characteristic note. Jenkins acknowledges only acquaintance with his feelings: one more form of controlling knowledge.

Like *The Prime of Miss Jean Brodie*, *A Question of Upbringing* depends for effect on perceived continuities between youthful and adult life. The extreme generational hostility of the Burgess and Sillitoe works does not exist here. Templer offers "a somewhat menacing picture of his father's habitually cantankerous behavior" which Jenkins fails to take seriously "because of Templer's tendency to impute bad temper to anyone placed in a position of authority in relation to himself" (p. 72). Templer's tendency, perhaps a milder version of Smith's in "The Loneliness of the Long-Distance Runner," does not characterize the novel's other young people, who, on the contrary, seek clues about life's mysteries from the conduct of their elders and who yield unprotestingly to authority or ignore it. From the point of view of the adult reader, however, the novel nonetheless offers little reassurance. Unlike earlier works, it encourages no nostalgia for the lost pleasure of youth. Adolescents appear afflicted with ignorance, not blessed by innocence. They do not enjoy themselves in any vivid way. When Jenkins nerves himself to make a romantic declaration to the French girl who attracts him, he finds himself speaking tenderly to a matron whose identity he has briefly confused. The contretemps epitomizes the adolescent situation, the plight of those ever at cross-purposes with themselves. They display no moral superiority to their elders: not the superiority of Tom Jones in his natural virtue nor that of Smith with his class integrity nor even that of Alex in his determination to remain himself. On the other hand, their elders demonstrate no superiority to them either. Although the young learn from the old—as they have, by the testimony of fiction and journalism and sermons, for several hundred years—they do not learn goodness: they learn only the ways of the world. The grown-ups in *A Question of Upbringing* occupy themselves with getting ahead in the financial or social world, with making use of those they know to consolidate a sense of worth. They teach the young to do the same.

The psychological satisfaction such fiction provides for adults partakes of the pleasures of self-castigation. Increasingly in the twentieth century, the novel of adolescence provides not only a device for criticizing the existing state of society (a function it has served from the beginning) but also a record of adult guilt. All grown-ups offer the young is knowingness. The awareness, the knowledge, that represent the goal of social and political education—the education that in fiction has replaced moral training—appear rather shabby attainments. As Erikson points out, the mature require confirmation by their juniors. Confirmation resides in imitation: but as Powell's adolescents imitate their adult models, they reveal the inadequacy of those models. The phenomenology of adolescence, as rendered in Powell's restrained and Burgess's flamboyant fiction, through the social sentimentality of Sillitoe and the social cynicism of Spark, exposes the barrenness of the adult world.

Epilogue

Like the death of parents, the growth of children speaks of mortality to the middle-aged. The adolescent rejects boundaries, blithely crosses them, refusing to stay put, to remain a child, to accept subservience, to be predictable. His or her ability to avoid restrictions as though none existed, to leap walls that keep grown-ups in their place, declares the power of beginnings. On the other hand, the adolescent lacks money and self-defined social status and power in the world of affairs. Because adults possess these commodities, they retain, after all, some capacity for controlling their juniors, or at least for limiting the consequences of their freedom.

The terms of this summary belong to the twentieth century, but its substance—except for the first sentence—echoes descriptions from the last three centuries. John Locke and Erik Erikson would recognize one another's portraits of youth. The assortment of texts examined in this study display striking unanimity in their descriptive evocations; they differ in the meanings they assign to the phenomena described. Few generalizations present themselves after one has read a mass of material about youth from the last three centuries: the same attitudes recur in every period; no period provides unanimous assessment.

The judgments of and prescriptions for adolescents that emerge in these texts arrange themselves along a single axis, between the polarities of an ideology of harmony and one of conflict. Influenced by Freud but also, I suspect, by our knowledge of national and international politics, we expect opposition as the norm of family relationships as we expect it in more public patterns of relation. Sir Richard Steele and Samuel Johnson noted the *fact* of such opposition as well: but Steele could argue for an ideal of intergenerational harmony as a goal toward which all should strive (although Johnson, like a twentieth-century psychologist, assumed the inevitability of generational clash).

Conflict versus harmony as the polarities for discussions of adolescence involves more, however, than the relations between generations. Assumptions and hopes about the relations between individuals and their society also influence the kinds of significance attached to adolescence. The adolescent is an outsider, not a full member of his society: virtually everyone who thinks about the subject perceives that. Is this position one of weakness or of strength? Should adults try to help the young adjust themselves to social reality, or should they defer to the fresher vision of the young? Such questions bear on the nature of ideological commitment. One aspect of the official "public" ideology shared by many adults in the last three centuries is reflected in the concept of developmental theory, regardless of the specific manifestations assigned to stages of development. Development implies growth; theories of development rest on the assumption that the movement from childhood to adulthood represents progress. Erikson's eight ages even more emphatically than Shakespeare's seven speak an optimistic mythology of accretion and improvement. The adult, such theories suggest, should nurture the less-developed young. Knowing more, understanding more, experiencing more, grown-ups have achieved mastery to which their juniors can only distantly aspire. The hierarchy can seem benign because everyone, simply by surviving, sooner or later reaches a position of relative power, but its benignity does not diminish its essential rigidity.

Public ideologies are not the only ideologies, now or in the past. The suspicion that "development" constitutes a social myth received forceful articulation in the nineteenth century, with its wistful celebrations of childhood; but despite the scientific support adduced for various developmental theories in our own century, the last seventy-five or eighty years have also generated a literature of antidevelopment. Even the eighteenth century offers evidence of suspicion that the manifest masteries associated with adulthood do not necessarily correspond to profound understanding or control of actuality: Tom Jones grasps more about the world than does Mr. Nightingale, in some ways more than Squire Allworthy.

On the other hand, theories of psychological development *do* correspond to the realities of public power. Social authority belongs to the old, as everyone knows; the notion of consistent development justifies the allocation. Our psychology confirms our sociology.

Adolescence has something subversive about it. The adolescent's perception of self does not necessarily fit orthodox psychological or social theory, nor do adolescent actions. As perceived by their elders, adolescents often embody the conflict of private and public ideologies, the young standing for the authority of the personal, the unique, against the generalizing assumptions of their seniors. Although theories of development leave room for temporary regressions and false starts, the individual young often suggest that such unchartable anomalies, rather than more orderly alternatives, represent the most significant truth. Adults have to deal with the young's reluctance to be categorized.

Although these observations derive more immediately from life than from literature, written texts confirm them. Three centuries' records of adolescence display a consistency of tension between perceptions of youthful and adult modes of mastery. The tension reveals itself sometimes between fictional and didactic texts, sometimes within examples of either genre. Although many writers in both modes offer firm pronouncements about the balance of virtue between young and old, their prose frequently betrays the strain of such firmness.

Didactic works in their nature usually propound public ideology, speaking for the professed ideals and standards of a society. Sermons, educational manuals, conduct books, even journalistic recommendations to parents and children: all assume knowledge of what should be, and rarely is that knowledge eccentric. The proliferation of admonitory works for and about the young itself suggests adult uneasiness about youthful impulse: only by pouring out verbiage do we keep the young in line. Only thus, perhaps, do we reassure ourselves that we *know*.

The moralistic writings of the eighteenth and nineteenth centuries consistently recommend compliance with social decorums, suggest that the young behaved better in the past than they do in the present, insist on the high importance of conventional good behavior. Their often frantic adjurations indicate the belief of their writers that all too often the young in actuality fail to behave in the ways recommended. The twentieth century has generated new modes of didacticism: not advice to the young and their parents, but descriptions, psychological and sociological, of how, in detail, the young *do* behave: norms of expectation rather than of recommendation. Such descriptions speak more directly of insubordination, nonconformity, defiance. Both kinds of writing, prescription and description, indicate the longing of the

291

adult world that their children should confirm their values—by living up to them even better than their parents have done or, at the very least, by paying lip service to them.

Twentieth-century commentators, sometimes nineteenth-century ones as well, may declare themselves, implicitly or explicitly, on the side of the young. That doesn't make much difference: even so, they render the same perceived or dreaded clash of values between the generations. Grown-ups, too, can claim the condition of outsiders, but they cannot readily avoid the discomfort of inhabiting a social universe divided into outside and inside.

Adolescents, much writing indicates, always remind us of the society's divisions. Symbolically representing one polarity—passion as opposed to reason, say; or dependency as opposed to power—they thus encourage adults to define themselves as other; at the very least, they evoke the ambivalence associated with passion and power and the rest. The teleological structure of didactic writing implies certainty: a teacher must know what he teaches. Eighteenth- and nineteenth-century moralists *did* know; they admitted no doubts about proprieties of thought and behavior. But Wetenhall Wilkes suggested fairly openly something implicit in many of his contemporaries and successors. As he explained that he knew how young people should behave precisely because he himself behaved badly as a youth, he raised the problem of identification between the mature and those whom they may see as versions of their younger selves. Seldom does one altogether reject an earlier self. With urgencies of advice the moralists sought to suppress inconvenient impulse; but the urgencies often imperfectly conceal wistfulness, longing, admiration. In the purportedly scientific descriptions of our own time, such emotions on occasion emerge with yet greater vividness.

In the punitive note of many didactic texts one can equally well discern more negative feelings toward the young: anger, fear, also compatible with the semiconscious realization that youthful objects of instruction bear some relation to previous avatars of the instructor. The young appear to embody inconvenient aspects of the self, inconvenient components of society, difficult to assimilate, impossible to eliminate. The contradictory feelings they evoke reflect adults' simultaneous awareness of civilization's discontents (grown-ups have already paid the price they demand that their juniors pay) and its rewards (we try to feel the gains are worth the cost, and to assure the young of the fact).

The testimony of uncertain feeling in didactic texts is less vivid than in fiction, which need not direct itself so insistently toward support of the orthodox. (Fiction, indeed, helps us to understand the moralizers more than they illuminate it.) Here the terms of ambivalence and conflict become more apparent; here we see more clearly the forms of the struggle for power between young and old, the politics of generations. Adolescents provide appropriate fictional material because they exist always (so we believe) in a condition of desire. They want intensely: want love, excitement, gain, supremacy, challenge—whatever. The moralists' urgings of subservience endeavor to control such want; the nineteenth-century warnings against ambition acknowledge it while denouncing it. Desire supplies energy, generates conflict, makes action—the stuff of novels. It also raises questions of value. The *Bildungsroman* structure nominally evades such questions by implying that growing up constitutes a goal as well as a process. The generations follow each other in orderly succession; the desires of the young provide, at most, temporary interruptions in the reassuring sequence.

Even in the eighteenth century, though, and more in the nineteenth century, and more still in the twentieth, novelists, as we have seen, sometimes suggested the losses implicit in growing up. To emphasize such losses involves implicit celebration of adolescent desire. The world denies fulfillment for most youthful dreams; to attain maturity implies relinquishing earlier fantasies. But fiction often reminds us how much we have given up in growing up, as it locates value and attraction in those too young to be sensible. Of course, the novelist who designates as adolescents characters dominated by fantasy thus provides in effect a ready-made explanation for their lack of realism: several centuries of expectation stand behind the view of the young as dreamers. Fantasy, hope, aspiration belong by well-established convention to teen-agers. No wonder fiction flourishes around them!

Didactic writers often implicitly assume that the young want, among other things, worldly success, that they yearn for prestige and power. Novelists rarely imagine such desires. On the contrary, fiction dwells on specifically those youthful desires most incompatible with social actuality: perfect love, impossible creativity, inconceivable moral improvement in the world. The adolescent in fiction thus allows the novelist to explore at least the imagining of alternatives to the given without making firm commitment to them. The fascination of the young as fictional subjects, one must suspect, has always derived partly from their anomalous relation to society. At precisely the same period when moralists were urging teen-agers to behave either like children or like grown-ups, novelists had already begun to enjoy the potentialities of their in-between stage of development.

The perception of adolescents as outsiders with the capacity either to deny or to confirm their societies by choosing or not choosing to enter the inside helps to account for one of the few clear trends emerging from this survey of writing about the young. In general, one can detect a movement toward increasingly intense identification with the young on the part of novelists who evoke them. More and more now, as social organization provides less satisfaction, *everyone* wants to be an outsider. The adolescent can appear heroic in not belonging; the novelist can express through adolescent characters a wistful longing to share their condition. Such longing rarely lacks ambivalence, as works like *A Clockwork Orange* and *Absolute Beginners* attest. The degree to which nonconformists are "punished" suggests not only the paranoia of novelists about their own traditional roles as outsiders, but the possibility of punitive impulse fostered by the dual identification with adolescents and with adult contemporaries.

In all periods, with varying vocabulary but unvarying perception, observers and imaginers of adolescence have associated this life stage with intense feeling. The perception is the most consistent observation of the young, and in many ways the most important—both for the literary emphases it generates and for those it causes writers to avoid. The young compel imaginative involvement as beings who care intensely what happens—to them especially, but also to others, on occasion even to the world at large. This fact (or persistent fantasy) provides another way of accounting for continuing fictional concentration on youth. In earlier periods than our own, however, the two kinds of intense emotion that most often manifest themselves in the young—those fundamental impulses of aggression and sexuality—have often been sharply criticized by the novelistic action (as in *Tom Jones*) or carefully obscured (as in *Evelina* and the works of Scott and Austen). Even Smollett, who allows his protagonists relatively free indulgence of their inclinations toward both open and covert aggression, causes them to reform in the end. The politics of generational relationship, as expressed in the writing of novels, involves a good deal of suppression. Only in the twentieth century does celebration of the *specific* feelings of the young correspond in intensity to the controlling devices that fiction allows.

The shapes of novels have changed in three centuries, even of novels that might reasonably be described as "realistic." The different range of permissible subject matter, of course, changes the raw material for plots. But the characteristic form of those plots has also altered. The typical eighteenth-century novel of adolescence moves toward a fairly definitive happy ending in which the protagonist symbolically enters his or her anticipated adulthood. By the nineteenth century, more ambiguous conclusions abound: heroes and heroines still grow up, often, and marry, but as early as Austen the action preceding such denouements raises questions about the possible value and fulfillment of conventional maturity. The twentieth-century fiction of adolescence moves typically toward indeterminate conclusions. Such shifts chart the decline in optimism and confidence familiar enough in other manifestations; they emphasize the degree to which adults' literary treatment of adolescents reflects their feelings about social possibility. Relative confidence in the viability of an existing social system allows the structuring of orderly plots with fortunate outcomes; the possibility of imagining the fortunate erodes along with that of believing in the rightness of the given.

The shifting shapes of these fictions speak also of changes in beliefs about how change occurs and what it means. In the eighteenth century, when Locke dominated thought about education, the conviction that adults bear responsibility for much that is written on the tablets of the child's mind implied the high importance of adults. Accepting responsibility for the moral and intellectual welfare of adolescents as well as children, accepting responsibility for orderly sequences of growth in the young, grown-ups reminded themselves of their power. If they bore the burden of guilt for adolescents who went wrong, even that declared that the mature made all conceivable difference in the world. The move toward inwardness in the early nineteenth century implied new notions of responsibility. If the quality of perception, of consciousness, counted, that was quite independent, most of the time, of adult influence. And degree of consciousness, unlike degree of knowledge, has little connection to chronological age. Society's elders no longer could be thought to control all change in the young. (They might continue to believe in, or to claim, their own power, but the young had new ideological weapons against them.) Change took place within, by incalculable laws of individual personality; novels turned to the subject of such change.

I am exaggerating, of course, the sharp difference between eighteenth- and nineteenth-century convictions. Neither the world nor the novels in it altered suddenly and definitively as the eighteenth century gave place to the nineteenth. There is nothing startling about the idea that people came more and more to value individual internal experience, or that the novel reflected the new emphasis. Less frequently observed is the correlation between emphasis on the inner life and interest in the adolescent as subject. The young, with intense feelings often readily proclaimed, provide plausible material for investigation of the inner life, for celebration of its intensities, for criticism of the obstacles society provides against its flowering. Fiction of the nineteenth and twentieth century has increasingly explored these opportunities.

The young embody our most profound vulnerabilities and our most intimate strengths. They speak to us of our past and of our future. We can imagine them as licensed transgressors, surrogates for ourselves, or as prophets of salvation; as violaters or precursors of system. In the past three centuries, writers *have* imagined them in all these ways. The struggle of father and son, mother and daughter, is no critical metaphor but a fact of experience—as is the love between generations. From such crucial facts, mythologies burgeon. The mythology of adolescence, recorded in fiction and in social, psychological, moral, and theological commentary, tells us of ourselves, our ancestors, and our descendants.

Notes

Chapter 1: "Exploration, Becoming, Growth, and Pain"

1. Sigmund Freud, "Family Romances," *Collected Papers,* ed. James Strachey, 5 vols. (New York: Basic Books, 1959), vol. V, p. 74.
2. Genesis 37:7.
3. Genesis 37:9.
4. Bruno Bettelheim, "The Problem of Generations," in *The Challenge of Youth,* ed. Erik H. Erikson (Garden City: Doubleday, 1965), pp. 76–109.
5. John and Virginia Demos, "Adolescence in Historical Perspective," *Journal of Marriage and Family* 31 (1969): 632.
6. See Kingsley Davis, "Adolescence and the Social Structure," *Annals of the American Academy of Political and Social Science* 235 (1944): 8.
7. Lawrence Stone, *The Family, Sex and Marriage in England 1500–1800* (New York: Harper & Row, 1977), p. 376.
8. *Le Grand Propriétaire de toutes choses,* quoted in Philippe Ariès, *Centuries of Childhood,* tr. Robert Baldick (New York: Vintage Books, 1962), p. 21.
9. Erik H. Erikson, *Childhood and Society,* 2nd ed. (New York: Norton, 1963), pp. 262–63.
10. John Locke, *Some Thoughts Concerning Education* (London: A. and J. Churchill, 1693), p. 254.
11. William Cobbett, *Advice to Young Men, and (Incidentally) to Young Women, in the Middle and Higher Ranks of Life* (London, 1829), letter III, p. 83.
12. Cyril S. Smith, *Adolescence: An Introduction to the Problems of Order and the Opportunities for Continuity Presented by Adolescence in Britain* (London: Longmans, 1968), p. 2.
13. Frank Musgrove, *Youth and the Social Order* (London: Routledge & Kegan Paul, 1964), p. 10.
14. Erik H. Erikson, *Life History and the Historical Moment* (New York: Norton, 1975), p. 222.
15. Kenneth Keniston, "Psychological Development and Historical Change," *Journal of Interdisciplinary History* 2:2 (1971): 331–32.
16. Introduction to *The Family in History,* ed. Charles E. Rosenberg (Philadelphia: University of Pennsylvania Press, 1975), p. 9.
17. Geoffrey H. Hartman, "A Short History of Practical Criticism," *New Literary History,* 10 (1979): 502.

Chapter 2: "Nobody's Power"

1. Henry Home, Lord Kames, *Loose Hints upon Education, Chiefly Concerning the Culture of the Heart,* 2nd ed. (Edinburgh: John Bell, 1782), p. 256.
2. *The Lady's Preceptor, taken from the French of the Abbe D'Ancourt, and adapted to the Religion, Customs, and Manners of the English Nation,* 2nd ed. (London: J. Watts, 1743), p. 28.
3. Michel Foucault, *A History of Sexuality,* tr. Robert Hurley (New York: Pantheon, 1978), p. 18.
4. Eliza Haywood, *The Female Spectator,* 4 vols. (London: T. Gardner, 1745), III, 179.

5. Samuel Johnson, *The Rambler*, ed. W. J. Bate and Albrecht B. Strauss, The Yale Edition of the Works of Samuel Johnson (New Haven: Yale University Press, 1969), no. 130, 15 June 1751; IV, 330.

6. *Rambler* no. 133, 25 June 1751; IV, 342.

7. Wetenhall Wilkes, *A Letter of Genteel and Moral Advice to a Young Lady* (London: M. Cooper, 1744), p. 81.

8. *The Early Diary of Frances Burney*, ed. Annie Raine Ellis, 2 vols. (London: Bell, 1889), entry for 27 March 1768; I, 4.

9. Samuel Richardson, *Pamela, or Virtue Rewarded* (New York: Norton, 1958), p. 176. Subsequent references to this edition will be incorporated in the text.

10. John Gay, *The Beggar's Opera*, 3rd ed. (London: John Watts, 1733) Act I, Scene v, p. 8.

11. Charlotte M. Yonge, *The Daisy Chain, or Aspirations: A Family Chronicle* (London: Macmillan, 1899), p. 163.

12. "A Fear for the Future," *Fraser's Magazine* 59 (1859): 245.

13. Dorothea Beale, "On the Education of Girls," *Fraser's Magazine* 74 (1866): 523.

14. Dinah Mulock, "In Her Teens," *Macmillan's Magazine* 10 (1864): 220.

15. "Female Education, and Modern Match-making," *Fraser's Magazine* 13 (1836): 309–10.

16. Charles Kingsley, "Thrift," *Sanitary and Social Lectures and Essays, The Works of Charles Kingsley*, vol. 18 (London, 1880), p. 78.

17. "A Fear for the Future," *Fraser's Magazine* 59 (1859): 243.

18. Elizabeth Garrett Anderson, "Sex in Mind and Education: A Reply," *Fortnightly Review* 15 n.s. (1874): 590.

19. Edith J. Simcox, "Custom and Sex," *Fortnightly Review* 11 n.s. (1872): 320.

20. "Women's Education," *Fraser's Magazine* 79 (1869): 537.

21. Harriet Martineau, *Household Education* (London: Edward Moxon, 1849), pp. 257–58.

22. Elizabeth Gaskell, *Wives and Daughters*, ed. Frank Glover Smith (Baltimore: Penguin, 1969), p. 35. Subsequent references to this edition will be incorporated in the text.

23. Doris Lessing, *Martha Quest* (New York: New American Library, 1970), pp. 7–8. Subsequent references to this edition will be incorporated in the text.

24. G. Prys Williams, London School of Economics, quoted by Harry Hopkins in *The New Look: A Social History of the Forties and Fifties in Britain* (London: Secker & Warburg, 1963), p. 423.

25. John Barron Mays, *The Young Pretenders: A Study of Teenage Culture in Contemporary Society* (New York: Schocken Books, 1965), p. 165.

26. John R. Gillis, *Youth and History: Tradition and Change in European Age Relations 1770–Present* (New York: Academic Press, 1974), p. 207.

27. Peter Laurie, *The Teenage Revolution* (London: Anthony Blond, 1965), p. 133.

28. E. M. Eppel and M. Eppel, *Adolescents and Morality* (London: Routledge & Kegan Paul, 1966), p. 61.

29. L. Joseph Stone and Joseph Church, "Pubescence, Puberty, and Physical Development," *The Psychology of Adolescence: Essential Readings*, ed. Aaron H. Esman (New York: International Universities Press, 1975), p. 83.

30. Cyril S. Smith, *Adolescence: An Introduction to the Problems of Order and the Opportunities for Continuity Presented by Adolescence in Britain* (London: Longmans, 1968), p. 75.

31. Elizabeth Douvan and Joseph Adelson, *The Adolescent Experience* (New York: John Wiley, 1966), p. 229.

Chapter 3: "Straight from Mother Nature"

1. Colin MacInnes, *Absolute Beginners, The London Novels* (New York: Farrar, Straus & Giroux, 1969), p. 261.

2. Samuel Johnson, *The Rambler*, ed. W. J. Bate and Albrecht B. Strauss, The Yale

Notes

Edition of the Works of Samuel Johnson (New Haven: Yale University Press, 1969), no. 84, 5 January 1751; IV, 81.

3. *The Spectator*, ed. George A. Aitken, 8 vols. (London: John C. Nimmo, 1898), no. 153, 25 August 1711; I, 342.

4. *Rambler*, no. 196, 1 February 1752; V, 258.

5. *The Connoisseur, The British Essayists*, ed. Alexander Chalmers (Boston: Little, Brown, 1856), no. 78, 24 July 1755; XXVI, 78–79.

6. Isaac Watts, *The Improvement of the Mind: Or, A Supplement to the Art of Logick* (London: James Brackstone, 1741), pp. 102–3.

7. Eliza Haywood, *The Female Spectator*, 4 vols. (London: T. Gardner, 1745), IV, 176–77.

8. Hannah More, *Essays on Various Subjects, Principally Designed for Young Ladies* (London: Wilkie and Cadell, 1777), pp. 92–93.

9. *Youth Persuaded to Obedience, Gratitude, and Honour to God and Their Parents* (Newcastle: I. Thompson, 1754), p. 7.

10. Wetenhall Wilkes, *A Letter of Genteel and Moral Advice to a Young Lady* (London: M. Cooper, 1744), pp. 64–65.

11. *Collected Works of Oliver Goldsmith*, ed. Arthur Friedman, 4 vols. (Oxford: Oxford University Press, 1966), IV, 18.

12. Charles Kingsley, "Fathers and Children," *Sermons for the Times, The Works of Charles Kingsley*, vol. XXIII (London, 1888), pp. 7–8.

13. Kingsley, "Sonship," *Sermons*, p. 106.

14. Herbert Spencer, *Education: Intellectual, Moral, and Physical* (New York, 1893), pp. 190–91. First edition 1860.

15. Thomas Hughes, *Tom Brown at Oxford* (London: Macmillan, 1914), p. 408. First published 1861.

16. Harriet Martineau, *Household Education* (London: Edward Moxon, 1849), p. 324.

17. William Cobbett, *Advice to Young Men, and (Incidentally) to Young Women, in the Middle and Higher Ranks of Life* (London, 1829), p. 30.

18. Samuel Smiles, *Self-Help, with Illustrations of Conduct & Perseverance* (London: John Murray, 1969), p. 232. First edition 1859.

19. Frederick Greenwood, "Reflections on My Daughter's Marriage," *Cornhill Magazine* 6 (1862): 804.

20. William Makepeace Thackeray, *The History of Pendennis* (London: Macmillan, 1911), p. 71. Subsequent references to this edition will be incorporated in the text.

21. William Makepeace Thackeray, "Roundabout Papers—No. I: On a Lazy Idle Boy," *Cornhill Magazine* 1 (1860): 127.

22. Cyril S. Smith, *Adolescence: An Introduction to the Problems of Order and the Opportunities for Continuity Presented by Adolescence in Britain* (London: Longmans, 1968), p. 2.

23. Peter Laurie, *The Teenage Revolution* (London: Anthony Blond, 1965), p. 9.

24. F. Musgrove, *Youth and the Social Order* (London: Routledge & Kegan Paul, 1964), p. 16.

25. John Barron Mays, *The Young Pretenders: A Study of Teenage Culture in Contemporary Society* (New York: Schocken Books, 1965), p. 15.

26. Edward Shorter, *The Making of the Modern Family* (New York: Basic Books, 1975), p. 8.

27. Harry Hopkins, *The New Look: A Social History of the Forties and Fifties in Britain* (London: Secker & Warburg, 1963), p. 423.

28. Clifford Geertz, "Religion As a Cultural System," *The Interpretation of Cultures* (New York: Basic Books, 1973), p. 100.

29. John Calvin, *Calvin's New Testament Commentaries*, tr. T. H. L. Parker (Grand Rapids, 1972), XI, 182–84; quoted by William J. Bouwsma, "Christian Adulthood," *Daedalus* 105 (1976): 80–81.

30. Erik H. Erikson, *Life History and the Historical Moment* (New York: W. W. Norton, 1975), p. 109.

31. *The Writings of Jonathan Swift*, ed. Robert A. Greenberg and William B. Piper (New York: Norton, 1973), p. 114.

Notes

Chapter 4: Perplexities of Passion: The Eighteenth Century

1. James Burgh, *Youth's Friendly Monitor: Being a Set of Directions, Prudential, Moral, Religious, and Scientific* (London: M. Cooper, 1756), pp. 58–59.

2. James Fordyce, *Addresses to Young Men*, 3rd ed., 2 vols. (London: Cadell, 1789), I, 64. First edition 1777.

3. Henry Home, Lord Kames, *Loose Hints upon Education, Chiefly Concerning the Culture of the Heart* (Edinburgh: John Bell, 1782), p. 249.

4. *Thraliana: The Diary of Mrs. Hester Lynch Thrale, 1776–1809*, ed. Katherine C. Balderston, 2nd ed., 2 vols. (Oxford: Oxford University Press, 1951), I, 462–63.

5. William Dodd, *Sermons to Young Men*, 3 vols. (London: Knox and Cadell, 1761), II, 87.

6. John Aikin, *Letters from a Father to a Son*, 2 vols. (New York: Garland, 1971), I, 8. Vol. I, written in 1792–93, was first published in 1796.

7. Henry Fielding, *Joseph Andrews and Shamela*, ed. Martin C. Battestin (Boston: Houghton Mifflin, 1961), p. 256. Subsequent references to this edition will be incorporated in the text.

8. Samuel Richardson, *Clarissa, or The History of a Young Lady*, 4 vols. (London: Dent, 1932), I, 486. Subsequent references to this edition will be incorporated in the text.

9. David Fordyce, *Dialogues Concerning Education*, 2nd ed. (London, 1745), p. 266.

10. Isaac Watts, *The Improvement of the Mind: Or, A Supplement to The Art of Logick* (London: James Brackstone, 1741), pp. 329–30.

11. *Youth Persuaded to Obedience, Gratitude, and Honour to God and Their Parents* (Newcastle: I. Thompson, 1754), p. 14.

12. "A New Method for Making Women As Useful and As Capable of Maintaining Themselves, As the Men Are," *Gentleman's Magazine* 9 (1739): 526.

13. James Burgh, *The Dignity of Human Nature*, 2 vols. (London: Johnson and Payne, 1767), I, 209.

14. *The Plain Dealer*, 2 vols. (London: Richardson and Wilde, 1730), no. 11, 27 April 1724; I, 78.

15. John Bennett, *Letters to a Young Lady*, 6th American ed. (Hudson: William Norman, 1811), p. 186. First edition 1789.

16. *The Polite Lady: Or A Course of Female Education, In a Series of Letters, from a Mother to her Daughter*, 2nd ed. (London: Newbery and Carnan, 1769), p. 114. First edition 1760.

17. John Bennett, *Strictures on Female Education: Chiefly As it Relates to the Culture of the Heart* (Norwich: Bushnell, [1788]), p. 123.

18. Isaac Watts, *A Treatise on the Education of Children and Youth*, 2nd ed. (London: J. Buckland, 1769), p. 158.

19. Tobias Smollett, *Roderick Random* (London: Oxford University Press, 1930), p. 498. Subsequent references to this edition will be incorporated in the text.

20. Hester Chapone, *Letters on the Improvement of the Mind, Addressed to a Young Lady*, 2nd ed., 2 vols. (London: J. Walter, 1783), II, 144. First edition 1773.

21. John Locke, *Some Thoughts Concerning Education* (London: A. and J. Churchill, 1693), pp. 255–56.

22. John Gregory, *A Father's Legacy to his Daughters*, 4th ed. (London: W. Strahan, 1774), p. 102. First edition also 1774.

23. See, for a few examples, James Fordyce, *Sermons to Young Women*, 4th ed., 2 vols. (London: Millar and Cadell, 1767), I, 212–13 ("warm fancy") and I, 292 ("natural Fire"); Mary Wollstonecraft, *Thoughts on the Education of Daughters* (New York: Garland, 1974; first published 1787), p. 146 ("warm affections"); Bennett, *Letters*, p. 76 (warm imagination); Gregory, p. 10 (warm imagination).

24. Hannah More, *Strictures on the Modern System of Female Education*, 2 vols. (London: Cadell and Davies, 1799), I, 202.

25. William Dodd, *Sermons to Young Men*, 3 vols. (London: Knox and Cadell, 1771), III, 180–81. See also III, 238–39; II, 197; II, 72.

26. Philip Dormer Stanhope, Earl of Chesterfield, *Letters to His Son*, 2nd ed., 4 vols. (London: Dodsley, 1774), 26 July O.S. 1748; II, 31 and 13 Dec. O.S. 1748, II, 114. See also

27 May O.S. 1748, II, 7; 12 Oct. O.S. 1748, II, 78; 30 July O.S. 1749, II, 190; 8 Feb. O.S. 1750, II, 344–45.

27. George Lillo, "The London Merchant," II, i, in *Eighteenth-Century Plays,* ed. Ricardo Quintana (New York: Random House, 1952), pp. 305–6.

28. Maria Cooper, *The History of Fanny Meadows,* 2 vols. (London: T. Becket, 1775), I, 118–19.

29. Frances Burney, *Evelina, or the History of a Young Lady's Entrance into the World,* ed. Edward A. Bloom (London: Oxford University Press, 1970), pp. 30–31. First published 1778.

30. Henry Fielding, *The History of Tom Jones, A Foundling* (New York: New American Library, 1963), bk. IX, ch. i, p. 412. First published 1749.

Chapter 5: Annals of Anxiety

1. Hannah More, *Essays on Various Subjects, Principally Designed for Young Ladies* (London: Wilkie and Cadell, 1777), pp. 145–46.

2. Henry Home, Lord Kames, *Loose Hints upon Education, Chiefly Concerning the Culture of the Heart,* 2nd ed. (Edinburgh: John Bell, 1782), pp. 255–56.

3. Maria Edgeworth and Richard Lovell Edgeworth, *Practical Education,* 2 vols. (London: J. Johnson, 1798), II, 528.

4. Erasmus Darwin, *A Plan for the Conduct of Female Education* (Philadelphia: John Ormrod, 1798), p. 13.

5. *Thraliana: The Diary of Mrs. Hester Lynch Thrale, 1776–1809,* ed. Katharine C. Balderston, 2nd ed., 2 vols. (Oxford: Clarendon Press, 1951), 15 March 1784, pp. 590–91.

6. Hannah More, *Strictures on the Modern System of Female Education,* 2 vols. (London: Cadell and Davies, 1799), I, 103.

7. Mary Wollstonecraft, *Thoughts on the Education of Daughters* (New York: Garland, 1974), p. 95. First edition 1787.

8. Mary Wollstonecraft, *A Vindication of the Rights of Woman,* ed. Carol H. Poston (New York: W. W. Norton, 1975), p. 162. First edition 1792.

9. Catharine Macaulay, *Letters on Education,* ed. Gina Luria (New York: Garland, 1974), p. 217. First edition 1790.

10. John Bennett, *Letters to a Young Lady, on a Variety of Useful and Interesting Subjects,* 6th American ed. (Hudson: William Norman, 1811), Advertisement. First edition 1789.

11. Mary Hays, *Memoirs of Emma Courtney,* 2 vols. (New York: Griffith, 1802), I, 14. First edition 1796.

12. Charlotte Lennox, *The Female Quixote, or, The Adventures of Arabella,* ed. Margaret Dalziel (London: Oxford University Press, 1970), p. 5. First edition 1752.

13. Charlotte Palmer, *Female Stability: Or, The History of Miss Belville,* 5 vols. (London: Newbery, 1789), I, 125.

14. Robert Bage, *Man As He Is,* 4 vols. (London: William Lane, 1792), I, ii–iii.

15. Mary Ann Hanway, *Ellinor; or, The World As It Is,* 4 vols. (London: Minerva Press, 1798), preface, I, iii.

16. Ann Radcliffe, *The Mysteries of Udolpho,* 2 vols. (London: Dent, 1931), II, 63. First edition 1794.

Chapter 6: The Generations: Imagination and Growth

1. Sir Walter Scott, *Waverley or 'Tis Sixty Years Since,* 2 vols., The New Abbotsford Edition of the Waverley Novels (Boston: Dan Estes, 1900), I, xvi–xvii. Subsequent references, to the same edition, will be incorporated in the text.

2. Isaac Taylor, *Home Education,* 7th ed., revised (London, 1867), p. 33. First published 1837.

3. Isaac Taylor, *Advice to the Teens, or, Practical Helps Towards the Formation of One's Own Character* (Boston: Wells and Lilly, 1820), p. 30. First published 1818.

4. Hannah More, *Coelebs in Search of a Wife, Works,* Vol. VIII (London: Bohn, 1853), p. 106. First published 1809.

5. Jane Austen, *Northanger Abbey and Persuasion, The Novels of Jane Austen,* ed. R. W. Chapman (Oxford: Clarendon, 1923), V, 243. Subsequent references, to the same edition, will be incorporated in the text.

6. Eaton Stannard Barrett, *The Heroine, or, Adventures of Cherubina,* 1st American, from 2nd London, ed., 2 vols. (Philadelphia: M. Carey, 1815), II, 16. First published 1813.

Chapter 7: The Generations: Submerged Conflict

1. Sir Walter Scott, *Rob Roy,* The New Abbotsford Edition of the Waverley Novels (Boston: Dan Estes, 1900), VIII, 260. Subsequent references will be incorporated in the text.

2. *Mansfield Park, The Novels of Jane Austen,* ed. R. W. Chapman (Oxford: Clarendon, 1923), III, 91. Subsequent references to this edition will be incorporated in the text.

3. *Sense and Sensibility, The Novels of Jane Austen,* I, 101.

4. *Pride and Prejudice, The Novels of Jane Austen,* II, 3.

5. *Letters from a Father to a Son,* 2 vols. (New York: Garland, 1971), I, 330–31. Vol. I written 1792–93, published 1796; vol. II written 1798–99, published 1800.

6. Mary Wollstonecraft, *A Vindication of the Rights of Woman,* ed. Carol H. Poston (New York: Norton, 1975), p. 112. First published 1792.

7. *Monthly Review* 54 (1807): 17.

8. Notice of J. Taylor, *A Summary of Parental and Filial Duties, Monthly Review* 54 (1807): 320.

9. Review of *Letters Addressed to a Young Man on His First Entrance into Life . . .,* by Mrs. West, *Gentleman's Magazine* 90 (1801): 735.

10. Isaac Taylor, *Home Education,* 7th ed., revised (London, 1867), p. 163.

11. Samuel Taylor Coleridge, *The Friend: A Series of Essays,* 3 vols. (London: Rest Fenner, 1818), III, 2–3.

12. Jane Austen to Cassandra Austen, 11 October 1813; *Letters,* ed. R. W. Chapman (London: Oxford University Press, 1952), p. 344.

13. Robert Bage, *Hermsprong; or, Man As He Is Not,* 3 vols. (London: William Lane, 1796), III, 241.

14. "Thoughts on Novel Writing," *Blackwood's Magazine* 4 (1819): 394.

Chapter 8: Us or Them: Some Victorians

1. Philippe Ariès, *Centuries of Childhood,* tr. Robert Baldick (New York: Vintage, 1962), p. 32.

2. Frederick Greenwood, "Reflections on My Daughter's Marriage," *Cornhill Magazine* 6 (1862): 811.

3. See John R. Gillis, *Youth and History: Tradition and Change in European Age Relations 1770–Present* (New York: Academic Press, 1974), pp. 74–75, 105 ff.; Kenneth Keniston, "Youth: A 'New' Stage of Life," *American Scholar* 39 (1970): 631–32; Edward Shorter, *The Making of the Modern Family* (New York: Basic Books, 1975), passim.

4. *Stray Papers on Education,* by B. H., quoted in E. Lyttelton, *Mothers and Sons or Problems in the Home Training of Boys* (London, 1892), pp. 19–20.

5. Harriet Martineau, "Middle-Class Education in England: Girls," *Cornhill Magazine* 10 (1864): 555.

6. Henry Maudsley, "Sex in Mind and in Education," *Fortnightly Review* 15 n.s. (1874): 473.

7. "Women's Education," *Fraser's Magazine* 79 (1869): 541.

8. Dinah Mulock, "In Her Teens," *Macmillan's Magazine* 10 (1864): 219.

9. Penelope Holland, "Two Girls of the Period: I. Our Offence, Our Defence, and Our Petition," *Macmillan's Magazine* 19 (1869): 324.

10. *The Mill on the Floss, The Complete Works of George Eliot* (London: Postlethwaite, Taylor and Knowles, 1908), II, 201. Subsequent references, to this edition, will be incorporated in the text. First published 1860.

11. "Our Public Schools—Their Discipline and Instruction," *Fraser's Magazine* 50 (1854): 407.

12. Samuel Smiles, *Self-Help, with Illustrations of Conduct & Perseverance* (London: John Murray, 1969), p. 229. First published 1859.

13. William Cobbett, *Advice to Young Men, and (Incidentally) to Young Women, in the Middle and Higher Ranks of Life* (London, 1829), letter V, p. 281.

14. Herbert Spencer, *Education: Intellectual, Moral, and Physical* (New York, 1893), p. 191. First published 1860.

15. Charles Kingsley, *Sermons for the Times, The Works of Charles Kingsley* (London, 1858), sermon VII, "Sonship," XXIII, 109–10.

16. "Our Modern Youth," *Fraser's Magazine* 68 (1863): 115.

17. *Great Expectations, The Works of Charles Dickens* (London: Chapman and Hall, n.d.), V, 311. Subsequent references, to this edition, will be incorporated in the text. First published 1861.

18. *Adam Bede, Complete Works of George Eliot*, I, ii, 349. (Two volumes, with separate pagination, are printed in one.) Subsequent references, to this edition, will be incorporated in the text.

19. "An Inquiry into the State of Girls' Fashionable Schools," *Fraser's Magazine* 31 (1845): 703.

20. Charlotte M. Yonge, *The Daisy Chain, or Aspirations: A Family Chronicle* (London: Macmillan, 1899), p. 16. First published 1864. Subsequent references, to this edition, will be incorporated in the text..

21. Thomas Hughes, *Tom Brown's School Days* (Boston: Phillips, 1920), p. 163. First published 1857.

22. Dorothea Beale, "On the Education of Girls," *Fraser's Magazine* 74 (1866): 521.

23. William Johnston, *England As It Is, Political, Social, and Industrial, in the Middle of the Nineteenth Century*, 2 vols. (London, 1851), I, 289.

24. *The Monthly Packet* (January 1851), quoted in Marion Lochhead, *Young Victorians* (London: John Murray, 1959), p. 89.

25. Anthony Trollope, *Orley Farm* (New York: Knopf, 1950), p. 29. Subsequent references, to this edition, will be incorporated in the text.

26. Anthony Trollope, *The Bertrams*, 2 vols. (Leipzig: Tauchnitz, 1859), II, 374. Subsequent references, to this edition, will be incorporated in the text.

27. Anthony Trollope, *The Small House at Allinghum*, 2 vols. (Boston: Houghton Mifflin, 1929), I, 36. Subsequent references, to this edition, will be incorporated in the text.

Chapter 9: Heroes: The Early Twentieth Century

1. G. Stanley Hall, *Adolescence: Its Psychology and Its Relations to Physiology, Anthropology, Sociology, Sex, Crime, Religion, and Education*, 2 vols. (New York: Appleton, 1904), I, 311. Subsequent references, to this edition, will be incorporated in the text.

2. Arnold Bennett, *Hilda Lessways* (New York: Dutton, 1911), p. 4. Subsequent references, to this edition, will be incorporated in the text.

3. Arnold Bennet, *The Lion's Share* (New York: Doran, 1916), p. 4. Subsequent references, to this edition, will be incorporated in the text.

4. D. H. Lawrence, *Sons and Lovers* (New York: Viking, 1958), p. 212. Subsequent references, to this edition, will be incorporated in the text.

5. James Joyce, *A Portrait of the Artist as a Young Man* (New York: Viking, 1964), p. 203. Subsequent references, to this edition, will be incorporated in the text.

Notes

Chapter 10: Guilt and Responsibility: The 1950s and the 1960s

1. Erik Erikson, "Youth: Fidelity and Diversity," *The Challenge of Youth,* ed. Erik H. Erikson (Garden City, N.Y.: Doubleday, 1965), p. 24.

2. Anthony Burgess, *A Clockwork Orange* (New York: Norton, 1963), p. 41. Subsequent references, to this edition, will be incorporated in the text.

3. Erik H. Erikson, *Chilhood and Society,* 2nd ed., revised and enlarged (New York: Norton, 1963), p. 36. First published 1950. Subsequent references, to this edition, will be incorporated in the text.

4. Erik H. Erikson, *Young Man Luther: A Study in Psychoanalysis and History* (New York: Norton, 1962), p. 14. Subsequent references, to this edition, will be incorporated in the text.

5. Doris Lessing, *Martha Quest* (New York: New American Library, 1970), pp. 7, 8. First published 1964.

6. Alan Sillitoe, *The Loneliness of the Long-Distance Runner* (New York: New American Library, 1959), p. 15. Subsequent references, to this edition, will be incorporated in the text.

7. E. M. and M. Eppel, *Adolescents and Morality* (London: Routledge & Kegan Paul, 1966), p. 213.

8. Mark Abrams, "The Facts of Young Life," *Encounter* 6 (May 1956): 41–42.

9. Martha Gellhorn, "So Awful to Be Young," *Encounter* 6 (May 1956): 48.

10. Muriel Spark, *The Prime of Miss Jean Brodie* (New York: Dell, 1969), p. 10. First published 1961. Subsequent references, to this edition, will be incorporated in the text.

11. Anthony Powell, *A Question of Upbringing, A Dance to the Music of Time/1 (Spring)* (New York: Popular Library, 1976), p. 220. First published 1955. Subsequent references, to this edition, will be incorporated in the text.

Index

Index

Index